NOVELL'S®

Novell's® Guide to Integrating
NetWare and TCP/IP

NOVELL'S®

Novell's® Guide to Integrating NetWare and TCP/IP

DREW HEYWOOD

Novell Press, San Jose

Novell's® Guide to Integrating NetWare and TCP/IP

Published by
Novell Press
2180 Fortune Drive
San Jose, CA 95131

Library of Congress Catalog Card No.: 96-75756

ISBN: 1-56884-818-8

Printed in the United States of America

10 9 8 7 6 5 4

1A/RW/QU/ZW/FC

Distributed in the United States by IDG Books Worldwide, Inc.

Distributed by Macmillan Canada for Canada; by Computer and Technical Books for the Caribbean Basin; by Contemporantea de Ediciones for Venezuela; by Distribuidora Cuspide for Argentina; by CITFC for Brazil; by Ediciones ZETA S.C.R. Ltda. for Peru; by Editorial Limusa SA for Mexico; by Transworld Publishers Limited in the United Kingdom and Europe; by Al-Maiman Publishers & Distributors for Saudi Arabia; by Simron Pty. Ltd. for South Africa; by IDG Communications (HK) Ltd. for Hong Kong; by Toppan Company Ltd. for Japan; by Addison Wesley Publishing Company for Korea; by Longman Singapore Publisher Ltd. for Singapore, Malaysia, Thailand, and Indonesia; by Unalis Corporation for Taiwan; by WS Computer Publishing Company, Inc. for the Philippines; by WoodsLane Enterprises Ltd. for New Zealand.

For general information on Novell Press books in the U.S., including information on discounts and premiums, contact IDG Books at 800-434-3422 or 415-655-3000. For information on where to purchase Novell Press books outside the U.S., contact IDG Books Worldwide at 415-655-3021 or fax 415-655-3295. For information on translations, contact Waterside Productions, Inc., 2191 San Elijo Avenue, Cardiff, CA 92007-1839, at 619-632-9190. For sales inquiries and special prices for bulk quantities, call IDG Books Worldwide at 415-655-3000. For information on using Novell Press books in the classroom, or for ordering examination copies, contact the Education Office at 800-434-2086 or fax 817-251-8174.

John Kilcullen, *President & CEO, IDG Books Worldwide, Inc.*

Brenda McLaughlin, *Senior Vice President & Group Publisher, IDG Books Worldwide, Inc.*

The IDG Boooks Worldwide logo is a trademark under exclusive license to IDG Books Worldwide, Inc., from International Data Group, Inc.

Rosalie Kearsley, *Publisher, Novell Press, Inc.*

Novell Press and the Novell Press logo are trademarks of Novell, Inc.

Welcome to Novell Press

Novell Press, the world's leading provider of networking books, is the premier source for the most timely and useful information in the networking industry. Novell Press books cover fundamental networking issues as they emerge—from today's Novell and third-party products to the concepts and strategies that will guide the industry's future. The result is a broad spectrum of titles for the benefit of those involved in networking at any level: end-user, department administrator, developer, systems manager, or network architect.

Novell Press books are written by experts with the full participation of Novell's technical, managerial, and marketing staff. The books are exhaustively reviewed by Novell's own technicians and are published only on the basis of final released software, never on prereleased versions.

Novell Press at IDG is an exciting partnership between two companies at the forefront of the knowledge and communications revolution. The Press is implementing an ambitious publishing program to develop new networking titles centered on the current version of NetWare and on Novell's GroupWise and other popular groupware products.

Novell Press books are translated into 12 languages and are available at bookstores around the world.

Rosalie Kearsley, Publisher, Novell, Inc.
David Kolodney, Associate Publisher, IDG Books Worldwide, Inc.

Novell Press

Publisher
Rosalie Kearsley

Associate Publisher
David Kolodney

Market Development Manager
Colleen Bluhm

Associate Acquisitions Editor
Anne Hamilton

Communications Project Specialist
Marcy Shanti

Managing Editor
Terry Somerson

Associate Developmental Editor
Amy R. Marks

Copy Editor
Ron Hull

Technical Editor
Amit Satoor

Editorial Assistant
Jean Leitner

Production Director
Andrew Walker

Supervisor of Page Layout
Craig A. Harrison

Pre-Press Coordination
Tony Augsburger
Patricia R. Reynolds
Theresa Sanchez-Baker

Media/ Archive Coordination
Leslie Popplewell
Kerri Cornell
Michael Wilkey

Project Coordinator
Ben Schroeter

Graphics Coordination
Shelley Lea

Production Staff
Diann Abbott
Vincent F. Burns
Laura Carpenter
Stephen Noetzel
Andreas Schueller
Elsie Yim

Production Associate
Chris Pimentel

Proofreaders
Mick Arellano
Kathleen Prata

Indexer
Matthew Spence

Illustrators
Mark Mandrell
Greg Maxson

Cover Design
Archer Design

Cover Photographer
Gregg Whitaker

For Lauren, *ma petite danceuse.*

About the Author

Drew Heywood is a networking professional who has been working with NetWare since 1987. He has managed WANs and LANs in government and industry. Drew has written extensively about networking, including several popular books: *Inside NetWare 3.12, Inside NetWare 4.2,* and *NetWare: The Professional Reference.* In total, he has authored and/or coauthored more than 150,000 books in print.

Preface

WHO SHOULD READ THIS BOOK?

Ten years ago, I never thought about TCP/IP. Now, however, for all us LAN administrators, TCP/IP knowledge is a vital job skill. If you need your PCs to talk to a UNIX computer through your LAN, you need to know TCP/IP. Heck, if you need to talk to just about any computer, you need to know TCP/IP. And if you want to connect your LAN to the Internet—who doesn't these days—you need to know TCP/IP. Don't try to avoid it—TCP/IP is everywhere, and eventually every LAN administrator's resume will need to list TCP/IP as a skill area.

This book is intended to help experienced administrators of NetWare 3 and 4 make the transition to TCP/IP. I'll assume that you know the basics of administering your NetWare server and that utilities such as SYSCON and NWADMIN aren't mysteries to you. But I don't assume that you know anything about protocols or communication theory. Don't worry if you don't know the difference between a protocol and a protractor. It's my job to orient you with the right data communications knowledge.

WHAT'S IN THIS BOOK

This book provides you with two kinds of knowledge: theoretical knowledge about what TCP/IP is and how it works and practical knowledge about the NetWare products that implement TCP/IP. In fact, these two types of knowledge define the organization of this book:

Part I: TCP/IP Concepts

This section provides the theory. The overall organization is taken from the structure of the TCP/IP protocol model, with its four layers: network access, internet, host-to-host, and process/application. These layers break down the functionality of TCP/IP into chunks that are more nearly bite-sized than TCP/IP as a whole, although each layer still has a lot to chew on. Here's how the chapters are organized.

▸ Chapter 1 (Introduction to TCP/IP) prepares you to do your own research on TCP/IP. The many protocols that make up the TCP/IP protocol suite are documented in Request for Comment (RFC) documents, which now number nearly 2000 and date back to the origins of the ARPANET in 1969. To appreciate and understand this rich set of documentation, you need to understand how the ARPANET has evolved, ending up in the Internet we know today. More important, you need to know how standards are established on the Internet. Then, you can retrieve RFCs for yourself and learn about TCP/IP from the horse's mouth.

▸ Chapter 2 (TCP/IP and Network Communication) builds some theoretical models of network communication. Starting with the 7-layer OSI Reference Model and moving on to the 4-layer TCP/IP model, you will learn how network communication works. My goal in this chapter is to provide you with a rich set of conceptual hooks on which you can hang the many facts you encounter in the next four chapters.

▸ Chapters 3 through 6 provide layer-by-layer coverage of the TCP/IP protocol suite. You might react to the length of these chapters, saying perhaps, "I don't need to know much at all about IPX. Why is there over 50 pages about the network access layer alone?" The unfortunate answer is that TCP/IP was designed for function and not for simplicity, and TCP/IP is considerably more complex to configure and manage than the Novell IPX/SPX protocols. TCP/IP administrators perform tasks that are unheard of with IPX/SPX, such as manually addressing each TCP/IP computer with a network and host identification number. No, all of the information in these chapters isn't essential. I could have gotten you started with a bit less, but then I wouldn't have answered the many questions that are sure to arise as you become more deeply involved in TCP/IP.

Part II: Implementing NetWare TCP/IP

Part II is where theory meets practical fact, where you put your knowledge from Part I to work building TCP/IP into your NetWare network.

- ▶ Chapter 7 (Introducing NetWare TCP/IP) builds the bridge, demonstrating how TCP/IP in general is realized with NetWare products. Here we review the NetWare protocol architecture, the Open Datalink Interface (ODI). And we briefly examine the various NetWare products that provide TCP/IP support.

- ▶ Chapter 8 (Implementing TCP/IP on NetWare Servers) shows how TCP/IP works on NetWare 3 and NetWare 4 servers. You learn how to install, configure, activate, and manage the protocols on both types of NetWare servers.

- ▶ Chapter 9 (Installing TCP/IP on NetWare Clients) shows how to get TCP/IP running on DOS and DOS/Windows workstations. We examine the LAN WorkGroup and LAN WorkPlace products, which combine TCP/IP support with an extensive array of TCP/IP applications.

- ▶ Chapter 10 (Internetworking NetWare TCP/IP) moves beyond simple networks to see how TCP/IP is configured on large, routed networks. You learn how to configure static routing as well as the routing protocols RIP and OSPF. And you learn how to use IP tunneling to enable your NetWare IPX LANs to communicate through a TCP/IP network.

- ▶ Chapter 11 (Managing NetWare TCP/IP) shows how to configure Simple Network Management Protocol (SNMP) management on your NetWare TCP/IP network. You learn how to configure NetWare servers and clients so that they can be managed using SNMP, and you learn how to use the management consoles that are included with NetWare 3 and 4 and with LAN WorkPlace.

- ▶ Chapter 12 (NetWare/IP) examines the product that enables you to operate your NetWare network using only TCP/IP. Organizations that wish to run a single-protocol LAN use NetWare/IP to eliminate IPX.

KEEP IN TOUCH

Thanks for choosing this book. I sincerely hope it meets your needs and that you will turn to it many times as you learn about and operate NetWare TCP/IP on your LAN. I've been a LAN administrator for a long time and hope I have a pretty good idea what my colleagues need to know. But I know there is always room for improvement.

This is about the tenth book on NetWare that I've written or co-authored, and I haven't written the perfect book yet. There's always something I should have included or a better way to make a point, and so help me, there is an occasional error as well. The fastidious editors at Novell Press and my excellent technical editor have already done a lot to help me fine-tune this manuscript, but I'm very sure there is more to be done.

Nothing tests a book like having a few thousand readers tear through it. You, the readers, are a vital part of the process of making my books—and the computer book industry as a whole—better and more responsive to your needs. So please, if you have a comment, be it praise or poison, let us know.

As this book is published, my Internet address is dheywood@iquest.net. Please feel free to write with your comments and questions. I'll do my best to answer all your e-mail promptly.

Acknowledgments

I have reached the ten-year mark of my affiliation with NetWare, and with this book I have tried to make my own small contribution to the huge body of work that is NetWare as we know it today. To everyone who has designed, coded, documented, supported, or dreamed the dream of making NetWare better, my humble thanks for producing products worth writing about.

I have also nearly reached the four-year mark in my affiliation with Rose Kearsley, Publisher of Novell Press. Rose has been keeping me supplied with products and information throughout my four years of writing about NetWare, and I am thrilled to at last have the opportunity to write a book for her. Rose, I hope you like it.

Marci Shanti has been my primary contact at Novell for quite awhile, and lately she's had the task of rushing product and literature to me, all in the "(ta da) nick of time!" So thanks, Marci, for accepting my panicked phone calls so calmly and rushing to my aid.

An author can have no better friend than an editor who won't let anything get by, and Amy Marks at IDG has been among the best editors I have worked with. Thanks, Amy, for your dilligence and for keeping me honest and on track.

IDG Books Worldwide has managed to build an impressive staff and seems to have handily taken up the challenge at Novell Press. One asset is Publisher David Kolodny, who remains with Novell Press through it's move to IDG. Another is Anne Hamilton, my acquisitions editor. Both worked to get this project going and rushed to my aid in times of troubles. Thanks!

I have received technical support from several people. To Amit Satoor at Novell, my gratitude for the diligent technical edit. Special thanks to Keith Brown for his many prompt and insightful answers to my questions, and also to Adam Goodman for filling in the gaps on LAN WorkGroup 5. Also, to Peter Kuo, thanks for letting me take up your busy time with my e-mails.

Finally, to my business partner, my friend, and my wife: Thank you Blythe for your support, patience, and tolerance. We've survived another book together.

(IDG Books Worldwide would like to give special thanks to Patrick J. McGovern, founder of International Data Group, who made this book possible.)

Contents at a Glance

Contents

Introduction

I first met NetWare about ten years ago, and let me tell you, back then it was a thrill just see a LAN work. The idea that PCs could connect to a NetWare server, print, and share files was pretty heady stuff. It seldom crossed our minds in the mid-1980s that LANs were in their nursery period and that eventually they would have to toddle out and meet the rest of the world. With surprising rapidity, however, LANs have assumed a crucial place in business computing. No longer is it sufficient for LANs to live in isolation. They must communicate with other computers on other networks.

As you will learn in Chapter 1, a variety of technologies enable different types of computers and networks to communicate. A 3270 gateway, for example, enables PCs on a LAN to communicate with an IBM mainframe computer in a very limited way by making the PC appear to be a 3270-type terminal. Gateways, however, are special-purpose connectivity solutions, designed to connect one specific type of device to another specific type. What is needed is a more universal solution that can connect any given pair of devices.

The universal solution most widely in use, in fact the only comprehensive universal connectivity solution, is TCP/IP. Originally developed for the ARPANET, an experimental network operated by the United States Department of Defense, TCP/IP has evolved over more than 20 years into a mature and comprehensive technology for networking all sorts of computers.

You may not have heard of the ARPANET, but I'll bet you've heard of the Internet, unless of course you've been buried under a rock. The Internet is the modern incarnation of the ARPANET, which was cut loose from military control in the mid-1980s. For a long time, the ARPANET/Internet has been used to connect educational and corporate institutions that were involved in defense research, and the many wizards at those many institutions have grown TCP/IP into the 800-pound gorilla of network protocols, the protocol that can sit anywhere it wants and be welcome.

NETWARE AND TCP/IP

Novell has known about TCP/IP for a long time, and included support in NetWare 3 starting in 1987. Since that time, a comprehensive set of products has been introduced that enable NetWare servers to provide many of the services that generally are associated with UNIX. I'm not going to recite product names here, because the features won't make much sense until you have some background information. You will learn more about the Novell products in Chapter 6. Suffice it to say that the list is quite extensive.

For this book, I have chosen to cover the most central aspects of NetWare TCP/IP, focusing on setting up and managing TCP/IP on NetWare servers and clients (workstations). Even then, because of the richness of NetWare TCP/IP, I had to pick and choose among the features. My goal has been to give you the background needed to understand NetWare TCP/IP and then to show you the essentials everyone needs to know about getting TCP/IP running on NetWare LANs. Basically, I have followed the old proverb of teaching you to fish so that you can feed yourself. When you finish this book, you will have the skills you need to comprehend any of Novell's TCP/IP-related products.

LEARNING TCP/IP

When you consider the complexity of the job it is performing, NetWare is a very simple product to administer. On a simple network, IPX (Novell's counterpart to TCP/IP) is practically invisible. Typically, the only configuration information you need to enter are network numbers for the internal and external networks. Everything else comes automatically. Routing, the capability of forwarding data through complex networks, is built into NetWare. You don't have to do a thing to turn on routing other than to add a second network card to a server. The folks at Novell are justifiably proud of their network architecture, which performs well and practically snaps together.

All that changes with TCP/IP. The wonderful plug-and-play world of IPX is left behind, and you enter the realm of a protocol where everything—and I mean everything—can and probably must be configured. In other words, you can't do TCP/IP unless you know how and often why TCP/IP works. That's where this book comes in. Within these covers you will find everything you need to know to put TCP/IP to work on your NetWare network.

## PART I

TCP/IP Concepts

## CHAPTER 1

Introduction to TCP/IP

Imagine a room filled with people from different countries. Suppose there is a German, a Finn, an Italian, a Korean, and a Saudi Arabian. All have an urgent need to communicate, but there is a problem: no two people speak the same language.

Until recently, the realm of computer networking resembled that room. Computers communicate with one another using languages called network *protocols*. Unfortunately, unless all of the computers in a network use the same protocols, communication may be impossible.

For example, IBM computers have traditionally used System Network Architecture (SNA) network protocols to exchange data. Computers made by Digital, however, have traditionally been connected through Digital Network Architecture (DNA) networks. As a result, exchanging data between IBM and Digital computers can be quite difficult. In the 1970s and 1980s, different computer vendors such as IBM, Digital, Sperry, Burroughs, Honeywell, and Tandem (among others) promoted their own protocols. Although a few vendors supported other vendors' network protocols, the majority did not. A particular vendor may have decided not to support others' protocols for a variety of reasons:

▸ Certain protocols may not have coincided with the vendor's own particular network design philosophy.

▸ The vendor may have regarded its own protocols as superior to others.

▸ Proprietary protocols could serve to tie customers to one brand of equipment.

▸ Changing protocols for a computer network architecture involved a major effort.

▸ By and large, customers were loyal to a particular computer brand and there was no need for them to connect with other brands.

Local area networks (LANs) led the computing world into a new age. However, LANs tended to remain strongly tied to their own "homegrown" protocols. LANs were essentially isolated islands, much like their mainframe cousins. Although Novell promoted an excellent set of protocols called the IPX/SPX protocol suite early on, those protocols were not implemented by many vendors for quite some time. Microsoft and IBM relied on NetBEUI. Apple introduced its own AppleTalk. Even though Novell began supporting other protocols such as AppleTalk and SNA, variations in the architectures of IPX, AppleTalk, and SNA continue to hinder seamless interoperability between different computer systems. For example, an IBM mainframe cannot connect seamlessly with a NetWare LAN that uses only IPX protocols.

All of this "netspeak" — SNA, DNA, AppleTalk, NetBEUI, and so forth — may seem a little puzzling to you at first. I simply want to demonstrate all of the confusion that existed in the early years of the network industry.

The Need for Common Protocols

When people need to overcome language barriers, they often use translators. For example, the United Nations General Assembly uses a large body of translators to facilitate communication. A similar approach can be used to allow different kinds of computers to communicate.

Translation is a common tool for enabling network communication. Certain kinds of translators, called *gateways*, exchange data between different environments — for example, between a NetWare and an SNA environment. One way to allow different vendors' networks to interconnect is simply to use different gateways for the various types of networks, just like the UN employs different translators for communication among the various nations.

Although using gateways is an effective means of connecting networks, in the long run it is not a very practical solution. Gateways are difficult to design, and they are seldom foolproof. Furthermore, each gateway must be purchased, installed, and maintained. Finally, gateways complicate LAN communication, which should be kept as simple as possible. In short, gateways do not provide the kind of seamless communication that most networks require.

There is an alternative approach that solves many of the problems presented by gateways. That alternative involves agreeing on common protocols that can be used by *all* computers to communicate through a network. Although having a common set of protocols would seem to be an obvious solution, it nevertheless took a long time for that solution to be realized. For the reasons mentioned above, manufacturers continued to adhere to their own protocol suites.

Until very recently, the most common means of transporting data between different computer brands was to store the data on a disk or magnetic tape and then physically transport the magnetic media to another computer. It was not uncommon for a computer system in a small- to medium-sized company to resemble the one shown in Figure 1.1. In this configuration, the accounting, sales, and finance data are stored on an IBM mainframe, engineering data are stored on a VAX, and end users are connected to a Novell LAN, which supports the company's personal productivity programs. This kind of setup caused many problems. For example, for a long time there was only one way to take data from a report produced by an IBM mainframe and use it in a Lotus spreadsheet: You needed to have someone manually reenter the figures from a green-bar printout into the spreadsheet.

FIGURE 1.1

A Multi-Protocol Network

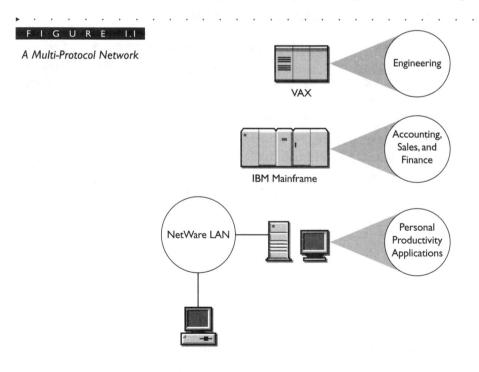

Fortunately, users did not have to wait for manufacturers to give in and agree on common protocols. By the late 1980s, those protocols already existed. The protocols were Transmission Control Protocol/Internet Protocol (TCP/IP), the protocols developed for the Internet. These protocols are mature, robust, and extensive. They are open protocols, defined in public forums. They were not designed to meet the specific requirements of a particular company. As organizations began to see the potential of TCP/IP to unify their network environments, they began to push for TCP/IP support in all of their computing environments. One-by-one, vendors have yielded. Today, TCP/IP is available on virtually every computing platform.

NOTE **The term TCP/IP is derived from the two most prominent components of a vast suite of protocols: the Transmission Control Protocol (TCP) and the Internet Protocol (IP). You will learn more about TCP, IP, and many other related protocols in this book.**

To understand why the TCP/IP protocol suite has become the common language of the modern network, you need to understand a little about the evolution of TCP/IP and how TCP/IP standards are set. The remainder of this chapter explores the processes by which TCP/IP continues to evolve to meet the changing needs of its users.

The Origins of TCP/IP

The US Department of Defense (DoD) was one of the first organizations to realize a need for wide area networking. As far back as the 1960s, the DoD infrastructure included hundreds of computers around the world. Some of these computers were operated by the DoD itself, but many belonged to defense contractors and universities that were doing work for the DoD.

In the early 1960s, computers exchanged data through dedicated communication channels. If a pair of computers needed to communicate, they were connected by a dedicated circuit. As more computers were added, separate lines were installed to connect each computer to every other computer in the network. This setup is called a *mesh*. See Figure 1.2. A mesh network functions very well, but it is costly. Today, many mainframes still use dedicated communication channels. The problem with this approach is that the number of required lines increases rapidly as the number of computers grows. Very soon the configuration becomes unwieldy.

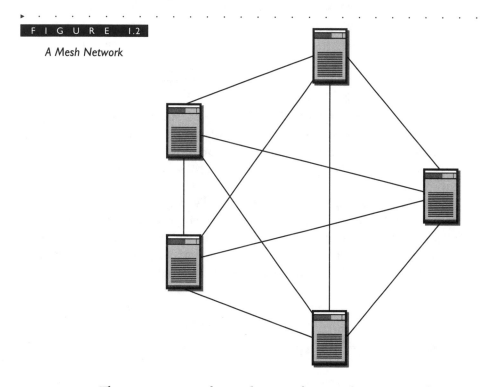

The next step in the evolution of networking was to have some hosts route messages between other hosts, as shown in Figure 1.3. This strategy enabled network designers to reduce the number of communication links, but it also created complications because it required several computers to share the same communication lines. You can see in Figure 1.3 how a system that uses hosts necessitates shared communication lines.

There are two ways communication lines can be shared:

▶ By permitting a single computer to monopolize a line until its message has been sent. This technique is known as *circuit switching*. With circuit switching, extra channels are needed to allow several conversations to take place at the same time.

▶ By breaking messages into small units so that parts of different messages can take turns on the same line. This technique is called *packet switching*. It enables many computers to share a single communication channel.

In the late 1960s, the Advanced Research Projects Agency (ARPA) of the DoD decided to focus its research on the second technology — i.e., packet switching.

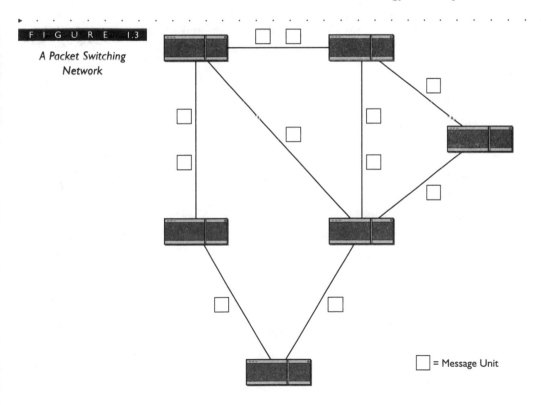

FIGURE 1.3

A Packet Switching Network

☐ = Message Unit

The DoD required several things from its networks:

- **Standard protocols.** The DoD purchases computer equipment from the lowest bidder. Therefore, the DoD required a standard set of protocols that could be used for all computer configurations. It was essential to develop protocols that enabled different computer brands to interoperate.

- **Reliability.** The DoD needed to be prepared for wartime conditions. At the time ARPA decided to initiate packet switching research, long-distance communication technologies were primitive and prone to trouble. Consequently, ARPA required protocols that could cope with a lot of stress.

- **Flexibility.** Networks constantly change, and the protocols had to allow the changes to be made smoothly without interrupting service.

HISTORY OF THE INTERNET

The particular wide area network that eventually became the Internet began in 1968. It connected four sites: SRI International, the University of California at Santa Barbara (UCSB), the University of California at Los Angeles (UCLA), and the University of Utah. Dubbed the ARPANET, the network grew to include 20 hosts by 1972.

Remember that in 1972 all computers were so-called *host* computers: mainframes and minicomputers that serviced large numbers of people through time-sharing or batch processing. At that time, it was hardly imaginable that an individual person might have his or her own computer to work on. The convention of calling all computers on a TCP/IP network "hosts" derives from those early days of shared computers.

As the ARPANET grew, it gradually came to function as much more than simply a means of communication between the DoD and its contractors. Soon, the ARPANET connected a majority of colleges and graduate schools, as well as a large number of technology vendors. By the mid-1980s, the ARPANET had expanded far beyond its DoD origins and had gained a momentum of its own.

Consequently, in the mid-1980s, ARPA (now called DARPA, or the Defense Advance Research Project Agency) decided to end the ARPANET experiment. The DoD had established MILNET for U.S. military data communication, and the ARPANET was left to its own devices.

In 1986, the ARPANET was replaced by a higher-performance network funded by the National Science Foundation (NSF). This network, called NSFNET, now serves as the backbone of the Internet. NSFNET is managed by Advanced Network Services (ANS).

NSFNET represented the first step toward privatizing the Internet. Since NSFNET was established, management of the network has become more and more privatized, although oversight of network standards still belongs to a public organization, the Internet Activities Board (IAB).

Development of the TCP/IP protocols began in the early 1980s, and in 1983 the ARPANET converted to TCP/IP. Availability of the TCP/IP protocols received a significant boost when TCP/IP was included in version 4.2 of Berkeley Standard Distribution (BSD) UNIX. Because use of BSD UNIX was free to educational institutions, it was widely adopted by universities and in a variety of industries. Additionally, BSD UNIX became the foundation of several commercial UNIX products, including Digital's Ultrix and Sun's SunOS. As BSD UNIX was disseminated through the educational and research computing communities, TCP/IP soon became the dominant network protocols in those environments.

By the mid 1980s, TCP/IP had two big advantages:

▶ It was readily available to those who needed it (primarily industrial and educational researchers).

▶ It was the protocol of the ARPANET, to which those researchers were connected.

The result was widespread use of TCP/IP in communities of users who were on the leading edge of computing technology. TCP/IP's evolution took off. By 1990, TCP/IP had gained momentum and was poised for the next critical stage in its evolution. TCP/IP was ready to enter the business world.

TCP/IP AND OPEN COMPUTING STANDARDS

As TCP/IP was maturing, another trend was emerging. Although corporate information systems departments were still relying heavily on mainframe computing, the personal computer had begun to infiltrate business operations. The business world began to explore new ways of using computers beyond the established paradigm of computing using shared hosts.

By about 1985 (the year the IBM AT computer was introduced), the number of personal computers on corporate desktops had reached critical mass, and companies began to demand network connectivity. Users were no longer willing to transfer files via "sneakernet" and modems. LANs, which previously had been niche products, began to flourish. Some of the more reliable and versatile LAN products — most notably NetWare — began to change the way organizations did their computing.

Soon managers of information systems (often collectively referred to as *MIS*) began to realize that they had a problem. Users wanted to expand the range of their desktop computers. They wanted to access the corporate mainframe from their PCs. For example, some users wanted to obtain sales data from a VAX so that they could manipulate it using Lotus 1-2-3. Other users wanted to send files to branch offices without having to set up dial-in and dial-out modems. Basically, users were asking for seamless communication — that is, they wanted their computers to be able to communicate freely with all other computers. The problem of integrating computing had to be dealt with.

No single vendor had a comprehensive strategy for dealing with the problem. In fact, as the demand for connectivity grew among users, computer vendors tended to focus on improving their own protocols rather than building bridges with other protocol suites.

To achieve their goal of interconnecting their companies, MIS needed protocols that were not tied to a particular vendor's network. Out of this need developed a movement that came to be called *Open Computing,* which sought to establish non-proprietary computing standards.

Even though TCP/IP was available as an open standard, many people viewed TCP/IP with skepticism because it is not governed by an international standardization body. Therefore, many industry authorities supported a different approach for developing open network standards. For awhile, the most popular interconnectivity movement was Open Systems Interconnection (OSI), which is a set of network standards being developed by the International Organization for Standardization (ISO). The government of the United States was deeply involved with OSI, and at one time it announced that all agencies of the U.S. government would convert to Government OSI Profile (GOSIP), which is a set of standards derived from OSI.

However, the excitement about OSI soon dissipated. As with many international negotiations, it has proved difficult to establish a final product that satisfies everyone involved. Work on the OSI protocols has progressed slowly. The GOSIP initiative has foundered, and the DoD has continued to use TCP/IP for its networks.

As OSI bogged down, MIS realized what the TCP/IP community had known all along: TCP/IP could be used to integrate the computer world. People began to realize that TCP/IP standards are not as unreliable as previously thought. Although TCP/IP is not standardized by an official international body, the standardization process is exceptionally responsive to input. There are no closed-door decisions, and all standards are available to the public. In short, TCP/IP has the two main features the corporate world was looking for: openness and connectivity independent of any particular computer brand or brands.

Later in this chapter, you will see how TCP/IP standards are developed. The process is extraordinarily inclusive. In fact, you yourself could get involved. TCP/IP has attracted some of the brightest and most imaginative people in network computing, and the protocols have achieved a remarkable richness. Here are just a few of the services that are readily available through TCP/IP protocols:

- **FTP (File Transfer Protocol).** Used to transfer and manage files among networked computers. This is a widely implemented service.

- **Telnet.** Provides remote terminal service that enables users to log onto remote computers.

- **DNS (Domain Name Service).** Makes TCP/IP networks more comprehensible by providing a hierarchical directory of users' names that identify network hosts.

> ▸ **SMTP (Simple Mail Transfer Protocol).** Delivers electronic mail through internetworks.

> ▸ **SNMP (Simple Network Management Protocol).** Used for managing network devices.

This book examines all of these protocols, among others.

TCP/IP and Internet Standards

Standards for TCP/IP are set somewhat indirectly. Unlike other protocols, the TCP/IP protocols are not standardized by an international treaty organization. Under the authority of the NSF, the Internet Activities Board (IAB) sets all standards for the Internet and therefore sets standards for TCP/IP, which is used on the Internet. Anyone who wants to connect to the Internet — which today is practically everyone — must use protocols approved by the IAB. As a result, the TCP/IP protocols running on most networks are standardized by a group that has no real authority other than its charter to manage the Internet. The process may not be ideal, but as you will see it works very well.

In 1983, the IAB received its charter to design, engineer, and manage the Internet. The IAB charter describes the organization as "an independent committee of researchers and professionals with a technical interest in the health and evolution of the Internet system." The IAB has established two groups to oversee the short-term and long-term evolution of the Internet: the Internet Engineering Task Force (IETF) and the Internet Research Task Force (IRTF). The various groups involved in Internet standards are shown in Figure 1.4.

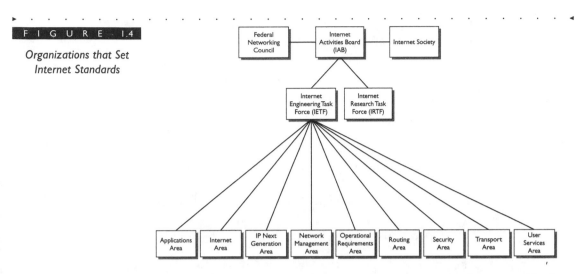

*Organizations that Set
Internet Standards*

The most prominent organization is the Internet Engineering Task Force, which is responsible for specifying the Internet architecture and protocols. The charter of the IETF describes the organization as follows:

> The IETF is not a traditional standards organization, although many specifications are produced that become standards. The IETF is made up of volunteers who meet three times a year to fulfill the IETF mission. There is no membership in the IETF. Anyone may register for and attend any meeting.

A document named *The Tao of IETF* provides insight into the organization and function of the IETF as well as a description of the organization's meetings. Later in this chapter, I will explain how to find this document on the Internet, along with other related documents. See "Obtaining Internet Documentation" later in this chapter.

The IETF is organized into a number of technical areas. The specific areas evolve with the needs of the Internet community. At present, the IETF's technical areas are:

- Applications
- Internet
- IP Next Generation
- Network Management
- Operational Requirements

- Routing
- Security
- Transport
- User Services

The Internet Engineering Steering Group (IESG) oversees the IETF and is responsible for formally recommending standards to the IAB. The IESG members are the directors of the various IETF technical areas.

The Internet Research Task Force conducts Internet research. In reality, it is difficult to draw a line between the IRTF and the IETF because membership overlaps considerably. Membership overlaps not only because the participants have similar interests, but also because this overlapping promotes the transfer of technology among participants.

Two outside organizations have close ties with the IAB. The Federal Networking Council represents agencies of the US government and coordinates the agencies' use of the Internet. The Internet Society is a public organization made up of people from education, industry, government, and the general Internet-user community. The Internet Society promotes use of the Internet and gives its members a forum for contributing input into the Internet standards process. For information contact:

```
The Internet Society
Suite 100
1895 Preston White Drive
Reston, VA 22091
USA
E-mail: isoc@isoc.org
703-648-9888
```

Day-to-day operation of the Internet is now performed by private firms under contract with the NSF. The groups responsible for these operations are collectively referred to as the InterNIC (Internet Network Information Center), which consists of two different organizations:

> ▸ **InterNIC Directory and Database Services,** operated by AT&T. This service consists of a wide variety of informational databases on topics that deal with virtually every aspect of the Internet.

> ▸ **InterNIC Registration Services,** operated by Network Solutions. This service has primary responsibility for registering addresses and names on the Internet.

INTERNET DOCUMENTATION

Discourse related to the development of the Internet is open to the public. All documents are freely available on the Internet through a variety of access methods. Among the public documents are minutes of IETF meetings, existing standards, standards under development, and miscellaneous memoranda that are of interest to the Internet community.

Requests for Comments

The documents you hear about most often are Requests for Comments (RFCs). All Internet standards are published as RFCs. For example, the Transmission Control Protocol (TCP) is documented in RFC 793. The official document that lists all Internet standards is itself an RFC entitled *Internet Official Protocol Standards* (currently RFC 1800). This document is updated periodically.

If you scan the index of RFCs, you will find documents on a wide variety of subjects. (I'll tell you how to access the index a little later in this chapter.) Here are some typical entries from the index:

```
1866   PS   T. Berners-Lee, D. Connolly, "Hypertext Markup
             Language - 2.0", 11/03/1995. (Pages=77) (Format=.txt)

1850   DS   F. Baker, R. Coltun, "OSPF Version 2 Management
             Information Base", 11/03/1995. (Pages=80)(Format=.txt)
             (Obsoletes RFC1253)
```

```
1132  S    L. McLaughlin, "Standard for the transmission of 802.2
           packets over IPX networks", 11/01/1989. (Pages=4)
           (Format=.txt)

1796  I    C. Huitema, J. Postel, S. Crocker, "Not All RFCs are
           Standards", 04/25/1995. (Pages=4) (Format=.txt)

1791  E    T. Sung, "TCP And UDP Over IPX Networks With Fixed
           Path MTU", 04/18/1995. (Pages=12) (Format=.txt)

0968       V. Cerf, "Twas the night before start-up",
           12/01/1985. (Pages=2) (Format=.txt)

0740  H    R. Braden, "NETRJS Protocol", 11/22/1977. (Pages=19)
           (Format=.txt) (Obsoletes RFC0599)
```

The letter to the right of each RFC number indicates which category the RFC belongs to. There are several formal RFC categories, as follows:

- **Standard (S).** An official standard Internet protocol.

- **Draft Standard (DS).** A protocol that is in the final stages of development and is nearing approval as an Internet standard.

- **Proposed Standard (PS).** A proposal that is under consideration as a possible future standard.

- **Experimental (E).** Protocols that are being tested but are not yet on the standards track.

- **Historical (H).** Obsolete protocols or protocols that are no longer standards.

- **Informational (I).** RFCs that provide the Internet community with general information. Some of these RFCs document standards that, although not actual Internet standards, are commonly used on the Internet.

- **Unclassified (no code).** RFCs of a miscellaneous, sometimes frivolous nature (for example, RFC 968).

It is important to understand that not all RFCs are standards. For example, the Network File Service (NFS) protocol developed by Sun Microsystems is in widespread use on the Internet, but NFS is not an Internet standard. Making NFS an Internet standard would place it under the jurisdiction of the IETF, rather than Sun, which licenses the protocol to many vendors of TCP/IP products. Nevertheless, there is a need for the Internet community to be informed about the protocol. Therefore, NFS v. 3 is documented in RFC 1814, which is an informational RFC. For a list of the RFCs that document Internet standards, consult the RFC named *Internet Official Protocol Standards*.

Not all Internet standard protocols are mandatory. Instead, the protocols are assigned varying degrees of requirement. The different levels are:

▸ **Required.** All systems on the Internet must implement the protocol.

▸ **Recommended.** The protocol should be implemented.

▸ **Elective.** The protocol may be implemented.

▸ **Limited.** The protocol may be useful in some situations. This requirement level may be assigned to historical, experimental, and specialized protocols.

▸ **Not Recommended.** Historical, experimental, and specialized protocols that are not recommended for use on the Internet.

Only certain levels are associated with each category of RFC. Table 1.1 summarizes the levels that correspond to each category.

T A B L E 1.1

Levels of Requirement Associated with RFC Categories

	REQUIRED	RECOMMENDED	ELECTIVE	LIMITED	NOT RECOMMENDED
Standard	✔	✔	✔		
Draft Standard	✔	✔	✔		
Proposed Standard			✔	✔	
Experimental				✔	
Historic					✔

You should keep in mind that specific RFCs are never updated. Once a document is assigned an RFC number, it is effectively cast in stone. Any modifications that are approved by the IETF result in a new RFC with a new number. The RFC index entries shown earlier include two examples of RFCs that make previous RFCs obsolete. Although the obsolete RFCs remain in distribution, they are typically categorized as historic. Therefore, while you need to be sure that you use the most recent RFC that describes a given protocol, you never need to worry that there may be a more recent version of a particular RFC, such as RFC 793.

The procedure for establishing Internet standards is conservative. An entity as enormous as the Internet cannot afford to be governed by rash decisions. Many proposed protocols do not survive, but the ones that do tend to have a broad consensus of support. Those protocols also tend to be fairly long-lived. The TCP protocol described in RFC 793 has existed since September 1981. Figure 1.5, adapted from a diagram in RFC 1800, illustrates the life cycle of an Internet protocol. Each transition to a new classification requires an explicit decision of the IAB based on the recommendations of the IESG.

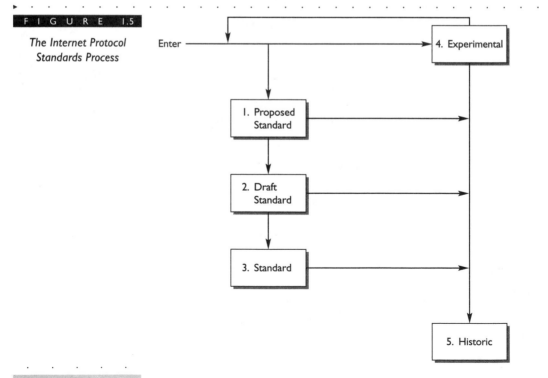

The stages in the cycle are as follows:

1 • When a proposal enters the standards process it is assigned an initial status, often as a proposed standard. Many protocols undergo extensive scrutiny by the IETF before they enter the standards track. That is why certain subjects are never introduced into the RFC cycle. You won't find experimental RFCs related to IP next generation (IPng), a very hot topic at the IETF, because the RFC process is too slow and cumbersome for topics that generate a lot of debate.

   Classification of a protocol as a proposed standard places the protocol on track as a candidate for future standardization. A proposal may enter the standards track only with the approval of the IESG.

2 • A proposed standard can only be promoted to a draft standard by specific action of the IESG. A protocol must remain a proposed standard for at least six months. In general, a proposed standard is only promoted after there have been at least two independent implementations of the protocol and after the IESG has made a recommendation.

   Classification of a protocol as a draft standard notifies the Internet community that the protocol is nearing standardization. Unless significant objections are made, a protocol that is a draft standard will most likely become a standard after about six months.

3 • A draft standard is promoted to a standard only by approval of the IESG. The protocol must have been a draft standard for at least six months. In order to be promoted to a standard, a protocol must have operational experience, and it must demonstrate interoperability in at least two implementations.

4 • Protocols classified as experimental are *not* on the standards track. The IESG may assign an experimental classification to a protocol that is under consideration when it feels the proposal is not yet ready for standardization. Experimental protocols may reenter the standards track as they mature, or they may be removed from consideration altogether and classified as historic.

5 • When a protocol becomes obsolete or when it is declassified as a standard for some other reason, it is designated as historic. Any experimental or standard protocol can be removed from further standards evaluation in this way.

Internet-Drafts

Much of the work being done on protocols is often published in documents called Internet-Drafts. Protocols that are not yet ready to enter the standards track are typically documented in Internet-Draft form. Unlike RFCs, Internet-Drafts are subject to modification at any time, so you need to keep up with the latest versions. A great deal of the IETF's work is ongoing. The information may be hard to find, but documentation is generally available.

OBTAINING INTERNET DOCUMENTATION

RFCs, Internet-Drafts, and other Internet documents are readily available through the Internet. The majority of documents may be acquired using a variety of methods, including FTP, electronic mail, the World Wide Web, and WAIS. This section discusses several approaches (see Chapter 6 for more detailed information).

RFCs are stored in *primary and secondary repositories*. Primary repositories receive RFCs immediately after they are published. Secondary repositories receive copies of RFCs from primary repositories. Updates of secondary repositories may, therefore, be delayed to some degree, depending on the site.

An index of RFCs, available from the InterNIC Directory Services, is extremely useful for finding out more information about the Internet and TCP/IP. The index file named `rfc/rfc inde.txt` can be obtained via e-mail or anonymous FTP. Both methods are discussed in detail in the following subsections.

Electronic Mail

An excellent way to get started is to use the RFC-INFO service, which lets you obtain RFCs, FYI documents, and Internet Monthly Reports (IMRs) using e-mail. This technique is available to anyone who can send e-mail to the Internet directly or through an Internet gateway. To obtain current instructions on obtaining RFCs and other documents, send e-mail addressed to `rfc-info@isi.edu`. The message text should be `help: ways_to_get_rfcs`. A help document will be returned to you via e-mail.

Requests made to the RFC-INFO service consist of keywords placed in the message text. To obtain help documents, start with the following requests:

- ► `Help: Help.` Obtains a brief command list.

- ► `Help: Manual.` Obtains a complete manual for the service.

- ► `Help: List.` Shows you how to use the List request.

- ► `Help: Retrieve.` Shows you how to use the Retrieve request.

If your primary goal is to retrieve RFCs, basically all you need to know is how to use the Retrieve request. The message you would use to retrieve RFC 793 is:

```
Retrieve: RFC

Doc-ID: RFC0793
```

Notice that the RFC number must be four digits. (If necessary, you may need to add a 0 at the beginning.) Consult the help documents for ways to retrieve documents using standards numbers, as well as methods for retrieving FYIs and other Internet documents. Documents will be sent to you in text format. If you require files that are preformatted for PostScript printers, you may want to retrieve them from an FTP site.

Besides the help documents, you may wish to obtain directories of available documents. Because there are so many documents available, different search criteria can be used to narrow the search. (These criteria are described in the help documentation.) For example, to obtain a list of FYI documents published in 1994, the message would be:

```
List: FYI

Dated-after: Dec-31-1993

Dated-before: Jan-01-1995
```

You can also use the `List: RFC` and `List:IMR` requests to obtain lists of FYI and IMR documents.

Another way to obtain RFCs via e-mail is to send a message to `mailserv@ds.internic.net`. **In the message include the text** `file /ftp/rfc/rfcnnnn.txt` **where** `nnnn` **is the RFC number. Do** *not* **include leading zeros in the RFC numbers.**

NOTE

FTP

Probably the most common way that documents circulate on the Internet is using *file transfer protocol* (FTP). FTP is a protocol that is used to configure FTP servers, which make parts of their file systems available to users running FTP client software. Although FTP can be used to manage remote file systems — for example, to create and remove directories — the most common use of FTP is to transfer files.

RFCs and other Internet documents are widely available on *anonymous* FTP servers. These servers are called "anonymous" because they permit anyone to log in without a specific user account. Users simply enter `anonymous` as a login name. Typically, a user is requested to enter his or her e-mail address as a password. Anonymous FTP users are very limited in what they can do, but anonymous FTP is a convenient way for organizations to make files readily available to Internet users. I show you how to use FTP to obtain documents from the InterNIC document service in Chapter 6.

The most up-do-date sources of RFCs are the primary RFC repositories. At this time, the primary repositories are:

```
DS.INTERNIC.NET (InterNIC Directory Services)

NIS.NSF.NET

NISC.JVNC.NET

FTP.ISI.EDU

WUARCHIVE.WUSTL.EDU

SRC.DOC.IC.AC.UK

FTP.NCREN.NET

FTP.SESQUI.NET

NIS.GARR.IT
```

Often, as with the DS.INTERNIC.NET server, RFCs are stored with the path `rfc/rfcnnnn.txt` where `nnnn` is the number of the RFC. Leading zeros are not included in the filename. Thus, RFC 793 would be stored in the file `rfc793.txt`.

You can also obtain RFCs in PostScript format by replacing the `.txt` filename extension with `.ps`.

World Wide Web

The World Wide Web is probably the easiest way to obtain Internet documentation and other information about TCP/IP. The InterNIC operates a Web site that accesses the InterNIC Directory and Database Services and the InterNIC Registration Service. The URL for the InterNIC Web site is `http://ds.internic.net/`. Figure 1.6 shows the Web page for the Directory and Database Services. This page accesses a variety of InterNIC information besides RFCs and FYIs. For example, InterNIC Directory Services maintains a "White Pages" directory with information about many Internet users.

FIGURE 1.6

World Wide Web Page for the InterNIC Directory and Database Services

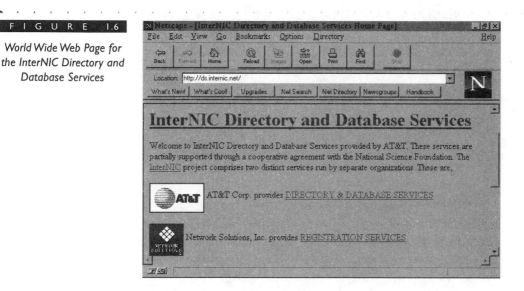

The IETF also maintains a Web page. You can access it through the InterNIC Web site, or can reach it using the URL `http://www.ietf.reston.va.us/`.

WAIS

The Wide Area Information Servers (WAIS) maintains an extensive, searchable database of documents on the Internet. You can access the InterNIC WAIS server using your own WAIS client software. Telnet access is also available. To access the WAIS server using Telnet, Telnet to DS.INTERNIC.NET and log in with the name wais. A password is not required. You will be connected to a WAIS client. The client is quite easy to use, but help is available if you need it. You can also conduct WAIS searches through the InterNIC Web server.

Gopher

Gopher is a service that indexes files related to many FTP sites on the Internet. You can use your own Gopher client software to access a Gopher server by connecting to INTERNIC.NET and using port 70. Or, you can reach a Gopher client via Telnet: Connect to DS.INTERNIC.NET and log in as gopher. No password is required. In Chapter 6, I use a Gopher search to demonstrate how to use of Telnet.

Archie

Internet documents are also cataloged on an Archie database. You can Telnet to an Archie server or perform searches with e-mail. To do an interactive search, Telnet to DS.INTERNIC.NET. Log in as archie without a password. Consult the on-line help for instructions.

Information about accessing Archie through e-mail can be obtained by sending e-mail addressed to archie@ds.internic.net. In the message, enter the help command.

What Is Inside the RFCs?

This chapter has given you an overview of the origins of TCP/IP, the processes that help TCP/IP to evolve, and ways to gain access to the enormous amount of information that is available about TCP/IP. You now know what an RFC is, and you know how to get all the RFCs you could ever desire. Now it is time to discuss the contents of RFCs. However, before I get too specific, you need some background on what communication protocols do and how they are organized. Therefore, next I will examine some different models of network communication.

## CHAPTER 2

TCP/IP and Network Communication

If you have been working with NetWare for any length of time, you may take for granted the ease with which network protocols can be configured. Adding IPX protocol support to a network card is as simple as typing the command BIND IPX TO NE2000 NET=1234. You have probably never had to configure IPX routing, supply the addresses of computers on a network, or enter tuning parameters for network protocols. One source of NetWare's reputation as an easy-to-manage network operating system is the plug-and-play nature of NetWare's protocols.

As you work with TCP/IP, however, you must deal with a more complex environment — not impossible, just complex. You need to be more knowledgeable and you need to plan more for setting up the network because each computer on the network must be assigned an address that conforms to a master address scheme. On each host, you must configure files that enable it to locate gateways (routers) and to access directories of host names. With NetWare, you never have to worry about computer names because NetWare takes care of the names for you. With TCP/IP, names must be administered. Also, you need to know more about your own specific network because TCP/IP functions differently on some networks than on others.

The chapters in Part I prepare you to work as a TCP/IP administrator. In them you will learn, layer-by-layer, how TCP/IP functions, how it relates to the network, and how it relates to NetWare and the IPX protocol. Chapter 2 provides valuable background information about the layers of a TCP/IP network and how network protocols work.

You have probably seen layered models of networks before — most likely the Open Systems Interconnection (OSI) seven-layer reference model. Layers are exceptionally useful tools for understanding network communication. Networks are built in layers because layers make networks easier to understand, easier to design, and easier to reconfigure.

This chapter begins with a discussion of communication in general. I use a layered model to describe an example or real-world, human communication in order to illustrate basic principles of network design. If you are not comfortable with the concept of network protocol stacks, you should take some extra time to review the communication process described here.

Once you thoroughly understand network protocol stacks, you will be ready to look at some real network models. This chapter covers not just one, but two. I first introduce you to the OSI Reference Model because that is the model Novell uses to discuss NetWare protocols. The Open Datalink Interface (ODI) standard, which guides design of network protocol drivers for NetWare, follows the OSI model. Therefore, in order to understand NetWare TCP/IP, you must understand the seven layers of the OSI model.

However, the OSI model did not exist when TCP/IP was created. The designers of TCP/IP instead used their own four-layer model. Although the TCP/IP protocols can be forced to fit the OSI model, they can be better understood in the context of their original four layers.

Layered Communication

You can learn a lot about data communication by looking closely at how people exchange information. Many seemingly simple everyday processes are more complicated than you may realize.

When people converse, there is always the possibility that they will misunderstand each other. Subtleties in choice of words, in the inflection of voice, and in body language can affect the way others interpret your meaning. That is why many people prefer the telephone over electronic mail. Because subtle cues are left out when you send an e-mail message, your precise meaning is more likely to be misunderstood.

Techniques have been devised to improve communication in a number of different settings. Diplomats have long been aware of the need for clear communication, and diplomatic protocols have been established to reduce miscommunication. *Robert's Rules of Order* is a set of guidelines that in part are intended to reduce the potential for miscommunication that is inherent when communication becomes disorderly. In business letters, certain conventions are used so readers can quickly see what's important. In electronic correspondence, a whole system of symbols (called *emotion icons* or *emoticons*) has developed to ensure that the writer's meaning is properly understood. You have undoubtedly come across a :-) or a ;-) at one time or another.

MODEL OF EVERYDAY COMMUNICATION

Consider a complex human process that closely parallels network data communication: the process of bringing clothes along on an airplane trip.

The process starts when you place your clothes in a suitcase. You attach an identification tag so that your luggage will not be lost. At the airport, you hand your suitcase to an attendant who attaches a tag that indicates your destination. When you have arrived at your destination, you pick up your suitcase. But, how does your luggage get to the same place? What steps need to be taken?

The complete process is surprisingly complex — especially because so many different people are involved. Here are the steps when you travel from, say, Indianapolis to Los Angeles.

1 • You place your clothes in a suitcase.

2 • You label the suitcase with an identification tag.

3 • You take the suitcase with you to the airport and hand it to an attendant.

4 • The attendant examines your ticket to determine your destination and then attaches another tag that indicates the appropriate airport code. The attendant then sends the suitcase to the airplane.

5 • Baggage handlers examine the suitcase's destination information to decide which plane it belongs on.

6 • If you need to change planes along the way — for example, at Denver — baggage handlers at the intermediate airport must examine the suitcase's routing information to determine what to do with your suitcase. (For example, they determine that your suitcase must be transferred to another plane headed for Los Angeles.)

7 • When your plane arrives in Los Angeles, baggage handlers again must examine the tag to determine where to route your suitcase. At this point, your suitcase is sent to a luggage carousel.

8 • You retrieve your suitcase case and take it with you to your hotel room.

9 • You open the suitcase and unpack your clothes.

I've gone through these steps in detail because the process provides a useful analogy to many of the concepts applied to data networks. Figure 2.1 shows a model of the baggage-handling process.

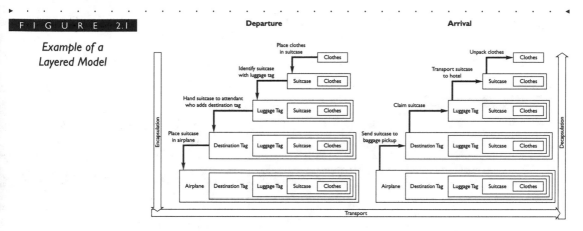

FIGURE 2.1

*Example of a
Layered Model*

The first concept to note is *encapsulation* — that is, placing something inside a container. You place your clothes in a suitcase so you can keep them all together and so you can label them all at once. Likewise, your suitcase is encapsulated in the plane. All of the suitcases for your flight are placed on the same plane so that they all arrive at the proper destination at the same time.

The reverse of encapsulation is *decapsulation* — that is, opening containers and removing their contents. When you arrive at your destination, the luggage from your plane is removed so that each suitcase can be individually routed. Similarly, when you arrive at your hotel, you remove your clothes from the suitcase that you used to encapsulate them.

Another important concept is *routing*, which takes place at three points in the scenario:

▶ In Indianapolis, the suitcase is routed to your plane.

▶ At the intermediate airport in Denver, your suitcase is routed again. Baggage handlers examine the suitcase and decide whether it should remain in Denver or be forwarded to another flight.

> ▸ In Los Angeles, baggage handlers again examine the suitcase and determine that it has reached its final destination. They therefore route the suitcase to the local baggage claim area.

Figure 2.2 shows the big picture. The diagram should look familiar to you. If you substitute computers for airports, the picture resembles a typical network diagram. The difference is that, on the one hand, suitcases and airplanes are used to route clothes from one location to another. On the other hand, computer networks route data through cables. The general principles, however, are the same.

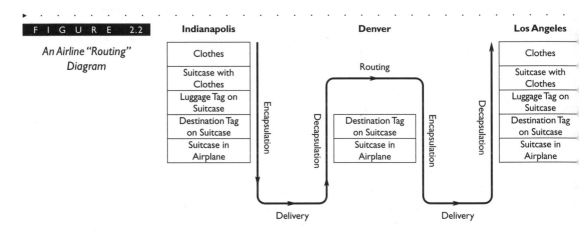

FIGURE 2.2

An Airline "Routing" Diagram

In Figure 2.2, you can see that the routing in Denver does not require complete decapsulation. Your clothes are partially decapsulated when your suitcase is unloaded from the plane, but your clothes nevertheless remain encapsulated in your suitcase. Only enough decapsulation occurs to allow baggage handlers to properly route your clothes. Keep this analogy in mind later on when I discuss network routers. (Later, you will see that routers need not always implement a complete set of protocols. They only need to implement enough protocols to allow routing to occur.)

Another key concept is *addressing*. In the suitcase analogy, routing depends on one critical piece of information: the destination tag placed on your suitcase at the beginning of the trip. This tag indicates where your suitcase needs to be delivered. The tag can be regarded as yet another form of encapsulation: Your clothes become encapsulated in a suitcase bearing a destination tag.

Routing can be performed efficiently only if a consistent labeling system is recognized at all of the locations through which luggage must be routed. Imagine the confusion that international travel would cause if every country in the world had its own unique tagging system that was not recognized in other countries. At best, travel would be much slower. At worst, your luggage would wind up lost forever. Fortunately, international agreements have resulted in fairly uniform standards for regulating commercial air travel. The common standards work fairly well because they are universally recognized.

The concept of *layering*, subdividing a complex task into multiple distinct steps, can also be understood in light of the luggage analogy. The task of transporting your suitcase from one place to another can be broken into discrete steps that occur more or less independently. The interfaces between the steps must be clearly defined. When you hand your suitcase to an attendant at your departure airport, you must present a ticket that identifies your destination. When the attendant transfers the suitcase to baggage handlers, it must have a destination tag. At each step along the way, certain previously defined conditions must be met before a transfer from one layer to another can occur.

Layering is a key concept. It involves compartmentalizing complex processes into elementary steps. Imagine how complex baggage handling would be if each passenger had to devise a method for delivering his or her bags and personally had to execute that plan. Each passenger would want to do things differently, and chaos would ensue. As it is, the passenger is only responsible for starting and ending the process. Someone else takes care of the steps in between.

Layering allows you to deal with the individual processes at each layer separately. Different layers can function in their own unique ways. For example, the baggage handling in Indianapolis might proceed differently from the baggage handling in Denver. Indianapolis could use a system in which people manually transfer luggage from a conveyor belt to a cart and then onto the airplane. Denver might instead use an automated system that transfers luggage mechanically and that performs routing with a computer. As long as common interfaces are used, the steps that occur at each layer can be different.

Another concept that is illustrated by the luggage analogy is *peer-to-peer communication*. Each layer communicates with corresponding layers at other locations. When the airline attendant places a destination tag on your suitcase, the attendant is not using the tag to communicate with you. The attendant is communicating with other baggage handlers at other airports. In other words, the baggage handler is communicating with *peers*.

Finally, you should be familiar with the concept of *error handling*. Given the volume of luggage transported every day, mistakes naturally occur. Those mistakes can be very costly, especially when valuable items are lost. In almost every case, more effort must be expended to correct an error than to deliver an item properly the first time. Although the airline industry spends far less on its error-correction mechanisms than on its primary luggage-delivery system, its error handling system is nevertheless important.

SUMMARY OF LAYERED COMMUNICATION

Here is a summary the concepts the luggage analogy should help you understand:

- ▶ **Encapsulation.** The process of enclosing messages in packages so they can travel through different layers during communication.

- ▶ **Routing.** Procedures that ensure packages follow the most efficient paths through complex systems.

- ▶ **Addressing.** Conventions that are used to identify packages.

- ▶ **Layering**. The organization of complex processes into discrete steps that are connected to each other by certain well-defined interfaces.

- ▶ **Peer-to-peer communication.** Communication between corresponding layers in different locations.

- ▶ **Error handling.** Mechanisms that are used to detect and, if possible, correct errors.

By looking at a computer-based model (namely, the OSI Reference Model), you can see more clearly how these principles apply to network data communication.

The OSI Reference Model

The OSI model is important because unless you understand it, you will have trouble understanding the organization of Novell protocols. Novell's Open Datalink Interface (ODI) technology is based on the OSI model, and discussion of the IPX and TCP/IP protocols necessarily involves OSI terminology. Therefore, you must be familiar with the OSI model if you want to understand NetWare TCP/IP fully.

Figure 2.3 illustrates the OSI model. At the risk of enraging OSI purists, I use a nine-layer model instead of a seven-layer model. I feel the additional layers are necessary for the following two reasons:

▶ The OSI Reference Model does not address network cabling or other media. The physical layer describes only the protocols, interfaces, and signaling for the medium. It does not include the hardware and cabling. I have added the media layer (layer 0) to represent hardware and cabling in network communication.

▶ The OSI Reference Model does not include end-user applications, such as word processors. The application layer describes the interface between user applications and the network. It does not deal with the applications themselves. I have added the user layer (layer 8) to show how end-user applications fit into the picture.

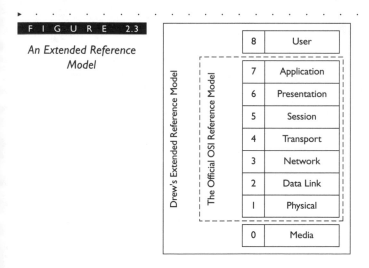

FIGURE 2.3

An Extended Reference Model

The following sections describe my extended OSI Reference Model layer by layer.

NOTE

Figure 2.3 shows why suites of protocols are commonly called protocol stacks. A suite of protocols consists of several protocols that are grouped by layer to fulfill a specific network communication function.

THE MEDIA LAYER (LAYER 0)

All communication requires a medium through which the communicated information can travel. For speech, the medium is the air. For sight, the medium is light. For electronic data, the medium can be just about anything that scientists find a way to adapt.

By far the most common medium is copper cable, but fiber optics, infrared light, radio waves, and microwaves are all alternative media. Each particular medium has its own advantages and disadvantages. For example, copper is cheap and easy to install, and it performs well for most applications. But copper is not as effective when data rates are too high. Microwave, by contrast, supports high data rates and can be used to send data anyplace within the line of sight, but microwave is unbelievably expensive. Therefore, very few organizations can afford private microwave links.

The different media use a variety of methods to convey information. Information may be transmitted using high and low voltages, voltage transitions, light pulses, or changes in analog carriers. However, regardless of the method used, computer data must be transmitted as *bits*. One signal represents a 1; another represents a 0. That is all that is going on as far as the medium is concerned.

You need not understand how the different media operate. The basic point is this: The medium is only important at the physical layer. TCP/IP couldn't care less whether messages are routed through a coax Ethernet or a laser beam. Layers make it unnecessary to adapt TCP/IP to the medium because TCP/IP isn't even aware of the medium.

THE PHYSICAL LAYER (LAYER 1)

The first layer of the traditional OSI model is the physical layer. The physical layer is responsible for transmitting data bits to the network medium and receiving data bits from the medium. Protocols at the physical layer perform two functions that complement each other, as follows:

- ▸ When data moves down the protocol stack toward the network medium, the physical layer receives streams of bits from the data link layer and sends the data in electrically encoded form to the medium.

- ▸ When data moves up the protocol stack from the medium to the upper layers, the physical layer receives bits from the network and sends them to the data link layer.

Figure 2.4 shows how the physical layer functions. The message unit at the physical layer is the *bit*. The physical layer receives a stream of bits from the data link layer which it transmits as an electrical waveform on the network. The physical layer deals only with the mechanical, electrical, and procedural interfaces required to send bits to the medium and to receive bits from the medium. Examples of issues that relate to physical layer include:

- ▸ What voltages should represent different bit values?

- ▸ How long should a bit last?

- ▸ Is communication one- or two-way?

- ▸ Which wires should carry specific signals?

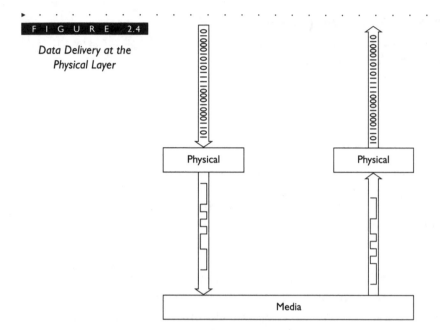

F I G U R E   2.4

*Data Delivery at the
Physical Layer*

THE DATA LINK LAYER (LAYER 2)

The data link layer is responsible for delivering message units between devices on the same network. There are several different names used to describe network devices. The most common name for network devices is probably *nodes*. The data link layer is responsible for node-to-node delivery of message units. Message units are usually called *frames* at the data link layer, but they are also commonly referred to as *packets*.

The data link layer performs two functions:

▸ It provides an address mechanism that uniquely identifies each node on the local network.

▸ It receives message units from upper layers, formats the data into frames, and sends the frames as bits to the physical layer.

In local area networks (LANs), many nodes are attached to the same network medium. Therefore, each node sees every message that is transmitted. A node addressing scheme allows each node to tell which messages are intended for it. Node addresses uniquely identify every piece of hardware connected to a network.

In Figure 2.5, node B sends a frame to node C. To do so, node B merely creates a frame addressed to C and passes the frame to the physical layer. The frame travels through the network to nodes A and C. Node A does not recognize the node address as its own, so it discards the frame. Node C recognizes the address and therefore receives the frame.

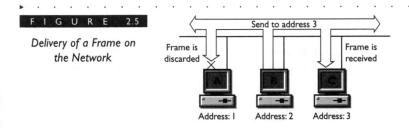

FIGURE 2.5

Delivery of a Frame on the Network

Node addresses are often referred to as *physical addresses* because these addresses are typically coded into the network interface's hardware. Node addresses are also sometimes called *MAC addresses* because the IEEE (Institute of Electrical and Electronics Engineers) protocols such as 802.3 (IEEE Ethernet) and 802.5 (Token Ring) define a *medium access control* (MAC) sublayer at which addressing takes place. I prefer to use the term "physical address."

The information needed to deliver data is encoded into frames, which the data link layer constructs. The format of a typical frame is shown in Figure 2.6. A frame consists of several parts called *fields*. The various fields are as follows:

- ▶ **Start Indicator.** A bit pattern that indicates where a frame begins.

- ▶ **Destination Address.** The physical address of the destination node.

- ▶ **Source Address.** The physical address of the node that sent the frame.

- ▶ **Control Information.** Protocol-dependent data that serves a variety of control functions.

- ▶ **Data.** Data received from upper layers. This is the frame's payload.

- ▶ **Error Control.** A value that can be used to determine whether a frame has been damaged during transmission.

Start Indicator	Destination Address	Source Address	Control Information	Data	Error Control

Because the physical layer can only handle bits, the data link layer must organize bits into the proper message structure. The data link layer accomplishes this by adding special bit patterns to the beginnings and ends of frames. After adding the framing information to a frame, the data link layer transmits the frame to the physical layer in the form of a stream of binary digits.

Examples of data link layer protocols are Ethernet and Token Ring. (Both protocols are also used at the physical layer.) I explain these protocols, among others, in Chapter 3.

THE NETWORK LAYER (LAYER 3)

The message delivery depicted in Figure 2.5 is very basic. But what happens when more than one network is involved? Figure 2.7 shows what happens when data travels from one network to another. When B sends a frame to E, the frame circulates throughout network 1, where it originated. However, none of the devices on network 1 will find its address in the destination address field. Although C is connected to both network 1 and network 2, some functionality above and beyond the data link layer must be added to allow C to forward the frame from one network to another. The term *bridging* is used to describe the transfer of frames between networks. (I discuss bridging in more detail later in this chapter.)

F I G U R E   2.7

Delivering a Frame on an Internetwork

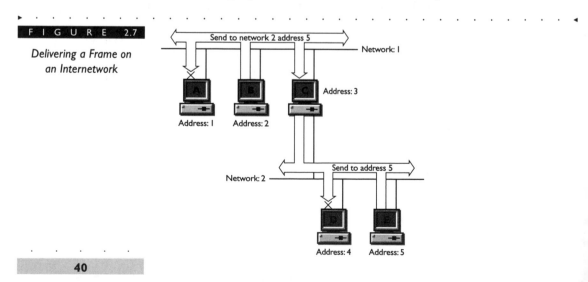

The network shown in Figure 2.7 is typically called an *internetwork* because it is a "network of networks." Node C, which is connected to both networks, is called a *router* because it routes messages from one network to another. Often, routing involves the selection of the best route through a complex internetwork.

In order for routers to work, each network must have its own unique *network address*. Routers build tables that contain network addresses for all of the networks on an internetwork. These network addresses must be encoded into messages at the network layer. When a router finds a network address in a message, it sends the message on its way to the appropriate destination network. Each node on an internetwork can be identified by the combination of its network address and its physical address.

Consequently, nodes on an internetwork can be categorized in two ways:

▶ *End nodes* are the endpoints of a communication. At the network layer, end nodes add network addresses to message units. End nodes do not perform routing. The OSI term for an end node is *end system*. The traditional TCP/IP term for an end node is *host*.

▶ *Intermediate nodes* are routers. They forward messages through internetworks. Intermediate nodes must be equipped with a routing function so they can determine routes and forward messages. A router can be a dedicated piece of equipment, or it can be a device that also serves another purpose (such as a NetWare server or a TCP/IP host to which a routing function has been added). The OSI term for intermediate node is *intermediate system*. The TCP/IP term has traditionally been *gateway*, but the term *router* has recently become more popular.

Network-layer message units are usually called *packets*. Novell's network-layer protocol is Internet Packet Exchange (IPX). The TCP/IP network-layer protocol is the Internet Protocol (IP). IP's message units are called *datagrams*, which I discuss later in this chapter under the heading "Packet Switching."

THE TRANSPORT LAYER (LAYER 4)

Here are some of the transport layer's functions:

▸ If a message is too big for layers 0 through 3 to handle, the transport layer breaks the message into smaller units that the network can handle.

▸ The transport layer can make delivery more reliable by detecting errors and requesting that damaged message units be resent.

▸ On multitasking hosts, the transport layer ensures that messages are delivered to the correct processes.

I discuss each of these important functions in the subsections that follow.

Message Fragmentation and Reassembly

When you are determining the maximum message size that your network will accommodate, you must strike a balance. If the maximum message size is too large, a single transmission could monopolize the network for too long. Therefore, a relatively small cap is usually placed on network frame size. An Ethernet data frame, for example, accepts a maximum of 1500 bytes of data.

Because the majority of messages on your network will probably exceed 1500 bytes in length, you need some way to break up large messages into small pieces. That method is called *message fragmentation*. The transport layer accepts a continuous stream of data from upper-layer protocols and buffers the data until the amount reaches the maximum that a frame can accommodate. Each message fragment, called a *segment*, is tagged with a sequence number. The sequence numbers are used at the receiving end to reassemble the segments in their original order and recover the message. Segment numbers are necessary on packet switching networks because segments may not arrive in the order they were sent. Figure 2.8 illustrates how segments may take different routes through an internetwork and arrive out of order.

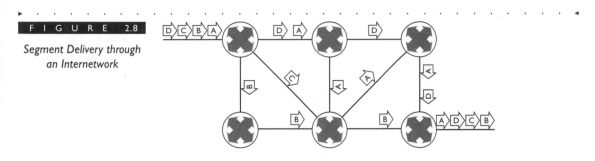

FIGURE 2.8

*Segment Delivery through
an Internetwork*

Error Detection and Recovery of Data

Although error detection and recovery of data may occur at any protocol level, these functions are usually performed by the transport layer protocols. The transport layer protocols ensure that all the segments related to a message are received without error. That task makes the process of detecting errors and recovering data extremely complicated. Typically, transport layer protocols employ a system of acknowledgments. The transport layer at the receiving node must acknowledge that it has received individual segments or groups of segments. The sending transport layer then resends segments for which it has not received acknowledgments.

When a network's messages need to be absolutely free of errors, that network can employ *reliable delivery* protocols. When you use reliable delivery protocols, errors may still occur, but the errors are detected and then corrected. Certain costs are associated with reliable delivery. Acknowledgments take up network bandwidth, and additional processing is required when the sending and receiving nodes must track each segment and determine whether it has been acknowledged.

Because reliable delivery can be costly, sometimes it makes sense to assume that messages will be delivered properly. For example, if messages are short and relatively unimportant, it probably does not matter if a few messages are occasionally lost. You probably don't need reliable delivery for your network management data. If a device sends an alert that is lost, it can always resend the message after a delay. Also, reliable delivery can unnecessarily add overhead to networks that are basically pretty reliable, such as LANs.

When the cost of reliable delivery outweighs the benefits, network designers turn to *unreliable delivery* methods. With unreliable delivery, errors will *not* be automatically detected and corrected. However, if the transport layer does not perform error recovery, a higher level protocol (or even an application) can take on the responsibility of detecting errors.

Usually, NetWare does not provide reliable delivery at its transport-level protocol. Because LAN delivery is generally free of error, NetWare's designers decided not to sacrifice performance for the sake of reliable delivery. Error recovery is performed by the NetWare Core Protocols (NCP), which work in conjunction with IPX at the network layer. When reliable delivery is required, NetWare uses the Sequenced Packet Exchange (SPX) protocol.

In the TCP/IP protocol suite, the Transmission Control Protocol (TCP) provides reliable delivery. Because TCP/IP is commonly used in relatively unreliable wide area network (WAN) environments, the majority of TCP/IP services rely on TCP for reliable delivery. When unreliable delivery is acceptable, the User Datagram Protocol (UDP) can be substituted for TCP.

Protocol Multiplexing

The majority of computers are multitasking devices, meaning that they can run several processes at once. Multitasking complicates things on a network. Not only does a network need to deliver messages to the right computers, each message must be directed to the correct process on each computer.

The OSI protocol model solves this problem by assigning a *service access point* (SAP) to each protocol. A SAP is a number that serves as an address. Each message has three identifiers: a network address, a physical address, and an SAP. The combination of these three numbers ensures the message will reach the correct process on the correct computer. Figure 2.9 illustrates how SAPs are used to deliver messages to processes.

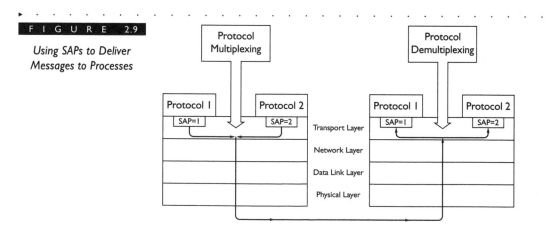

F I G U R E   2.9

Using SAPs to Deliver Messages to Processes

Service access points allow the transport layer to combine messages from several processes and send those messages through a common network interface. That process is called *multiplexing*. At the receiving end, the transport layer does the reverse: It recovers separate messages from the single incoming stream of data. The process of recovering the original messages is called *demultiplexing*.

THE SESSION LAYER (LAYER 5)

Usually, network computers engage in two-way communication. In other words, computers typically have *dialogs*. The primary function of the session layer is to control those dialogs.

There are three modes of communication between computers. The three modes are:

- **Simplex.** Data travels in one direction. One node transmits and the other receives.

- **Half-Duplex.** Data travels in both directions. Both nodes can transmit and receive. However, the nodes must take turns because the medium cannot accommodate simultaneous transmissions.

- **Full-Duplex.** Data travels in both directions. Both nodes can transmit and receive data simultaneously. (Each node can send and receive at the same time.)

Figure 2.10 illustrates the three modes.

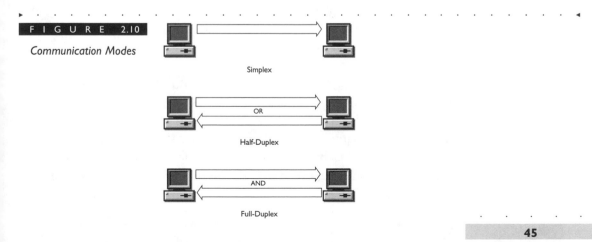

FIGURE 2.10

Communication Modes

Simplex

Half-Duplex

Full-Duplex

Full-duplex operation is the most desirable mode of network communication. To make full-duplex work, a network need some form of flow control so that a node does not send data more rapidly than the data can be received. On data networks, the orderly exchange of data between two nodes is called a *session*. (In reality, most LANs do not permit multiple messages on a medium at a given time. Therefore, full-duplex communication is not — strictly speaking — simultaneous. Nevertheless, from the end nodes' standpoint, full-duplex communication does appear to be simultaneous.)

A session establishes a *virtual connection* between two computers on a network. The computers behave as though a dedicated communication channel existed between them, even though they are sharing a medium with many other computers. A virtual connection is necessary for reliable delivery.

The session layer's primary job is management of sessions. Each session has three phases:

1. • **Connection establishment.** This is the special process during which two computers agree to communicate. Many things can be decided during connection establishment, including the protocols to be used, the error control parameters, and the limitations on the size of messages.

2. • **Data exchange.** During most of the session, the computers exchange data in an orderly manner. A session may last a short time or it may be of indefinite duration.

3. • **Connection release.** This is the distinct process in which the computers terminate the connection. (The process is also sometimes called tear down.) Failure to release a connection can invalidate the data transmitted, or it can leave the processes in limbo.

Connections often make considerable demands on a system. Those demands may be justifiable when network errors are likely — for example, on WANs — or when errors cannot be tolerated. However, sometimes the cost of having connections cannot be justified. For example, if a node only transmits short, infrequent messages, it may require more effort to build, maintain, and tear down connections than to send the data. That would be a disproportionate use of network bandwidth. In cases where the cost of having connections cannot be justified, connectionless delivery can be used. With connectionless delivery, a connection need not be established or released. The sending computer simply transmits data without any assurance that it will be received.

THE PRESENTATION LAYER (LAYER 6)

Not all computers are alike. For example, the majority of computers use ASCII character codes, but IBM mainframes use a system called EBCDIC. The numerous differences among computers make it difficult for computers to exchange data.

The presentation layer's job is to overcome those differences by presenting data to upper-layer protocols in a uniform format. This often involves using a standard to represent data so that the data can be understood by different computer hardware and software systems. Computers typically do not arrive from the factory with the standards included, but all computers can be programmed to understand standard formats. In the OSI realm, the standard is called Abstract Syntax Notation, Revision 1 (ASN.1). In TCP/IP, an example of a standard format is the External Data Representation (XDR) format, which Sun's Network File System (NFS) protocol uses. You will learn more about NFS in Chapter 6.

The presentation layer can also be used for encryption and decryption and for compression and decompression of data. When data formats are converted as data travels from an application to a network, the conversion can be performed at the presentation layer.

In practice, presentation layer protocols are seldom implemented. The presentation layer often simply passes data unaltered between the session and application layers. For example, data encryption and decryption are often performed by the applications themselves. Likewise, data compression and decompression are often performed by network hardware, such as compression modems. In reality, presentation layer protocols are very rare.

THE APPLICATION LAYER (LAYER 7)

From its name, you might assume that the application layer involves familiar applications like WordPerfect and Lotus 1-2-3 — that is, the applications that users operate directly. However, you would be mistaken. In the OSI Reference Model, the term "application layer" means something else. The application layer is the interface that allows applications to connect to the network.

Some application layer protocols provide the foundation of network services. For example, Novell's Message Handling Service (MHS) and TCP/IP's Simple Mail Transfer Protocol (SMTP) are protocols that enable e-mail applications to send, receive, and manage electronic mail.

Application program interfaces (APIs) are an important component of the application layer. An API is an interface that programmers use to connect their programs to a system. For example, Novell's NetWare Core Protocol (NCP) is an API that programmers use to build NetWare-aware applications. In TCP/IP, some common APIs are:

- Berkeley Sockets (or BSD Sockets), popularized by 4.3BSD UNIX

- Streams Transport Layer Interface (TLI), developed by AT&T

- Windows Sockets (WinSock), designed for the Microsoft Windows environment and based on BSD Sockets

NetWare servers support applications written for the Sockets and TLI APIs.

Application-level protocols are associated with a wide variety of network services in addition to electronic mail. Here are some others:

- **Remote file services.** Application-level protocols are necessary for the remote file services provided by systems such as Novell's NetWare and Sun's NFS. NetWare enables user applications to access files on NetWare servers. NFS enables TCP/IP hosts to mount remote file systems and use them as if they were local.

- **Remote job execution.** This service enables users to initiate programs that execute on remote computers.

- **Naming services and directories.** These services provide a catalog of a network's computers and shared resources. The catalogs use logical names so users and applications do not need network and node addresses.

- **Network management.** Some protocols — for example, Simple Network Management Protocol (SNMP) — enable computers to send alerts and statistics to management consoles. These protocols also allow management consoles to change operating parameters of network devices.

THE USER LAYER (LAYER 8)

The final layer of my extended version of the OSI model is the user layer. The user layer consists of the programs that the end users run. Depending on the interface with the application layer, certain programs may be able to access the network without being network-aware. Because networks have become so popular, most applications now conform to one or more APIs. You may have already specified API calls without realizing what you were doing. For instance, when you install WordPerfect and specify NetWare operation, you are in fact indicating which API calls you want WordPerfect to use.

The DoD Protocol Model

Although there are several different names for the protocol model associated with TCP/IP, the model is usually referred to as the DoD model because the protocols originated at the Department of Defense.

The DoD model was created before the OSI model existed. Consequently, the four-layer Internet model does not fit neatly into the OSI model. Nevertheless, in Figure 2.11 you can see how the layers of the Internet model correspond more or less to the layers of the OSI Reference Model.

F I G U R E   2.11

Comparison of the DoD and OSI Protocol Models

OSI Reference Model	Internet Model
Application	Process/Application
Presentation	
Session	
Transport	Host-to-Host
Network	Internet
Data Link	Network Access
Physical	

NOTE **Because the layers of the two models do not correspond exactly, you may find variations on this diagram in other sources. Different people are bound to conceptualize the layers differently. There is not a single "right" way to compare the two models.**

The following paragraphs give you an overview of the layers of the DoD protocol stack. I examine each layer in more detail in later chapters.

The network access layer enables TCP/IP hosts to communicate with other hosts on a network. The network access layer corresponds roughly to the data link and physical layers of the OSI model. At the network access layer, hosts are identified by physical addresses that are used for local delivery of messages. You should keep in mind that TCP/IP was designed to operate over existing network types. The creators of TCP/IP have not defined their own network types. You may occasionally need to adapt TCP/IP to a particular type of network. Several RFCs discuss adaptation issues. The network access layer is the subject of Chapter 3.

The internet layer — which I cover in Chapter 4 — delivers messages through internetworks. The internet layer corresponds to the network layer of the OSI model. The internet layer is primarily associated with one protocol, the Internet Protocol (IP), which delivers messages (called *datagrams*) between hosts on an internetwork. The internet layer uses logical addresses to identify hosts. The logical addresses (called *IP addresses*) incorporate both network and host identifiers that IP uses for routing. An address resolution protocol (ARP) is used to map IP addresses to the network access layer's physical addresses.

The host-to-host layer corresponds to the OSI transport layer. The host-to-host layer performs message fragmentation and assembly, as well as message multiplexing. The host-to-host layer may provide reliable delivery. The Internet uses two protocols at this level. The Transmission Control Protocol (TCP) provides fully reliable service, and it is therefore used most often. When unreliable service is acceptable, the User Datagram Protocol (UDP) can be employed. You will learn more about the host-to-host layer in Chapter 5.

The process/application layer — which I discuss in Chapter 6 — includes a wide variety of protocols, processes, and applications that depend on the host-to-host layer to provide a network interface. You can see the richness of TCP/IP at the process/application layer. Here are just a few examples of the many of services supported by TCP/IP:

▸ **File Transfer Protocol (FTP).** Supports transfer of files between systems and allows users to access file systems remotely.

▸ **Telnet.** Provides remote terminal capability. With Telnet, users can utilize different networked computers for terminal sessions.

▸ **Simple Mail Transfer Protocol (SMTP).** Serves as the standard protocol for delivering electronic mail over the Internet.

▸ **Simple Network Management Protocol (SNMP).** Allows network administrators to collect network management information and to manage network devices remotely.

▸ **Network File System (NFS).** Enables users to mount remote file systems as if files were local. NFS allows users to share file systems on remote computers.

The process/application layer does not correspond exactly to the layers of the OSI model. Some applications perform functions that correspond to several OSI levels. FTP, for example, manages user sessions. As I mentioned earlier, session management is a function of the session layer in the OSI model. FTP also converts file formats when they are transferred between different systems. In the OSI model, format conversion is handled by the presentation layer. FTP can also be used for file transfers, which is a function of the application layer in the OSI model.

Figure 2.12 shows several important TCP/IP protocols and how they correspond to the DoD protocol model.

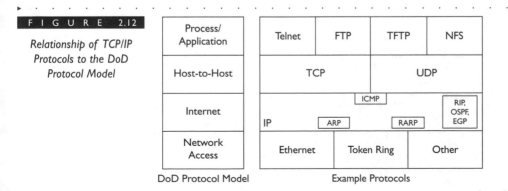

FIGURE 2.12

Relationship of TCP/IP Protocols to the DoD Protocol Model

More on Protocol Models

Now that you have seen two different protocol models, a few additional observations may be made.

As you know, protocol layers must communicate with each other. For example, the network layer of one computer sends network addresses to the network layers on other computers. In order for communication between corresponding layers to take place, you need to use message formats that can be understood by all of the layers in the sending and receiving protocol stacks. Effective communication between all of the layers is possible because each layer builds on what it receives from other layers.

The OSI term for the messages that a protocol layer sends to the next lower layer is *protocol data units* (PDUs). Each layer adds its information in the form of a *header* that is appended to the start of the PDU received from an upper layer. Figure 2.13 illustrates the process for the network and transport layers. The network layer constructs a network PDU by appending its header information to the transport layer PDU that is to be sent. When the network layer receives a frame from the network, it strips off the network header to recover the original transport layer PDU, which is forwarded to the transport layer.

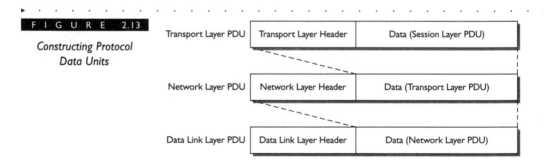

FIGURE 2.13

Constructing Protocol Data Units

The process of packaging information from higher layers into new PDUs is called *encapsulation*. In Figure 2.13, transport layer data is encapsulated in the network layer PDU, and network layer data is encapsulated in the data link layer PDU. The processes of encapsulation and decapsulation take place at each layer of sending and receiving protocol stacks. Figure 2.14 illustrates the complete process. Notice that the data link layer typically adds a trailer as well. This trailer contains codes that can be used to detect network transmission errors.

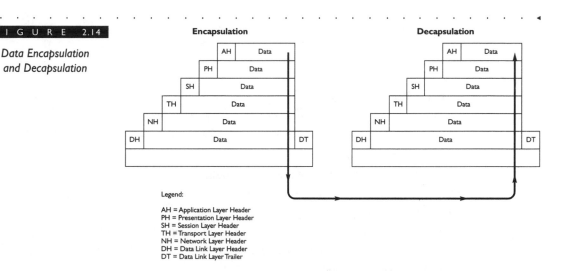

FIGURE 2.14

Data Encapsulation and Decapsulation

Legend:

AH = Application Layer Header
PH = Presentation Layer Header
SH = Session Layer Header
TH = Transport Layer Header
NH = Network Layer Header
DH = Data Link Layer Header
DT = Data Link Layer Trailer

Each layer (except possibly the physical layer) has a specific header format. This header information is used by the corresponding layer at the receiving end. In other words, each protocol communicates with its *peer* protocol in the receiving computer. This type of communication is called *peer-to-peer communication.*

Data Communication Technologies

Network communication is a complex process. Large networks can have many computers that all need to communicate with each other. Combinations of different network types can make network communication even more complicated. In this section I discuss several important technologies that make complex networks possible. I address the following questions:

▶ When several messages must be sent through a single communication channel, how can the messages share the channel yet still retain their distinct identities?

▶ When messages travel through complex networks, how can the messages be switched through the available paths?

▸ When messages are switched through different paths, how does the network determine the best route for messages to take?

MULTIPLEXING

Often, many data streams need to share the same communication channel. Sometimes only a single channel is available. Or it may be too costly to pay for more than one channel. Or a channel may have very high bandwidth, and it may be inefficient to dedicate the entire channel to a single data stream. The technology that allows multiple streams of data to share a single communication channel is called *multiplexing.*

This section examines two types of multiplexing: *protocol multiplexing,* which occurs in protocol stacks, and *signal multiplexing,* which takes place in data communication channels.

Protocol Multiplexing

You saw an example of protocol multiplexing earlier in this chapter in the section about the transport layer. Using service access points, the transport layer delivers messages to the appropriate protocols in higher layers. But the transport layer is not the only layer that uses protocol multiplexing. For example, protocol multiplexing is used in other layers in each of the following cases:

▸ When the data link layer must recognize several different types of Ethernet frame types and enable them to share a network interface card.

▸ When the data link layer must determine where to deliver messages (that is, which is the appropriate protocol stack). For example, both IPX and TCP/IP protocol stacks may be present.

▸ When the network layer must determine where to deliver messages (that is, which is the correct transport protocol). For example, the network layer might have to decide between TCP and UDP.

▸ When the transport layer must deliver messages to the correct upper-layer application, such as FTP, Telnet, or SMTP.

Figure 2.15 illustrates how protocol multiplexing can take place at virtually any protocol level.

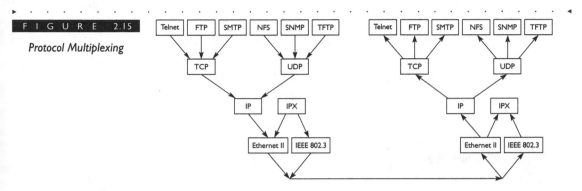

F I G U R E   2.15

Protocol Multiplexing

Signal Multiplexing

Baseband media are media that support a single data stream. LANs often use baseband media. Ethernet and Token Ring assume a baseband medium is in use, and they both employ mechanisms to ensure that only one node can transmit at a time.

Broadband media are media that can carry multiple data steams simultaneously. Broadband media are common as well. Microwaves, fiber optics, and coaxial cables are all examples of broadband media. With these media, multiplexing is necessary so that multiple data streams can share the bandwidth of the medium at the same time.

Digital data can be multiplexed using a technique called *time-division multiplexing* (TDM). The bandwidth of the medium is broken into multiple time slots, which are allocated to the data streams transmitted. Figure 2.16 illustrates how TDM works. The multiplexer and demultiplexer are synchronized. They associate each time slot with the correct data stream. The data streams take turns using the data capacity of the medium.

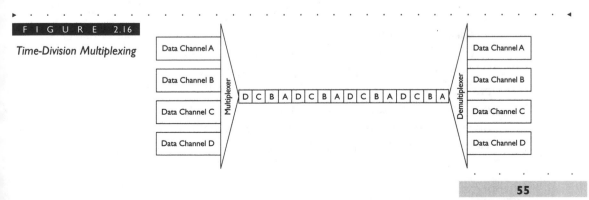

F I G U R E   2.16

Time-Division Multiplexing

Time-division multiplexing works well if all data streams are equally busy. If the traffic levels in the data streams are uneven, however, some time slots may be underutilized, and other time slots may not be able to handle the data streams that are allocated to them. A technique called *statistical TDM* allocates time slots based on how busy the data streams are. Figure 2.17 illustrates statistical TDM. In Figure 2.17, the time slots are no longer allocated in a fixed sequence. Each time slot is assigned a data stream based on need. In the diagram, data stream B is the busiest, and therefore it receives the most time slots. Data stream D is silent, and so it does not receive any time slots.

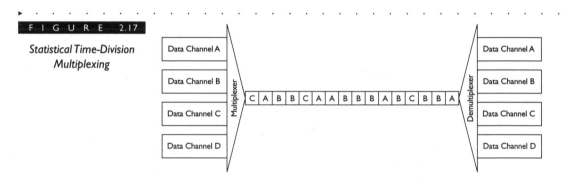

FIGURE 2.17

Statistical Time-Division Multiplexing

SWITCHING DATA THROUGH INTERNETWORKS

Networks are frequently designed so that two or more paths are available between nodes. Having multiple paths provides a backup in case one of the paths fails. Furthermore, having multiple paths can increase network data capacity because you then have the option of using all of the pathways simultaneously, if necessary. However, multiple paths present a problem: How should messages be switched through the available pathways to reach their destinations? There are two common techniques for switching messages: circuit switching and packet switching.

Circuit Switching

Circuit switching works much like the public telephone system. When you pick up a phone and call a friend, the telephone system creates a path between your phone and your friend's phone. A circuit is established between the two telephones. (At one time, the circuit consisted of an actual copper wire that you could trace from one phone to the other. Today, several types of media are used.) From your point of view, a portion of the network is dedicated completely to your personal use.

A circuit-switched data network is shown in Figure 2.18. When two nodes establish a session, a circuit is created through the internetwork. All traffic between the endpoints travels through this circuit. The connected computers are guaranteed a certain amount of bandwidth devoted to their use. Also, circuit switching pre-establishes a path through the network. Because there is a pre-established path, circuit switching delivers messages reliably and with few delays.

FIGURE 2.18

Circuit Switching

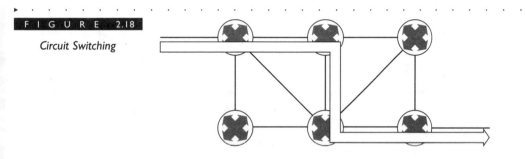

Circuit switching has disadvantages, however. If the circuit's dedicated bandwidth is not fully used, a portion of the network's overall bandwidth is wasted. Furthermore, if the network temporarily requires extra capacity, the circuit may need to be torn down and reestablished with greater bandwidth. Therefore, circuit switching is seldom used for data communication. (One exception is asynchronous transfer mode, or ATM. In Chapter 3 you will see how ATM is able to benefit from the advantages of circuit switching without the problem of inefficient bandwidth utilization.)

In real-world implementations, it is highly unlikely that a dedicated physical circuit could ever be traced through a network. Circuits are usually multiplexed through high-bandwidth media. Nevertheless, from the standpoint of the users at both ends, a dedicated circuit appears to exist.

Packet Switching

Because circuit switching typically wastes network capacity, the vast majority of LANs and WANs employ *packet switching*. With packet switching, messages are broken into pieces, and each piece contains information that identifies the source and destination computers. (In the early days of the technology, the pieces were usually called *packets*. Today, they are often called *frames*.) The identification information is used by the switches to route the pieces through the network. Refer back to Figure 2.8 for a diagram of how packet switching works.

Packet switching has several advantages over circuit switching. With packet switching, bandwidth is available on demand. Bandwidth is not dedicated, and therefore bandwidth is never wasted. Also, because a circuit is not established through the network, switches may change the routes they use from time to time. If a switch discovers that a new route would be more efficient (for example, when the current route is congested), the switch can choose the new path.

Two types of service are available on packet switching networks:

▸ *Connectionless* service does not establish a formal connection between the end nodes. Each packet is treated as a separate entity, and is routed through the internet independently, based on address information embedded in the packet. Packets that are treated in this manner are referred to as *datagrams*, and connectionless service is sometimes called *datagram service*. Because a formal connection is not established, connectionless service is *unreliable*. In other words, the network cannot be counted on to detect errors. With connectionless service, error detection and correction are the responsibility of upper-layer protocols.

▸ *Connection-oriented* service establishes a formal connection that gives the packet switching network the appearance of a dedicated circuit (at least from the perspective of the endpoints). Because this type of service behaves like a dedicated connection, the circuits established are called *virtual circuits*. Virtual circuits provide reliable delivery, and errors are detected and corrected.

An example of unreliable (connectionless) communication in the real world occurs when a company sends out a direct mail advertisement. The recipients do not expect to receive the communication. Furthermore, short of calling everyone who receives the mailing, there is no way for the company to confirm delivery. The individual pieces of mail sent out by the company are comparable to the datagrams transmitted during connectionless service.

NOTE

The terms physical and virtual are often used when networks are discussed. As a rule, you can distinguish the physical from the virtual by following these rules:

▸ **If you can see or touch it, it is physical.**

▸   **If you can't see or touch it, it is virtual.**

What you see on a network isn't always what you get. For example, you may think a computer is using a dedicated circuit, but the circuit may in fact be multiplexed. In that case, the circuit is called a "virtual circuit."

BRIDGING AND ROUTING

You have learned that packets can be switched through internetworks. But I have not yet explained how routes are selected. The two main techniques used to select routes are *bridging* and *routing*. The protocol layer where the routing decision takes place determines which term should be applied.

Bridging

At the data link layer, *bridging* uses physical addresses to make routing decisions. Figure 2.19 illustrates a typical bridging network. Bridges examine all of the frames that pass by them. Eventually, a bridge can ascertain the physical addresses that can be reached from the various networks connected to the bridge.

In the diagram, bridge A can not tell whether node B is attached to a nearby network or a distant one. Bridge A knows only that if it receives a frame from network 1 that should go to node B and that the frame should be forwarded to network 2. Bridge A is totally unaware that B is on a remote network.

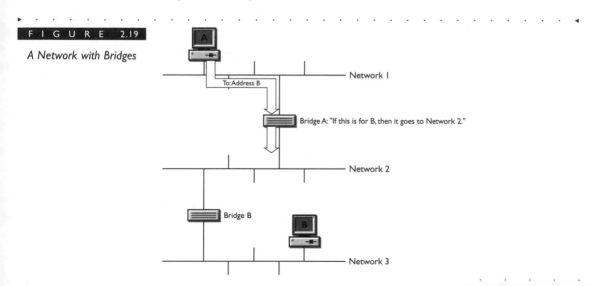

FIGURE 2.19

A Network with Bridges

Bridging takes place at the data link layer of the protocol stack. Figure 2.20 illustrates what takes place at the bridge. An incoming frame is forwarded to the data link layer, where the address information is recovered. The address information is used to select the interface that should be used to forward the frame, which is then sent down through the protocol stack and on to the appropriate destination.

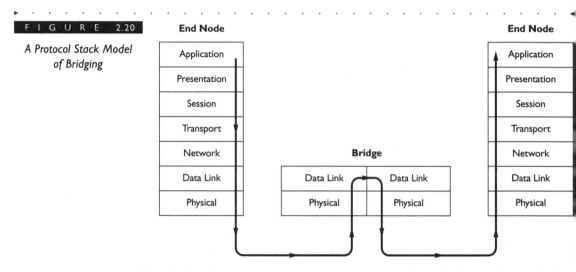

FIGURE 2.20

A Protocol Stack Model of Bridging

Notice that the bridge implements a separate protocol stack for each attached network. In theory, these protocol stacks could be different and a bridge could be used to connect one type of network to another — for example, an Ethernet to a Token Ring. In practice, this is seldom the case. As you will see in Chapter 3, networks at the physical layer are quite different from networks at the data link layer. Consequently few bridges have been developed that can successfully connect different types of networks.

Bridging has some limitations. The principle limitation is that bridging cannot handle networks that provide multiple routes to a destination. Loops develop and the network clogs with endlessly circulating traffic. An approach called the *spanning-tree algorithm* enables bridging networks to include redundant paths, but the network is logically configured so that redundant paths are only used if one of the paths fails. Then the extra paths are used to provide new routes. Spanning tree does not enable bridges to select the best possible routes. Nor does it give bridges the ability to use different routes when network conditions change.

Source routing is an alternative to traditional bridging. With source routing, a node broadcasts a frame called a *discovery frame* to the network. Each time the discovery frame crosses a bridge, it collects the route information. When a discovery frame reaches the destination node, it has collected enough information to describe a complete route between the endpoints. The discovery frame then returns to the original node, which adds the route information to each frame it transmits. Although Token Ring uses source routing to route packets, processing takes place at the data link layer. Therefore, Token Ring really uses bridging. However, because each Token Ring frame includes complete routing information, bridging decisions need not be made *en route*.

NOTE

Hybrid devices exist that perform various combinations of bridging and routing. These devices are called bridging routers, or routing bridges, or *brouters*. There is no one accepted method to combine bridging and routing functions. Therefore, in this book I discuss only bridges and routers, and I do not attempt to describe all of the variations that exist.

Routing

At the network level, route decisions are made by a process called *routing,* which uses the network addresses. Network address information is used to build a logical picture of a network in the form of a *routing table* that describes how messages should be routed to destination networks. Because routers deal with relatively few networks, routing tables can make fairly complex routing decisions. A routing table can build a detailed picture of where networks are and the best way to reach them.

Figure 2.21 shows an internetwork consisting of four distinct networks.

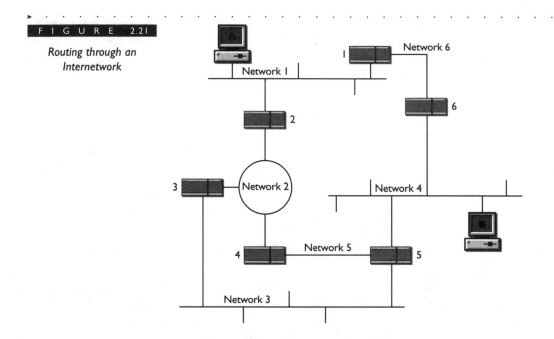

FIGURE   2.21

Routing through an
Internetwork

The most common algorithm for making route decisions uses *hop count*, which involves counting the number of networks that must be crossed to reach the destination network. Consider a packet being routed from computer A to computer B. When counting hops, the originating network counts as one hop. Therefore, the hop counts for the various possible routes are:

ROUTE	NUMBER OF HOPS
A-1-6-4-B	3 Hops
A-1-2-5-4-B	4 Hops
A-1-2-3-4-B	4 Hops

An estimation of the cost of routing is called a *metric*. By the hop count metric, the shortest route would be through routers 1 and 6. This simplistic approach could lead to poor choices, however, if the lines connecting the various routers operate at different speeds. Suppose network 6 operates at 56 kilobits per second while all the other lines operate at 1.2 megabits per second. In that case, the A-1-2-5-4-B route would probably deliver data faster. This problem can be corrected by assigning larger metrics to certain paths. For example, a hop count of ten might be assigned to network 6. The slow connection would then be used only if the other routes were unavailable.

As I mentioned earlier, routing operates at the network level. Figure 2.22 shows a protocol stack model of routing. The router implements a protocol stack for each network interface. The advantage of routing is that the network level is independent of the physical network. Different kinds of networks can share exactly the same network layer. This makes it easy for routers to forward data from one type of network to another. A common network layer could operate over an Ethernet data link layer for one interface and a Token Ring layer for another interface. Because of this capability, routers are the primary tool for connecting different types networks.

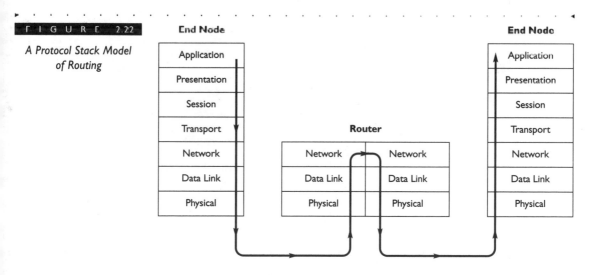

FIGURE 2.22

A Protocol Stack Model of Routing

From Theory to Practice

In this chapter, I have given you a theoretical context for the next four chapters. Although you have seen in general terms how networks function layer-by-layer, you have not yet encountered any real protocols in this book. Now it is time to get down to specifics. In Chapter 3, I begin to discuss TCP/IP in particular. I show you how TCP/IP network designers have built these functions into real networks and real protocols. In Chapter 4, I examine the network access layer, which is at the bottom of the DoD protocol model.

The Network Access Layer

TCP/IP comes into play at the network access layer. The Department of Defense did not design a network architecture specifically for TCP/IP. Rather, TCP/IP was designed with a layered approach so that it could be adapted to future network standards. As you will see in this chapter, TCP/IP has been used with many different types of networks. The following network standards are discussed in this chapter:

- Ethernet II

- IEEE 802.3 Ethernet

- IEEE 802.5 Token Ring

- Digital Data Services

- X.25 Packet Switching

- Frame Relay

- Asynchronous Transfer Mode (ATM)

The primary goal of this chapter is to show how TCP/IP can be adapted to these different networks. I explain a little about how each network works, as well.

Ethernet II

Ethernet and TCP/IP have had a long history together. Ethernet grew out of work by Robert Metcalf, Daniel Boggs, and their colleagues at the Xerox Palo Alto Research Center (Xerox PARC), and Ethernet was already well-defined when TCP/IP was being developed for the ARPANET. Ever since the inception of TCP/IP, the two have been closely related. The vast majority of TCP/IP implementations are designed with Ethernet II in mind.

There have been two generations of Ethernet. The first generation emerged in 1980. It was developed through the cooperation of Digital, Intel, and Xerox. This first generation is generally referred to as *Ethernet I* (or *DIX 1.0*). An updated version was introduced in 1982. The updated version was dubbed *Ethernet II* (or *DIX 2.0*). Nowadays, Ethernet I is seldom used, although you may still encounter it on older hardware. Ethernet II, by contrast, is very common on TCP/IP networks.

HOW ETHERNET NETWORKS WORK

The majority of LANs use baseband media, which allow only one computer to transmit data at a time. Therefore, network designers must decide how to enable multiple computers to share a medium. A mechanism that determines how computers share a medium is called an *access control method.*

The access control method that Ethernet uses is very basic. Essentially, a node that needs to transmit on an Ethernet network simply listens to the network before sending. If the network is silent, the node begins to transmit. The official name for this type of access control method is *carrier-sensing multiple access* (CSMA). *Carrier-sensing* merely means that the nodes listen before they talk.

If that were the whole story, Ethernet would be simple indeed. Unfortunately, it takes time for electrical signals to travel through wires, and that delay causes a problem. Two different nodes may sense a quiet network at the same time and then begin to transmit simultaneously, producing two signals on the network. That event is called a *collision.* Figure 3.1 shows how collisions can happen.

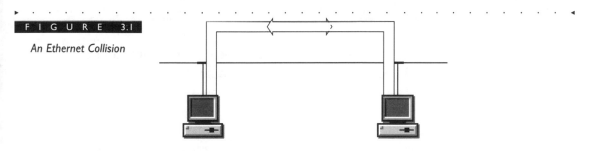

An Ethernet Collision

When a collision occurs, no valid data is transmitted. Each node continues to listen to the network as it transmits and senses that a collision has occurred. (A collision can be easily sensed because the two signals result in higher than normal voltages.) If a transmitting node senses a collision, it transmits a *jamming signal* that invalidates the frame and notifies all other nodes that a collision has taken place. Then the sending nodes stop transmitting for awhile. The period of time each node waits before transmitting again is determined randomly. The random delay makes it less likely that the nodes' transmissions will collide again. The mechanism for detecting collisions is called *collision detection* (CD). The full name of the access control method developed for Ethernet is "carrier-sensing multiple access with collision detection." Because that name is a mouthful, the mechanism is usually referred to as *CSMA/CD* for short.

One problem with collision-detection mechanisms is that collisions between very short frames might not be detected. Nodes listen for collisions only during transmission. If the transmission ends before a collision occurs, the collision will not be detected. Figure 3.2 shows how a collision might be undetected. To ensure that all collisions are detected, a minimum frame length must be specified. The minimum length ensures that all frames reach all nodes in the network before transmission is complete. The transmitting nodes will therefore always detect collisions before the nodes stop transmitting.

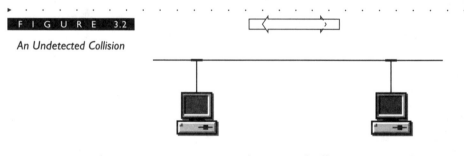

FIGURE 3.2

An Undetected Collision

Ethernet CSMA/CD is an elegant and efficient protocol. On a properly loaded network, very little of the network bandwidth needs to be devoted to Ethernet's operation. When there are relatively few collisions, the collisions do not critically impair network performance.

However, when many collisions occur, they can become a problem. CSMA networks are commonly called *contention-based networks* because nodes contend for network access. When too many nodes contend for network access, collisions start to dominate the network, and performance deteriorates. See Figure 3.3. Eventually, transmission becomes difficult because the majority of attempts produce collisions. In theory, collisions could prevent all nodes from accessing the network. Because nodes are not guaranteed an opportunity to transmit (in other words, because there is only a probability that a node will be able to transmit), Ethernet is sometimes referred to as a *probabilistic network*.

Nevertheless, Ethernet (that is, Ethernet II and IEEE 802.3, which I discuss later) remains the most popular network standard. It works well in the vast majority of situations. Furthermore, it is simple, and the network components it requires are relatively inexpensive.

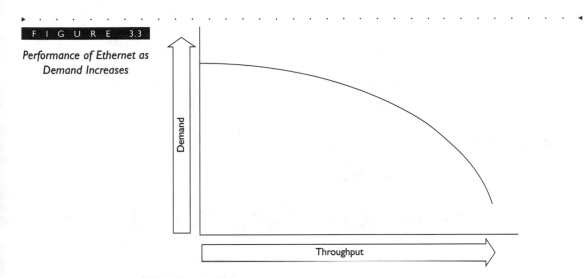

F I G U R E   3.3

Performance of Ethernet as Demand Increases

ETHERNET MEDIA

The original Ethernet medium is a thick coaxial cable referred to as *Thick Ethernet* or simply *ThickNet*. The cable can be used for network segments up to 500 meters in length. The cable can support up to 100 nodes, and it operates at 10 megabits per second (Mbps). However, Thick Ethernet's cables — and the hardware components it requires — are fairly costly. The popularity of Thick Ethernet has waned as cheaper alternatives have become available.

The other medium developed specifically for Ethernet consists of a thinner coaxial cable. Not surprisingly, this cable is called *Thin Ethernet* or *ThinNet*. Networks that use Thin Ethernet are limited to 185-meter segments and 30 nodes. Like Thick Ethernet, Thin Ethernet operates at 10 Mbps. The hardware required for Thin Ethernet is much simpler than the hardware required for Thick Ethernet. Therefore, Thin Ethernet costs considerably less.

Both varieties of Ethernet media — thick and thin — were adopted for standardization when the IEEE sought to develop an industry standard for CSMA/CD networks. I explain these Ethernet media in more detail when I discuss the IEEE 802.3 standard later in this chapter.

THE ETHERNET FRAME FORMAT

The Ethernet II frame format is particularly relevant to TCP/IP Ethernet II and TCP/IP fit together perfectly. When you adapt TCP/IP to other types of networks, you must do some extra work.

Figure 3.4 shows the Ethernet II frame format. In general, frame format diagrams show a frame's first bit on the left-hand side. Therefore, you should read the diagram from left to right to see the frame format from start to end. Table 3.1 summarizes the fields in an Ethernet II frame. The term *octet* is used in many protocol standards to describe a group of 8 bits. (Because an octet is the same thing as a byte, many newer standards use the term "byte" instead.)

F I G U R E   3.4

*Format of an
Ethernet II Frame*

Preamble (8 octets)	Destination Address (6 octets)	Source Address (6 octets)	Type (2 octets)	Data (46-1500 octets)	FCS (3 octets)

T A B L E   3.1

*Fields in an
Ethernet II Frame*

FIELD	PURPOSE
Preamble	An 8-octet (64-bit) field signals the beginning of an Ethernet frame. It begins with seven octets that have the bit pattern 10101010 and ends with one octet that has the bit pattern 10101011. This distinctive pattern marks the beginning of a frame, but the preamble is not part of the frame and it is not counted in the frame length.
Destination address	A 6-octet (48-bit) address indicates the physical of the address node that is the frame's destination. The receiving node examines this field to determine whether it is the destination of the frame.
Source address	A 6-octet (48-bit) address indicates the physical address of the node where the frame originated. This address is used by receiving nodes to address reply frames.
Type	A 2-octet (16-bit) field describes the type of data that the frame carries. The information in this field is generally referred to as the EtherType.
Data	This field contains the protocol data unit received from upper layers. This field has a minimum length of 46 octets and a maximum length of 1500 octets. If the data field is shorter than 46 octets, upper-layer protocols must pad it with octets of 0 value to achieve the minimum length.

TABLE 3.1	FIELD	PURPOSE
Fields in an Ethernet II Frame (continued)	Frame check sequence (FCS)	A 4-octet (32-bit) code detects errors during transmission. The code is derived using an algorithm called a *cyclic redundancy check* (CRC). The receiving node recalculates the CRC and compares its result to the value to the frame check sequence. A match indicates the frame was not corrupted.

If you add up the lengths of all fields, you find that an Ethernet frame has a maximum length of 1518 octets (6 + 6 + 2 + 1500 + 4 = 1518) and a minimum length of 64 octets (6 + 6 + 2 + 46 + 4 = 64). The 64-octet minimum combined with the 8-octet preamble results in a minimum frame length of 576 bits, which is long enough to ensure detection of all collisions.

ETHERNET ADDRESSING

Ethernet uses a very simple mechanism to deliver frames on a network. The sending node inserts the destination node's address in the destination address field. The frame is then placed on the network where it is examined by all nodes. The node that recognizes its own address in the destination address field receives the frame.

For this scheme to work, each node on a network must have a unique number. The designers of Ethernet created a scheme that ensures every Ethernet device *in the whole world* has a unique number.

Figure 3.5 shows the format of an Ethernet address, which consists of 48 bits arranged in three fields. Bits are numbered from bit 0 (the low-order bit) to bit 47 (the high-order bit). The first bit on the left of the address is the high-order bit, and addresses are arranged like conventional binary numbers — going from higher- to lower-bits as you read left to right.

FIGURE 3.5	
Structure of an Ethernet Address	47 ... Vendor Code (23 bits) ... Globally Administered Address (24 bits) ... 0

Physical/Multicast Bit

Typically, Ethernet addresses are expressed as six two-digit hexadecimal numbers. This is easy to do because each group of 8 bits maps to two hex digits. An example would be 06 02 AD 01 20 1D. Hex representation makes it easier for humans to scan the addresses. Figure 3.6 illustrates how to create a hexadecimal representation of an Ethernet address. Hex is so easy to use that it is seldom necessary to worry about the binary form of an Ethernet address.

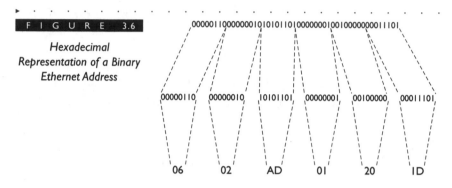

Hexadecimal Representation of a Binary Ethernet Address

Bit 47 (the high-order bit) is the Physical/Multicast (P/M) bit. When this bit has a value of 0, the frame specifies the physical address of a node on the network. When this bit has a value of 1, the address is a *multicast address*. Multicast addresses are used to send messages to groups of designated computers.

The first three octets of an Ethernet address comprise a vendor code. Each manufacturer of Ethernet equipment is assigned one or more 24-bit identification codes by a central registry. (All vendor codes begin with a P/M bit value of 0.) Registration was originally performed by Xerox but has been delegated to the IEEE. Table 3.2 lists some typical vendor codes, which are documented in RFC 1700, entitled *Assigned Numbers*.

TABLE 3.2

Examples of Ethernet Vendor Codes

VENDOR CODE	VENDOR
00 80 C2	IEEE 802.1 Committee
00 AA 00	Intel
08 00 09	Hewlett-Packard
08 00 14	Novell
08 00 2B	DEC
08 00 56	Stanford University
08 00 69	IBM

The remainder of the address is a 24-bit code that uniquely identifies each device the vendor manufactures. The combination of the unique vendor codes and a unique code for each piece of hardware results in a unique Ethernet address for each piece of hardware created. These addresses are typically burned into the hardware and are often called *physical addresses*. Because the addresses are registered on a global basis, they are also called *globally administered addresses*.

 It is possible to override the physical address of an Ethernet adapter by changing parameters in the network drivers. Addresses that are created locally are called locally administered addresses.

NOTE

One more Ethernet address should be mentioned. An address consisting entirely of 1s is the standard Ethernet *broadcast address,* which is represented in hex as FF FF FF FF FF FF. The route of messages sent using the broadcast address depends on the network layer. With some protocols, messages sent to the broadcast address are allowed to cross routers and are forwarded to all nodes on the internetwork. In other protocols (notably TCP/IP), broadcast messages are not permitted to cross routers and are distributed to the local network only.

To summarize, there are three categories of Ethernet addresses:

▸ Globally administered addresses (physical addresses burned into hardware) which have a Physical/Multicast (high-order) bit value of 0

▸ Multicast addresses, which have a Physical/Multicast (high-order) bit value of 1

▸ Broadcast addresses, which consist entirely of 1s

ETHERTYPE

The *type field* (or *EtherType field*) plays a significant role in relation to TCP/IP. This field identifies the type of data that is carried in the data field. The EtherType value is used in protocol multiplexing to ensure that data is delivered to the correct upper-layer protocol stack. RFC 1700, entitled *Assigned Numbers,* lists EtherType numbers that have been assigned to specific protocols and organizations. Table 3.3 shows some common EtherType values listed in RFC 1700.

T A B L E 3.3	ETHERTYPE (DECIMAL)	ETHERTYPE (HEXADECIMAL)	DATA TYPE
Examples of EtherType Values	2048	0800	Internet IP (IPv4)
	2053	0805	X.25 Level 3
	2054	0806	ARP
	33023	80FF – 8103	Wellfleet Communications
	32873	8069	AT&T
	33079 – 33080	8137 – 8138	Novell, Inc.

NOTE

In the IEEE 802.3 version of Ethernet (see below), the type field has been replaced by a length field, which has a maximum value of 1500. All EtherType values are 1501 (5DDh) or greater. Therefore, systems can distinguish between 802.3 and Ethernet II frames by examining the value of the type or length field.

IEEE LAN Standards

The main organization that sets international LAN standards is the Institute of Electrical and Electronics Engineers (IEEE), the largest professional organization in the world. Network standards are handled by the 802 committee — so called because the committee first met in 1980 in the month of February. The International Standardization Organization (ISO), which establishes international LAN standards, has adopted the IEEE 802 standards in ISO standard 8802. (The ISO standard based on IEEE 802.3 is called ISO 88023.)

Figure 3.7 illustrates the architecture of the IEEE 802 standards. Notice that the OSI data link layer has been subdivided into two sublayers in the diagram. The subdivision allows the IEEE to designate a common layer above all LAN protocols. The responsibilities of the data link layer have been divided between the sublayers as follows:

▸ *Logical link control* (LLC) provides a common interface between lower-level IEEE protocols and the network layer. The LLC sublayer delivers data between nodes that reside on the same network segment.

▸ *Medium access control* (MAC) is the mechanism that enables nodes to share a common network medium.

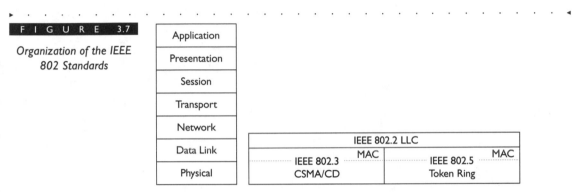

Only the standards that are discussed in this chapter are shown in Figure 3.7. This chapter examines three of the 802.x standards:

▸ 802.2, which defines the LLC sublayer

▸ 802.3, which defines the MAC and physical layers for a CSMA/CD network derived from Ethernet II

▸ 802.5, which defines the MAC and physical layers for a token-passing network derived from IBM's Token-Ring network

Notice in Figure 3.7 that the 802.2 LLC protocol serves as a common protocol that is used above 802.3 and 802.5 networks. This approach simplifies adaptation of network layers to different types of LANs. Each of these protocols is discussed in later sections. First, however, I examine the addressing scheme of 802 networks.

IEEE 802 ADDRESSING

Node physical addresses are used for local delivery of data frames. When the physical address format was being developed, the IEEE required a format that could be used for all 802 protocols. The address format that was chosen closely resembles the address format of Ethernet II. In the IEEE model, physical addresses are functions of the MAC protocol sublayer. Therefore, physical addresses are frequently referred to as *MAC addresses*.

The IEEE defined both 16- and 48-bit address formats. However, because 16-bit addresses are seldom used, I do not discuss them here.

All nodes on a network must be configured to use the same address format. Figure 3.8 illustrates the format of a 48-bit address. This address format has been adopted for IEEE 802, ISO 8802, and other network standards such as Frame Relay. Although the format resembles addresses for Ethernet II, some differences exist.

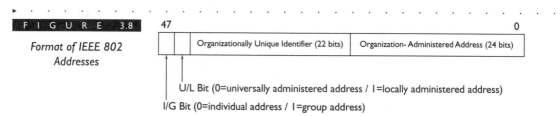

FIGURE 3.8

Format of IEEE 802 Addresses

The high-order bit (bit 47) designates the address as an *individual* or a *group address*, and it is therefore called the *I/G bit*. If the value of the I/G bit is 0, the address is an individual address. (An individual address is comparable to an Ethernet II physical address.) If the value of the I/G bit is 1, the address is a group address. (A group address is comparable to an Ethernet II multicast address.) In other words, apart from the difference in terminology, the I/G bit has the same purpose and function as the Ethernet II P/M bit.

Bit 46 designates the address as either a *universally* or *locally administered* address. Therefore, bit 46 is referred to as the *U/L bit*. If the value of the U/L bit is 0, then the address is universally administered. A universally administered address is based on a 22-bit identifier that is unique to a particular organization and a 24-bit address that is assigned by the organization to each device it manufactures. Universal addresses can be overridden by parameters that configure the drivers for the network adapter. If the value of the U/L bit is 1, then the address is locally administered.

The combination of an organizationally unique identifier and a unique address assigned by the organization results in global uniqueness for each device that is assigned an IEEE 802 address. The IEEE now assigns organizationally unique identifiers — a responsibility that was transferred to the IEEE from Xerox. In general, universally administered addresses are preferable because they prevent conflicts from occurring.

IEEE 802.2 LOGICAL LINK CONTROL

The LLC sublayer performs two basic functions: frame delivery and protocol multiplexing and demultiplexing. Many of the services at the LLC sublayer are optional and can be performed instead by upper-layer protocols.

Protocol Multiplexing and Demultiplexing

The multiplexing capability of the LLC sublayer enables it to support multiple upper-layer protocol stacks. This function is performed by the EtherType value in an Ethernet II frame. 802.2 LLC uses a different mechanism called the *link service access point* (LSAP). Each upper-layer protocol is assigned an LSAP, which functions as a logical address. The LSAP identifies the protocol stack that is associated with each frame and enables LLC to deliver frames to the correct protocol stack.

The most significant difference between the IEEE protocols and Ethernet II is the difference between the LSAP and EtherType mechanisms. To support TCP/IP, an extension of the LLC protocol called the *Subnetwork Access Protocol* (SNAP) must be employed. (SNAP is discussed later in the section "IEEE 802.3 CSMA/CD.")

Delivery Services

LLC is responsible for delivering data between computers. The delivery services have two functions: flow control and error recovery. LLC provides three levels of delivery services that offer different degrees of communication integrity.

Flow Control   Communication devices are equipped with *receive buffers* — memory that can store data while it is waiting to be processed by a device. If data arrives faster that the device can pull the data from its receive buffers, some of the data may be lost. One responsibility of LLC is to prevent buffer overflow. Two primary mechanisms are used to manage communication flow:

▶ *Stop-and-wait* is an uncomplicated method that requires the receiving device to acknowledge each frame it receives. An acknowledgment signals the receiver's ability to receive more data. The sending device waits for an acknowledgment before it sends more data. This technique is effective, although it is inefficient because the acknowledgment process slows down transmission. Also, because each data frame spawns an acknowledgment frame, this technique almost doubles the amount of network traffic.

▶ *Sliding-window* enables the receiver to acknowledge several frames at once. A *window* is the number of frames that can be traveling at any given time. When two devices connect for an exchange of data, they agree on an appropriate window. The sending device can transmit only as many frames as the window designates. When that number is reached, the sending device must pause. The receiving device can acknowledge more than one frame with the same message. When frames are acknowledged, the window moves forward so that the sender can transmit more frames. In a full-duplex dialog that enables the sender to both send data and receive acknowledgments simultaneously, sliding-window results in much smoother data flow. Because multiple frames can be acknowledged with a single message, the increase in network traffic is not as noticeable as with stop-and-wait.

Error Recovery   Error recovery may be performed by LLC, depending on the service that is selected. The MAC sublayer detects errors but does not perform error recovery.

LLC error recovery uses an *automatic repeat request* (ARQ) technique. With ARQ, the receiving node must acknowledge each frame that it receives correctly. There are two types of ARQ:

▶ **Stop-and-wait ARQ.** The sending device waits for an acknowledgment of each frame that is received intact. Any unacknowledged frame is retransmitted after a short delay.

▶ **Go-back-N ARQ.** The receiving device can request retransmission of specific frames. Connection-mode service is required.

Delivery Service Modes LLC has three different delivery-service modes, which implement different combinations of flow control and error recovery techniques. The available services are:

▸ **Unacknowledged datagram service (Type 1 service).** This mode is connectionless. It supports point-to-point, multipoint, and broadcast transmission. Flow control and error recovery are not performed.

▸ **Virtual circuit service (Type 2 service).** This mode is connection-oriented. It provides flow control, frame sequencing, and error recovery.

▸ **Acknowledged datagram service (Type 3 service).** This mode is a combination of Type 1 and Type 2 services. It supports point-to-point datagram service with message acknowledgments.

Type 1 service is the most common. LLC is seldom implemented with Type 2 or Type 3 service. Type 1 service promotes efficiency in lower-layer protocols. In the TCP/IP protocol suite, the TCP protocol provides reliable service when it is necessary. It would be redundant to perform the same service at both the network layer and the data link layer.

Format of LLC Data The protocol data unit (PDU) constructed by the LLC sublayer is shown in Figure 3.9.

FIGURE 3.9

Format of an LLC Protocol Data Unit

DSAP	SSAP	Control	Data

Table 3.4 describes the different fields of an LLC PDU.

TABLE 3.4

Fields of an LLC Protocol Data Unit

FIELD	DESCRIPTION
Destination Service Access Point (DSAP)	The link service access point specifying the protocol stack on the receiving node at the data's destination.
Source Service Access Point (SSAP)	The link service access point specifying the protocol stack on the sending node where the data originated.

(continued)

T A B L E 3.4	FIELD	DESCRIPTION
Fields of an LLC Protocol Data Unit (continued)	Control	Control information that varies depending on the function of the PDU.
	Data	The payload of the PDU. In other words, the data received from the network layer.

IEEE 802.3 CSMA/CD

Digital, Intel, and Xerox — who jointly developed Ethernet II — submitted the new technology to the IEEE for standardization. The 802.3 committee took on the task of developing LAN standards based on Ethernet CSMA/CD technology. IEEE 802.3 is similar to Ethernet II in most respects. However, there are some differences between the two as a result of the IEEE's decision to implement 802.2 as a common LLC layer for all LAN protocols.

IEEE 802.3 LANs use the same signaling techniques and — with a very minor exception — the same hardware as Ethernet II. As a result, the two Ethernet varieties coexist fairly smoothly. 802.3 and Ethernet II frames can be multiplexed on the same medium without difficulty, and Novell's ODI architecture supports both frame types on the same network adapter.

> **NOTE** The name "Ethernet" was coined at Xerox. It refers to "luminiferous ether," a substance physicists once believed to be the medium through which light travels.

There has been considerable debate about whether IEEE 802.3 should in fact be called "Ethernet." The dispute is likely to continue as long as both Ethernet II and IEEE 802.3 are in use. Xerox long ago surrendered the Ethernet trademark, and some people (including Robert Metcalf) argue that the term should be applied to the latest version of Ethernet, which is IEEE 802.3.

> **IMPORTANT** I use the term "Ethernet" to describe both standards. When I need to point out a difference between the standards, I refer specifically to Ethernet II or Ethernet 802.3.

The IEEE 802.3 Frame Format

The format of an IEEE 802.3 frame is shown in Figure 3.10.

Preamble (7 octets)	Start Frame Delimiter (1 octet)	Destination Address (6 octets)	Source Address (6 octets)	Length (2 octets)	Data (46-1500 octets)	FCS (3 octets)

Table 3.5 describes the fields in an IEEE 802.3 frame.

T A B L E   3.5

*Fields in an
IEEE 802.3 Frame*

FIELD	DESCRIPTION
Preamble	A 56-bit field consisting of seven octets with the bit pattern 10101010.
Start frame delimiter	A single octet field with the bit pattern 10101011 that signals the start of a frame.
Destination address	A 6-octet (48-bit) address that indicates the physical address of a frame's destination node. Receiving nodes examine this field to determine which frames they should receive.
Source address	A 6-octet (48-bit) address that indicates the physical address of the node where the frame originated. Receiving nodes use this address to send reply frames.
Length	A 2-octet (16-bit) field that specifies the number of octets in the LLC data field. The number of octets can vary from 46 to 1500.
LLC data	The field that contains the protocol data unit received from the LLC sublayer. This field has a minimum length of 46 octets and a maximum length of 1500 octets. If the protocol data unit is shorter than 46 octets, 0-value octets are added to attain the minimum length.
Frame check sequence (FCS)	A 4-octet (32-bit) code used to detect errors during transmission. The code is derived using an algorithm called a *cyclic redundancy check* (CRC). The receiving node recalculates the CRC and compares the result to the value of the frame check sequence. A match indicates that the frame was not corrupted.

Figure 3.11 compares the formats of Ethernet II and IEEE 802.3 frames. The most significant difference is that an IEEE 802.3 frame has a length field instead of a type field. Otherwise, the two frame types are essentially the same. If 48-bit addresses are used, the length of both IEEE 802.3 and Ethernet II frames can range from 64 through 1518 octets.

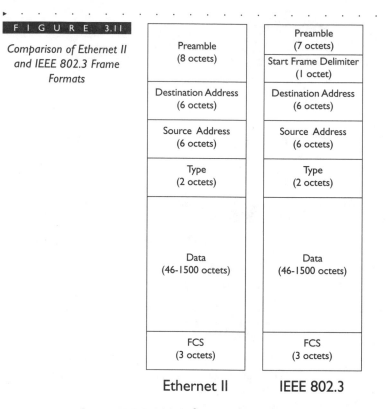

FIGURE 3.11

Comparison of Ethernet II and IEEE 802.3 Frame Formats

Ethernet II
Preamble (8 octets)
Destination Address (6 octets)
Source Address (6 octets)
Type (2 octets)
Data (46-1500 octets)
FCS (3 octets)

IEEE 802.3
Preamble (7 octets)
Start Frame Delimiter (1 octet)
Destination Address (6 octets)
Source Address (6 octets)
Type (2 octets)
Data (46-1500 octets)
FCS (3 octets)

In an IEEE 802.3 frame, the combination of the 7-octet preamble and the 1-octet frame start sequence is comparable to the 8-octet preamble of an Ethernet II frame.

Although 16-bit MAC addresses are possible with IEEE 802 LANs, they are seldom used. Because the IEEE address format was adapted from Ethernet II, address fields are functionally identical when 48-bit address are used.

The one functional difference between the frame formats is the distinction between an Ethernet II frame's type field and an IEEE 802.3 frame's length field. These two fields perform different functions in the different networks. The protocol multiplexing function of the EtherType field is performed by the 802.2 LLC protocol for IEEE LANs. As I mentioned earlier, it is easy to distinguish Ethernet II frames from IEEE 802.3 frames. If the value of the type or length field is 1501 or greater, then that field represents an EtherType value, and the frame is therefore an Ethernet II frame. If the frame's length is anywhere from 46 through 1500, then the frame is an IEEE 802.3 frame.

Implementing TCP/IP over IEEE 802.3 Networks

Although TCP/IP may be adapted to any network, it fits most naturally on Ethernet II LANs. NetWare TCP/IP is typically implemented using Ethernet II frames.

To run TCP/IP with networks that do not incorporate the type field of Ethernet II, the EtherType information must be encoded using the Subnetwork Access Protocol (see RFC 1042), which extends the LLC header to include the EtherType. Figure 3.12 shows the format of an LLC PDU with the Subnetwork Access Protocol (SNAP) extensions. To indicate that the PDU utilizes SNAP encapsulation, the values of the Destination Service Access Point (DSAP) and Source Service Access Point (SSAP) fields must be set to 170, the control field must be set to 3 (unnumbered information), and the organization code should be set to 0.

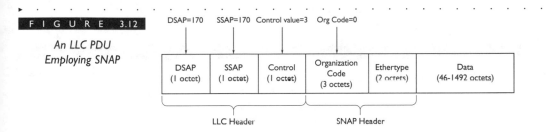

FIGURE 3.12

An LLC PDU Employing SNAP

The SNAP data is encoded as the first 8 octets of the data field. This unfortunately reduces the number of bytes that an IEEE 802.3 frame can carry when SNAP encapsulation is used. The maximum length of an Ethernet frame is 1518 octets. The maximum length allows at most 1500 octets for data because SNAP encapsulation reduces that payload by 8 octets. This may complicate matters if frames are routed between Ethernet II and IEEE 802.3 networks.

SNAP is a general-purpose extension that is applicable to all IEEE 802.x LANs. NetWare uses SNAP encapsulation to run TCP/IP over token ring physical layers, for example. SNAP can also be used to mate TCP/IP to networks such as Frame Relay and ATM.

IEEE 802.3 Media

The IEEE has assumed responsibility for standardizing all Ethernet media. Both Thick Ethernet and Thin Ethernet have been adopted as part of the IEEE 802.3 media options. However, the committee has broadened Ethernet media choices considerably. The most notable addition is a standard that enables Ethernet to run on unshielded twisted-pair cable. More recently, 100 megabit per second (Mbps) networks based on CSMA/CD have been added.

I do not discuss the different media options at great length in this book because the type of cable used is irrelevant to the way TCP/IP works. Therefore, I only briefly mention here the different media options offered by the 802.3 standard.

Each option is identified by a three-part name (for example, 10BASE5). The first number in the name indicates the nominal speed of the network — for instance, 10 signifies 10 Mbps. The middle part (e.g., BASE) indicates the network's operating mode (for example, baseband). The final characters reflect the physical characteristics of the network. For example, 5 indicates that a 10BASE5 network accommodates cable segments up to 500 meters in length. The current IEEE 802.3 media options are listed in Table 3.6.

T A B L E 3.6	MEDIUM	DESCRIPTION
IEEE 802.3 Media Options	10BASE5	The IEEE version of Thick Ethernet. It employs a thick, 50-ohm coaxial cable and operates in baseband mode. Cable segments can extend to 500 meters without bridges or routers. It operates at 10 Mbps.
	10BASE2	The IEEE version of Thin Ethernet. It employs a thin, 50-ohm coaxial cable and operates in baseband mode. Cable segments can extend to 185 (the 2 indicates approximately 200) meters without bridges or routers. It operates at 10 Mbps.
	10BASE-T	Ethernet using unshielded twisted-pair (UTP) cable. It operates at 10 Mbps. It is wired in a star. Cables connecting nodes to wiring concentrators may be up to 100 meters in length.
	10BROAD36	Broadband Ethernet. Supports multiplexing of multiple 10 Mbps Ethernet channels through a single 75-ohm coaxial cable.
	100BASE-TX	One of several 100 Mbps standards being considered by the IEEE. Many of the 100 Mbps standards being considered use unshielded twisted-pair cable. These standards differ in the number of pairs and in the quality of cable they require. Also being considered is 100BASE-TF, for use with optical fiber cable.

IEEE 802.5 TOKEN RING

The technology standardized in the IEEE 802.5 token ring network originated out of research at IBM. Token ring is the second most popular LAN physical layer. Although at one time token ring was poised to surpass Ethernet, the plummeting cost of Ethernet components has helped Ethernet to remain the market leader. Ethernet is more popular than token ring for several reasons:

- ▶ Ethernet's mechanisms are much simpler than token ring's. As a result, the hardware required for Ethernet is significantly cheaper.

- ▶ For a long time, token ring was perceived as proprietary technology of IBM, despite its availability as an IEEE standard. Buyers have perceived Ethernet as more open — that is, not as controlled by a single vendor.

- ▶ TCP/IP has grown in popularity. Many buyers recognize that TCP/IP fits most naturally with Ethernet.

There are, however, compelling reasons to consider token ring in some cases. To understand when token ring might be appropriate, it is necessary to examine how token ring functions.

How Token Ring Networks Work

The basic operation of token ring is easy to understand. Nodes are arranged in a ring, as shown in Figure 3.13. Frames pass from station to station around the ring. To control access to the network, a special *token frame* is circulated around the network. A node needing to transmit must wait until it receives the token frame. Only the node that has control of the token may transmit. This restriction prevents more than one node from accessing the network at a given time. After a node has transmitted its frame, the node transmits a new token frame around the ring so that other nodes can transmit.

FIGURE 3.13

Operation of a Token Ring

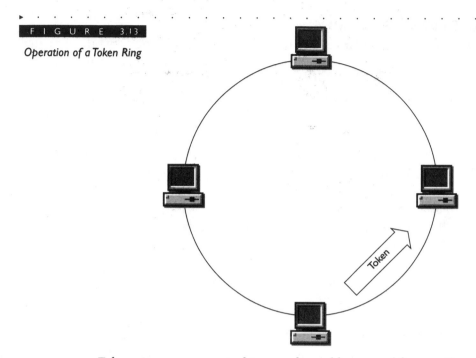

Token ring access control is complicated by several factors. Frames can become lost or damaged. More importantly, if a token were lost, the network would grind to a halt. The token ring designers therefore had to design a mechanism that could create a new token if the old one were lost. Another complication in token ring stems from the fact that one node is designated as an *active monitor* that oversees network operation. Token ring designers had to create a mechanism for designating a new active monitor if the old one were to fail. There are at least a dozen other problems that further complicate token ring's design.

Why did IBM bother to design a more complicated network than Ethernet? To understand the answer to that question, you need to understand one of Ethernet's main weaknesses. Each time a node transmits, there is a chance that a collision will occur. The probability of collisions rises as the network gets busier. Eventually, the network can reach a point where nodes experience transmission delays — or even complete failures. In many systems, the uncertainty inherent in Ethernet transmissions cannot be tolerated. For example, in manufacturing, a delay or a failure of a warning signal could cause expensive equipment to be damaged.

Token ring is immune to such problems. Every node on the network is guaranteed a chance to transmit each time the token goes around the ring. There is no chance that a node will be unable to transmit because of collisions. Moreover, token ring has a priority mechanism that allows you to designate certain critical systems. (That feature is not available in Ethernet.)

It is hard to compare the general performance of token ring with Ethernet's performance. Nevertheless, I'll venture to say that when demand on a network is within reasonable limits, a 16 Mbps token ring and a 10 Mbps Ethernet have similar performance. Ethernet is extremely simple. Apart from collisions, no network bandwidth is used solely for the purpose of operating the network. A high percentage of Ethernet's capacity is available to transmit data. Token ring, on the other hand, requires a variety of control mechanisms to keep the network running. The control mechanisms use network bandwidth and therefore reduce the capacity of the network to carry data. However, token ring performs better on heavily loaded networks. With Ethernet, busy networks can experience gridlock when too many collisions are occurring.

In general, the capabilities of Ethernet — coupled with its low cost — make Ethernet more popular. Token ring is usually only chosen by buyers who have a need for its special capabilities and who can justify the additional expense.

Token Ring Media

Although the IEEE 802.5 standard specifies certain things like data rates and interface requirements, the standard does not include the details of cabling a token ring network. As a result, the majority of vendors and customers use the IBM Cabling System, which was designed with token ring in mind.

IBM's approach to cabling token ring is called a *star-wired ring*. Frames circulate around a ring, but the ring is concealed by a star wiring plan. Figure 3.14 illustrates how wiring hubs can be configured so that a network can be wired as a star but still function as a ring.

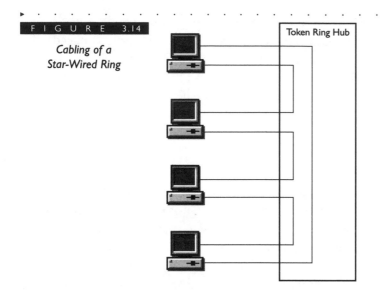

F I G U R E   3.14

*Cabling of a
Star-Wired Ring*

The majority of early token rings were cabled with IBM Type 1 cable — a fairly heavy cable that featured two twisted-pairs of wires enclosed by a shield. IBM approved of having token ring networks operate at 4 Mbps and 16 Mbps data rates over Type 1 cable. IBM also recommended 4 Mbps operation over Type 3 cable (data grade, unshielded twisted-pair). However, IBM was reluctant to approve 16 Mbps networks using UTP cable. IBM introduced a higher-speed standard for UTP only after several other vendors brought out networks that offered 16 Mbps operation over Type 3 cable. IBM has since revised their cable system to support operation up to 100 Mbps.

The IEEE 802.5 Frame Format

Figure 3.15 shows the format of an IEEE 802.5 frame. The frame is divided into three major sections:

- **Start-of-frame sequence (SFS).** Indicates the beginning of a frame.

- **Data section.** Includes control information, upper-layer data, and the frame check sequence.

- **End-of-frame sequence (EFS).** Indicates the end of the frame and includes several control bits.

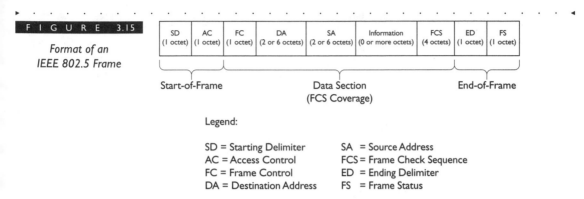

FIGURE 3.15

*Format of an
IEEE 802.5 Frame*

SD (1 octet)	AC (1 octet)	FC (1 octet)	DA (2 or 6 octets)	SA (2 or 6 octets)	Information (0 or more octets)	FCS (4 octets)	ED (1 octet)	FS (1 octet)

Start-of-Frame   Data Section   End-of-Frame
                     (FCS Coverage)

Legend:

SD = Starting Delimiter   SA = Source Address
AC = Access Control   FCS = Frame Check Sequence
FC = Frame Control   ED = Ending Delimiter
DA = Destination Address   FS = Frame Status

Table 3.7 describes the fields of an IEEE 802.5 frame. As you can see, a token ring frame contains no counterpart to an Ethernet II frame's type field. SNAP encapsulation allows TCP/IP to run over a token ring network. NetWare uses the TOKEN-RING_SNAP frame type for this purpose.

TABLE 3.7

*Fields in an
IEEE 802.5 Frame*

FIELD	PURPOSE
Starting delimiter (SD)	A 1-octet field comprised of electrical signals that are not permitted elsewhere in the frame. The SD field purposely violates data encoding rules (it stands out like a sore thumb) and it contains no data. The SD signals the beginning of a frame.
Access control (AC)	A 1-octet field that includes control bits used to set priority and to carry out a variety of token ring control functions.
Frame control (FC)	A 1-octet field that indicates whether or not the frame is a MAC control frame. MAC control frames are used to manage operation of the token ring network.
Destination address (DA)	A 2- or 6-octet field that contains the 802-format address of the destination node.
Source address (SA)	The 802-format address of the node that originated the frame.
Information	Contains LLC data or data related to the control operations of a MAC protocol frame.
Frame check sequence (FCS)	A 32-bit cyclic redundancy check value used to detect errors in transmission.

(continued)

T A B L E 3.7	FIELD	PURPOSE
Fields in an IEEE 802.5 Frame (continued)	Ending delimiter (ED)	A 1-octet field comprised of electrical signals that are not permitted elsewhere in the frame. The ED field purposely violates rules for encoding data and contains no data. The ED signals the end of a frame.
	Frame Status (FS)	A duplicate of the ED. Because the ED field is not covered by the FCS, this copy of the ED is used to check for errors.

Digital Data Services

In this section, I discuss the protocols used to build WANs, which can range in size from networks that cover a radius of only a few miles to networks that cover the whole world. To build a private WAN — or to connect to a public one — you need a way to set up data communication lines across large distances. In virtually all cases, this means leasing a communication line from a digital data service (DDS). This chapter introduces you to different options that are available, including dedicated and switched digital services.

DEDICATED LEASED LINES

A *dedicated leased line* is a communication line that permanently connects two points. Users are usually unaware of the specifics of connections, which make use of a variety of technologies including copper cables, fiber optics, and microwaves. From a user's perspective, the important thing is that a certain capacity for data transmission has been dedicated exclusively to the user's needs.

Dedicated leased lines are expensive. The cost is significantly greater for higher data rates. Typically, data rates on dedicated leased lines are substantially lower than on the average LAN. Although a wide variety of services are available in both analog and digital, the use of high-speed modems and analog lines to connect computer sites is becoming increasingly less common. The majority of lease lines are digital, and data rates are usually 56 Kbps or higher.

T1, originally developed for digital voice channels, is the most widely available DDS. A T1 line can multiplex 24 digital voice channels, but T1 is useful for computer data, as well. T1 supports point-to-point full-duplex communication at a data rate of 1.544 Mbps. The international equivalent of T1 is E1, which operates at a data rate of 2.048 Mbps.

Because T1 supports multiple, discrete channels, some service providers offer leases on part of the capacity of a T1 line. *Fractional T1* enables customers to lease one or more of the 64 Kbps channels at a reduced cost. Other digital data rates in the United States are T2 (6.312 Mbps), T3 (44.736 Mbps), and T4 (274.176 Mbps). The comparable international services — standardized by the International Telecommunications Union (ITU) — are 8.848, 34.304, and 139.264 Mbps. (The ITU was formerly known as the International Telegraph and Telephone Consultative Committee, or CCITT.)

It is entirely possible to build a private network using only leased lines. However, usually only large corporations can afford to pay the high cost. The Internet consists largely of dedicated lines, but the cost of ownership has been spread across the entire Internet community. In the past, an organization that wanted to connect to the Internet would lease a line that connects to a willing host. In turn, the organization would let other organizations connect to the Internet through its network.

Leased lines are also used to connect to public data services, such as X.25 and Frame Relay networks. (See the sections named "X.25" and "Frame Relay" later in this chapter.) When a network provider is local, you can usually save money by leasing a local line to a network provider rather than leasing private lines to all of your remote sites.

Leased lines are both costly and inflexible. When you lease a line, you need to lease a fixed data capacity that allows for your peak demands. During quiet periods, much of the capacity you are paying for is unused. If your network demands are irregular, you may want to consider a switched digital connection. (See the following subsection.)

Several pieces of equipment are required to connect a network to a digital leased line. Figure 3.16 shows how a leased line can be used to connect two LANs. The wide-area connection consists of the following components:

▶ A bridge or router configured to direct traffic from the LAN to the leased line

▶ A channel service unit/digital service unit (CSU/DSU) to translate LAN signals into the format required by the leased line

▶ A network interface supplied by the communication provider

NetWare's MultiProtocol Router can be used to connect to a DDS (see Chapter 10).

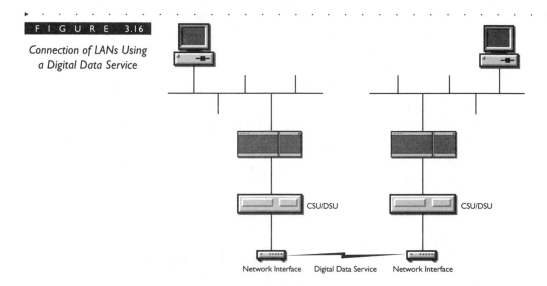

FIGURE 3.16

Connection of LANs Using a Digital Data Service

SWITCHED DIGITAL SERVICES

At one time, a *switched data connection* meant a standard analog telephone line and a modem. Unfortunately, standard modems seldom provided the performance required to connect LANs. As a result, most organizations were forced to lease dedicated lines — even though their communications might have been infrequent.

In recent years, however, a variety of services have made switched connections possible. Switched digital services and switched 56-Kbps CSU/DSUs are both now available.

The emerging technology that seems likely to replace the analog modem is the *Integrated Services Digital Network* (ISDN), which is a fully digital service designed for switched connections. Many levels of ISDN service are available. A common service provides two 64 Kbps digital channels. These channels offer a potential bandwidth of 128 Kbps, but they must be aggregated by equipment at the customer site. ISDN has the potential to make switched digital service available at reasonable cost. Recently, several major communication providers have committed to making ISDN available in their service areas. At present, however, ISDN's availability remains spotty.

X.25

Leased circuits have many significant disadvantages. Dedicated lines are costly. Furthermore, it is expensive to reconfigure a network based on leased circuits, because the setup fees are high. That is why the majority of organizations obtain their wide-area connectivity from public data networks.

Public data networks are owned and operated by network providers, who establish a high-capacity network to cover a specific geographic area. Customers lease bandwidth on the network. The only leased lines involved are the lines that connect the customers' sites to the local network's point of presence. Although public data networks aren't cheap, they can be much more cost-effective than networks based on leased lines — particularly when a number of sites must be connected.

Some public data networks offer dial-in capacity, which can make it easy to implement a mobile computing strategy.

TIP

X.25 was one of the earliest WANs. Despite unspectacular performance by today's standards, X.25 remains widely available. Virtually any network environment can be connected to an X.25 network. X.25 is a packet switching network that supports both switched and permanent virtual circuits. *Permanent virtual circuits* can be established to provide reliable connections between computers that must remain in constant communication. *Switched virtual circuits* enable devices to establish temporary connections that are torn down when no longer needed, much like the connection you have when you make telephone call.

X.25 was developed when communication lines were slow and not very trustworthy. The upper limit on X.25 data rates is 64 Kbps, which was more than enough when the majority of networks carried traffic between dumb terminals and host computers. Today, however, the performance constraints of X.25 make it unsuitable for linking LANs.

Because X.25 networks initially often relied on unreliable analog media, the X.25 protocol was designed for robust error detection and recovery. Each X.25 switch is responsible for detecting and recovering errors. Therefore, error checking occurs many times along the way as a packet is switched through the network. Modern digital lines are far more reliable, so X.25's frequent error checking is often unnecessary.

Figure 3.17 illustrates LANs connected through a packet switching network. Packet switching networks are commonly represented by a cloud because the inner workings of the network are hidden from outside observers. Data enters the network at one point and exits at another. What happens in between is the packet switching network's concern.

The networks shown in Figure 3.17 can run any protocols. When they run TCP/IP protocols, for example, the IP messages are encapsulated in X.25 frames and are decapsulated at the receiving end. The encapsulation and decapsulation process is very transparent.

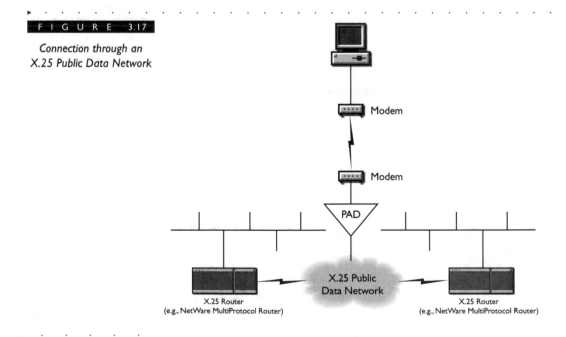

FIGURE 3.17

Connection through an X.25 Public Data Network

Devices connect to an X.25 network using a *packet assembler-disassembler* (PAD). The PAD could be located at the customer site, interfaced to a LAN through a router, and linked to the X.25 network through a leased or dial-up connection. Another option would be to locate the PAD at the network service provider and make it available through a dial-up modem connection.

X.25 is recommended by the International Telecommunications Union (ITU), which is the agency of the United Nations responsible for international communication standards. The protocol model for X.25 is shown in Figure 3.18.

The X.25 Protocol Stack

| Application |
| Presentation |
| Session |
| Transport |
| Network |
| Data Link |
| Physical |

| X.25 Packet Level Protocol |
| Link Access Protocol Balanced (LAPB) |
| X.21 or X.21 *bis* |

The protocol model for X.25 consists of three layers:

▸ X.21 provides the physical layer for digital circuits. X.21 *bis* is the comparable standard for analog circuits.

▸ Link Access Procedure Balanced (LAPB) is the data link layer protocol. It provides full-duplex, synchronous communication.

▸ X.25 is a network layer protocol that provides flow control and reliable delivery.

As I have already indicated, X.25 is an extremely limited protocol that remains popular primarily because it is readily available. But X.25 is not well-suited to LANs for a variety of reasons. LANs tend to produce traffic that is characterized as "bursty" — that is, traffic that has extremely variable data requirements. Frame Relay, which was derived from X.25, offers bandwidth on demand and therefore works better for most LAN communication.

Frame Relay

Frame Relay is essentially a modernized X.25 network. The ITU designed Frame Relay as a streamlined packet switching network that could provide broadband service. Frame Relay accommodates bursty LAN traffic by offering bandwidth on demand. Therefore, Frame Relay can adjust to varying rates of data flow.

Subscribers to a public Frame Relay network contract for a guaranteed data rate called a *committed information rate* (CIR). Depending on the service provider, subscribers may be permitted to exceed the CIR on a temporary basis. Subscribers pay for additional bandwidth as necessary. This flexibility enables customers to purchase Frame Relay service that closely matches their normal requirements. At the same time, customers still have the option of obtaining more bandwidth on a temporary basis.

Frame Relay is connection-oriented. It supports switched virtual circuits (SVCs) and permanent virtual circuits (PVCs). Establishing a PVC configures a fixed path through the network that enables devices to communicate efficiently because very little processing is needed to move each frame through the network. A PVC can multiplex up to 1024 logical connections.

The data field of a Frame Relay frame is called the *payload*. The capacity of the payload field is configurable. Therefore, when you implement a Frame Relay network, you can fine-tune the network to different requirements.

> **SNAP encapsulation must be used to support TCP/IP over Frame Relay.**
>
> NOTE

Frame Relay accommodates much higher data rates than are available with X.25. Also, Frame Relay can operate over high-speed digital services such as T1 and T3. In fact, data rates of up to 44.6 Mbps are possible.

Frame Relay's performance is better than X.25's because Frame Relay's designers were able to assume that data communication lines would be reliable. This assumption frees Frame Relay of the need to perform error detection and recovery each time a frame is switched. Although Frame Relay detects errors and discards bad frames, upper-layer protocols are responsible for requesting retransmission of bad or missing frames. In general, moving error recovery to upper-layer protocols enhances network performance. Figure 3.19 shows the Frame Relay protocol stack, which corresponds to the data link and physical layers of the OSI Reference Model.

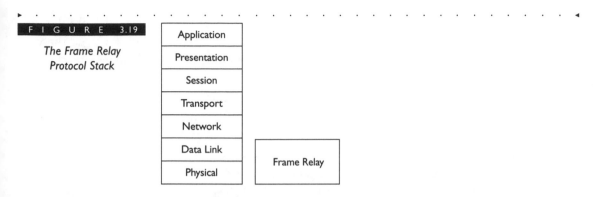

FIGURE 3.19

The Frame Relay Protocol Stack

A typical Frame Relay network is shown in Figure 3.20. LANs connect to the Frame Relay network using a *Frame Relay Interface* (FRI), which often is incorporated into a router. Frame Relay is one of the WAN options of the NetWare MultiProtocol Router. Frame Relay networks can be either public or private data networks.

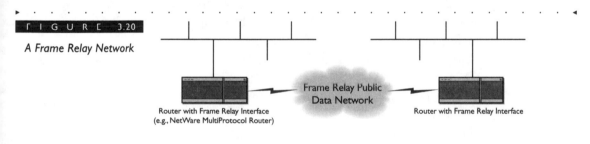

FIGURE 3.20

A Frame Relay Network

Asynchronous Transfer Mode

If there were such a thing as a high school yearbook for networks, *asynchronous transfer mode* (ATM) would undoubtedly be voted Most Likely to Succeed. ATM is an emerging technology that promises to solve a host of problems faced by computer network administrators. To understand why there is currently so much interest in ATM, you need to know something about the different kinds of services that LANs are now being asked to provide.

In the mainframe era, network traffic consisted primarily of character data being transferred between terminals and host computers. Terminal traffic could be supported with limited bandwidth, and 56 Kbps data links were pretty hot stuff.

But the emergence of LANs has changed all that. New technologies such as Ethernet, ARCnet, and token ring (which operate at about 10 Mbps) have changed the way distributed processing is done. In the early days of LANs, users primarily transferred files, ran programs, and printed documents through the network. The networks that emerged in the 1980s were capable of handling all of these tasks satisfactorily.

Now, however, new LAN applications are emerging. The problem isn't just that more data must be handled. Today, users want their LANs to support new types of data such as voice and video. Video, in particular, places heavy demands on a network. Not only does video require a great deal of bandwidth (as much as 6 Mbps for a single channel), but video also relies on two different streams of data (video and audio) that must remain synchronized as data is delivered through the network. Traditional LANs — even fast ones — simply aren't up to the task of delivering synchronized data streams.

ATM has unique capabilities that position it to satisfy these new requirements. All types of data can be accommodated by ATM, including data, voice, and video. ATM offers bandwidth on demand, very high throughput, and the ability to synchronize the delivery of multiple data streams, such as the components of a video signal.

ATM evolved from broadband ISDN (B-ISDN), a technology that is an extension of the narrowband ISDN developed in 1988 by the CCITT (now known as the ITU). The ITU governs the primary standards of ATM but has not addressed issues of LAN implementation.

The ATM Forum is a consortium of network industry partners that addresses the issues involved in employing ATM with LANs. The Internet Engineering Task Forum (IETF) also looks at ATM issues, and several Internet-Drafts address topics related to ATM.

HOW ATM WORKS

ATM stands for *Asynchronous Transfer Mode*. In order to understand how ATM works, you must first know something about transfer modes in general. A *transfer mode* is a method of transporting data units through a network. Transfer modes are closely related to the concepts of multiplexing and packet switching, which are discussed in Chapter 2.

Synchronous Transfer Mode (STM) makes use of time-division multiplexing. Multiple data streams are assigned time slots. The data streams share the communication bandwidth by taking turns. STM allocates each data stream a guaranteed bandwidth and offers synchronous delivery of multiple data streams. As such, STM is well-suited to voice and video. However, STM is too inflexible to support data. Also, because time slots must be configured, STM has trouble accommodating variable data transfer requirements.

Packet Transfer Mode (PTM) employs packet switching, which provides the kind of flexible service required for computer data. PTM is not bound by time slots that have fixed sizes, so it can accept data units of varying sizes. However, PTM cannot provide synchronous delivery.

In many ways, ATM is a hybrid of STM and PTM. ATM can be adapted to data, voice, and video. ATM employs fixed-size data units called *cells,* which are switched through virtual circuits. ATM cells are 53 bytes in length. With ATM, switching operations are more efficient, because switching can be optimized for a standard-size data unit. Virtual circuits ensure that cells arrive in the order in which they were transmitted, because all cells are switched through the same path.

To accommodate the needs of voice and video, ATM provides *cell synchronous service.* ATM can synchronize delivery of multiple data streams, and it provides guaranteed bandwidth. In especially critical situations, ATM can provide *constant bit rate service,* in other words, service that delivers data at a constant rate that compensates for delays in transmission. For computer data only, ATM offers bandwidth on demand and is highly responsive to bursty LAN traffic.

ATM is connection-oriented, and devices must establish a virtual circuit in order to communicate. The virtual circuit defines a path through the ATM network that is dedicated to the use of the connected devices. Figure 3.21 illustrates how a virtual circuit is defined.

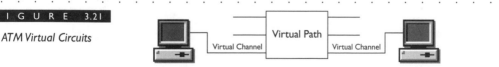

FIGURE 3.21

ATM Virtual Circuits

In a virtual circuit, two ATM devices are connected by at least one *virtual path,* which typically corresponds to a media channel. The path is called "virtual" because it does not correspond to a specific dedicated physical path through a medium. Bandwidth is dedicated to the virtual path only when the connection is used to transfer cells. Because bandwidth is not dedicated to any connections, bandwidth is available to all connections on demand.

A virtual path can accommodate over 16 million virtual channels, although most equipment accommodates fewer. A virtual circuit between two switches is defined by the virtual path and virtual circuit assigned to it. As shown in Figure 3.22, each pair of switches may assign a different virtual path and virtual circuit to the connection. Virtual path and virtual circuit information is encoded in the header of the ATM cell. Figure 3.23 shows the format of an ATM cell.

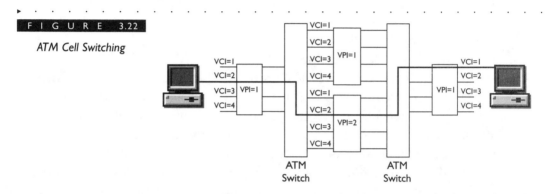

The cell's connection information is encoded in the *virtual path identifier* (VPI) and *virtual circuit identifier* (VCI) fields. The VPI and VCI fields are the only fields I discuss here because these two fields are key to understanding how ATM routes cells. Figure 3.22 shows how cells are switched through an ATM network. The bold line indicates the path associated with a particular virtual circuit. Between each pair of switches, a VPI and a VCI are associated with the virtual circuit. Each switch maintains a database that describes how cells for each connection should be switched. The VPI and VCI fields are updated as cells are forwarded from switch to switch using data stored in databases maintained by the switches. Switches consult their databases to determine which path to use when forwarding a cell that arrives from a virtual circuit.

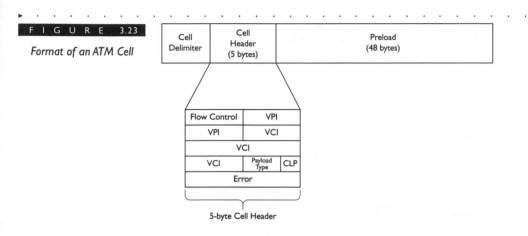

FIGURE 3.23

Format of an ATM Cell

The ITU has defined the protocol model for B-ISDN. That protocol model is shown in Figure 3.24. Although ATM protocols correspond to the first three layers of the OSI Reference Model, all switching is performed below the network layer in order to achieve greater efficiency.

The layers of the ATM protocol model are as follows:

- **ATM adaptation layer (AAL).** This layer provides an interface between upper-layer protocols and ATM switching. IEEE 802.2 LLC encapsulation is used. SNAP must be used to support TCP/IP. The AAL is responsible for message fragmentation and reassembly. The AAL provides either connection-oriented or connectionless service. Variable and constant bit rate services are supported.

- **ATM layer.** This layer defines cell formats. It is responsible for cell delivery. The ATM layer supports permanent virtual circuits (PVCs) and switched virtual circuits (SVCs).

- **ATM physical layer.** This layer transports cells through the network and defines signaling requirements.

The ATM physical layer does not define data rates or media types. ATM can be adapted to virtually any medium and any performance level.

ATM Adaptation Layer (AAL)
ATM Layer
ATM Physical Layer

ATM MEDIA

There are no inherent restrictions on ATM data rates or media, and different combinations of media and data rates are bound to appear. IBM, for example, has offered a 25 Mbps ATM product that is designed to bring ATM to the desktop.

Four ATM interfaces have been defined by the ATM Forum:

- ▸ 45 Mbps DS3 WAN

- ▸ 155 Mbps OC-3 SONET

- ▸ 155 Mbps multimode optical fiber based on Fiber Channel

- ▸ 100 Mbps multimode optical fiber based on Fiber Distributed Data Interface (FDDI)

The DS3 service interface supports copper and fiber media and can be used to interface LANs to telecommunications networks.

Synchronous Optical Network (SONET), developed by BellCore, is a common ATM carrier. SONET data rates are specified by *optical carrier* (OC) *levels.* Available data rates range from 52 Mbps (OC-1) to 2.5 Gbps (OC-48).

The FDDI interface is most likely to be incorporated into LANs. This interface is designed to take advantage of newer developments in FDDI such as FDDI over copper (CDDI). FDDI is a fault-tolerant network based on token ring operating at 100 Mbps.

A unique benefit of ATM is that networks can incorporate a mix of data rates. A 25 Mbps desktop connection could be switched to a 100 Mbps FDDI backbone, which could in turn be switched into a 466 Mbps public network. This scalability could make ATM the dominant network standard in coming decades.

ARCHITECTURE OF ATM LANS

The ATM Forum has been most responsible for defining an ATM LAN architecture. Figure 3.25 shows a typical ATM LAN. ATM networks consist of *endstations* and *switches*. The ATM Forum has defined two network interfaces:

- **User-Network Interface (UNI).** An endstation is connected to a switch through this interface.

- **Network-Network Interface (NNI).** A switch connects to another switch through this interface.

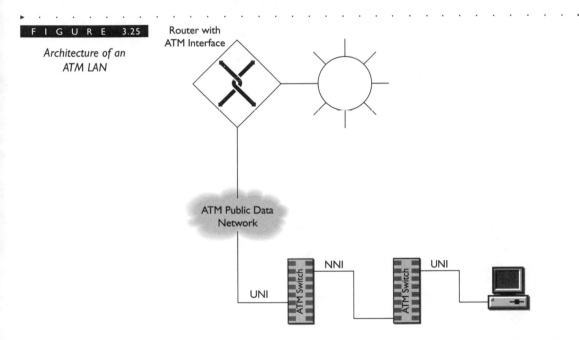

ATM sounds great, but don't rush out and sell your Ethernet boards. ATM LANs are still nascent. Several years will be required before you will see standards that can be turned into cost-effective products. ATM remains an expensive technology that is ready only for those organizations that require ATM's unique capabilities.

A Note on Network Evolution

The needs of network users are evolving rapidly. There is no sign that a few trusted standards will be universally adopted any time soon. In fact, the market is expanding for network products that satisfy specific market niches. Some of the network standards that have been around for awhile are still emerging technologies. Even good old Ethernet continues to evolve into ever-faster versions. In this chapter, I have tried to make you aware of the many different options available.

In Chapter 2, I explained that the function of the network access layer is fairly limited. The network access layer is responsible for delivering frames (or other small message units) between nodes on a network. There are many other tasks that the network layer does not perform. TCP/IP can be used to carry out many of those tasks. In the next chapter, I examine the internet layer, which is the first TCP/IP protocol layer.

## CHAPTER 4

The Internet Layer

The Internet Protocol (IP) is a required protocol at the internet layer. IP is really at the heart of the DoD protocol stack. At other layers, you will learn about alternative protocols that serve specialized purposes. At the internet layer, however, there is only IP, which has three key responsibilities:

- Addressing

- Delivery of datagrams on the internetwork

- Datagram fragmentation and reassembly

RFC 791, as amended by RFCs 919, 922, and 950, sets forth IP's specifications. Although IP is the powerhouse protocol at the internet layer, several other protocols assist IP. The protocols that assist IP are discussed in detail later in this chapter, but here is a general overview of the services they provide:

- The *Internet Control Message Protocol* (ICMP) enables destination hosts to communicate errors to source hosts. ICMP also allows destination hosts to provide other hosts with limited routing information.

- The *Address Resolution Protocol* (ARP) and the *Reverse Address Resolution Protocol* (RARP) help IP *resolve* (match) addresses used at the internet level to physical addresses used at the network access level.

- The *Routing Information Protocol* (RIP) and the protocol called *Open Shortest Path First* (OSPF) assist IP with routing. IP uses information from routing tables to route data, but IP cannot gather routing information to update routing tables. RIP and OSPF are designed to gather network path information and maintain the routing tables used by IP.

In order to understand IP itself, you must first learn a little about *IP addressing*. TCP/IP uses distinctive addresses called *IP addresses* to identify hosts at the internet level and at higher layers. IP addresses are unique to TCP/IP.

IP Addressing

TCP/IP predates many other protocols and, in fact, predates the vast majority of physical network standards. When IP was first conceptualized, there were no network node identification standards like IEEE 802's globally administered addresses. TCP/IP needed an addressing scheme that could be independent of network hardware so that a uniform address scheme could be applied to all hosts, regardless of type.

Consequently, at the layers above the network access layer, hosts are identified by logical IP addresses. Each IP address includes a network address and a node address so that every host on an internetwork can be uniquely identified by its IP address.

TCP/IP's logical IP addresses have some administrative benefits. When a TCP/IP host is set up, its configuration includes information that identifies several critical hosts on the network. For example, each host is configured with the address of a default router. Also, when a naming service is operating, each host is configured with the address of the host operating as a name server. Suppose that dozens of hosts have been configured using the physical address of a particular router. The address would change if the network board in the router were replaced. In that case, you would need to reconfigure all of the hosts that use the router. However, a router can retain the same logical IP address even though its network board is changed. If the router's IP address is used in the hosts, no other hosts need to be reconfigured when the network board in the router is replaced.

As you can see, IP addresses promote stability in the network. This stability is important to end users as well as administrators because the end users may need to access hosts using addresses. When commonly used host addresses are changed, all users on the network must be informed or else the users will not be able to access the hosts.

> **Using a name service alleviates this problem. A name service enables users to access hosts by name rather than address. The TCP/IP Domain Name Service is discussed in Chapter 6.**
>
> TIP

NOTE

Many TCP/IP concepts have no counterparts in the IPX/SPX protocols that support standard NetWare communication. IPX relies on physical addresses, and NetWare uses dynamic mechanisms such as the Service Advertising Protocol (SAP) to advertise the availability of services. With NetWare, node names are collected and updated automatically.

Formats of IP Addresses

An IP address consists of 32 bits arranged in two fields. The two fields of IP addresses are as follows:

▸ The *netid* field specifies the address of the network to which the host is attached.

▸ The *hostid* field specifies a unique logical identifier for each host on a given network.

The netid is used to route data through the internetwork. An *IP network* consists of a group of hosts that share the same netid. All hosts with a given netid should be attached to a common network segment so that they can communicate directly. Hosts separated by a router will be unable to communicate even though they have the same netid. Hosts with different netids *must* communicate through a router — even though they may be attached to the same network segment.

When the IP addressing scheme was designed, its creators assumed that networks would vary greatly in size and number. This assumption led them to create several IP address classes that could support networks of different sizes. The five address classes are as follows:

▸ *Class A* addresses were designed to support a few very large networks. The netid is contained in the first octet. The hostid is contained in the remaining three octets. Class A addresses begin with the high-order bit set to 0.

▸ *Class B* addresses were designed to support a moderate number of networks of intermediate size. The first two octets are devoted to the netid. The remaining two octets are the hostid. Class B addresses begin with the high-order bits 10.

▶ *Class C* addresses were designed to support a large number of small networks. The first three octets are the netid. Only the final octet is devoted to the hostid. Class C addresses begin with the high-order bits 110.

▶ *Class D* addresses support multicasting, enabling messages to be sent to defined-groups of hosts. The use of multicast addresses is defined by the network implementation. Class D addresses begin with the high-order bits 1110.

▶ *Class E* addresses are reserved for experimental purposes and begin with the high-order bits 11110.

Figure 4.1 shows the classes of IP addresses. Notice that a 32-bit IP address is divided into four octets, which form the basis of the address classes.

F I G U R E   4.1

Structure of IP Addresses

Using Dotted-Decimal Notation

You will discover that there are times when it is necessary to work with IP addresses in their binary form. However, bit patterns of IP addresses aren't very easy to read or remember. An address that reads 10001111 01010111 11000111 00100001 is not likely to stick in your memory for very long.

Because binary numbers are not very easy to deal with, an alternate format has been developed for IP addresses. The majority of IP addresses you see are expressed in *dotted-decimal notation*. The conversion is simple. Each of the four octets is converted to an equivalent decimal value from 0 through 255. The complete address is represented by separating the decimal numbers with periods. The dotted-decimal equivalent of the address listed above is:

143.87.199.33

Dotted-hexadecimal notation is also used for IP addresses, but it is not as common. In dotted-hex, the above address would be represented as follows:

    8F.57.CF.21

NOTE

The calculator that ships with Microsoft Windows has a scientific mode that converts hex, binary, and decimal numbers. Turn on scientific mode by selecting the Scientific command in the View menu. Alternatively, Appendix B includes a table that lists decimal, binary, and hexadecimal equivalents. (Appendix A explains briefly how the numbering systems work.)

Rules for Assigning IP Addresses

Some IP addresses are designated for special purposes. Therefore, certain addresses *cannot* be assigned to hosts. Here are some of the addresses that cannot be used for hosts:

- ► A hostid with all bits set to 0 identifies the network itself. (For example, the IP address 128.1.0.0 refers to the network with the netid 128.1.) A hostid cannot consist entirely of octets with the value 0.

- ► A netid with all bits set to 0 refers to "this network." (For example, the IP address 0.5.127.240 refers to host 5.127.240 on the current class A network.) Therefore, a netid cannot consist entirely of octets with the value 0.

- ► An octet that is all 1s (decimal 255, hex FF) indicates a broadcast address. Thus, the IP address 255.255.255.255 identifies a message that is to be broadcast to all hosts on the current network, and the IP address 199.38.87.255 identifies a message that is to be broadcast to all hosts on network 199.39.87.

- ► The netid 127 (binary 01111111) is reserved for use as a *loopback address*. If a host sends a message to 127.0.0.1 (or any address on network 127) the message will not reach the network. The message will be reflected back to the sending process. The loopback address is a useful troubleshooting tool.

▸ The final octet of an IP address cannot be 0 or 255.

These restrictions limit the addresses that are available in each address class. Table 4.1 summarizes the IP addresses that are available for addressing hosts.

T A B L E 4.1

Available IP Addresses

CLASS	FROM (BINARY)	FROM (DECIMAL)	TO (BINARY)	TO (DECIMAL)	AVAILABLE NETWORKS	AVAILABLE HOSTS
A	00000001	1	01111110	126	126	16,777,214
B	10000000	128	10111111	191	16,384	65,534
C	11000000	192	11011111	223	2,097,152	254

NOTE The only network likely to run out of available IP addresses is the Internet. Until recently, even the Internet had plenty of available addresses. Now, however, even class C addresses are becoming scarce. In 1992, only about 2% of the available class C addresses were taken. In 1994, that figure had reached 25%. Current indications suggest that available Internet addresses will be exhausted by about 1997. This looming crisis is driving the effort to develop the next generation of IP (called IPng or IPv6).

ASSIGNING IP ADDRESSES TO HOSTS

In most cases, IP addresses are manually assigned to host computers by entering the IP address into the host configuration files. This manual procedure is perhaps the single most time-consuming task an administrator faces when setting up a TCP/IP network. The network administrator must devise a plan for assigning each network a unique netid and each host a hostid that is unique on the host's network.

In many cases networks are segmented to form internetworks. Figure 4.2 shows an example of a TCP/IP internetwork that incorporates network segments with class A, B, and C addresses. Address classes can be mixed freely on an internetwork.

Notice that routers are essentially TCP/IP hosts that interface to two or more networks. Each interface must be assigned an IP address that is correct for the network it attaches to.

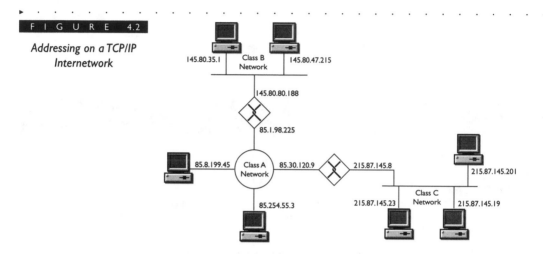

FIGURE 4.2

Addressing on a TCP/IP Internetwork

145.80.35.1 Class B Network 145.80.47.215

145.80.80.188

85.1.98.225

85.8.199.45 Class A Network 85.30.120.9 215.87.145.8 215.87.145.201

85.254.55.3 215.87.145.23 Class C Network 215.87.145.19

There are a number of reasons to segment a network. Here are a few:

▸ If a network is congested, properly designed segmentation reduces traffic on each segment. With the best design, the majority of traffic will be between hosts on the same network segment.

▸ LAN cabling systems accommodate maximum numbers of connected devices. To exceed those limits, the network must be segmented.

▸ LANs can accommodate different LAN technologies to meet different requirements. A token ring network might be required in manufacturing, for example, whereas Ethernet is used elsewhere. Routers can interconnect different types of LANs.

▸ WAN technologies enable a network to grow beyond local limits. Routers are used to keep unnecessary traffic off the wide-area connection.

▸ Security may be enhanced by isolating parts of the network. Routers can be configured to filter traffic so that critical data does not reach other local or remote networks.

Routing theory is addressed later in this chapter, under the heading "Delivering Datagrams on Internetworks." Chapter 10 covers the installation and configuration of NetWare routers for TCP/IP.

OBTAINING ADDRESSES FOR THE INTERNET

The Internet can only run smoothly if each network and each host is uniquely addressed. So if you want to connect your network to the Internet, you need to apply for enough addresses to support your network.

Internet addresses can be obtained from the InterNIC Registration Service. However, if you are connecting to the Internet through an Internet access provider (IAP), the InterNIC will probably refer you to your IAP to obtain an address. IAPs are assigned blocks of addresses that they make available to their customers.

Address registration forms are available via anonymous FTP from DS.INTERNIC.NET, or from the World Wide Web, with the URL http://ds.internic.net/.

Applications may be submitted by mail or e-mail to:

Network Solutions
InterNIC Registration Services
505 Huntmar Park Drive
Herndon, VA 22070

```
HOSTMASTER@INTERNIC.NET
```

At this point, you are not likely to obtain anything other than a class C address. Class A addresses were depleted long ago by organizations such as the DoD and IBM. A few class B addresses are still available, but they are in high demand. Even class C addresses are running out, so obtain your address as soon as possible.

If you plan to connect your network to the Internet in the near future, obtain a registered address now and use it to configure your network. That will save you the trouble of having to reconfigure your TCP/IP computers when you actually hook up to the Internet.

SUBNETTING

A class A or B address can accommodate *a lot* of users. Not many networks can physically support 65,534 hosts without a few routers. So what's an administrator to do? Should you use a class B address for a 500-node LAN and let the rest of the available addresses go to waste? If you're attached to the Internet, you can't really do that because your organization probably won't be assigned sufficient IP addresses to let you configure every network with a separate netid. So what should you do?

Subnetting is a technique that enables you to spread a single IP address more thinly so that its address pool can be shared by several network segments. Even if your organization has a single class C address, subnet addressing enables you to support a LAN with several segments. Subnetting is defined in RFC 950.

Figure 4.3 shows the theory behind subnetting. Ordinarily, an IP address is read like this:

```
netid + hostid
```

When subnetting is used, an IP address has three fields:

```
netid + subnetid + hostid
```

The bits necessary to create the subnetid field are borrowed from the hostid field. You lose some of the bits that could be used to configure hosts, but you gain in the number of network segments your lone IP address can support.

F I G U R E   4.3

A Class B Address with and without Subnetting

| Without Subnetting | 10111100 00100001 | 01111011 00100011 |
| | netid | hostid |

| With Subnetting | 10111100 00100001 | 01111011 | 00100011 |
| | netid | subnetid | hostid |

Introduction to Subnet Masks

Subnetting is achieved using a subnet mask. *Subnet masking* is the tool that designates bits for the subnet mask. I'll warn you right now: Subnet masking is an area where there's no substitute for getting down to the bit level. Dotted decimal equivalents just don't allow you to see what's going on. So if you're uncomfortable with binary, now is the time to review number notation schemes in Appendix A.

Figure 4.4 shows how subnet masking can be applied to class A, B, and C addresses. Of course, you have more bits available for subnetids with a class A or B address, but class C addresses can be productively subnetted.

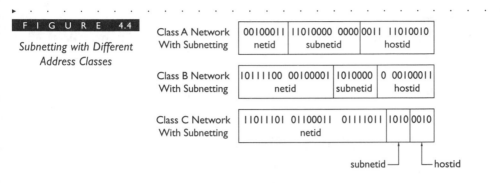

FIGURE 4.4

Subnetting with Different Address Classes

The subnet mask is simply a 32-bit binary number that matches an IP address digit-for-digit. A 1 in the subnet mask indicates that the corresponding bit in the IP address is part of the netid or subnetid. A 0 in the subnet mask indicates that the corresponding bit in the IP address is part of the hostid.

Like IP addresses, subnet masks are frequently represented in dotted-decimal form. However, dotted-hex is also common. In fact, NetWare generally represents subnet masks in dotted-hex notation. See Appendix A for further explanation.

In most cases, the 1s in a subnet mask are adjacent, high-order bits. As a result, there are only eight subnet masks you will commonly encounter. If you memorize the information in Table 4.2, you will know the most popular subnet masks.

TABLE 4.2

Common Subnet Masks

BINARY	DECIMAL
00000000	0
10000000	128
11000000	192
11100000	224
11110000	240
11111000	248
11111100	252
11111110	254
11111111	255

The majority of TCP/IP implementations require that IP addresses be assigned a subnet mask even though the network may not be segmented into subnets. When IP addresses are used without subnetting, a *default subnet mask* must be specified, which simply includes a 1 that corresponds to each digit in the standard netid field. Table 4.3 lists the default subnet masks for the three IP address classes.

T A B L E 4.3

Default Subnet Masks

ADDRESS CLASS	BINARY SUBNET MASK	DOTTED-DECIMAL MASK	DOTTED-HEX MASK
A	11111111 00000000 00000000 00000000	255.0.0.0	FF.00.00.00
B	11111111 11111111 00000000 00000000	255.255.0.0	FF.FF.00.00
C	11111111 11111111 11111111 00000000	255.255.255.0	FF.FF.FF.00

The subnet mask must contain as many bits as are required to define the hostid field for the address class of the IP address. A subnet mask of 255.255.0.0 is invalid for a class C IP address.

Identifying Subnetids and Hostids

Here are a few examples to help you understand subnet masks (see also Figure 4.5). Suppose a class A network identified by 65.0.0.0 is to be subnetted with the subnet mask 255.255.0.0. What are the subnetid and netid for host 65.210.185.33? To determine the values, the numbers must be examined in binary form:

IP Address	01000001	11010010	10111001	00100001
Subnet Mask	11111111	11111111	00000000	00000000
Subnetid		11010010		
Hostid			10111001	00100001

Therefore, the IDs for this host are as follows:

Netid	65
Subnetid	210
Hostid	185.33

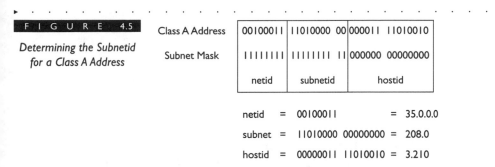

FIGURE 4.5

Determining the Subnetid for a Class A Address

Things get a bit more complicated when the subnet mask doesn't fall on an even octet boundary. Here are some more examples. Suppose a class B network with the address 128.100 is to be given the subnet mask 255.255.240. What will be the subnetid and netid for host 128.100.158.200? Here are the binary equivalents:

IP Address	10000000	01100100	10011110	11001000
Subnet Mask	11111111	11111111	11110000	00000000
Subnetid			10010000	
Netid			00001110	11001000

When the subnetid is expressed in decimal form, trailing zeros are added to complete an octet. In decimal form, the IDs for this host are:

Netid	128.100
Subnetid	144
Hostid	14.200

Here is another example. A class C network with the address 200.85.123 will be subnetted with the mask 255.255.255.224. What are the subnetid and hostid for host 200.85.123.45?

IP Address	11001000	01010101	01111011	00101101
Subnet Mask	11111111	11111111	11111111	11100000
Subnetid				00100000 (32 decimal)
Netid				00001101 (13 decimal)

Therefore, the IDs in decimal form are:

Netid	200.85.123
Subnetid	32
Hostid	13

NOTE **RFC 905, which defines IP subnet addressing, specifies that subnetids cannot consist entirely of 0s or 1s. This significantly reduces the number of subnets that can be defined, particularly for class C addresses.**

A number of TCP/IP implementations, including Novell's, permit use of subnet 0. If you choose to implement subnet 0 on your network, be sure that all systems on the network support it. (Examples in this book will not use subnet 0.) When subnetting is applied, the rule remains in effect that the hostid cannot consist entirely of 0s or 1s.

Example: A Class C Network with Subnets

Because so few bits are available for subnetting, class C addresses present the greatest challenge when setting up subnets. Therefore, here is a more complex example of a class C network that consists of an internetwork with four subnets. The subnetid must occupy three bits, giving a total of six subnets to work with. The subnet mask, therefore, is 255.255.255.224. Table 4.4 lists the ranges of addresses that a three-bit subnet mask makes available (assuming that subnet 0 will not be supported). Remember the following rules, which restrict the available subnetids and netids:

- ▸ The subnetid cannot be all 0s or all 1s.

- ▸ The netid cannot be all 0s or all 1s.

T A B L E 4.4

*IDs Available on a Class C Subnet
with Subnet ID 255.255.255.224*

SUBNETS ADDRESS	FIRST IP ADDRESS (BINARY)	LAST IP ADDRESS (BINARY)	FIRST IP ADDRESS (DECIMAL)	LAST IP HOSTIDS (DECIMAL)	AVAILABLE
00100000	00100001	00111110	33	62	30
01000000	01000001	01011110	65	94	30
01100000	01100001	01111110	97	126	30
10000000	10000001	10011110	129	158	30
10100000	10100001	10111110	161	190	30
11000000	11000001	11011110	193	222	30

If subnet 0 is not used, the three bit subnet mask enables you to configure six subnets with 30 hosts each for a total of 180 hosts. With subnet 0, you can configure 210 hosts on seven subnets. Although you lose between 45 and 75 potential hostids in the process, that may be a small price to pay if it can allow your class C address to handle a WAN.

Figure 4.6 shows an internet with four subnets. The internet is configured with a class C address, and the subnet mask is 255.255.255.224.

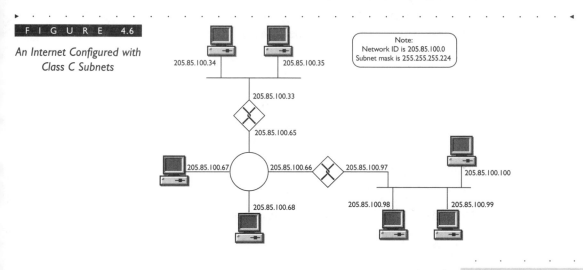

F I G U R E 4.6

*An Internet Configured with
Class C Subnets*

Note:
Network ID is 205.85.100.0
Subnet mask is 255.255.255.224

205.85.100.34
205.85.100.35
205.85.100.33
205.85.100.65
205.85.100.67
205.85.100.66
205.85.100.97
205.85.100.100
205.85.100.68
205.85.100.98
205.85.100.99

Class C subnets are pretty quirky, and there are some subnet masks that aren't very useful. Table 4.5 shows what different subnet masks (not including subnet 0) can achieve.

T A B L E   4.5

Effects of Class C Subnet Masks

NUMBER OF MASK BITS	MASK (BINARY)	MASK (DECIMAL)	AVAILABLE SUBNETS	HOSTS PER SUBNET	TOTAL HOSTS AVAILABLE
1	10000000	128	0	N/A	0
2	11000000	192	2	62	124
3	11100000	224	6	30	180
4	11110000	240	14	14	196
5	11111000	248	30	6	180
6	11111100	252	62	2	124
7	11111110	254	126	0	0
8	11111111	255	254	0	0

Calculating Available Subnets and Hostids

You can use two simple formulas to determine the number of subnetids and hostids-per-subnet you can configure with a given subnet mask:

Available subnets = $2^{(number\ of\ masked\ subnet\ bits)} - 2$
Available networks = $2^{(number\ of\ unmasked\ bits)} - 2$

To demonstrate, I will apply the formulas to a class B address with the subnet mask 255.255.248.0. This mask designates five bits for the subnetid and leaves eleven bits for the netid. Here are the calculations:

Available subnets = $2^5 - 2 = 30$
Available networks = $2^{11} - 2 = 2046$

Now that you have seen how IP addresses are structured, you are ready to learn how they are used for message delivery.

Delivering Datagrams on Internetworks

IP provides connectionless delivery of messages through an internetwork. RFC 791, which outlines the IP standard, refers to IP messages as "datagrams." A *datagram* is a message that is sent individually — without any formal connection or error checking. When connection-oriented delivery is necessary, TCP provides it at the host-to-host layer.

Routing is performed at the IP protocol layer. Originally, IP routers were called *gateways*, but the term "gateway" is also used to describe an upper-layer protocol translator that connects dissimilar systems. (For example, a gateway might be used to connect a LAN to an IBM SNA network.) Therefore, there has been a trend away from using the term "gateway" to describe devices at the IP protocol layer. Instead, the devices are simply called *routers*.

IP is responsible for delivering datagrams to the correct network, but the data link layer handles delivery of the data to the correct computer. Consequently, two different address schemes are involved: IP addresses are used to route datagrams to the right network, and physical addresses are used to deliver the message to the proper computers. The following subsection explains how data delivery is carried out in a simple scenario involving a single network segment.

BASIC DATAGRAM DELIVERY

When a frame's source and destination nodes are connected to the same network, a very simple mechanism can handle delivery of the data. The source codes the physical address of the destination into the destination address field (or DA field) of the frame and sends the frame out on the network. Every node on the network looks at the frame and checks the DA field. If a node recognizes its own address in the DA field, it receives the frame and passes it to the network layer. If the node's address does not match the address in the frame, the frame is ignored.

However, as I mentioned earlier, IP works with IP addresses, which are *not* used by the data link layer. Before IP can send a datagram on its way, IP must know the physical address of the destination computer. To get that information, IP relies on an auxiliary protocol called the *Address Resolution Protocol* (ARP).

Address Resolution Protocol

ARP has one purpose, and that is to supply IP with physical addresses. Figure 4.7 shows how IP and ARP work together.

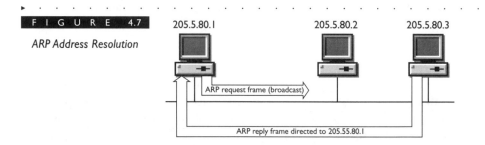

F I G U R E 4.7

ARP Address Resolution

Here are the steps that allow IP to obtain the physical address of the host 205.5.80.3:

1 • IP calls ARP, passing ARP the address 205.5.80.3.

2 • ARP generates an ARP request frame, which is broadcast to the local network. (Broadcasts to Ethernets and IEEE LANs are sent to the physical address FF FF FF FF FF FF.) The ARP request frame includes the sending host's IP address and physical address. The frame also includes the IP address ARP is attempting to resolve.

3 • The broadcast ARP request frame is received by all hosts on the local network. (IP broadcasts do not cross routers.) Each host attempts to match its own IP address to the IP address in the ARP request frame.

4 • If a host discovers a match, it generates an *ARP response frame* by adding its own physical address in a space provided in the ARP request frame. The ARP response frame is then returned directly to the host that originated the ARP request frame.

5 • ARP in the original host receives the ARP response frame, extracts the physical address, and passes the address to IP.

ARP maintains a cache table of recently resolved addresses. Before generating a request frame, ARP consults the table to see whether the address has been recently matched. This reduces the network traffic that would be generated if ARP were required to resolve addresses for each datagram sent. Entries in the cache table remain there for a limited period of time, which is determined by the network administrator. ARP regains addresses that have expired.

Reverse Address Resolution Protocol (RARP) compliments ARP by resolving physical addresses to their corresponding IP addresses.

Delivering a Datagram Locally

Once IP has identified the physical address of the destination host, IP uses the network access layer to deliver the datagram.

The process of delivering a datagram locally is as follows:

1 • IP receives data from an upper layer protocol, which includes the IP address of the destination host.

2 • IP examines the netid portion of the destination IP address and compares it to its own netid. If the destination and source netids match, the data can be delivered on the local network.

3 • IP queries ARP to obtain the physical address of the destination host.

4 • IP constructs a datagram that includes the source and destination IP addresses.

5 • IP passes the datagram to the network access layer. With the datagram, IP passes the source and destination IP addresses.

6 • The network access layer builds a frame that includes the source and destination physical addresses. The datagram received from IP is stored in the data portion of the frame.

7 • The network access layer sends the frame on the network.

8 • The host whose physical address matches the destination address in the frame receives the frame. Delivery is accomplished.

IP's job is quite simple when it must deliver a datagram to a local network. Understanding local delivery is essential to understanding internetwork delivery. Every hop through an internet is accomplished through local datagram delivery.

Delivering a Datagram to a Remote Network

When data is delivered to a remote network, delivery involves routing. Figure 4.8 shows a simple internetwork consisting of two network segments separated by a single router. Note: An IP router is essentially a TCP/IP computer that is equipped with two network interfaces. A TCP/IP host that is connected to two or more networks is called a *multihomed* host. A router may be a dedicated device, in which case, protocols above the internet layer will probably not be implemented. There is no need for TCP when you have a dedicated router because the datagrams are never sent above the internet layer. However, a router can also be a working computer. A NetWare server, for example, can route IP datagrams as well as perform file services.

Routers need routing information that pertains to all of the remote destinations where the datagrams are to be sent. This information is stored in a *routing table,* which lists the destination networks and the best IP address to use for each network. Information can be added to routing tables in three ways:

- By an automated route discovery program

- Manually

- In response to ICMP messages

NetWare uses all three methods. In the present chapter, I discuss two different route discovery programs: RIP and OSPF. Later on, in Chapter 10, I discuss manual and automated routing.

When a routing table does not contain information about a destination, a router may check a *default router* (also called a *default gateway*). The IP address of a default router is entered manually when a host is configured.

Figure 4.8 depicts delivery of a datagram to a remote destination.

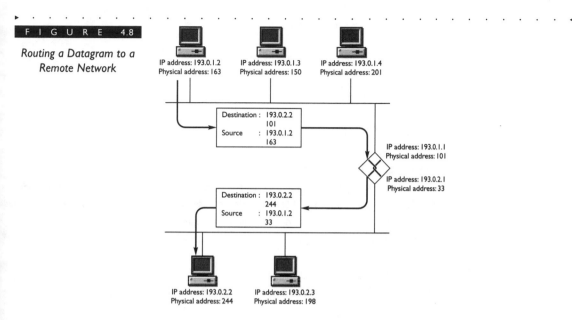

FIGURE 4.8

*Routing a Datagram to a
Remote Network*

IP address: 193.0.1.2
Physical address: 163

IP address: 193.0.1.3
Physical address: 150

IP address: 193.0.1.4
Physical address: 201

Destination : 193.0.2.2
101
Source : 193.0.1.2
163

IP address: 193.0.1.1
Physical address: 101

IP address: 193.0.2.1
Physical address: 33

Destination : 193.0.2.2
244
Source : 193.0.1.2
33

IP address: 193.0.2.2
Physical address: 244

IP address: 193.0.2.3
Physical address: 198

In Figure 4.8 a datagram is routed from host 193.0.1.2 to host 193.0.2.2. Delivery
is performed as follows:

1 • IP in host 193.0.1.2 examines the datagram and determines that it
must be routed to a remote network. (The netid portion of the
destination IP address is not 193.0.1.)

2 • IP consults its routing table to obtain the IP address of the interface
that should receive datagrams destined for network 193.0.2. The best
next interface is 193.0.1.1.

3 • IP performs an ARP request to determine the physical address of
interface 193.0.1.1. ARP responds with the physical address 101.

4 • IP constructs an IP datagram and sends it to the network access layer,
along with the hardware address obtained from ARP. The address
information sent to the network access layer is as follows:

▸ Destination IP address: 193.0.2.2

▸ Destination physical address: 101

▸ Source IP address: 193.0.1.2

▸ Source physical address: 163

NOTE **The destination IP address and the destination physical address do not correspond to the same host. When the datagram is routed, the IP address always refers to the ultimate destination. The physical address refers only to the source and destination interfaces for the current hop.**

5 • The network access layer constructs a frame and deposits it on the network. The router recognizes its physical address and receives the frame.

6 • IP on the router recovers the datagram, examines the IP address and learns that the destination is on network 193.0.2. Because the destination netid does not match the netid of the interface that received the datagram, the frame must be routed. IP consults its routing table and learns that the network can be reached from interface 193.0.2.1.

If IP on the router determines that the netid in the destination address matches the netid of the interface that received the datagram, the datagram will be discarded. Only datagrams destined for other networks will be routed.

7 • IP calls ARP to obtain the physical address of the destination host. ARP responds with the physical address 244.

8 • IP constructs a datagram and sends it to the network access layer with the physical address information as follows:

▸ Destination IP address: 193.0.2.2

▸ Destination physical address: 244

- Source IP address: 193.0.1.2

- Source physical address: 33

    Here again, the IP addresses refer to the original source host and the *ultimate* destination. The physical addresses reflect the current hop only.

9 • The network access layer constructs a frame and forwards it to the network.

10 • The network layer of host 193.0.2.2 recognizes its physical address, receives the frame, and recovers the original datagram.

As you can see, the IP address remains constant when a frame is routed. In order to send its reply, the receiving host does not need to know the physical address of the source host. Only the source IP address is necessary.

ROUTING TABLES

Routing tables and the programs that maintain them are vital tools on internetworks. They determine how efficiently datagrams will be delivered and how well routers adjust to changes in the network. There are two approaches to maintaining routing tables: static and dynamic.

Static Routing

When relying on *static routing,* the network administrator uses a software tool to manually maintain the information in the routing table. Any changes made to the network must be entered in the routing tables of all routers on the network. Consequently, static routing can be a tedious task. However, static routing may be appropriate in some cases. Here are some examples of cases where static routing makes sense:

- The network is small enough that network administrators are comfortable with manual maintenance.

- The network changes infrequently.

▸ The network does not have alternate routes to destinations. (Static routing cannot take advantage of alternate routes when a primary route fails.)

Another reason for turning to static routing is that static routing generates no network overhead. Dynamic routing protocols require routers to communicate to exchange routes. In some instances the traffic generated to maintain routing tables can overwhelm the network, particularly when slow, wide-area links are involved.

With NetWare, static routing table entries can be entered in two ways:

▸ Using the INETCFG NetWare Loadable Module (NLM)

▸ Using the TCP/IP Console (TCPCON.NLM) to reconfigure hosts via the Simple Network Management Protocol (SNMP)

In the vast majority of cases, the difficulty associated with static routing outweighs whatever advantages it might offer, especially now that efficient routing protocols are widely available for use in dynamic routing.

Dynamic Routing

Dynamic routing involves using protocols to monitor the network, identify routes, and create entries in routing tables. Dynamic routing protocols can automatically adjust to changes in the network. These protocols allow hosts to take advantage of alternate paths when primary paths become unavailable. NetWare supports four TCP/IP protocols related to routing:

▸ Routing Information Protocol (RIP)

▸ Open Shortest Path First (OSPF)

▸ Exterior Gateway Protocol (EGP)

▸ Internet Control Message Protocol (ICMP)

RIP and OSPF are classified as *interior gateway protocols* (IGPs) or *interior routing protocols* (IRPs). An IGP is used to determine routes within an *autonomous system* (AS) — that is, within a group of hosts that share the same routing protocol. You can use these protocols to configure routing on your NetWare TCP/IP networks.

Exterior gateway protocols (EGPs), also called exterior routing protocols (ERPs), perform routing between autonomous systems. Figure 4.9 illustrates the relationship of IGPs and EGPs.

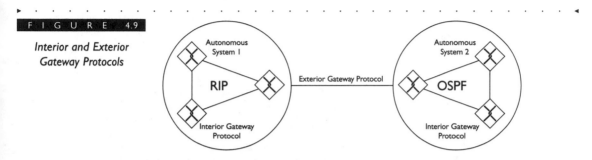

FIGURE 4.9

Interior and Exterior
Gateway Protocols

Routing Information Protocol

Routing Information Protocol (RIP) is a very widely used internet routing protocol. RIP is classified as a "distance vector routing" protocol. Distance vector routing is a technique for describing routes to a destination network in terms of the "cost" to reach the destination using a particular IP address. Cost is simply a metric ranging in value from 1 to 15. Typically, cost represents the number of hops required to reach the destination via a particular route. One hop is counted for each network that must be crossed.

The original implementation of RIP, now known as RIP I (RFC 1058) was written prior to several RFCs that extended the functionality of IP. A particularly problematic limitation of RIP I is that it does not support subnet addressing. This limitation prevents RIP I from advertising subnet routes. Although RIP I can be used with subnets, RIP I advertises only network routes, and numerous restrictions apply. (For example, RIP I does not support variable-length subnets.)

RIP II (RFC 1723) is a draft standard that is supported by NetWare TCP/IP. RIP II extends RIP I by adding support for subnet masks and also supports the use of subnet 0. RIP II incorporates the following enhancements:

▸ Passwords may be used for authentication.

▸ Subnet masks are supported. A subnet mask is associated with each destination, supporting use of variable-length subnet masks.

▶ RIP II routing packets can be multicast, reducing the load on hosts that are not listening for RIP packets. The RIP II multicast address is 224.0.0.9.

NetWare 4.1 and the NetWare MultiProtocol Router can support RIP I and RIP II simultaneously.

A RIP routing table entry must include — at a minimum — the following data:

▶ The IP address (or host name) of the destination

▶ A metric representing the total cost to reach the destination

▶ The IP address (or host name) of the next router used to reach the destination

▶ A flag indicating the route has been recently updated

▶ Timers

Each routing table must contain an entry specifying a *default router*. When the routing table does not contain enough information to forward a particular datagram, the datagram is relayed to the default router. By convention, the default router is specified by the destination IP address 0.0.0.0. Typically, the routing tables of non-routing hosts (such as user workstations) will be configured with the default router only, specifying a router on the local network. The routing tables of routers contain routes for all destinations in the internet.

IMPORTANT

TCP/IP's RIP routing protocol is not the same as the NetWare RIP protocol you may be familiar with. Both RIP implementations were derived from the Xerox XNS protocol, but they function separately and operate somewhat differently. For example, NetWare RIP advertises routing information at one-minute intervals, whereas TCP/IP RIP advertises routes at 30-second intervals. Of course, they are also designed to route different protocols.

RIP Route Convergence   The basic RIP mechanism is extremely simple. Each router periodically broadcasts its entire routing table. Other routers use these broadcasts to update their own routing tables. Eventually, each router learns all of the available routes in the internetwork. The process that enables each router to arrive at an accurate picture of the internetwork is called *route convergence*.

Before you can understand the shortcomings of RIP, it is necessary to examine how route convergence takes place. Figure 4.10 illustrates an internetwork consisting of five segments (N1 – N5) connected by four routers (R1 – R4).

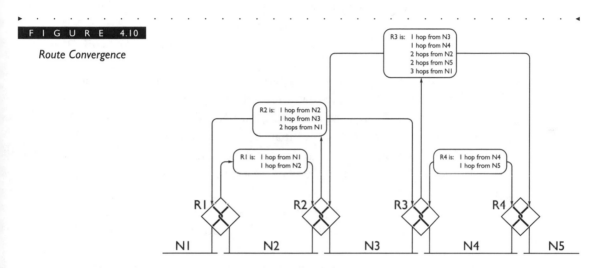

FIGURE   4.10

Route Convergence

The following steps explain how R1 initializes its routing table and how R1's information is propagated throughout the internet (assuming all routers have been newly initialized with empty routing tables):

1 • When a router is initialized, it has information only about the networks to which it is directly attached. R1 is aware of N1 and N2, and, because they are directly attached, R1 knows them to be one hop away.

2 • R1 broadcasts a *RIP response packet* stating that R1 is one hop from N1 and one hop from N2.

3 • R2 receives the RIP response packet from R1. Because R2 has a direct attachment to N2, R2 discards the information it receives about N2.

4 • R2 now knows that it is one hop away from R1 because they are both one hop from N2. To determine the distance to N1, R2 adds its cost to reach R1 to R1's cost to reach N1. R2 concludes that it can reach N1 through R1 at a cost of 2.

5 • R2 broadcasts a RIP response packet with its routing table entries. From R2's broadcast, R1 learns that it has a route to N3 at a cost of 2. Also, R3 learns that it has a route to N2 (cost of 2) and to N1 (cost of 3).

Each router broadcasts its routing table at 30-second intervals. While the above exchanges are taking place, R4 has also been at work transmitting its routing table so the other routers can learn about routes to N5. Eventually, each router receives information about every other destination in the internet, along with the costs to reach those destinations. If multiple routes exist, the router selects the route that has the lowest cost. If a new, lower-cost route later becomes active, the router discards the old route.

In the scenario above, I ask you to assume something that is very unlikely (namely, that all routers have been newly initialized). In practice, this is seldom the case. A newly started router can converge on the network fairly quickly by issuing a RIP request packet soliciting routing information from established routers.

RIP Convergence Problems   The basic RIP algorithm is not perfect. In particular, it can take a long time for routers to converge after a network change occurs.

Figure 4.11 shows a typical network. Notice that a cost of 1 has been assigned to all connections except the connection between R2 and R4, which has a cost of 10. There are two main reasons why a network administrator might assign a higher cost to that connection. The cost at that link may be higher because of a slower WAN link that ought to be avoided if a more efficient path exists. The cost at that connection might also be higher because several other routers (not shown in the diagram) come between R2 and R4.

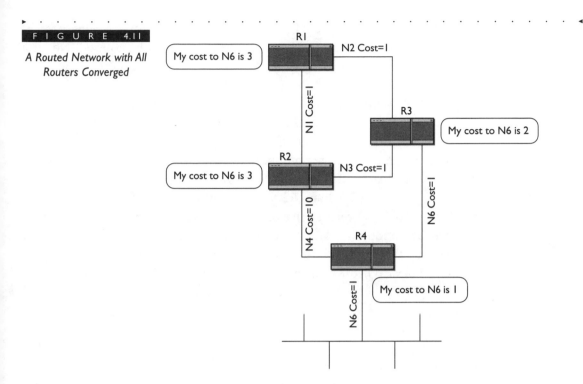

A Routed Network with All Routers Converged

When all channels are functioning properly, the routers have the following entries in their routing tables:

- ▸ R1 can reach N6 via R3 at a cost of 3

- ▸ R2 can reach N6 via R3 at a cost of 3

- ▸ R3 can reach N6 via R4 at a cost of 2

- ▸ R4 can reach N6 directly at a cost of 1

What happens if the link between R3 and R4 fails? Then the routers' cost information becomes invalid. R1, for example, must now route through R2 to reach N6, at a cost of 12. The routers cannot adjust to the network change very quickly at all.

R3 would become aware of the problem fairly quickly through a time-out mechanism. If it has not received a route response packet from R4 within 180 seconds, R3 purges any routes in its table that are directed through R4. When that happens, R3 must find a new route to N6.

Finding a new route is more complicated than discovering the original route because, under the basic RIP algorithm, R1 and R2 have both advertised that they can reach N6 at a cost of 3. R1 and R2 do not know the cause of the failure. When, after 180 seconds R3 advertises that its route to N6 is gone, R1 and R2 begin searching for a new route. And that's the root of the problem. A route advertisement announces only that a route exists. An advertisement does not identify the path that the data takes. When R1 advertises that it can reach N6 in 3 hops, the other routers are ignorant of the fact that the advertised route may depend on a failed network segment.

Suppose R2 continues to advertise that it can reach N6 at a cost of 3. R1 may pick up on this and conclude that R1 can now reach N6 through R2 at a cost of 4. R1 now advertises that it can reach N6 at a cost of 4. R3 sees these advertisements and assumes that it can reach N6 through R1 at a cost of 5. Figure 4.12 shows how each of the routers would advertise its cost at this point.

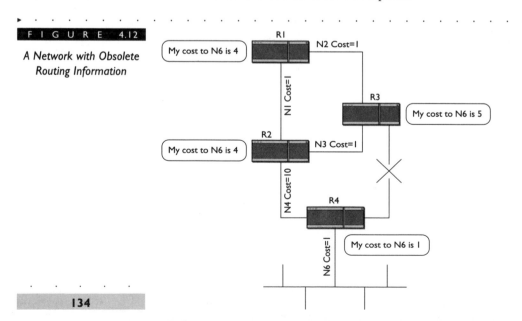

FIGURE 4.12

A Network with Obsolete Routing Information

R1 — My cost to N6 is 4 — N2 Cost=1

N1 Cost=1

R3 — My cost to N6 is 5

R2 — My cost to N6 is 4 — N3 Cost=1

N4 Cost=10

R4 — My cost to N6 is 1

N6 Cost=1

Suppose now that R1 and R2 receive R3's routing advertisement and use it to update their routing tables. Using R3's misinformation, R1 and R2 assign a cost of 6 to the routes. This prompts R3 to update its routing table to reflect a route through R1 at a cost of 7, forcing R1 and R2 to update their cost estimates.

In this way, the costs slowly ratchet up until R2 concludes that its route through R4 is the most efficient route available. This causes R2 to advertise that it can reach N6 in 11 hops. R1 and R3 recognize that R2 is now the low-cost route to N6 and update their routing tables as shown in Figure 4.13.

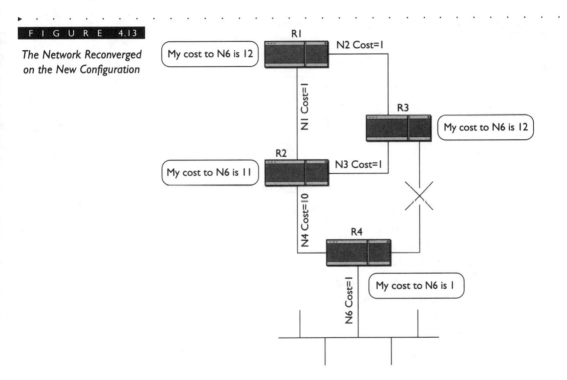

FIGURE 4.13

The Network Reconverged on the New Configuration

Routing tables gradually converge on the new values as RIP advertisements are sent at 30-second intervals. Eventually, if a valid route exists, the routers converge on the new configuration. This process could take a considerable amount of time and, in the meantime, no datagrams would be routed to N6.

The Count-to-Infinity Problem A more serious problem occurs when a network failure renders a destination unreachable. Consider the simple network in Figure 4.14. Under normal operation, R1 can reach N2 through R2 at a cost of 2.

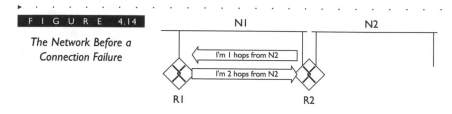

FIGURE 4.14

The Network Before a
Connection Failure

Now, consider what happens when R2's connection to N2 fails, as shown in Figure 4.15.

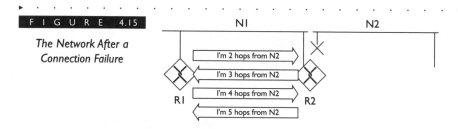

FIGURE 4.15

The Network After a
Connection Failure

R2 immediately discovers the failure and searches its routing tables for an alternate route. Because R1 has been advertising that it can reach N2 in 2 hops, R2 decides to use that route. Now, R2 announces that it can reach N2 in 3 hops.

When R1 learns that R2's cost to N2 is 3, R1 concludes that its cost to reach N2 must now be 4. Therefore, R1 begins to advertise that its cost to reach N2 is 4. But R2 has assumed it can reach N2 through R1. Now R2 learns that its cost to reach N2 is 5.

In reality, N2 is no longer reachable. (This is a sinister scenario indeed.) R1 and R2 can never converge on a correct route to N2 because no such route exists, and their hop counts continue to escalate as the routers count to infinity. The solution to this problem is to designate a certain number as infinity — in other words, to set a limit on the number of counts. For RIP, the limit is 16. Any route that is advertised with a cost metric of 16 is assumed to be unreachable. However, it can take a while for the routers to realize that the destination is unreachable.

In the preceding examples, when a router realizes a route is no longer available, it simply purges the entry from its routing table. Nothing indicates to the other routers that the destination is unreachable. A simple modification could greatly reduce the time it takes the routers to realize a destination is unreachable. Instead of simply discarding the table entry, R2 could also announce that its cost to reach N2 is now 16. Then, R1 would immediately realize that the network cannot be reached. The routers never even begin the time-wasting count to infinity.

With distance-vectors algorithms, the value of infinity represents a design compromise between the time it takes routers to converge and the size of network that can be supported. Because RIP designates a metric of 16 as infinite, no two destinations on the internet may be more than 15 hops apart. This limits the size of the networks that RIP can support. The designers of the RIP protocol did not feel that it could adequately support networks with diameters larger than 15 hops.

NetWare TCP/IP supports three techniques that help avoid loops and speed convergence:

▸ Split horizon

▸ Triggered updates

▸ Poison reverse

The following subsections explain how these techniques work.

Split Horizon   If you refer back to Figure 4.13, you will see that problems arise because R1 advertises routes to R2 that have been obtained *from R2*. This leads R2 to the erroneous conclusion that R1 has its own route to N2, independent of R2.

Split horizon is a technique based on the observation that it is never advantageous for a router to advertise a route back to the interface from which the route was received. In other words, if R1 has received a route from a network, R1 should never advertise that route back to the same network. Split horizon prevents routers like the ones shown in Figure 4.13 from entering a self-referential loop because R1 would never inform R2 that R1 could reach N2.

Figure 4.16 shows split horizon in action. R1 advertises to network N3 R1's cost to N2. However, R1 does not advertise that cost to N1 because R1 based its calculation of the cost on information received from N1.

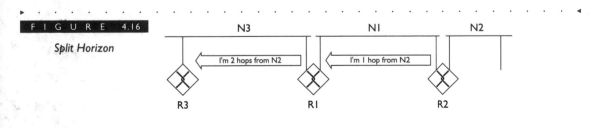

FIGURE   4.16

Split Horizon

Split horizon works best when routers are adjacent. Figure 4.17 illustrates a more complex network. If the connection between R3 and N4 fails, N4 becomes unreachable and R3 stops advertising its route to N4. Because R1 and R2 no longer receive information about the route to N4, after about 90 seconds the route *times out* (expires), and information about the route is removed from the routing tables of R1 and R2.

Even so, a loop might still be created. Thanks to split horizon, R1 and R2 cannot advertise routes they learn from R3 back to R3. However, a path between R1 and R2 is still possible, which is all it takes for a loop to get started. Here's how:

1 • R1 times out its route to N4 before R2.

2 • R2 continues to advertise its route to N4, and the route is picked up by R1, which now assumes that it has a route to N4 via R2 at a cost of 2.

3 • R1 advertises to N2 that it can reach N4 at a cost of 3 hops.

4 • R3 receives the route advertisement from R1, adds the route to its routing table, and advertises the route to N3.

5 • R2 times out its route entry for N4.

6 • R2 receives a route advertisement from R3 and assumes that it can reach N4 through R3 at a cost of 4 hops.

7 • R2 advertises its new route to N1 and a loop is created.

As you can see, split horizon does not solve the count-to-infinity problem when network routers are arranged in loops. In Step 1, the routers update their routing tables at different times, so phantom routes persist in routing tables. To solve this problem, vestiges of old routes must be eliminated as quickly as possible. *Triggered updates* is a technique that can be used to speed up the removal of old routes.

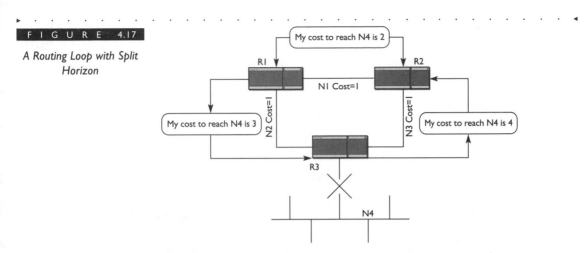

FIGURE 4.17

A Routing Loop with Split Horizon

> **Routing loops can be avoided by eliminating redundant pathways in your networks. However, that means sacrificing fault tolerance. The best way to prevent routing loops is to avoid RIP altogether. The Open Shortest Path First (OSPF) protocol, which I discuss in the next section, does not suffer from the routing-loop problem and has many other benefits as well.**

NOTE

Triggered Updates   Triggered updates force a router to send a RIP update immediately after learning of a route change. The router does not wait to broadcast its regular router response packet. The update contains information only about the change. In Figure 4.17, R3 would immediately advertise that N4 is unreachable. That advertisement would force R1 and R3 to update their routing tables almost simultaneously. If necessary, triggered updates propagate to other routers in the network so routers converge on the new configuration rapidly.

> **Triggered updates can cause excessive broadcast traffic and should be used with caution.**

WARNING

Poison Reverse   *Poison reverse* is an alternative to split horizon. With poison reverse, when a router receives information about a route from a particular network, the router *does* advertise the route back to that network. However, the router advertises a metric of 16, which indicates that the destination is unreachable. In Figure 4.18, if R1 reaches N2 through R2, then R2's route to N2 must not go back through R1. To reinforce this, R1 advertises to R2 that R1's cost to reach N2 is 16 (virtual infinity). Therefore, R2 concludes that N2 is unreachable through N1. Poison reverse informs routers of invalid routes immediately, eliminating the delay caused when routing table entries must time out.

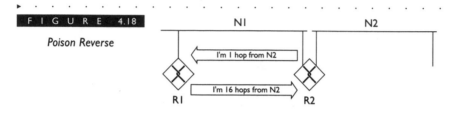

F I G U R E 4.18

Poison Reverse

N1

N2

I'm I hop from N2

I'm 16 hops from N2

RI

R2

Although poison reverse enables networks to converge on changes more rapidly than split horizon, poison reverse also increases router traffic. Every route that is learned must be advertised back with a metric of 16. This is especially a problem on networks where many routes must be advertised. In those cases, split horizon may work better.

With NetWare, split horizon is automatically invoked if poison reverse is deactivated.

NOTE

Conclusions About RIP Many people believe that OSPF has made RIP obsolete. Nevertheless, RIP remains in wide use partly because of the many operating routers that support RIP but not OSPF. Fortunately, RIP remains a viable protocol that operates reliably. RIP provides fairly rapid convergence, and the overhead it requires is not unreasonable on a properly configured network. However, if your network uses RIP, you should be aware of the following limitations:

▸ RIP imposes a maximum network diameter of 15 hops, limiting the scope of your network.

▸ Convergence can take considerable time.

▸ RIP routers advertise their complete routing tables every 30 seconds. On a large internet having many routers, considerable traffic can be generated, monopolizing an unacceptable amount of network bandwidth. This is especially troublesome when router traffic must cross WAN links.

For all these reasons, you should consider migrating your network to a link-state routing protocol such as OSPF. As the next subsection indicates, link-state protocols do not suffer from any of RIP's aforementioned disadvantages.

Open Shortest Path First

OSPF (RFC 1583) is a draft standard protocol on the Internet Standards track. OSPF is becoming increasingly popular as the Internet community becomes less willing to cope with the limitations of RIP. Perhaps the most significant problem in moving to OSPF is that although OSPF is more network-friendly and uses less bandwidth, OSPF requires more processing capability in the router. Therefore, many older routers cannot be upgraded to support OSPF.

OSPF is a *link-state* routing protocol. Unlike RIP routers, which view networks merely in terms of adjacent routers and hop counts, OSPF routers build a comprehensive picture of networks that fully describes all possible routes along with their costs. This picture, called a *topological database*, takes the form of a hierarchical tree. Each router places itself at the root of a database tree and constructs a complete picture of the network from the router's own perspective.

Building the Topological Database   The network shown in Figure 4.19 will be used to illustrate the process by which link-state algorithms build topological databases. Each link between routers is identified with a cost. Because OSPF is not subject to routing loops, a much more flexible cost metric can be used than with RIP. In fact, with OSPF, you can use costs that range up to 65,535. Administrators can assign costs to each link and adjust the costs to fine-tune network traffic patterns.

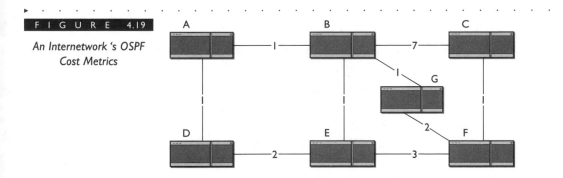

F I G U R E   4.19

An Internetwork 's OSPF Cost Metrics

The information routers require to build their databases is provided in the form of *link-state advertisements*. Routers do not advertise entire routing tables. Instead each router advertises only its information regarding immediately adjacent routers. These link-state advertisements are used to build a hierarchical database, similar to the one shown in Figure 4.20, which describes the network in Figure 4.19 from the perspective of router F.

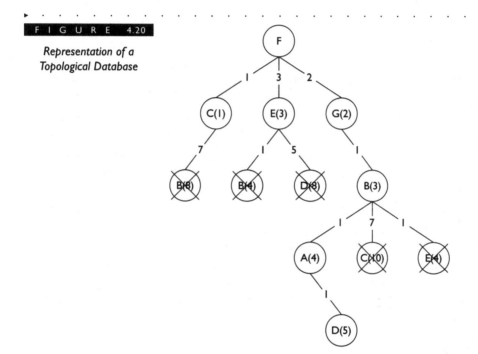

A topological database describes the most efficient route to each destination. Efficiency is determined by the total of all cost metrics encountered on the path. Only the most efficient route is maintained. As Figure 4.20 shows, less efficient routes are discarded. Therefore, F retains the route F-G-B (whose total cost is 3) as the least costly route to B, and F discards the route F-E-B (which has a total cost of 4).

What happens if several equally efficient routes are available? F has two routes to D that have a cost of 5: F-E-D and F-G-B-A-D. Then, OSPF can perform *load balancing*, which distributes traffic across the available routes. This capacity, which RIP lacks, is a big advantage of the OSPF protocol.

Relationships Among OSPF Routers   With OSPF, routers form two types of relationships with one another. The two kinds of relationships are as follows:

- *Neighborhood* exists between two routers that connect to the same network segment.

- *Adjacency* exists between neighboring routers that share routing information. Not all neighbors form adjacencies. Adjacent routers exchange routing information that enables them to synchronize their databases.

When an OSPF router starts up, it first uses a protocol called the *hello protocol* to discover which routers are its neighbors on the network segment. On networks that support broadcasts (such as Ethernet and token ring), a router can dynamically identify its neighbors by multicasting *hello packets* to all routers on the local network. On networks that do not support broadcasts (for example, connection-oriented networks such as X.25 and frame relay) neighbors must be manually entered into the router configuration.

After a router identifies its neighbors, the router attempts to form adjacencies with its neighbors. Once adjacencies have been established, the router advertises its information to adjacent routers by transmitting *link-state update packets*. A router's link-state advertisements include only firsthand information about the specific networks the router is directly attached to. (This prevents routers from advertising routes about which they have no direct knowledge.) As a link-state update packet is passed from router to router, each router adds its own link-state advertisements to the packet.

One router on each network acts as the *designated router* (DR). The DR performs two functions:

- It generates link-state advertisements on behalf of the network.

- It coordinates the distribution and synchronization of advertisements.

When there is no DR, neighbors select a new DR based on priority values carried in hello packets. At that time, a backup DR is also selected. Both the DR and the backup DR maintain adjacency relationships, but only the DR is responsible for generating network advertisements.

DRs simplify the process of synchronizing routers. Refer back to Figure 4.19. If router A and the DR are synchronized, and router B and the DR are synchronized, there is no need for A to synchronize with B. Therefore, if all neighbors synchronize with either the DR or the backup DR, the neighbors obviously must be synchronized with each other. In practice, therefore, routers establish adjacencies with the DR and the backup DR but not with other routers on the network. The DR serves to keep all routers in the network synchronized.

Administrators can designate *areas*, which are groups of routers that may or may not be on the same local network. Routers advertise their current state to all routers in their area by means of link-state update packets that are flooded throughout the area. The packets are propagated to all routers that belong to the area. A reliable delivery mechanism ensures that all routers in the area receive the advertisements.

Each router uses the information in the link-state update packets to construct its own topological database. Although the database is customized from the perspective of each router, all routers have exactly the same information. This is in sharp contrast to RIP, in which each router has an eccentric and incomplete knowledge of the network.

OSPF generates considerably less traffic than RIP for a variety of reasons:

▸ Routers transmit link-state advertisements at infrequent intervals. RIP requires each router to broadcast its entire routing table every 30 seconds.

▸ Between periodic updates, OSPF router advertisements only take place when a change is observed in the network.

▸ Link-state update packets are sent to adjacencies and are not broadcast. Adjacencies forward link-state update packets to other routers in the area. All packets are transmitted point-to-point eliminating broadcast traffic.

▸ Link-state update packets are flooded within an area, but the area may be defined by the network administrator to control the impact of OSPF updates on the Internet.

▸ A single link-state update can carry link-state advertisements for many routers.

Autonomous Systems and Areas   An *autonomous system* (AS) is a group of routers that exchange information using a common routing protocol. When an AS is joined to a network that uses a different protocol, the router connecting the dissimilar networks is called an *autonomous system border router* (ASBR). Figure 4.21 shows an ASBR used to connect an OSPF AS to a RIP AS.

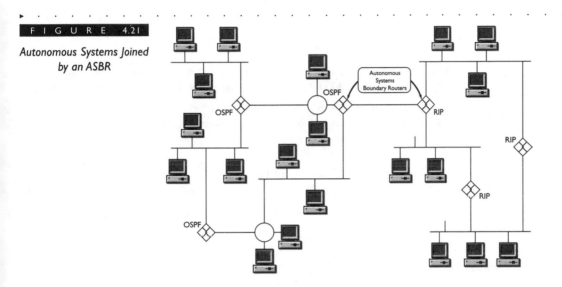

F I G U R E   4.21

Autonomous Systems Joined by an ASBR

Areas are administrative subdivisions of an OSPF autonomous system. By defining areas, administrators can determine which routers will participate in exchanging link-state updates.

By default, the entire AS is configured as a single area. It is possible, however, to logically subdivide the AS into two or more areas. When link-state updates are flooded, they will only be flooded to routers that participate in the same area. This selectiveness has several benefits:

- ▸ The amount of internetwork traffic is reduced.

- ▸ The routers maintain a smaller database, reducing memory and other CPU requirements.

- ▸ Routers can process changes more quickly because they have less to process.

Two rules must be followed when defining areas:

▸ An area must consist of contiguous routers. In other words, parts of an area cannot be separated by another area.

▸ The organization must be hierarchical. There must be one top-level area to which all other areas are connected. The top-level area is called the *backbone.*

NOTE

Link-state routing applies only within each area. If the areas are not organized hierarchically, loops can develop. A NetWare router acts as an intra-area router within each area. A NetWare router does not pass route information between non-backbone areas, and it therefore does not cause loops.

Figure 4.22 illustrates an AS that is organized in three areas. Connections between areas are made using *area border routers* (ABRs). Routers within the areas receive routing information for other areas from the ABRs, and ABRs are responsible for exchanging routing information with the backbone. ABRs serve as filters to determine what routing information should be propagated to adjoining areas. (Because ABRs carry heavy workloads, Novell recommends not using low-end computers as ABRs.)

Figure 4.22 illustrates the relationship of the backbone area (area B) to the areas it joins. All other areas must be directly connected to the backbone. If non-backbone areas are joined, loops may develop. Area C is connected to the backbone through two ABRs. This arrangement provides redundant paths, enabling the area to sustain a single router failure. Areas fall into two categories:

▸ *Stub areas* are connected to the backbone through a single ABR. To reduce routing network traffic, the ABR advertises itself as the default router within the area. No ASBRs are permitted within a stub area. In Figure 4.22, area A is an example of a stub area.

▸ *Transit areas* have two or more connections to the backbone. Area C in Figure 4.22 is an example of a transit area.

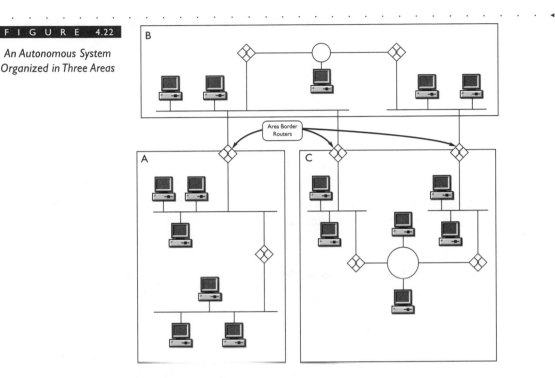

FIGURE 4.22

An Autonomous System Organized in Three Areas

Conclusions About OSPF

The network world is headed in the direction of link-state routing, although the remaining base of older routers is slowing the transition. NetWare supports two link-state protocols:

▸ NLSP (NetWare Link Services Protocol) for IPX

▸ OSPF for IP

Regardless of the protocols your network is running, you should consider implementing link-state routing. Even if your network is modest in size, you will observe a reduction in routing traffic. In summary, the advantages of link-state routing protocols over distance-vector protocols (such as RIP) are as follows:

▸ Network size is virtually unlimited.

▸ Bandwidth utilization is significantly lower.

▶ Packet sizes are smaller and increase in size less rapidly as the network grows.

▶ Updates are infrequent.

▶ Loops cannot develop within areas.

▶ Network changes propagate rapidly.

The primary disadvantage of link-state routing is that routers require more powerful hardware. Essentially, OSPF removes much of the responsibility for routing from the network and increases the responsibilities of the router. RIP uses a simpler algorithm that places greater demands on the network.

EXTERIOR GATEWAY PROTOCOL

RIP and OSPF are examples of *interior routing protocols,* which support routing within an autonomous system. Most administrators deal with this type of routing protocol.

External routing protocols are used to route between autonomous systems. Figure 4.23 illustrates an internetwork that uses an exterior gateway protocol to route between an OSPF AS and the Internet.

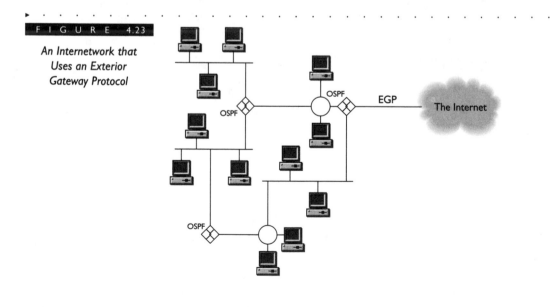

F I G U R E   4.23

An Internetwork that Uses an Exterior Gateway Protocol

NetWare supports the Internet *Exterior Gateway Protocol* (EGP) (RFC 827/904), which was introduced in 1982. EGP functions in a very simple manner. First EGP establishes neighbor relations with other directly connected routers. Then EGP determines which networks can be reached through each of its neighbor routers. Finally, EGP advertises route availability. EGP routers exchange periodic routing update messages to maintain current reachability databases.

EGP is extremely limited in its operation. An EGP router advertises only that it can reach a given remote network. No cost metric is used and no load balancing or route optimization are performed. This limitation also limits use of EGP to tree-shaped network configurations. All networks must connect to a central backbone.

EGP obtains its information about an AS from the IGPs within the AS. The information EGP receives must be specified by means of route filters — a precaution that prevents unwanted data from being propagated to external networks.

INTERNET CONTROL MESSAGE PROTOCOL

ICMP (RFC 792) was designed to compensate for IP's failure to provide a reliable protocol. ICMP reports many of the errors that are be detected at the Internet layer. Although ICMP is a separate protocol and uses IP datagrams to perform message delivery, ICMP is an integral part of IP, and it is required for every IP implementation.

ICMP messages typically report errors in the delivery of datagrams. However, because IP is not a reliable protocol, some errors may go undetected. It is possible for datagrams to be lost without generating ICMP messages. To give you a sense of ICMP's responsibilities, here are a few of the messages reported by ICMP:

- *Destination Unreachable* messages report when a net, host, protocol, or port is unreachable.

- *Time Exceeded* messages report that a datagram is undeliverable because the time-to-live field is zero and the datagram must be discarded.

- *Parameter Problem* messages report parameter problems and identify the octets in which problem are detected.

- *Source Quench* messages report that a gateway has been forced to discard a datagram because its input buffers are full.

▸ *Redirect* messages are sent by routers to inform hosts that a destination can be reached more efficiently by another router. This message can be used by the source host to update its router table.

▸ *Echo* and *Echo Reply* messages exchange data between hosts.

▸ *Time Stamp* and *Time Stamp Reply* messages enable hosts to exchange time stamp data.

▸ *Information Request* and *Information Reply* messages tell hosts the network numbers of attached networks.

ICMP Router Discovery Messages (RFC 1256) are an extension of ICMP. They provide hosts an alternative to using static configuration files to locate local routers when the hosts are initialized.

ICMP router advertisement messages are used by routers to advertise their presence on the network. These messages are either broadcast or multicast to all hosts on the network. Each message includes the IP address of the router along with a preference level. Hosts select the router that has the highest preference level. These messages are sent to the IP multicast address 224.0.0.1.

ICMP router solicitation messages enable hosts to solicit router advertisement messages from all routers on the network. These messages are sent to the IP multicast address 224.0.0.2.

Datagram Fragmentation and Reassembly

IP accepts fairly large datagrams from upper-layer protocols (as large as 65,535 bytes). This size far exceeds the size limits imposed by most networks. Ethernet, for example, can accommodate at most 1500 octets of upper-layer data in a frame.

One of IP's functions is to fragment large datagrams into smaller datagrams that are compatible with the network access protocols in use. The header of the IP datagram contains fields that allow receiving hosts to identify the position of each datagram in the overall structure and to reassemble the original datagram.

IP Datagram Format

Figure 4.24 shows the format of a IP datagram header. Many operational characteristics of IP can be tuned by placing different values in these fields.

FIGURE 4.24

Format of the IP Datagram Header

Table 4.6 summarizes the fields in an IP datagram header.

TABLE 4.6

Fields of an IP Datagram Header

FIELD	DESCRIPTION
Version	A 4-bit field that specifies the format of the Internet header. The current version of IP is version 4 as specified in RFC 791.
Internet Header Length (IHL)	A 4-bit field that specifies the length of the internet header in 32-bit words.
Type of Service	An 8-bit field that specifies the quality of service that is required. Figure 4.25 expands the details in this field. The effect of values in the precedence fields depends on the network in use. These values must be configured accordingly. Some of the options are incompatible. Low delay, high reliability, and high throughput are mutually exclusive because better performance in one area degrades performance in another.
Total Length	A 16-bit field that specifies the length of the datagram in octets, including the header and data. The size of this field limits IP datagrams to a maximum size of 65,535 octets. The IP standard recommends that all hosts should be configured to receive datagrams with a minimum size of 576 octets in length.

(continued)

Fields of an IP Datagram Header
(continued)

FIELD	DESCRIPTION
Identification	A 16-bit field containing information used to reassemble fragmented datagrams. Flags (3 bits). Contains the following control flags: Bit 0. Reserved; must be 0. Bit 1 (DF). 0 = may fragment; 1 = do not fragment. Bit 2 (MF). 0 = last fragment; 1 = more fragments. If a datagram is fragmented, the MF bit will be 1 in all datagram fragments except the last.
Fragment Offset	A 13-bit field that specifies the position of a fragment within the complete datagram if a datagram has been fragmented.
Time to Live	An 8-bit field that specifies the length of time a datagram may remain on the network. Typically, this value represents seconds. Each IP module that handles the datagram is required to decrement time to live by at least one. When time to live reaches 0, the datagram must be discarded. This ensures that undelivered datagrams cannot circulate endlessly on the network.
Protocol	An 8-bit field that specifies the upper-layer protocol associated with this datagram. See the RFC *Assigned Numbers* for the numbers associated with many protocols.
Header Checksum	A 16-bit error checksum that covers the header only. Whenever the header is modified, the checksum must be recalculated.
Source Address	Specifies the 32-bit IP address of the host that originated the datagram.
Destination Address	Specifies the 32-bit IP address of the host that should receive the datagram.
Options	May contain 0 or more 32-bit words that contain options as specified by RFC 791.

0	1	2	3	4	5	6	7
Precedence			D	T	R		

Legend:

Bits	0-2:	Precedence		
Bit	3:	Delay	(0=Normal Delay	1=Low Delay)
Bit	4:	Throughput	(0=Normal Throughput	1=High Throughput)
Bit	5:	Reliability	(0=Normal Reliability	1=High Reliability)
Bits	6-7:	Reserved		

Precedence

111	Network Control
110	Internetwork Control
101	CRITIC/ECP
100	Flash Override
011	Flash
010	Immediate
001	Priority
000	Routine

IP Version 6

The current version of IP, version 4 (IPv4), has done an admirable job supporting the Internet for nearly 15 years. However, this protocol is starting to show its age, particularly in light of the rapid expansion of Internet in recent years. IP addresses are getting scarce. Furthermore, IP is ill-suited to some tasks many people are demanding from the Internet (for example, secure exchanges of financial data).

The IP next generation (IPng) working group of the IETF is building a successor to IPv4. The new protocol, IP version 6 (IPv6), is currently in the draft standards process. Among the goals set for IPv6 are the following:

▶ The current 32-bit addresses will be extended to 128 bits. Address hierarchies will be supported. Automatic configuration of addresses will be improved.

▶ Support for authentication will enable IP to support private, secure data and to ensure data integrity.

▶ The header format will be simplified, with several fields being dropped.

▶ Greater support will be provided for extending the protocol and adding options.

If you are interested in learning about IPv6, you will find numerous Internet-Drafts available from the sources I mention in Chapter 1. At the time of this writing, the draft standard is found in the document DRAFT-IETF-IPNGWG-IPV6-SPEC-02.TXT.

Who Could Ask for Anything More?

IP is the central protocol in all TCP/IP configurations. It is the one protocol that will always be present. From this central position, IP bears the crucial responsibility of delivering message units through both simple and complex internetworks. IP could provide all of the message delivery necessary to run applications on a network.

It could, that is, if all applications had the same delivery requirements. If all applications could withstand unreliable delivery of 64-KB messages, IP would suffice. But often applications must transfer huge amounts of data, and application designers don't always want to divide the data into 64-KB chunks. Also, usually applications cannot tolerate faulty message delivery.

So IP isn't enough. Several additional features are necessary for a complete and versatile set of message delivery capabilities. Those features include reliable data delivery and fragmentation of large messages. The next chapter, which deals with the host-to-host layer, explains how those capabilities can be added to a network.

## CHAPTER 5

The Host-to-Host Layer

We have reached the point in our tour of TCP/IP where the network has the capability of probably delivering any message up to 65,535 bytes in size anywhere in any size internetwork. That's an amazing capability when you think about it, but I can see you're not all that excited. You'd probably like to transfer a 5-MB file with all the data for your office football pool, or you just don't think "probably" is good enough when the data going through the network will be used to cut you a paycheck. Well, relax, because relief is at hand in the guise of the host-to-host layer.

The host-to-host layer builds on the capabilities of the internet layer by adding two features to the network protocol stack:

▸ A network interface that enables upper-layer protocols to utilize the network without worrying about the logistics of message fragmentation.

▸ The capability of delivering messages between hosts either reliably or unreliably, as the situation demands.

The host-to-host layer is not one protocol but two. Transmission Control Protocol (TCP) provides reliable delivery, and User Datagram Protocol (UDP) provides unreliable delivery. These two protocols provide network protocol designers with a choice of host-to-host services: fast and unreliable, or slow and practically bulletproof.

TCP provides for reliable host-to-host communication. TCP will use every trick it knows to deliver your data, and it will let you know if the attempt fails. TCP will check for errors and resend data as required to accomplish delivery. If delivery cannot be performed (for example, if the only router is down), TCP will let upper-layer processes know that the delivery attempt failed. TCP had to be good, because it was given the task of delivering data on the ARPANET at a time when WAN technology was pretty iffy. Unfortunately, all this reliability comes at a price — TCP has a lot of overhead that generates network traffic and slows performance. At times, these disadvantages are too costly, which is why there are two protocols at the host-to-host layer.

UDP provides unreliable delivery when efficiency is more important than foolproof delivery. *Datagrams* are independent messages delivered on a "best-effort" basis. UDP sends the datagram down the protocol stack but doesn't spend any effort to determine if the datagram reaches the destination host. If an upper-layer protocol wants to know about failed delivery attempts, the upper layer must check things out on its own. Before you decide that UDP is good only for casual communications, guess again. Sun's Network File System (NFS) uses UDP as the host-to-host protocol. NFS performs extremely sophisticated remote file services, but its designers wanted the most efficient transport mechanism available and chose to implement NFS over UDP, providing reliable messaging in NFS itself.

The host-to-host layer is in the middle of the TCP/IP protocol stack and ties together upper-layer processes and the network. Figure 5.1 illustrates the TCP/IP protocol stack, showing several prominent protocols at the process/application layer. This figure gives you an idea how the pieces fit together and also demonstrates which protocols rely on TCP and which on UDP. So that you can understand how TCP and UDP service upper-layer protocols, the first topic this chapter addresses is protocol multiplexing.

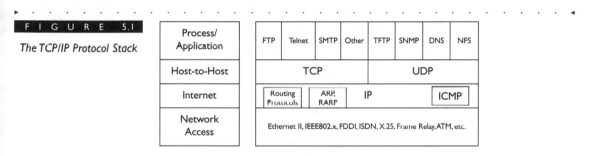

FIGURE 5.1

The TCP/IP Protocol Stack

Host-to-Host Layer Protocol Multiplexing

Chapter 2 introduced you to the concept of *protocol multiplexing,* which enables lower-layer protocols to maintain message streams for multiple upper-layer protocols. If you look at Figure 5.1, you can see that TCP and UDP must have access to a mechanism that enables them to sort out the data that is received from and that must be delivered to each upper-layer protocol.

But TCP must do more than just deliver data. TCP is a connection-oriented protocol that enables processes to engage in reliable, full-duplex dialogs with the corresponding protocols on another host. This turns out to be a pretty demanding job.

The interface between the host-to-host layer and upper-layer processes is the *port,* which is simply a mechanism for identifying data that is associated with specific protocols. TCP and UDP use the ports to deliver data to the correct protocol.

A port is identified by a *port number.* Although protocol designers can specify custom port numbers, a large number of port numbers, called *well-known ports,* have been reserved for specific protocols and organizations. Well-known ports and other official Internet numbers are assigned by the Internet Assigned Numbers Authority (IANA) and are specified in an RFC titled *Assigned Numbers* (RFC 1700).

A process is specified fully by the port together with the IP address of the host on which the process is running. The combination of a port number and IP address is called a *socket.* Because each host on an internetwork will have a unique IP address, each process running on the internetwork will have a unique socket.

A connection between two processes is specified fully by the sockets assigned to the processes. With sockets, the host-to-host layer provides a mechanism that supports full-duplex dialogs between end processes. Figure 5.2 shows how process-to-process communication takes place.

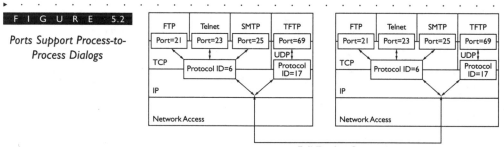

FIGURE 5.2

Ports Support Process-to-Process Dialogs

Sockets provide an application program interface (API) between processes and TCP and UDP. Programmers use the API to enable their applications to interface with the network. NetWare supports two common APIs:

- **Sockets.** An API that gained wide distribution in Berkeley Standard Distribution (BSD) UNIX.

- **STREAMS Transport Layer Interface (TLI).** An API developed by AT&T.

Transmission Control Protocol

TCP (RFC 793) provides a connection-oriented transport mechanism that enables hosts to engage in reliable dialogs. TCP communicates through the network much the same way we communicate through a telephone, with complete indifference to the complex mechanisms that enable communication to take place. Although TCP establishes connections pretty much by "dialing" the remote computer's number, TCP knows nothing about the network. In fact, TCP is quite indifferent to the network. IP worries about the network. TCP concerns itself with communicating with its peer TCP protocols on other hosts. This capability enables TCP to provide reliable delivery on any network, regardless of size or technology.

The philosophy behind TCP's design is spelled out in RFC 793: "Be conservative in what you do, be liberal in what you accept from others." TCP modules should be designed to accept a certain amount of variation in incoming data so that processes don't malfunction because of trivial errors. TCP is intended to be a forgiving protocol, but a protocol that provides rock-solid reliability.

TCP has several responsibilities:

- Enabling upper layer processes to send streams of data through the network

- Maintaining connections between processes

- Providing reliable communication

Let's take a look at each of these capabilities before moving on to the TCP data format.

DATA STREAM MAINTENANCE

Processes and applications know even less about the network than does TCP. They aren't used to fragmenting messages into byte-sized pieces, for example. When they need to send data, they pretty much just send data, in a continuous stream. One of TCP's responsibility is to enable these streams of data to be delivered through the network so that the peer process receives the same data in the same stream.

Figure 5.3 shows how the entire process works. Here is what happens as data flows down the protocol stack of the sending host, through the network, and up the protocol stack of the receiving host:

1 • TCP receives a continuous stream of data from the upper-layer process.

2 • If the amount of data exceeds what IP can handle in a datagram, TCP fragments the data stream into segments sized to meet the maximum size requirements of IP.

3 • IP receives the segments and, if necessary, fragments the segments into datagrams that conform to the maximum data capacity of a network frame.

4 • Network protocols encapsulate the datagram in a frame and transmit the frame to the network as a series of bits.

5 • Network protocols at the receiving host capture the bits and reconstruct the original frame.

6 • The datagram is extracted from the frame and passed up to IP.

7 • If the datagram is a fragment, IP reconstructs the original segment from the fragments. The segment is passed up to TCP.

8 • TCP reconstructs the original data stream from the segments that it receives and presents the data stream to the upper-layer process.

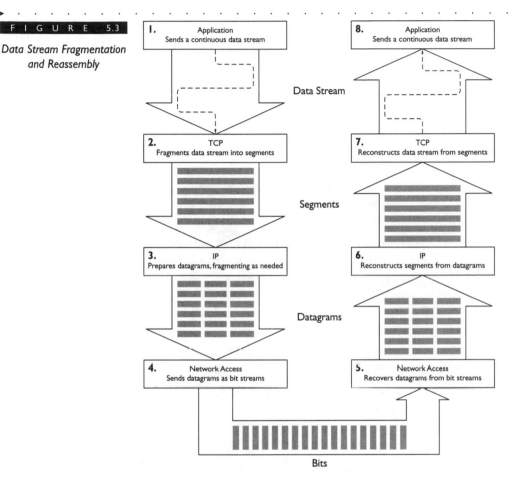

As all this data is being transferred between hosts, TCP is responsible for managing flow control via a process called *windowing*. When hosts set up a connection, they agree on a *window*, the number of unacknowledged octets of data that can be outstanding. If the sending host reaches the limit imposed by the window, it will cease transmitting until acknowledgments are received for some or all of the outstanding data. Acknowledgments move the window forward so that more data may be transmitted.

CONNECTION MAINTENANCE

TCP enables processes to establish connections with peer processes on other hosts. A connection must be explicitly opened or closed. When TCP issues an OPEN call, the call includes the local port and the remote socket. When the connection is established, the process that requested the connection is provided with a name that identifies the connection.

Connections may be active or passive:

▸ An *active open* is an explicit attempt to establish a connection with a remote process. In other words, an active open is one host reaching out to touch another.

▸ A *passive open* configures TCP to await incoming connection requests, enabling the process that requested the passive open to accept connections from remote processes. Passive opens are the tools that servers use to make services available on the network. Outside processes can then issue active opens to establish a connection.

The desirability of well-known ports becomes especially clear when considered with regard to passive opens. A remote host that wishes to connect to a service must be able to grab a handle on that service. That handle is the well-known port. For example, a remote FTP user's program knows that it can connect to an FTP server by requesting an active open using port 21.

When an open request is generated, TCP constructs a segment with the SYN (synchronize) control bit set. Control bits will be discussed in the section "TCP Header Format." When the remote TCP module receives the segment, it matches the remote socket to a local socket to establish a connection. The peer TCP modules exchange sockets and synchronize segment sequence numbers to complete the connection.

Connections must be explicitly closed. When a process asks TCP to close a connection, TCP constructs a segment with the FIN control bit set. Both ends must participate in closing the connection. The TCP that sends a CLOSE may continue to receive data until it receives a CLOSE from the remote TCP. This system enables both hosts to flush any outstanding data. Reliable data delivery continues until all data are received and both partners have closed the connection.

RELIABLE DELIVERY

TCP provides reliable delivery using a system of *segment sequence numbers* and *acknowledgments*. Every octet that is sent must be acknowledged or TCP will retransmit the data. When delivery begins, each octet is assigned a segment sequence number. The segment header specifies the segment sequence number of the first data octet along with an acknowledgment number. When a segment is sent, a copy is retained in a hold queue until the segment is acknowledged. Unacknowledged segments are resent.

When a receiving TCP acknowledges a particular segment sequence number, the sending TCP is relieved of responsibility for the data up to that point. The receiving TCP bears responsibility for reliably delivering data to the upper-layer process. These acknowledgments also form part of the windowing flow-control mechanism.

TCP DATA FORMAT

TCP applies a header to each segment that it constructs. The format of this header is shown in Figure 5.4. TCP segments are organized in 16-bit words and must contain an even number of octets. If the segment contains an odd number of octets, it is padded with an octet consisting of zeros. Table 5.1 describes the fields in the TCP header.

FIGURE 5.4

Format of the TCP Segment Header

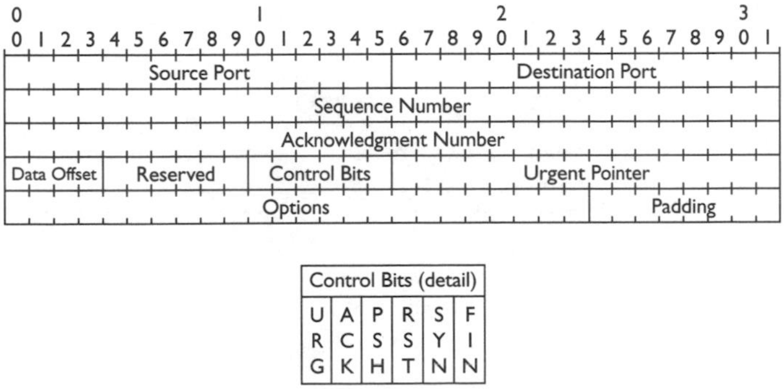

Fields in a TCP Segment Header

FIELD	PURPOSE
Source Port	A 16-bit field that specifies the port on the sending TCP module.
Destination Port	A 16-bit field that specifies the port on the receiving TCP module.
Sequence Number	A 32-bit field that specifies the segment sequence number of the first octet in the data field. If this segment opens a connection, the SYN control bit is set, the sequence number is the *initial sequence number* (ISN), and the first data octet is at sequence ISN+1.
Acknowledgment Number	A 32-bit field that specifies the next segment sequence number that the sending TCP expects. When a connection is active, TCP always sets the ACK control bit.
Data Offset	A 4-bit field specifying the number of 32-bit words in the TCP header. When options do not end on a 32-bit word boundary, the header is padded with zero-value octets.
Reserved	A 6-bit field reserved for future use. Its value must be zero.
Control Bits	A 6-bit field consisting of 6 control bits as follows: URG. 1 = Urgent Pointer significant; 0 = ignore Urgent Pointer. ACK. 1 = Acknowledgment Number is significant; 0 = ignore Acknowledgment Number. PSH. 1 initiates a push function. RST. 1 forces a connection reset. SYN. 1 = first segment of connection; synchronize counters. FIN. 1 = no more data; close the connection.
Window	A 16-bit checksum that provides error control for the header and data fields but does not cover padding that is added to make the header come out on an even 32-bit boundary. A 96-bit pseudo header is also covered.
Urgent Pointer	A 16-bit field that identifies the sequence number of the octet that follows urgent data. This pointer is a positive offset from the segment sequence number.
Options	A variable-size field that incorporates options.
Padding	A variable number of zero-value octets used to pad the header to an even 32-bit boundary.

In Table 5.1, the explanation of the window field mentioned a *pseudo header*. TCP uses a 12-octet data structure called a pseudo header to communicate with IP and to protect TCP from misrouted segments. The length of the pseudo header is not included in the value of the segment length field. The pseudo header format is shown in Figure 5.5.

FIGURE 5.5

Format of the TCP Pseudo Header

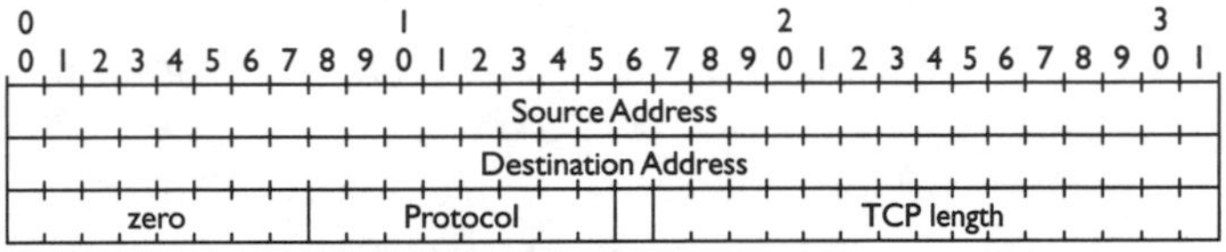

User Datagram Protocol

TCP is an aggressively conservative and formal protocol that communicates only in a connection-oriented environment. The overhead required to establish, maintain, and release a connection is justified in many situations when significant amounts of data must be communicated reliably. In many cases, however, the overhead is difficult to justify.

UDP (RFC 768) is a less fanatical protocol used by many processes that want to communicate with a minimum of fuss and bother and that can either tolerate an occasional error or provide error control themselves. UDP is a datagram protocol that does not need to process streams of data from upper layers. Because UDP is freed of the responsibilities of developing segments and maintaining connections, UDP is an extremely simple and efficient protocol.

When is UDP useful? Here are some examples:

▶ When messages are sporadic, the effort to establish and tear down a connection can exceed the effort required to transport the data. A good example of sporadic messaging is provided by SNMP, which generates network alerts called *traps* when specific network conditions occur. If a connection were established for each trap, overhead would slow delivery of traps and would bog down the network.

▶ When messages require no acknowledgment, a connection is wasted effort. SNMP traps are simply sent on the network. If network managers don't correct the cause of the trap, it will be generated again when necessary.

▶ When a protocol has special needs that don't fit with TCP, protocol designers may choose UDP because it imposes fewer limits. Sun's Network File System (NFS) was implemented over UDP so that the designers had more freedom to design the complete communication process.

Figure 5.6 shows the header format for a UDP datagram. The fields in the header are described in Table 5.2. Like TCP, UDP generates a pseudo header, which guards against misrouted datagrams. Figure 5.7 shows the data format of the pseudo header.

FIGURE 5.6	
Format of the UDP Datagram Header	

TABLE 5.2	FIELD	PURPOSE
Fields in a UDP Datagram Header	Source Port	An optional 16-bit field that specifies the port on the sending module when a reply is anticipated. When a reply is not required, the source port is 0.
	Destination Port	A 16-bit field that specifies the port on the receiving UDP module.
	Length	A 16-bit field that specifies the length of the datagram in octets, including the header and data fields. The minimum value of this field is 8. The maximum value imposes a maximum datagram size of 65,535 octets, with 56,527 octets available for data.
	Checksum	A 16-bit checksum that provides error control for the header, data, and pseudo header.

FIGURE 5.7

Format of the UDP Pseudo Header

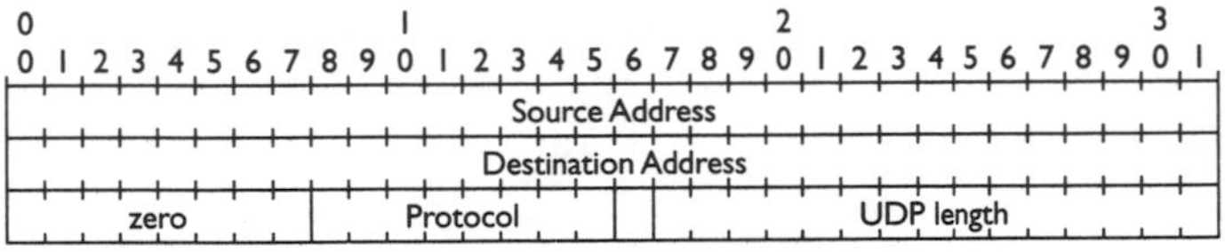

Ready for Work

Now, depending on the choice of transport protocol, the network can deliver huge messages with very high reliability. Or, if desired, the network can deliver small messages with great efficiency. The overall architecture of TCP/IP provides this versatility by offering a choice of host-to-host layer protocols.

The network is ready to go to work, but it doesn't yet have any work to do. Without taking one more step, the delivery capabilities of TCP/IP resemble an automobile without a driver's seat and steering wheel. The car can move, but it can't carry a payload. Unless we add some applications that enable end-users to "ride" the network, all we have is a technical curiosity. In the fourth and final protocol layer, we will at last encounter the reason for TCP/IP's existence: processes and applications that enable the network to accomplish real tasks.

## CHAPTER 6

The Process/Application Layer

The previous three chapters have shown you how TCP/IP can be used to build networks that can deliver messages reliably through a variety of media to anywhere in the world. That's all very impressive, but I'll tell you a secret. The network we've built to this point is a far cry from finished. It has no data to deliver, so even though the network is operational, it can't do useful work. We have built the infrastructure of the information highway, but we have yet to set a single vehicle in motion.

The process/application layer is the reason the lower layers exist. At this layer you find numerous protocols that support users directly or indirectly. At the process/application layer, it can be difficult to draw the line between a protocol and an application. Take the file transfer protocol (FTP) as an example. FTP enables hosts to offer a file transfer service to other hosts on an internet. FTP also enables remote users to connect with an FTP server and perform file operations. So FTP refers to both the server- and the client-side protocols. But it also behaves somewhat like an application in that users can enter protocol commands directly from the keyboard. You will see an example of this function later in this chapter when FTP is demonstrated.

NetWare client-server protocols function quite differently. Most NetWare services are made available via the NetWare Core Protocol (NCP). Users never see NCP protocols and never enter NCP commands directly. Instead, users interact with NetWare via familiar application and operating system commands. A NetWare shell or requester running on the workstation intercepts requests for network services and issues the proper NCP command to the network. In NetWare, network protocols are practically invisible.

With TCP/IP, users may interact directly with protocols at the process/application layer, or they may use applications that in turn access the network protocols. For example, you will seldom send TCP/IP e-mail by entering Simple Mail Transport Protocol (SMTP) commands directly, although you could. You are more likely to use an e-mail application that will generate the SMTP messages for you.

The process/application layer provides a protocol interface that enables upper-layer processes such as user applications to obtain network services. This chapter examines several protocols that are used widely on TCP/IP networks, including:

▸ File Transfer Protocol (FTP)

▸ Trivial File Transfer Protocol (TFTP)

▸ Telnet

▸ Simple Network Management Protocol (SNMP)

▸ Simple Mail Transport Protocol (SMTP)

▸ Network File System (NFS)

To provide a network interface for users, the process/application layer must put a friendly face on the network. How friendly would the network be if you had to access every host by its IP address? Could you remember the addresses of each of the dozens (or hundreds) of Internet hosts that you access to retrieve files, view Web pages, or send e-mail? Well, neither can anyone else, and the Internet community has long realized that if the Internet is to be usable, it must be possible to specify hosts by names rather than numbers. Because host naming is so central to using virtually all TCP/IP applications, before looking at the applications themselves, we will examine how TCP/IP host naming is performed.

Naming TCP/IP Hosts

NetWare administrators tend to take naming for granted. After a name is specified in a server's AUTOEXEC.NCF file, the server takes over the job of advertising the name to users. But TCP/IP lacks a protocol like NetWare's Service Advertising Protocol (SAP). Instead, host names are made available only if network administrators provide a naming service. Thanks to host naming, you can use the name DS.INTERNIC.NET instead of 198.49.45.10 to specify the InterNIC FTP host.

Naming is provided by two mechanisms — static hosts files and the Domain Name Service — which may be used separately or in conjunction. Because DNS grew out of the static hosts files system, we'll look at the use of static files first.

HOSTS FILES

Would you believe that the Internet was once fairly quiet? The ARPANET included a few hundred hosts and was fairly stable, at least compared to the recent frantic pace with which sites have been added to the Internet. Although current Internet growth is measured in hosts added per day, only a few hosts were added to the ARPANET in a given year. But even with a smaller, more stable network, it was important to provide users with a mechanism for naming hosts.

The mechanism involved a file named HOSTS.TXT, which provided a database that matched IP addresses to host name aliases. The master file was maintained at the Stanford Research Institute's Network Information Center (NIC). ARPANET site administrators would e-mail their name changes to the NIC, where they would be edited into the master HOSTS.TXT file. The HOSTS.TXT file would be compiled every few days to build a file named *hosts*, which would be made available on a host named SRI-NIC. System administrators would then use FTP to retrieve the master *hosts* file for use on their local hosts.

Each host at a site required access to the *hosts* file. For UNIX hosts, the convention was to store the file in the /etc directory on each host. Host processes would access the file to match hostnames to IP addresses. The *hosts* file is a text file with contents similar to the following:

```
#IP Address        Aliases
127.0.0.1          localhost loopback lb        #this host
165.88.100.1       eng1 bob.widgets.com bob
165.88.100.2       eng2 fred.widgets.com fred
165.88.150.1       sales1 mary.widgets.com mary
```

Entries in the *hosts* file contain three information fields separated by one or more spaces:

- ▸ An IP address.

- ▸ One or more aliases that serve as host names. Among the names included in the example are Internet domain names, such as mary.widgets.com.

- ▸ An optional comment, consisting of all text that follows the # character. Comments describe *hosts* file entries but are ignored when the file is processed.

Although *hosts* files could theoretically provide naming support on networks of any size, static naming files ran out of steam very early in the life of the ARPANET. Because the entire system depended on a single centrally administered file, updates could not take place as rapidly as was desired. Also, because one host served as the distribution point for the master file, FTP traffic to that host quickly became overwhelming. Even when the Internet consisted of a few hundred hosts, it became evident that static *hosts* files would soon be unsupportable. Today, when the Internet supports millions of personal computers, all configured as hosts, in a configuration that changes hourly, static naming would not be functional. That is why, in 1983, the ARPANET adopted the Domain Name Service as a more automated technology for providing a host naming service.

NOTE **Static hosts files remain a viable means of providing naming services on local TCP/IP networks, particularly if the networks are small in scope and change infrequently. Using static files, hosts can match names to addresses without generating network traffic. Administration of hosts files may be less labor intensive than maintaining a dynamic naming service. NetWare TCP/IP servers and clients use hosts files to map names to IP addresses.**

DOMAIN NAME SERVICE

The Domain Name Service (DNS; RFC 1034/1035) was designed to maintain a hierarchical database of host names. You are already familiar with another example of a hierarchical database: the system of directory and subdirectory trees that is used to organize files on DOS-based PCs and NetWare servers. Before looking at DNS, let's look at the characteristics of hierarchies in the familiar context of a file directory tree.

Example of a Hierarchical Data Structure

Figure 6.1 illustrates a hierarchical file system, using a portion of the directory structure on the SYS: volume of a NetWare 4 server. Before looking at the rules for constructing trees, let's name the components of a hierarchy.

- **Nodes**. These are the places where lines intersect. Each node is assigned an identifying name.

▸ **Root node**. One node, typically shown at the top of the tree is called the root node, or the *root directory* when it is part of a file system. Because there is only one root node, it is often unnamed. The DOS root directory is represented by a backslash (\). UNIX uses a forward slash (/). NetWare recognizes either.

▸ **Intermediate nodes**. Any node below the root is an intermediate node. With DOS and NetWare, intermediate nodes in the file system are called *directories*. In a hierarchy, intermediate nodes can contain sub-nodes. Each node is assigned a name, such as SYSTEM or PUBLIC.

▸ **End or leaf nodes.** A leaf node is the last node in a branch.

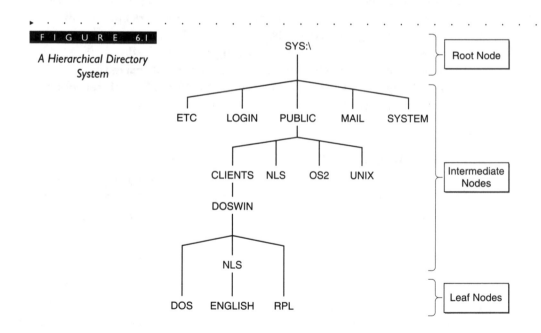

FIGURE 6.1

A Hierarchical Directory System

File systems typically permit files to reside in both intermediate and leaf nodes.

When moving up and down the hierarchy, nodes are often referred to as *parents* and *children*. A parent node is a node that contains one or more subordinate nodes, referred to as children. A child of one node can be the parent of another. Leaf nodes, however, are always children. Nodes that are children of the same parent are called *siblings*.

Figure 6.2 illustrates two rules about naming nodes. First, no two siblings may have the same node name. For example, the PUBLIC directory cannot contain two NLS directories. Second, two nodes may have the same name if the nodes are children of different parent nodes. If you browse around a NetWare 4 server, you will find several NLS subdirectories, but all will be under different directories.

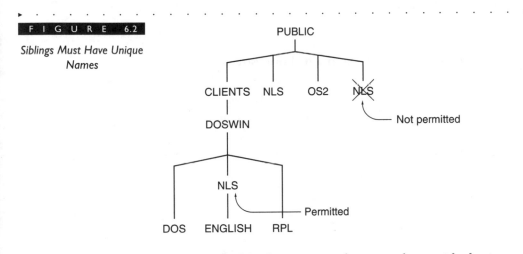

FIGURE 6.2

Siblings Must Have Unique Names

A node can be specified by listing its node name along with the intermediate nodes between itself and the root. In Figure 6.3, the directory containing English message files can be specified with the directory path \PUBLIC\CLIENT\ DOSWIN\NLS\ENGLISH. The complete name of a node, starting from the root and including every intermediate node name is called a *fully qualified name*. Because siblings cannot have the same node name, each node in the tree will have a unique fully qualified name.

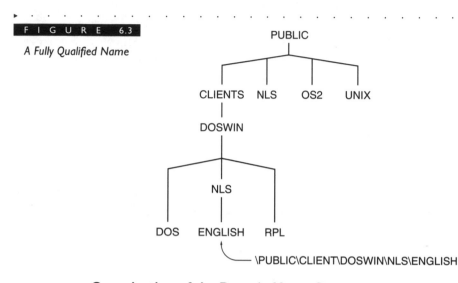

FIGURE 6.3

A Fully Qualified Name

\PUBLIC\CLIENT\DOSWIN\NLS\ENGLISH

Organization of the Domain Name Space

The DNS uses a hierarchical database called the *domain name space*. Figure 6.4 shows a simple domain name space that would be suitable for a small organization. Nodes in the domain name space are called *domains*. At the top of the hierarchy is a single root node called either *root* or the *root domain*. The root domain does not have a name and is often specified with a pair of empty quotation marks (" ").

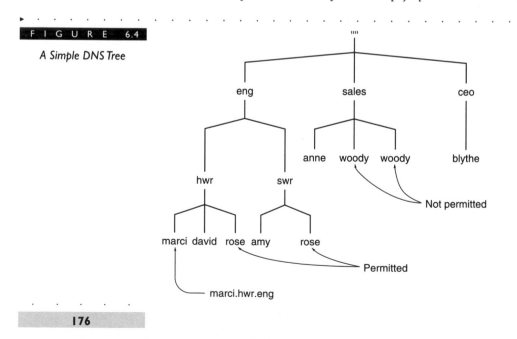

FIGURE 6.4

A Simple DNS Tree

Each node in the tree is assigned a name that may be up to 63-characters long. As with file systems, sibling nodes must be named differently. The full name of a node is specified by its *fully qualified domain name* (FQDN). Two important differences between DOS and DNS fully qualified names should be emphasized:

▶ Reading left-to-right, DNS names begin with the leaf node and proceed up the tree to the root. The period separating node names is read as "dot." DOS names begin with the root node on the left and proceed down through the tree to the subdirectory.

▶ A DNS fully qualified name does not usually include a symbol for the root. The root may be specified with a trailing dot (for example, rose.hwr.eng.), but the trailing dot usually is omitted. A DOS fully qualified name always specifies the root with a leading backslash (\) character.

A *domain* is simply a subtree of the domain name space, and you can change your perspective on the domain name space by selecting a different domain. The name of a domain is simply the FQDN of the topmost node in the domain. For example, in Figure 6.4, swr can be viewed as a subdomain of the eng domain. Alternatively, marci can be viewed as a subdomain of the swr.eng domain.

A domain cannot, however, consist of part of a subtree. In Figure 6.4, you cannot define a domain that includes nodes from hwr.eng and sales. A domain must consist of a parent node together with all nodes that are below the parent node in the hierarchy.

NOTE **DNS names are not case sensitive. The domain names hwr.eng, HWR.ENG, and Hwr.Eng are interchangable. However, domain names are most frequently expressed in lower-case characters.**

As you can see, the term *domain* is relative, depending on your perspective on the domain name space. Although every node can be viewed as a subdomain of the root domain, it is more convenient to identify an intermediate node as the domain that anchors a set of names. When it is necessary to classify domains based on their positions in the hierarchy, the following terms are used:

▸ A *first-level domain* is a child of the root domain. First-level domains are more commonly referred to as *top-level domains*.

▸ A *second-level domain* is a child of a first-level domain.

▸ A *third-level domain* is a child of a second-level domain (and so forth).

A domain name can serve multiple purposes. As the name of a node in the domain name space, the domain name serves as a point around which domain names can be defined. But a domain name can also provide a mapping to an IP address. On the Internet, for example, novell.com is associated with the IP address 192.31.114.4.

The Internet Domain Name Space

In some cases, organizations might implement private DNSs on an isolated network. A DNS is required on a network running NetWare/IP, for example. However, the largest incentive to implement DNS usually comes from a desire to integrate a private network with the Internet. Although name space administration is distributed fairly broadly, all organizations that wish to advertise a domain on the Internet must register a domain name. Registration prevents duplication of names and enables the process of resolving names to IP addresses to be coordinated among the many name servers on the Internet.

Ultimate authority for assigning Internet domain names belongs to the Internet Assigned Numbers Authority (IANA), which is administered by the Internet Registry (IR). Because the Internet name space is vast and changes daily, IANA has delegated registration authority for most lower-level domains to other organizations. Top-level domains are administered directly by Internet authorities.

The Internet name space can be divided into subdomains and zones to distribute administration. When a new second- or third-level domain is added, a management authority for the domain must be designated. In many cases, management of the domain will be performed by the organization that requested the domain, but management can also be delegated to other organizations as required.

The configuration of the Internet domain name space is described in RFC 1591, "Domain Name System Structure and Delegation." This document describes the overall domain name structure as well as guidelines for administering delegated domains. Figure 6.5 illustrates major features of the Internet domain name space.

Top-level domains (TLDs) fall into three categories:

- ► Generic world wide domains

- ► Generic United States domains

- ► Country domains

Before you can request a domain name, you need to decide where your organization fits in the overall scheme of things.

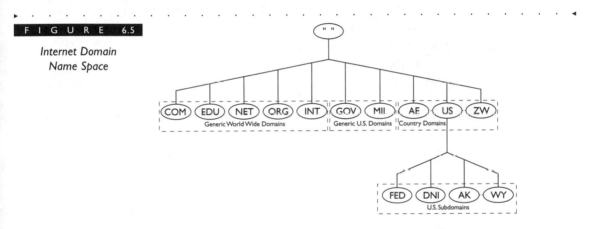

F I G U R E   6.5

*Internet Domain
Name Space*

Generic World Wide Domains

You will encounter generic world wide domains with the greatest frequency. Although each country is assigned a country domain, many organizations outside the United States are represented in these generic domains. To a degree, the place an organization registers is a matter of choice. The five generic worldwide domains are:

- ► **COM**. This domain is for commercial (business) organizations. The vast majority of companies with an Internet presence are registered in this domain. Because the COM domain is growing rapidly, there has been some discussion of subdividing it. Example: novell.com.

- ► **NET**. This domain includes network service providers and Internet administration authorities. Example: internic.net.

▸ **EDU**. This domain originally was intended for all educational institutions. But like COM, EDU has become quite extensive, and registration is now limited to four-year colleges and universities. All other schools are registered in their country domains. Example: berkeley.edu.

▸ **INT**. A domain for organizations established by international treaties.

▸ **ORG**. A miscellaneous domain for organizations that don't fit in the other domains.

Secondary domains beneath the generic world wide domains are the responsibility of the InterNIC. Contact hostmaster@internic.net via e-mail for registration information. The InterNIC is also responsible for registering new top-level domains.

Generic United States Domains

Two top-level domains have been created for use by the Unites States government:

▸ **GOV**. Although at one time any government organization could register in this domain, the GOV domain is now restricted to agencies of the United States federal government. State and local government agencies may register in state domains under the U.S. country domain.

▸ **MIL**. This domain is used exclusively by the United States Department of Defense.

Second-level subdomains in the GOV domain are registered by the InterNIC. Second-level domains under the MIL domain are registered by the DDN registry at nic.ddn.mil.

Country Domains

The IANA has no desire to get involved in international politics. Rather than attempting to decide whether a country is entitled to a country domain, the IANA defers to the ISO, an international organization with mechanisms in place to identify bona fide countries. Country top-level domains are derived from ISO 3166.

Registration of country domains has been delegated as follows:

> ▸ For Europe, the authority is RIPE NCC. Contact ncc@ripe.net.

> ▸ For the Asia-Pacific region, the authority is APNIC. Contact hostmaster@apnic.net.

> ▸ For North America and undelegated regions, the authority is InterNIC. Contact hostmaster@internic.net.

Appendix C lists the Internet top-level domains as of this writing, including country domains. I obtained this information from the WHOIS server at rs.internic.net. Later in the chapter, I will show you how to use WHOIS to obtain domain information.

Organization of the US Domain

The majority of United States organizations that are state-wide in scope (as opposed to national) are organized under the US country top-level domain, described in RFC 1480. Each state is assigned a second-level domain under US, named using the abbreviations established by the postal service. For example, CA.US is the domain assigned to California.

Two special subdomains of US designate organizations that have national scope:

> ▸ **FED**. Agencies of the U.S. federal government.

> ▸ **DNI**. Organizations that have a presence in multiple states or regions.

Although Internet administration does not manage state subdomains, RFC 1480 includes recommendations for organizing state domains. RFC 1480 describes the following state subdomains:

> ▸ **Locality**. A designation for the city, county, parish, or other locality in which the organization resides. Examples: Marvista.CA.US and Portland.OR.US.

▸ **CC**. Community colleges with a state-wide presence. Example: *<school>*.CC.MA.US.

▸ **CI**. As a subdomain of a locality, CI designates city government agencies. Example: Fire-Dept.CI.Los-Angeles.CA.US.

▸ **CO**. As a subdomain of a locality, CI designates county government agencies. Example: Fire-Dept.CO.San-Diego.CA.US.

▸ **GEN**. Entities that do not fit in the other categories. Example: *<organization>*.GEN.KY.US.

▸ **K12**. Public school districts. The PVT name may be included to designate private schools. Examples: *<school>*.K12.IL.US or *<school>*.PVT.K12.AZ.US.

▸ **LIB**. Libraries only. Examples: <library>.LIB.OR.US

▸ **STATE**. State government agencies. Example: <agency>.STATE.TX.US.

▸ **TEC**. Vocational and technical schools and colleges with a state-wide presence. Example: *<school>*.TEC.OR.US.

Figure 6.6 illustrates the organization of the US domain, including recommended subdomain names.

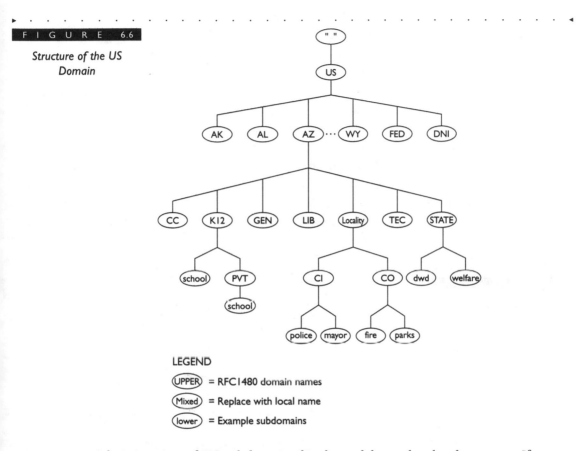

FIGURE 6.6

Structure of the US Domain

LEGEND

(UPPER) = RFC1480 domain names
(Mixed) = Replace with local name
(lower) = Example subdomains

Administration of US subdomains has been delegated to local contacts. If you wish to register a domain under US you will need to determine the appropriate contact person. Start by using FTP to retrieve the file in-notes/us-domain-delegated.txt from venera.isi.edu. This file can also be obtained via e-mail using the RFC-INFO service described in Chapter 1. Send e-mail to rfc-info@isi.edu with the following message:

```
help: us_domain_delegated_domains
```

Structure of Organization Domains

An organization that registers a domain on the Internet has complete freedom to design the domain as the organization sees fit. Of course, the organization's database tree must be configured within the organization's Internet domain. Figure 6.7 illustrates an example of a name space that might be established for the organization Widgets, Inc. This organization has been assigned the domain widgets.com and is responsible for managing the name space below that domain. Widgets will be required to maintain a DNS name server to handle all name resolution requests within its portion of the directory name space.

Because each organization is assigned a unique second-level domain name, every host in the Internet directory name space is identified by a unique FQDN. For example, no other host on the Internet will have the FQDN marci.swr.eng.widgets.com.

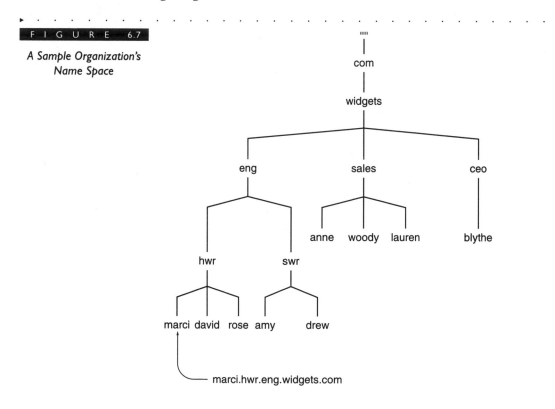

FIGURE 6.7

A Sample Organization's Name Space

Using WHOIS to Obtain Domain Information

WHOIS is a service that provides a "white pages" directory of people and organizations on the Internet. The information available is somewhat limited and reaches only the first two or three levels of the Internet name space. For example, only the second and third levels below the US domain are listed (for example, down to K12.CA.US). Nevertheless, WHOIS can be a valuable tool for obtaining information about domains and their contacts.

Entities within WHOIS are indexed by keywords. Top-level domains are indexed by the domain name followed by -DOM. To search for the EDU domain, you would search for EDU-DOM.

WHOIS searches may be conducted using client software, via the World Wide Web, or by using Telnet to access a WHOIS client on an InterNIC host.

If your host is equipped with a WHOIS client — many UNIX hosts are — you can conduct queries directly from the command line. The query to identify the contact for the COM domain is:

```
whois -h rs.internic.net com-dom
```

The InterNIC Web site can be used to conduct WHOIS searches. Reach the site with the URL **http://ds.internic.net**. From the InterNIC home page do the following:

1 • Select AT&T Directory and Databases.

2 • Select InterNIC Directory Services ("White Pages").

3 • Select WHOIS Person/Organization to generate a WHOIS query form.

4 • Enter a search word in the query form, and press Enter. The following databases will be searched and results will be displayed:

   ▸ InterNIC Directory and Databases Services (ds.internic.net), for domains other than MIL and for information other than point-of-contact.

   ▸ InterNIC Registration Services (rs.internic.net), for point-of-contact information.

   ▸ DISA NIC (nic.ddn.mil), for the MIL domain.

Using Telnet to access a WHOIS client on the INTERNIC host is an efficient way to obtain detailed WHOIS reports. After using Telnet to access rs.internic.net (no login is required), enter the command **whois** to access a WHOIS client. The following dialog shows a Telnet session with the results of querying for EDU-DOM:

```
Whois: edu-dom
Education top-level domain (EDU-DOM)

     Network Solutions, Inc.
     505 Huntmar park Dr.
     Herndon, VA 22070

     Domain Name: EDU

Administrative Contact, Technical Contact, Zone Contact:
     Network Solutions, Inc.  (HOSTMASTER)
     HOSTMASTER@INTERNIC.NET
     (703) 742-4777 (FAX) (703) 742-4811


Record last updated on 02-Sep-94.


Domain servers in listed order:

A.ROOT-SERVERS.NET            198.41.0.4
H.ROOT-SERVERS.NET            128.63.2.53
B.ROOT-SERVERS.NET            128.9.0.107
C.ROOT-SERVERS.NET            192.33.4.12
D.ROOT-SERVERS.NET            128.8.10.90
E.ROOT-SERVERS.NET            192.203.230.10
I.ROOT-SERVERS.NET            192.36.148.17
F.ROOT-SERVERS.NET            39.13.229.241
G.ROOT-SERVERS.NET            192.112.36.4


Would you like to see the known domains under this
top-level domain? n
```

Besides information about the EDU domain, this report lists the domain name servers that service top-level domains on the Internet. You can learn more about a specific host by searching on the host's IP address. An example in the following section shows details about one of the root name servers.

How DNS Works

DNS name resolution is performed by *name servers*, which are programs running on network hosts. Because the Internet is so extensive, DNS was designed so that many name servers could share the responsibility for resolving names. This is accomplished by dividing the complete name space into *zones*. Each zone can be serviced by its own name servers.

A name server that manages data for a zone is said to have *authority* for that zone. A name server will have authority for at least one zone, but a single name server can have authority for many zones if required. Figure 6.8 illustrates a name space that has been organized into zones. Notice that zones need not follow domain structures. Although a domain must consist of a connected subtree of the overall name space, zones need not consist of contiguous nodes. This flexibility enables a single name server to provide name resolution for multiple domains.

FIGURE 6.8

A Name Space Divided into Three Zones

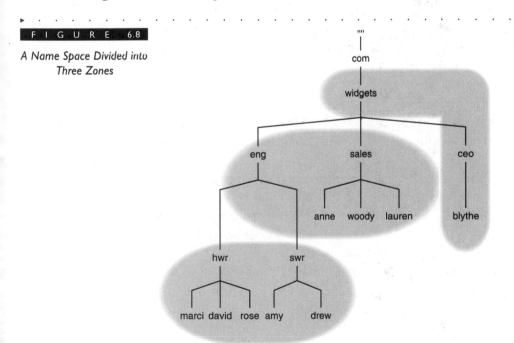

The principle name server for a zone is the *primary master name server*, which collects data for the zone from its configuration files. *Secondary master name servers* are redundant backups to primary servers and obtain data for the zones they service by performing *zone transfers* from the primary master name server for the zone. Secondary masters perform periodic zone transfers to keep up-to-date with changes in the zone. Configuration of two or more name servers for a zone provides fault tolerance and improves performance by distributing name-resolution processing across several hosts.

Assignment of primary and secondary master name servers is quite flexible. A name server can be authoritative for one or for several zones, and a given name server can function as a primary master for one zone and as a secondary master for another.

Because many name resolution attempts must begin with the root domain, the Internet root domain is serviced by nine root name servers, which include systems on NSFNET, MILNET, SPAN (NASA), and in Europe. These root-domain servers are authoritative for all top-level domains on the Internet. Authority for secondary- and lower-level domains is distributed across many name servers operated by the organizations that inhabit the Internet.

When an organization obtains a domain name and establishes a presence on the Internet, a name server must be designated that is authoritative for the domain. In most cases, the name server will be maintained on a host that is operated by the owner of the domain. It is not necessary for an organization to operate its own name server, however. Most Internet connections are now obtained from commercial Internet access providers. Many of these providers will maintain their client's zones on the provider's name servers. Contracting an Internet access provider to manage your domain name space is particularly desirable if your organization is small and cannot justify the labor costs to have DNS experts on staff or the hardware required to maintain a primary and a backup name server.

The complete Internet domain name space is maintained by many distributed name servers that have some degree of awareness of each other. This distributed network of name servers cooperates to provide name resolution for the complete Internet.

The client side of the name service is provided by *resolvers,* which are components of TCP/IP processes and applications that make use of DNS host names. The resolver is embedded in the software of each application, such as FTP or Telnet, enabling the application to contact one name server to initiate a name resolution query. The resolver in the application can construct a DNS query, but resolution of the query is the responsibility of the network name servers.

Figure 6.9 illustrates the process of resolving a query. The configuration of a TCP/IP host will include the IP address of at least one DNS name server. When an application requires name resolution service, it constructs a name service query and sends the query to a known name server. If the name server that is queried cannot resolve the name, it initiates a search starting with one of the available root name servers. The root name server provides the address of a name server that is authoritative for the first-level domain in the query. The search proceeds from first-to-second-to-lower-level domain name servers until a server is found that can respond to the query.

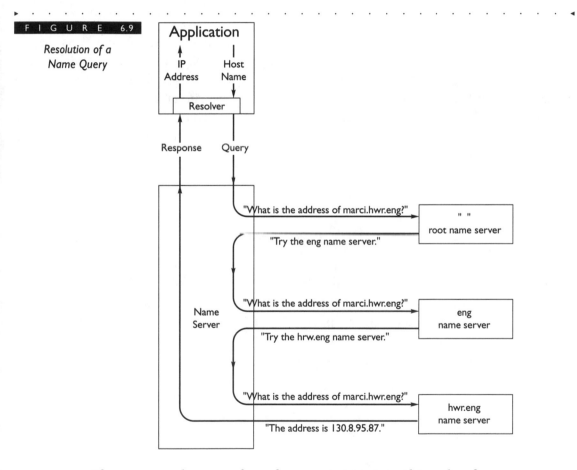

FIGURE 6.9

Resolution of a Name Query

The name search process depends on access to an intact hierarchy of name servers. If a functioning name server is unavailable at any level, name resolution will fail. That is why it is so important to have primary and secondary name servers available and why the Internet is serviced by nine servers at the root domain. Although lower-level servers reduce name resolution traffic by maintaining a cache of recently resolved names, if all root name servers on the Internet were to fail, all name resolution would eventually cease.

The most commonly used implementation of DNS is BIND (Berkeley Internet Name Domain), which is included in 4.3BSD UNIX. Now at version 4.8.3, BIND has been ported to a variety of UNIX and other platforms. BIND supports tree depths up to 127 levels, sufficient even for the Internet. In fact, all Internet root name servers are running an implementation of BIND.

BIND is a complex product, and DNS is an involved technology. This chapter should contain enough information for you to be able to configure and administer a basic DNS implementation. If you require more extensive information, I recommend the book *DNS and BIND* by Paul Albitz and Cricket Liu (O'Reilly & Associates, 1992).

NetWare/IP, a product that enables NetWare servers to operate NetWare services over TCP/IP protocols, includes domain name server software. See Chapter 12 (Managing NetWare/IP) for more information.

Common TCP/IP Applications

The remainder of this chapter examines some of the TCP/IP process protocols and applications you are most likely to encounter. Some, such as Telnet and FTP, are end-user tools that you will probably use frequently. Others, such as SMTP and SNMP, are protocols that support the functionality of end-user applications such as e-mail (SMTP) and network management (SNMP). We will examine the following process/application layer protocols:

- ► File Transfer Protocol (FTP)

- ► Trivial File Transfer Protocol (TFTP)

- ► Telnet

- ► Simple Network Management Protocol (SNMP)

- ► Simple Mail Transfer Protocol (SMTP)

- ► Network File System (NFS)

FILE TRANSFER PROTOCOL

FTP is the primary protocol used to move files around TCP/IP networks and is heavily used on the Internet. The name FTP refers to the protocol itself as well as to the program that users access to perform file operations. The FTP protocol can also be used by applications that need to perform network file operations.

FTP is a reliable, session-oriented protocol that operates over TCP. Users must log in before gaining access to the remote file system. Although FTP logins can be coordinated with user account names and passwords, FTP security is impaired because user names and passwords are not encrypted and, therefore, are accessible through the network. The majority of FTP sites you are likely to encounter offer *anonymous FTP* service, which means that any user can log in with the user name anonymous and a password that is usually the name of the user's e-mail account.

FTP Architecture

As shown in Figure 6.10, FTP operation requires client and server components. The host that will make its file system available to users runs FTP server software. Users run FTP client software that enables them to establish a network connection and perform file operations.

When the FTP server software is run on the server host, it performs a passive open, establishing a *socket* that can accept outside connections. When an FTP client issues an active open request, a *virtual circuit* is established between the sockets on the server and the client. A virtual circuit functions like a pipe through which data can be transferred reliably. The FTP connection enables the remote client to manipulate part of the server's file system as though the client were accessing the server directly.

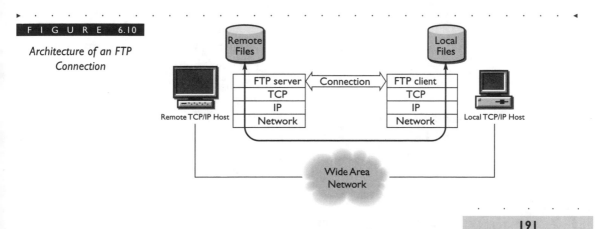

FIGURE 6.10

Architecture of an FTP Connection

NOTE

The NetWare FleX/IP product can be used to configure an FTP server on a NetWare file server. FTP client software is included with Novell's LAN WorkPlace and LAN WorkGroup products. LAN WorkPlace and LAN Workgroup also include FTP server software that supports a limited number of client connections. In Chapter 9, you will see how to set up an FTP server using LAN WorkPlace.

Guidelines for Using FTP

Most FTP servers are UNIX based, and the UNIX file system is somewhat different from the DOS file system you are probably familiar with. When you use FTP on the Internet, you need to be aware of the following differences between UNIX and DOS or NetWare:

▶ With NetWare and DOS, file and directory names are not case sensitive. For example, the filenames salesrpt.txt, SalesRpt.TXT, and SALESRPT.TXT are functionally identical and in a given directory refer to the same file. UNIX filenames and commands, in contrast, are case sensitive. The file This-Is-A-File.txt is different from this-is-a-file.txt, for example. Directory names also are case sensitive. In the UNIX environment, FTP commands are entered almost exclusively in lower case. The examples in this chapter will follow that convention.

▶ UNIX supports longer filenames than are possible with DOS-based file systems. The latter are limited to the familiar 8.3 naming convention (up to eight characters, followed by a period and an extension of up to three characters).

▶ Finally, DOS uses backslashes (for example, \DATA\REPORTS\SALES). When manipulating files on Novell servers, you have the option of using backslashes or forward slashes. In UNIX, however, forward slashes are used (for example, /data/reports/sales).

Sample FTP Session

Novell's LAN WorkPlace and LAN WorkGroup products include a utility called Rapid Filer that can be used to transfer files to and from FTP servers. Rapid Filer provides a simple, graphical interface to FTP, so you may never need to enter FTP commands directly. Then again, you may not always have a graphic utility available, you may need to use FTP capabilities that are unavailable in Rapid Filer, or you may be operating an FTP server that is available to outside users. In these cases, you will need to know how to use FTP from a command-line interface. LAN WorkPlace and LAN WorkGroup also include a DOS command-mode FTP client.

This section demonstrates how to use LAN WorkPlace's command-based FTP client. The following example shows you how to retrieve an RFC file from the InterNIC FTP server.

Before starting FTP, an Internet connection is required. The connection can be a network connection through a LAN that has a direct interface, or it can consist of a dial-up session through an Internet access provider. Once the connection is established, you can begin an FTP session. The following commands assume that you are using command-line FTP software on a DOS host.

Starting FTP   The first task is to start the FTP client software by typing **ftp** at the command prompt. In the following dialog examples, bold text is typed by the user:

```
C:> ftp
ftp>
```

When the FTP client software is activated, the prompt changes to ftp> indicating that FTP is active. At this point, only FTP commands will be accepted.

Opening a Connection with an FTP Server   The next task is to connect with a remote FTP server and log in. The session is initiated by using the **open** command:

```
ftp> open ds.internic.net
Connected to ds.internic.net
220-             InterNIC Directory and Database Services
220-
220-Welcome to InterNIC Directory and Database Services provided by AT&T
220-These services are partially supported through a cooperative agreement
220-with the National Science Foundation.
220-
220-Your comments and suggestions for improvement are welcome, and can be
220-mailed to admin@ds.internic.net.
220-
220-AT&T MAKES NO WARRANTY OR GUARANTEE, OR PROMISE, EXPRESS OR IMPLIED,
```

```
220-CONCERNING THE CONTENT OR ACCURACY OF THE INTERNIC DIRECTORY ENTRIES
220-AND DATABASE FILES STORED AND MAINTAINED BY AT&T. AT&T EXPRESSLY
220-DISCLAIMS AND EXCLUDES ALL EXPRESS WARRANTIES AND IMPLIED WARRANTIES
220-OF MERCHANTABILITY AND FITNESS FOR A PARTICULAR PURPOSE.
220-
220-
220-                          ****************************
220-
220-DS0 will be rebooted every Monday morning between 8:00AM and 8:30AM est.
220-
220-            Please use DS1 or DS2 during this period
220-
220-                          ***************************
220-
220-DS0 will be rebooted Monday, December 18, 1995 between 8 and 9 AM for
220-maintanence  reasons. Thereafter, it will be booted at the normal 8:00
220-to 9:00 slot.
220-
220-            ******************************************
220-
220 ds0.internic.net FTP server ready.
Remote User Name:
```

The previous dialog excerpts started the FTP client and opened a connection in two steps. If desired, you can perform both tasks in a single step by including the name of the FTP server as a command-line parameter. The following command starts the FTP client and attempts to connect to the InterNIC server:

```
C:> ftp ds.internic.net
```

Logging In   Many Internet FTP servers accept anonymous logins, allocating limited FTP privileges to users who do not have a personal user name and password. To accomplish an anonymous login, type **anonymous** when prompted for your user name. Most anonymous FTP sites request that you use your e-mail name as a password. Here is an example of an anonymous login process dialog:

```
Remote User Name: anonymous
331 Guest login ok, send ident as password.
```

```
Password: <e-mail name>
ftp>
```

NOTE

The FTP login process is not particularly secure. User names and passwords are not encrypted as they travel through the network, and anyone who has a network protocol analyzer (such as Novell's LANalyzer for Windows) can examine the packets and recover the login information. If you implement an FTP server that is accessible through a public network such as the Internet, you should ensure that the account names and passwords used for FTP are different from the names and passwords used to access secure systems.

Anonymous FTP isn't as risky as it might seem. All anonymous FTP users can be assigned strictly defined access to files and directories, limiting the damage they can do. In most cases, anonymous FTP users are only given read-only access to public directories.

Getting Help   During an FTP session, you can obtain help about the available commands by typing **help** as in the following dialog:

```
ftp> help
Commands may be abbreviated.  Commands are:

!          delete    lls       prompt     send
?          dir       lpwd      put        sendport
append     exit      ls        pwd        statistics
bell       force     mdelete   quit       status
bye        get       mdir      recv       user
cd         hash      mkdir     remotedir  verbose
close      help      mls       rename
copy       lcd       mget      rget
debug      lexec     mput      rmdir
defaults   ldir      open      rput
ftp>
```

The exact commands you see will depend on the commands available on the FTP software with which you are connected. Many of these commands remind us of FTP's origins in the UNIX community. Some will be familiar to DOS users, such as **dir, delete,** and **cd**. Others will be quite unfamiliar, such as **ls** (list files) and **pwd** (print working directory). Most commands are easy to grasp if you understand the logic behind the command name.

To obtain a brief description of a command, type **help** followed by the command name. For example:

```
ftp> help help
help            print local help information
```

Verbose and Sparse Responses   LAN Workplace FTP is configured so that by default it does not echo the command response messages that are produced by the FTP server. I have chosen to show these responses in this chapter by typing the command **verbose** at the ftp> prompt. Verbose mode is helpful when you are learning to use FTP because some messages contain information confirming that the command was carried out.

Navigating FTP Server Directories   When using FTP you are concerned with two current directories: one on your FTP client and another on the FTP server. Any files you copy will be copied between those two directories. The commands for changing directories are:

- **cd**, which changes the current directory on the FTP server

- **lcd** (local cd), which changes the current directory on the FTP client

The current directory on a UNIX computer is referred to as the *working directory*. When you first connect with an FTP server, your working directory will be root. The RFC documents on ds.internic.net are located in the /rfc directory. The following dialog takes place when changing the working directory to /rfc:

```
ftp> cd /rfc
250 CWD command successful
```

Notice the use of the forward slash to specify a UNIX directory. You must always enter file and directory specifications using the conventions of the host that the command is manipulating. You can determine the identity of the working directory with the **pwd** (print working directory) command, as in the following dialog, entered in the /rfc directory:

```
ftp> pwd
257 "/rfc" is the current directory
```

Here are some techniques that are useful when changing directories:

- ▸ To change to the parent directory of the working directory, issue the command **cd up** or **cd ..** (where .. is shorthand for the parent directory).

- ▸ To change to any directory in the file system, use a fully qualified directory name that starts from the root directory. The command **cd /ietf/ipngwg** will change the working directory to the ipngwg directory regardless of the current working directory. A fully qualified directory path is called an *absolute reference*.

- ▸ To change to a subdirectory of the working directory, you can use a *relative reference*. If your working directory is ietf and you wish to change to the /ietf/ipv6mib subdirectory, enter the command **cd ipv6mib**.

Figure 6.11 illustrates the use of absolute and relative directory references.

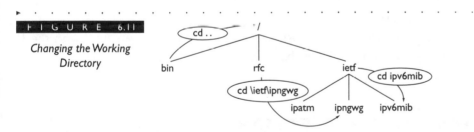

FIGURE 6.11

Changing the Working Directory

Navigating FTP Client Directories   Before copying files, you also need to set the current directory on the DOS client. If the files are to be copied to C:\RFCDOCS, enter the following command:

```
ftp> lcd \rfcdocs
Local directory now c:\rfcdocs
```

You can use absolute and relative directory references with the **lcd** command.

Examining Directories   In the above dialogs, the working directory on the FTP server was set to /rfc. You could now transfer files if you desired, but suppose you don't know the exact names of the files you want. How can you examine directory contents?

The **ls** command produces a basic listing of directory contents. But don't rush to enter an **ls** command, because the rfc directory contains about 2000 files. To display only a few of the files, you can use wildcard characters. FTP recognizes DOS * and ? wildcard characters. In the following listing, I've selected a filename parameter that will retrieve several files I want you to know about:

```
ftp> ls rfc-*.txt
200 PORT command successful.
150 Opening ASCII mode data connection for file list.
rfc-index.txt
rfc-instructions.txt
rfc-retrieval.txt
226 Transfer complete.
ftp>
```

The parameter rfc-* produced a listing of all files starting with the characters rfc-. The * character matches any series of characters and found several files in this example. The rfc-index file is mentioned in Chapter 1. This file includes an index to the current set of RFC documents. The other documents provide useful information on retrieving RFCs.

If the FTP server is a UNIX host, you can use several parameters with the **ls** command (see Table 6.1). Note that some of the following parameters must be entered in upper case:

T A B L E 6.1	PARAMETER	
Parameters for the ls Command	-a	All files will be listed, including hidden files.
	-C	A multi-column listing will be produced.
	-d	Only directory names will be listed.
	-F	File types will be included in the listing (directory or executable).
	-l	A long listing will be displayed.
	-R	A recursive (continuous) listing is produced.

Users familiar with the UNIX ls command might expect other options to be available as well. During an FTP session, however, the ls command is handled by FTP, not by the UNIX shell. Only the options supported by FTP are available.

Getting Files   At this point, we have set the working directories on the client and the server, and we have obtained a directory listing to confirm that the file we need resides in the working directory on the server. Once the working directories are set, retrieving a file is a piece of cake, as in this example:

```
ftp> get rfc1800.txt
200 PORT command successful
150 Opening ASCII mode data connection for rfc1800.txt (83648
bytes)
226 Transfer complete
85667 bytes transferred in 113 second(s) (758 bytes/s)
226 Transfer complete
ftp>
```

Files can be transferred in ASCII or binary modes. A binary transfer is a verbatim, byte-for-byte transfer of data that preserves the exact structures of program and data files. When transferring text files, however, it is preferable to use ASCII mode.

Text files have varying formats under different operating systems. UNIX files represent the end of a text line with a linefeed character. DOS represents the end of a line with the combination of a carriage return followed by a linefeed. If a text file is transferred between UNIX and DOS, a verbatim binary transfer will produce a file that does not conform to the file format of the destination system. An ASCII-mode FTP transfer will compensate for file format differences by translating the end-of-line characters so that they are correct for the destination file system.

If you want to perform an ASCII-mode transfer but don't want end-of-line character translation, use the **cr** command to disable character translation. Turn off character translation if a file will eventually end up on a system with an operating system that differs from the current FTP client. Suppose, for example, that you are using a DOS FTP client to retrieve a file from a UNIX FTP server. The file you retrieve, however, will eventually be copied to a UNIX computer. Use the **cr** command to turn off character translation so that the file will remain in UNIX format.

To switch to binary transfer mode, use the command **binary**. Switch back to ASCII mode with the command **ASCII**.

Closing the FTP Session When you have completed operations, you should close the FTP session. This can be done by entering the **close** command to close the connection to the FTP server, followed by the **bye** command to exit the FTP client software:

```
ftp> close
221 Goodbye
ftp> bye
C:\
```

Alternatively, you can simply enter the command **bye**, which both closes the connection and exits FTP.

FTP Command Reference

Although you will probably have access to a program that provides a graphical FTP interface, such as the Rapid Filer utility included with LAN WorkPlace, you may need to use the command-line approach at some point. In some cases, the command-line is more efficient because less data must be transferred to produce directory listings on the graphic client. Table 6.2 lists some of the commands available during FTP sessions. A complete list can be found in the *LAN WorkPlace for DOS User's Guide*.

NOTE

NetWare and DOS commands are not case sensitive. The example dialogs show the commands in lower case, but upper case could be used and is used in Table 6.1. When using FTP on a UNIX host, however, commands are case sensitive, and virtually all commands are entered in lower case. Be sure to check out the conventions of the environment in which you are using FTP.

T A B L E 6.2

Summary of FTP Commands

COMMAND	FUNCTION
APPEND *local remote*	Appends the contents of the workstation file *local* to the end of the server file remote. If the file specified by *remote* does not exist, the file is copied to a new file named local.
ASCII	Sets file transfer to ASCII mode, the default transfer mode. End-of-line characters will be translated as appropriate for the destination file system.
BELL	Turns on or off (toggles) a bell that sounds after completion of an FTP operation.
BINARY	Sets file transfer to binary mode. This mode should be used for data, program, and 8-bit ASCII text files.
BYE	Closes any active sessions and exits the FTP client to DOS.
CD *remote_path*	Changes the current working directory on the FTP server to the directory specified in *remote_path*.
CLOSE	Closes the host session but remains in FTP command mode.
COPY [-A] [-B] [F] [-I] [-R] *source destination*	Copies files. If *source* is a file, *destination* may be a directory or a fileIf *source* specifies multiple files or directories, *destination* must be a directory. Options are: -A Specifies ASCII file transfer. If the file has binary file characteristics the -A option is overridden and the transfer will be binary, unless the -F option is specified. -B Specifies binary file transfer. If the file has ASCII file characteristics the -B option is overridden and the transfer will be ASCII, unless the -F option is specified. -F Forces files to be transferred as specified by the -A and -B options. If an -A or -B flag is absent and COPY uses an open connection, COPY will use the same mode that was used for the previous COPY operation. If this is the first transfer, COPY defaults to ASCII. -I Forces COPY to ignore files that will be copied to a DOS computer if the files do not have valid DOS filenames. -R Copies recursively, including all subdirectories of the source directory. The source parameter may not include wildcards.
DEBUG	Sets debugging mode, during which FTP displays commands sent to the FTP server during a session. The default setting is off.
DEFAULTS	Restores DEBUG, SENDPORT, and VERBOSE to their default settings.
DELETE *remote_file*	Deletes the file named *remote_file* from the FTP server.

(continued)

T A B L E 6.2

Summary of FTP Commands
(continued)

COMMAND	FUNCTION
DIR [*remote_directory*]	Displays a detailed list of files in the working directory on the FTP server. If a directory parameter is included, displays a detailed list of files in the working directory specified by *remote_directory*.
FILE	Sets file transfer to file mode, unstructured byte streams.
FORCE	Determines whether file transfer parameters in effect for the connection are set automatically (the default setting), forcing FTP to transfer files according to the setting of the type parameter. When FORCE is off, FTP attempts to determine the file type prior to transfer. Setting FORCE to off has the same effect as specifying the -F option for the COPY command. Repeated entry of the FORCE command toggles the state between on and off.
GET *remote_file* [*local_file* | *local_directory*]	Retrieves the file *remote_file* from the FTP server and stores it either with the name *local_file* on the local host or with the name *remote_file* in the *local_directory*.
HASH	Prints a # character as each block of data is transferred. This slows file transfers. HASH is a toggle command, with the default value of off.
HELP [*command*]	Displays list of available commands, or, if a command is specified, a brief message about command.
LCD [*local_directory*]	Changes the working directory on the local computer.
LDIR [*local_directory*] [*local_file*]	Produces a detailed list of files in the current local directory or in the local directory specified by *local_directory*. Include a *local_file* parameter, which may include wild cards, to limit the display to specific files.
LEXEC ["*command*"]	Escapes to a DOS command shell. If a command parameter is included, the command will be executed. If the command includes spaces, enclose it in quotation marks ("").
LLS [*local_directory*] [*local_file*]	Lists files in the current local directory or in the local directory specified by *local_directory*. Include a *local_file* parameter, which may include wild cards, to limit the display to specific files.
LPWD	Displays the name of the working directory on the DOS workstation.
LS [{*remote_directory* | *remote_file*} [*local_file*]]	Lists files in the *remote_directory* on the FTP server, or files in the working directory on the FTP server that match the filename which may include wildcards. Include a *local_file* parameter to direct the results to a file on the DOS computer. On a UNIX host accepts UNIX ls options.
MDELETE *remote_file*	Deletes all files on the FTP server that match remote_file, which may include ? and * wild cards.

COMMAND	FUNCTION
MDIR [{remote_directory | remote_file} local_file]	Lists detailed contents of the remote_directory on the FTP server, or files in the working directory on the FTP server that match the filename remote_file, which may include wildcards. The last filename is interpreted as a local_file parameter, computer. On a UNIX host accepts UNIX ls options, specifying a file that will receive the results reported by MDIR. Enter a hyphen (-) as the local_file to direct output to the screen
MGET remote_file	Copies files from the FTP server that match remote_file, which may include ? and * wild cards.
MKDIR remote_directory	Creates the subdirectory named remote_directory on the FTP server.
MLS [{remote_directory | remote_file} [local_file]]	Lists contents of the remote_directory on the FTP server, or files in the working directory on the FTP server that match the filename remote_file, which may include wildcards. The last filename is interpreted as a local_file parameter, specifying a file that will receive the results reported by MDIR. Enter a hyphen (-) as the local_file to direct output to the screen
MPUT local_file	Copies one or more files specified by local_file to the ftp server. The local_file parameter may include ? and * wild cards.
OPEN hostname [port]	Open a connection to the specified hostname, which must be running FTP server software to accept the connection. The default FTP port is 21. If another port is used by an FTP server, it can be specified by the port parameter.
PROMPT	Switches prompting on or off during operations on multiple files (wild cards are used). You may find prompting irritating for routine operations such as MPUT and MGET, but may prefer to have prompting active for deleting files with MDELETE.
PUT local_file [remote_file | remote_directory]	Copies the local file local_file to the FTP host with the filename remote_file or to the remote_directory with the filename local_file.
PWD	Prints the working (current) directory on the FTP server.
QUIT	Terminates all FTP sessions and exits FTP to DOS.
RENAME I remote_new	Renames a file on the FTP host from the name remote_old to the name remote_new.
RMDIR remote_directory	Deletes the directory named remote_directory from the FTP server.
TYPE [type_name]	Displays the current file transfer setting. Include a type_name parameter to change the settings. Valid settings are ASCII (7-bit ASCII), BINARY (bit image) and LOCAL 8 (8-bit ASCII).
USER username	Initiates a login to the FTP host with the user name specified. FTP will prompt for a password.
VERBOSE	Switches VERBOSE mode on or off. Verbose mode provides information you may not care about such as file transfer statistics.

TRIVIAL FILE TRANSFER PROTOCOL

FTP was designed to provide robust file transfer service, with a measure of security, that could operate over unreliable WANs. Consequently the designers of FTP selected TCP as the host-to-host protocol. But providing reliable service with TCP comes at a cost. Network overhead is required to establish a virtual circuit, maintain a reliable dialog, and close the virtual circuit when the dialog is complete.

On some networks and for some purposes, the overhead associated with FTP is undesirable. When file transfer is informal and is performed on reliable networks, for example, a simpler protocol might do. That is why the Trivial File Transfer Protocol (TFTP; RFC 1350) was developed. TFTP operates in an unreliable, datagram environment using the UDP host-to-host protocol. No formal connection must be established or released, and no login is required.

TFTP is of particular value because it can be embedded into computer boot ROMs. This makes it possible to construct diskless, remote booting computers that operate in the TCP/IP environment. Sun UNIX workstations, for example, can use TFTP to download an operating system image from a central server when the computer is started.

But TFTP's complete lack of security can make it a security risk when a host is attached to a public network. Many system administrators will disable TFTP on their network hosts. If TFTP is enabled, careful attention should be paid to the areas of the file system that TFTP users can access.

TELNET

Another TCP/IP application you are likely to use is Telnet (RFC 854/855), a remote terminal program that enables users to engage in terminal dialogs with remote hosts on TCP/IP internetworks. The effect is much like using a telecommunications package and a modem to dial into an information service, but the entire process happens within the internetwork, without needing a dial-up connection.

Architecture of Telnet

Like FTP, Telnet operates in a client-server configuration. As Figure 6.12 illustrates, a host must run Telnet server software, which enables it to maintain a virtual terminal image that represents the client that will connect in. This virtual image is the key to making Telnet work, because the processes running on the

Telnet server interact with the virtual terminal just as though they were talking with a hardware terminal attached to a terminal port.

To initiate a Telnet connection, a user runs Telnet client software and logs onto the Telnet server. The Telnet server software receives keystrokes from the client and forwards the keystrokes to the virtual terminal where they become available to the application being used. When the application directs screen display data to the virtual terminal, the data are forwarded to the Telnet server process, which passes the characters on to the client. This process is a *double fooler.* The applications running on the server think they are interacting with a local terminal, and the user can behave as though the processing is taking place on the local client.

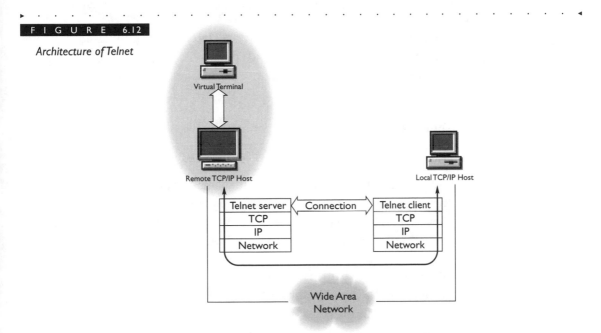

FIGURE 6.12

Architecture of Telnet

Telnet is a pretty basic telecommunications program, designed around text-based terminals, typically the Digital VT220, VT100/VT102, or VT52. Although these terminals are quite sophisticated as text terminals go, they will seem like pretty old technology to users who have come to know graphic user environments.

Although Telnet has a client and a server side, all the processing takes place at the server side. The client host might as well be a terminal since it operates in a pretty "dumb" mode. Telnet is not the first step toward distributed processing.

So, if Telnet is dumb and text-based, what is it good for? As it turns out, Telnet is good for quite a lot. The Internet community has evolved several text-based services that are well-suited to Telnet. Although graphic-based clients are available for many of these services, Telnet remains a viable tool for accessing the following services.

- **Archie.** This database service was originated by the McGill University School of Computer Science in Montreal, Canada. Archie catalogs the files on thousands of FTP servers on the Internet. You can retrieve informational files via anonymous FTP from archie.ans.net. Go to the directory /pub/archie/doc, and begin by retrieving the file whatis.archie.

- **Gopher.** This service was created at the University of Minnesota (home of the Golden Gophers) and can be used to gain access to a huge number of files and Internet services. To get information via anonymous FTP, connect to boombox.micro.umn.edu and get the file /pub/gopher/00README.

- **Veronica.** This service provides an indexing service for Gopher and indexes the majority of gopher sites. Now, since no serious computer techie would name a program after a comic book character, I'm sure you want to know the real meaning of the name Veronica. Well, it stands for "very easy rodent-oriented net-wide index to computerized archives." Now you know. To get an introduction to Veronica, use anonymous FTP to obtain the file /doc/net/uiucnet/vol6no1.txt from ftp.cso.uiuc.edu.

- **WAIS (Wide Area Information Servers).** This Internet search tool maintains indexes of catalogued resources. You can search for much of the published Internet documentation using WAIS, for example. You can access a WAIS client by using Telnet to connect with ds.internic.net. Log in with the user name wais. The service is easy to use and an on-line tutorial is available.

To show you how easily these services can be accessed, let's look at a sample Telnet session. In this case, Archie will be used to locate a file.

Accessing Archie via Telnet

You need a file that you know is available on an FTP server somewhere, but which server? And where is the file on the server? You could spend a great deal of time nosing around FTP sites until you found your file. That's where Archie comes in. Archie servers catalog files on thousands of FTP servers in a searchable index. You can access the Archie index by using Telnet to access an Archie server.

Table 6.3 includes a list of Archie servers. It is a good idea to use the Archie server that is nearest to your location to cut down on Internet WAN traffic. We will use the server archie.rutgers.edu.

T A B L E 6.3	
Archie Servers	

HOST NAME	LOCATION
archie.au	Australia
archie.univie.ac.at	Austria
archie.mcgill.ca	Canada
archie.funet.fi	Finland
archie.univ-rennesl.fr	France
archie.th-darmstadt.de	Germany
archie.ac.il	Israel
archie.unipi.it	Italy
archie.wide.ad.jp	Japan
archie.hama.nm.kr	Korea
archie.uninett.no	Norway
archie.rediris.es	Spain
archie.luth.se	Sweden
archie.switch.ch	Switzerland
archie.ncu.edu.tw	Taiwan
archie.doc.ic.ac.uk	United Kingdom
archie.unl.edu	USA (Nevada)
archie.internic.net	USA (New Jersey)
archie.rutgers.edu	USA (New Jersey)
archie.ans.net	USA (New York)
archie.sura.net	USA (Maryland)

LAN WorkPlace includes a Telnet client named TNVT220, which emulates a VT220 terminal. When using Telnet, it is important to match the terminal type you are emulating with the terminal type supported by the remote host. Otherwise, screen displays may contain garbage, and you may have trouble typing control characters. When you use Telnet, you are stepping into the remote computer's environment, and getting all the parameters right may take some tinkering at first. TNVT220 can be made to emulate a variety of terminals, including VT220, VT100, VT52, and ANSI. An UNKNOWN type implements Telnet without terminal emulation.

I started the sample Telnet session by entering the command **TNVT220 -T VT100 ARCHIE.RUTGERS.EDU**. This matched me to the VT100 terminal type that I knew the Archie server expected. After connecting, I received a login prompt:

```
login: archie
# Message of the day from the localhost Prospero server:

    Welcome to the Rutgers University Archie Server!
```

```
7/31/95  -   The Rutgers Archie server has been moved to its
             new home; A Sun SPARCserver 20/71!  Please let
             us know if you encounter any problems.
```

```
    Type "help" for information on how to use Archie.

# Bunyip Information Systems, Inc., 1993, 1994, 1995

# Terminal type set to 'vt100 24 80'.
# 'erase' character is '^?'.
# 'search' (type string) has the value 'sub'.
archie>
```

You can access on-line help for Archie by entering the command **help** at the archie> prompt. Press Ctrl+C to exit help.

My sample search is very unsophisticated. I want to see if any FTP servers have copies of the latest VLM update files (the files used to implement the DOS requester in the most recent NetWare DOS clients). (Yes, I could have gone straight to Novell's FTP server, ftp.novell.com, but I wanted to show you a search that was relevant to NetWare.)

Because I didn't think that many files would contain the letters "vlm" I entered the command **prog vlm** to search for files (programs) with the text vlm in the filenames. That search generated a very large listing with lots of files that I didn't want. (It seems that several very popular files have names starting with AVLMap.)

By default, Archie performs substring searches, which means that Archie will report every file in its database that contains the substring you specify with the `prog` command. That's why those AVLMap files showed up. If you find yourself · using Archie a lot, you should obtain a manual and learn how to conduct some more sophisticated searches. Start with the documents that are posted on archie.ans.net.

I knew that Novell typically calls update files DOSUP or WINUP or something like that, so I tried searching with the command **prog vlmup**. That got me closer. I only got a couple dozen items, including several versions of VLMUP. The most recent version seemed to be VLMUP4, so I searched for that. Here are the results:

```
archie> prog vlmup4
# Search type: sub.
# Your queue position: 1
# Estimated time for completion: 5 seconds.
working... =

Host nic.switch.ch     (130.59.1.40)
Last updated 03:29 22 Dec 1995

    Location: /mirror/novell/netwire/techfile
FILE  -rw-rw-r — 448237 bytes 08:59 23 Nov 1995 vlmup4.exe

    Location: /mirror/novell/updates/nwos/dwclnt11
FILE  -rw-rw-r — 448402 bytes 20:23 20 Dec 1995 vlmup4.exe

archie>
TNVT220 - Novell,Inc. archie.rutgers.edu (1) Rep  15:10 A
```

This information can guide you to an FTP server where you can retrieve the file. After you have completed an Archie search, enter the command **bye** to log out of Archie and end the terminal session.

Archie search results can be massive sometimes. If you have an e-mail account, you can have Archie mail you the results of the last search. To do so, enter the command mail followed by your mail ID.

SIMPLE NETWORK MANAGEMENT PROTOCOL

The "Network Management" in Simple Network Management Protocol (SNMP) refers to the task of collecting, reporting, responding to, and in some cases remotely changing data about devices on the network. SNMP is the most widely used network management protocol, and it is supported by many NetWare software products.

Actually, SNMP is one of three components that together make up the network management strategy for the Internet:

▸ SNMP is the protocol that supports communication between managed and managing devices.

▸ MIB is the *management information base*, which is the database that stores information about managed devices.

▸ SMI is the *structure and identification of management information*, which describes how object records in the MIB are constructed.

In Chapter 11, you will learn how to use SNMP to monitor and manage a NetWare network. Before you can configure SNMP, you need to know the components of an SNMP management system and how they are related.

The Management Information Base

A MIB is a management database consisting of *objects*. The MIB states what the objects are, but the structures of the objects are described by the SMI.

Three RFCs describe SNMP MIB standards:

► MIB-I (RFC 1156) was the first MIB specification and was originally published in 1988 as RFC 1066. MIB-I defines 8 object groups and 114 objects.

► MIB-II (RFC 1213) is the current Internet standard. MIB-II defines 10 object groups and 171 objects. NetWare 3 and NetWare 4 servers support MIB-II.

► RMON-MIB (RFC 1513/1217) defines objects oriented around managing network media rather than network devices.

MIBs are extensible and can be defined for special purposes. Vendors provide MIBs to support their products, for example, and a number of experimental MIBs are available. Experimental MIBs are MIBs that are undergoing trial for possible inclusion in the standard MIB-space.

Architecture of SNMP

Two types of devices make up the SNMP architecture. Figure 6.13 shows how the devices are related:

► Devices managed by SNMP run an *SNMP agent*, which is a background process that monitors operation of the device and communicates with the outside world. Each SNMP agent maintains a MIB that contains data about the device.

► SNMP agents are managed by *SNMP managers,* which are network management stations that collect messages from SNMP agents, generate reports, and in some cases manipulate data in the MIBs of managed devices.

A network management station gets its information either by requesting agents to send their data (a process called *polling*), or through *trap messages.*

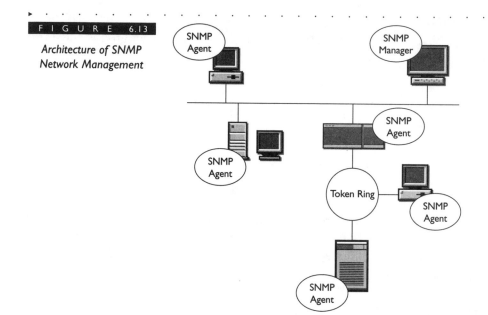

FIGURE 6.13

Architecture of SNMP Network Management

SNMP Functions

The use of SNMP (RFC 1157) is not limited to the Internet or even to TCP/IP. SNMP can be implemented independently of the TCP/IP protocols and can, for example, operate over IPX. In the TCP/IP environment, SNMP runs over the UDP transport.

All SNMP functions are based on the following five operations:

▸ **GetRequest**. The manager uses this command to poll an agent for information.

▸ **GetNextRequest**. The manager uses this command to request the next item in a table or array. The command is repeated to obtain all data in the table or array.

▸ **SetRequest**. The manager uses this command to change a value within an agent's MIB.

▸ **GetResponse**. An agent uses this command to satisfy a request from a manager.

▸ **Trap**. An agent uses this command to inform a manager of an event.

These messages enable SNMP computers to exchange data in two ways. Managers can poll agents for information, as shown in Figure 6.14. Polling occurs at spaced intervals to prevent network management traffic from using excess network bandwidth. Polling enables the SNMP manager to collect data about the network during normal operation. This data provides a baseline that can be used as a basis of comparison when performance degrades.

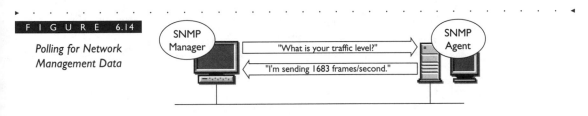

FIGURE 6.14

Polling for Network Management Data

When things go wrong, however, agents need to be able to make the problem known. As shown in Figure 6.15, agents can generate messages in response to events called *traps*. Network administrators configure traps that result when utilization thresholds are exceeded. The trap messages convey the information to the SNMP manager.

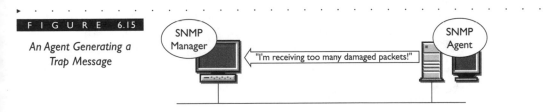

FIGURE 6.15

An Agent Generating a Trap Message

SNMP messages are exchanged within designated groups of computers that are identified by *community names,* which are 32-character, case-sensitive identifiers that serve much the same purpose as passwords, although they are not encrypted when transmitted and therefore are not secure. Three types of communities can be defined:

▸ The *monitor community* grants read access to MIBs. A manager must include the monitor community name in requests. The default monitor community is named *public*.

▸ The *control community* grants read and write access to MIBs.

▸ The *trap community* identifies all messages originated by agents in response to traps. An SNMP manager will receive those trap messages that match its trap community name.

The current SNMP standard, version 1, has significant limitations. Perhaps most significant is that community names are not encrypted as they are transmitted. As a result, anyone snooping the network with a protocol analyzer can learn the community names and gain access to considerable information about the network as well as gain the capability to manage network devices.

SNMP version 2 (RFC 1441 – 1452) is a proposed standard that encrypts messages to enhance security. SNMP improves the ability of the manager to retrieve network data by providing commands to retrieve entire tables without the need to read the table one record at a time with the GetNextRequest command.

NetWare SNMP Agents and Managers

Novell has designed SNMP agent capability into a variety of products. LAN Workgroup and LAN WorkPlace include SNMP agent software, as do NetWare 3 and NetWare 4 servers. The NetWare MultiProtocol router also incorporates an SNMP agent.

Basic SNMP management consoles in NetWare products include LWPCON in LAN WorkPlace for DOS, and TCPCON in NetWare 3 and 4. The NetWare Management System (NMS) is a full-featured, extensible SNMP management console that is available separately.

NetWare SNMP agents and managers will be examined in detail in Chapter 11 (Managing NetWare TCP/IP).

SIMPLE MAIL TRANSFER PROTOCOL

If the majority of Internet users were to name the application that they use most frequently, it would almost certainly be electronic mail. The protocol that supports Internet e-mail is the Simple Mail Transfer Protocol (SMTP), defined in RFCs 821 and 822. Generally speaking, users do not interface directly with SMTP. Access is generally gained through a *mail transfer agent* (MTA). The relationship between SMTP and MTAs is described in the following section.

Architecture of TCP/IP E-Mail

Figure 6.16 shows the relationships of the components of a TCP/IP electronic mail system. Overall management of messages is the responsibility of an MTA running on an e-mail server (also called a *mail exchanger*). The MTA performs three functions:

- ▸ Providing an interface that enables users and applications to interact with the mail system

- ▸ Sending and receiving messages

- ▸ Forwarding messages between mail servers

MTAs communicate with one another using the SNMP protocol.

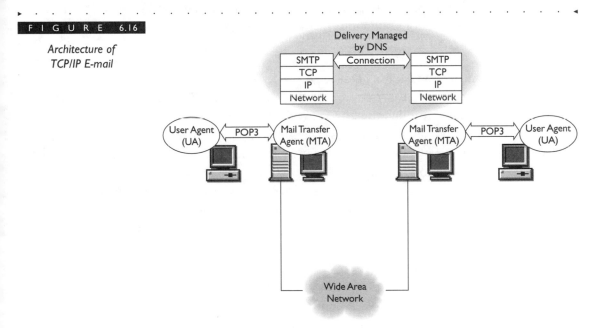

FIGURE 6.16

Architecture of TCP/IP E-mail

The familiar Internet e-mail addresses, such as GOOBER@foobar.com, are provided by MTAs. DNS does not know anything about GOOBER, but it does know about foobar.com. Also, DNS knows the addresses of mail exchangers that are running the MTAs that service the foobar.com domain. The division of labor is as follows:

▶ DNS delivers messages between mail exchangers. DNS maintains a directory of host names and of mail exchangers servicing a domain.

▶ Mail exchangers receive messages from user client software and enable user clients to receive messages.

End users interact with MTAs via *user agents* (UAs), which communicate with the MTA using a mail protocol such as the Post Office Protocol Version 3 (POP3; RFC 1460). Several UAs are available, but perhaps the best-known UA in the UNIX world is Eudora, although many e-mail packages can now interact with SNMP mail systems.

Internetwork Mail Delivery

Unlike data that support applications such as FTP and Telnet, e-mail data are not routed through the internetwork in real-time. E-mail routing is designed to be able to transfer high volumes of data in a reasonable period of time while minimizing the impact on network performance. The Internet delivers a lot of e-mail. If all of it traveled at top priority, the Internet would quickly be overwhelmed.

E-mail is transferred using a store-and-forward technique, illustrated in Figure 6.17. In this figure, mail exchanger 2 (MX2) is forwarding messages between MX1 and MX3. To improve efficiency, MX2 may wait until it has several messages to send to MX3, storing waiting messages on a hard drive until the data volume justifies opening a connection. MX2 might also improve efficiency by waiting until the network is quiet before transmitting, to minimize its impact on network performance. If messages in MX2 have waited more than a specified time, MX2 may be configured to send the messages even if the message volume is below the configured threshold. The goal is to produce a compromise between timeliness and network traffic impact.

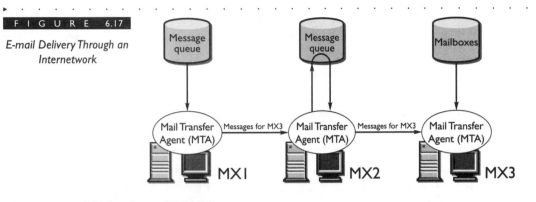

F I G U R E   6.17

*E-mail Delivery Through an
Internetwork*

Limitations of SMTP

SMTP grew up in the days when terminals were text only and when the fact that you could send electronic mail at all was pretty cool. Today, e-mail is referred to as *messaging*, and all sorts of data are riding on e-mail that were undreamed of in 1982 when SMTP became a standard. Voice, graphics, and even video are becoming part of the electronic messaging picture.

SMTP still has a few limitations, though. Because SMTP was designed around 7-bit ASCII text, we need to tap dance a bit to send binary data this way. The binary data must be encoded so that it fits into 7-bit ASCII messages. For UNIX, this typically involves a coding scheme called uuencode (UNIX-UNIX encode) to build the messages and the companion uudecode to recover the original binary data.

The Multipurpose Internet Mail Extensions (MIME; RFC 1521) are an elective Internet protocol that enables SMTP to carry non-text messages. Many e-mail packages for DOS and Windows support uuencode and MIME.

Another limitation of SMTP is that all messages are sent in open text. Security just wasn't a priority when the Internet was more a friendly community of users than a way to do business electronically that it has become. If you need to send sensitive data via SMTP, the data files should be encrypted.

NETWORK FILE SYSTEM

You've learned about FTP, which permits you to transfer files and manage remote file systems. And you've learned about Telnet, which lets you enter a remote terminal session with a remote host. But let's consider other activities. Suppose a remote computer has the files for a program that you want to run on your local computer. Or you want to place a spreadsheet file in a common location so that users can open it and enter their sales data. Neither of these scenarios presents any problem for NetWare. You simply store the files on a volume of the server, give users the required rights, and *voilá*, the files are shared. Users don't need to run FTP, retrieve the files, and FTP them back when the job is done. With NetWare, a shared file works like a local file, but it can be a local file for hundreds of users.

In the TCP/IP environment, the product that enables file volumes to be shared is the Network File System (NFS), developed by Sun Microsystems. An NFS server can export part of its directory tree. The exported directories can be mounted on NFS client workstations where they function as part of the local file system. A DOS user accessing files shared by a UNIX NFS server will perceive the shared directories and files as though they were stored using the DOS FAT file system. Figure 6.18 shows how NFS works.

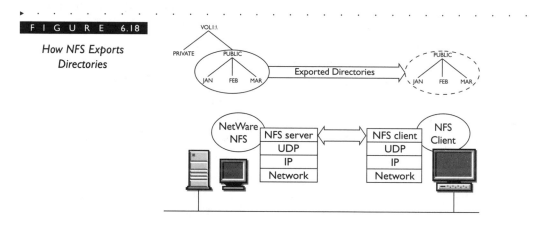

FIGURE 6.18

How NFS Exports Directories

Novell offers three NFS products for NetWare servers:

- ▸ **NetWare NFS.** This product enables NetWare 3.11 and 3.12 servers to provide NFS services. It adds an NFS name space to the NetWare server, enabling DOS, Macintosh, OS/2, and NFS clients to access the NetWare file system.

- ▸ **NetWare NFS Gateway.** This product enables NetWare clients to access remote NFS servers without requiring the clients to run NFS client software. Standard NetWare procedures may be used to access files on NFS servers.

▸ **NetWare NFS Services — NetWare 4 Edition.** This NFS server for the NetWare 4 environment supports NetWare Directory Services in NetWare 4.01 and later versions. NetWare NFS Services includes the NetWare NFS Gateway, FTP server, X-Windows, Line Printer Daemon to support UNIX printing, and much more.

The NetWare LAN WorkPlace and LAN WorkGroup products also include NFS client software for use in the DOS and Windows environments.

That's It for Theory

You now know the theory behind the complete TCP/IP architecture. You have seen how:

▸ The network access layer enables nodes to communicate.

▸ The internet layer extends communication throughout the internetwork.

▸ The host-to-host layer makes communications reliable and handles message fragmentation and reassembly.

▸ The process/application layer enables users to take advantage of the services that the lower layers provide.

The time has come to put theory into practice. In other words, you are about to put TCP/IP into action on your NetWare network. First, I'll tell you a bit about how Novell has implemented TCP/IP, and then we'll move on to the fun stuff. Just one more (short, I promise) chapter of background information, and then it's hands-on!

## PART II

Implementing Netware TCP/IP

## CHAPTER 7

Introducing NetWare TCP/IP

NetWare TCP/IP isn't really a product. I've used the expression in this book as a catch-all for the complete set of TCP/IP connectivity features that are available in the NetWare product line. Many NetWare products have built-in TCP/IP features. For example, NetWare 3.12 and 4.1 servers include everything you need to install a TCP/IP protocol stack on a NetWare server. And TCP/IP protocol support is included with several NetWare clients, enabling a variety of workstations to access NetWare and TCP/IP services.

But, as you have learned in the foregoing chapters, it isn't enough simply to enable hosts to exchange TCP/IP datagrams. Unless processes and applications are part of the picture, you really don't have a working network. That's where a lot of other NetWare products come in. Here are a few examples:

▸ LAN Workplace for DOS includes a variety of TCP/IP applications that enable users to access TCP/IP services, including FTP, Telnet, Gopher, and Netscape.

▸ FLeX/IP enables NetWare servers to function as FTP servers.

▸ NetWare NFS Services enables UNIX clients to access NetWare volumes that are shared using NFS.

▸ NetWare UNIX Print Services enables UNIX clients to print through NetWare-managed printers.

You will learn more about these and other TCP/IP-related products later in this chapter. Before cutting to the chase, however, you need to know the background plot: How do all the components of NetWare TCP/IP fit together? To get that part of the story, we need to look at the NetWare protocol architecture: Open Datalink Interface.

Open Datalink Interface

The OSI Reference Model and the DoD protocol model are just that: models. They present a general picture of network protocol stacks, but they do not describe specific implementations of the protocols. In other words, they don't tell you how a particular vendor has implemented the protocols in specific hardware and software modules.

One of the theoretical justifications for layered models is that different protocols can be plugged into different layers with a minimum of fuss. When vendors seek to develop a protocol environment that can integrate multiple protocol stacks, they must turn the theory into reality, and that turns out to be a bit complicated.

Novell's architecture for enabling NetWare servers and clients to flexibly support multiple protocol stacks is called Open Datalink Interface (ODI). As you will see, ODI enables NetWare servers to mix a variety of protocols and network interfaces, providing the flexibility required on a multi-protocol, enterprise internetwork. Because NetWare TCP/IP networks are typically multi-protocol networks, you need to understand how the parts of ODI fit together to grasp how protocols on your LAN are interrelated.

ODI LAYERS

Figure 7.1 illustrates the ODI model, filled in with some protocols that NetWare supports. As you can see, the ODI architecture enables NetWare to support three protocol stacks (IPX, TCP/IP, and AppleTalk), which in turn support three classes of services.

FIGURE 7.1

The ODI Model

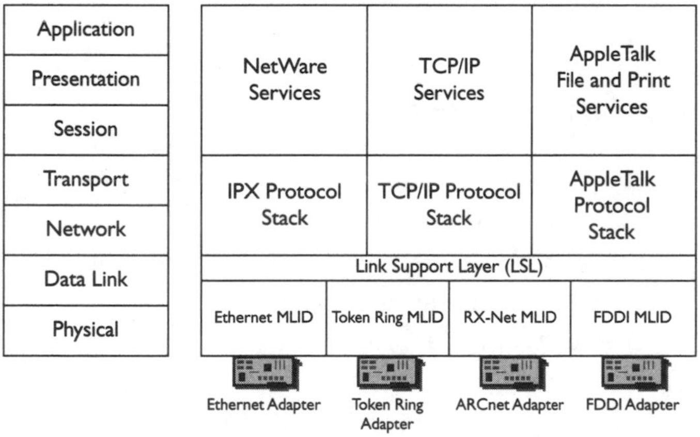

Anyone who has spent time managing a NetWare server has had to load and unload NetWare Loadable Modules (NLSs), the building blocks used to add features to NetWare 3 and 4 servers. Each box in Figure 7.1 corresponds roughly to an NLM loaded automatically or manually on a server. To start the TCP/IP protocols running on the server, for example, you load a TCP/IP NLM that consists of the file TCPIP.NLM. As you load modules on a server, or start drivers on a workstation, you can think in terms of where in the ODI model those modules and drivers fit. Let's start at the bottom of the figure and examine the layers.

Network Hardware

At the bottom of the model is the physical hardware, the network interface board or other communications hardware that enables the server to communicate with the outside. This hardware is not formally part of the ODI model, any more than Layer 0 is a part of the OSI Reference Model that was introduced in Chapter 2. But the hardware must be included in the picture to illustrate ODI's ability to link a given upper-layer protocol stack to given network hardware.

NetWare network drivers are able to support multiple network boards in a given computer. Why would you want to do that? With multiple network boards, you could segment your network to control traffic flow. Alternatively, you could connect your network to another network, which may or may not be the same network type as yours.

NetWare servers are particularly adept at supporting multiple LAN adapters and can handle as many as four. Any NetWare server that is connected to two or more network adapters is able to function as a router, forwarding network traffic between different attached networks.

Multiple Link Interface Drivers (MLIDs)

The next layer up the ODI model provides the software that enables upper-layer protocols to communicate with the network hardware. From the top of the model, all MLIDs look alike. At the bottom, each MLID provides a custom fit to a particular make and model of network board. This capability is the key feature that enables NetWare servers to mix and match network hardware.

The MLID completely isolates upper-layer protocols from the network hardware. IPX has no idea whether it is running over an Ethernet network or an FDDI network. As far as IPX is concerned, the network is irrelevant.

MLIDs must be able to support multiple network boards of the same type and multiple frame types. Think back to Chapters 2 through 6 and you will remember that protocol multiplexing is an important activity as message units travel up and down the protocol stack. At the MLID layer, protocol multiplexing is required to enable messages with different frame types to travel through the same MLID and the appropriate network interface. MLIDs have to be able to keep the various message streams sorted out.

Supporting Multiple Network Interfaces   When, as in Figure 7.2, a NetWare server needs to support two or more network interfaces that use the same driver, it can use a neat trick called *reentrant loading,* which enables the server to reuse the program code in an MLID. For example, suppose that a server has two NE2000 network adapters. The first time you load the NE2000.LAN network driver software, the driver program is loaded into memory. The second time you load the NE2000.LAN driver, NetWare is able to reuse the program that was loaded previously. This bit of programming magic uses memory more efficiently than loading the module two or more times.

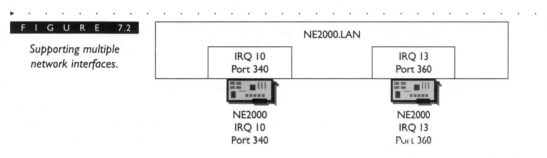

FIGURE 7.2

Supporting multiple network interfaces.

The MLID must have a way to direct message units to the appropriate network board. This is done by identifying each board with unique interface parameters. At the least, these parameters will consist of a unique interrupt (IRQ) and a unique I/O address (called a *port*) for each board. Each time the MLID module is loaded, it is loaded with a unique set of interface parameters that enables it to keep the various network boards sorted out.

Supporting Multiple Frame Types   Chapter 3 demonstrated that many types of networks support multiple frame types. Nowhere is this more evident than with Ethernet. NetWare supports no less than four Ethernet frame types and two token ring frame types. The Ethernet frame types are:

▸ **ETHERNET_II.** The original Ethernet frame type and still the champion on TCP/IP networks.

▸ **ETHERNET_802.2.** A frame type that fully complies with IEEE 802 specifications.

▸ **ETHERNET_802.3.** A frame type that Novell developed before the IEEE 802.2 specification was nailed down. Although this frame type is still available on all NetWare platforms, it is not recommended.

▸ **ETHERNET_SNAP.** The IEEE 802.2-compliant Ethernet frame type with SNAP encapsulation to support TCP/IP and other SNAP-compliant protocols.

NetWare also supports two token ring frame types:

▸ **TOKEN-RING.** The standard token ring frame type used in most environments.

▸ **TOKEN-RING_SNAP.** Token ring with SNAP encapsulation for use with TCP/IP and AppleTalk.

Many other frame types are supported for other network interfaces, but the above examples illustrate the problem faced by NetWare. If messages with several frame types are arriving from a single network through a single network adapter, NetWare must be able to send the appropriate frame type to the appropriate upper-level protocols.

This is accomplished by creating *virtual network adapters.* A given network adapter, identified by its IRQ and I/O address, is virtualized by identifying each virtual adapter with a frame type. Figure 7.3 illustrates an MLID that is maintaining two physical adapters, which are installed as four virtual adapters. Each virtual adapter is identified by a combination of an IRQ, a port, and a frame type. For any given MLID, these identifiers must be unique. Therefore, you can't load the same driver with the same parameters more than once.

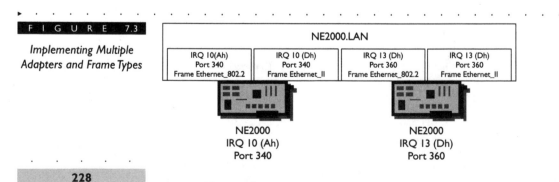

FIGURE 7.3

Implementing Multiple Adapters and Frame Types

Loading MLIDs on the Server   Server MLIDs are found in NLM files that have a LAN filename extension. Like all NLMs, the MLIDs are installed on the server with the LOAD command. Parameters entered on the command line specify the unique network board hardware characteristics as well as the frame type. Here is an example of a LOAD command for an NE2000 network board:

```
LOAD NE2000 INT=A PORT=340 FRAME=ETHERNET_802.2
```

Because each virtual network board must be unique, the same LOAD command can be entered only once on a given server.

To provide a shorthand for referring to a specific virtual network board, each is typically given a name, which is assigned with a NAME parameter in the LOAD command as in this example:

```
LOAD NE2000 NAME=NE2000_1_E82 INT=A PORT=340 FRAME=ETHERNET_802.2
```

Although you can name your boards any way you wish, the above example follows the convention of a three-part name:

▸ The name of the board driver

▸ A number identifying each board of that type. If the NE2000 driver is loaded for a different hardware adapter, the second adapter will be board 2.

▸ A shorthand for the frame type. E82 is, for example, shorthand for the ETHERNET_802.2 frame type.

The Link Support Layer

Take another look at Figure 7.1. Above the MLIDs is the Link Support Layer (LSL). The LSL acts as a switch, performing protocol multiplexing to ensure that the appropriate message units from the various MLIDs are directed to the appropriate upper-layer protocols. When MLIDs and upper-layer protocols are loaded, they register with the LSL, which assigns a logical identifier to each MLID and protocol stack. The LSL uses these logical identifiers to route incoming data from an MLID to the appropriate protocol stack, or to route outgoing data from a protocol stack to the correct MLID.

A given upper-layer protocol stack is associated with a given virtual network adapter through a process called *binding*. For example, a binding might declare that the frame type Ethernet_II loaded on adapter NE2000 number 2 will be associated with the IP protocol.

Recall from the discussion in Chapter 2 that the OSI network layer identifies each network using a unique network identifier. The situation is a bit more complicated in reality, because many MLIDs can support two or more frame types. The LSL's life is complicated by the need to route data between a given frame type in a given MLID to the appropriate protocol stack.

When ODI prepares a frame for the network, a protocol ID (PID) is appended to the start of the frame. The 6-byte PID identifies the frame type and the communication protocol that the frame encapsulates. For example, a PID of 8137h identifies an Ethernet II frame containing IPX data. A PID of 800h identifies a frame with IP data. These PID values are used by the LSL to route data to the correct protocols and MLIDs, which are identified by the registration tables the LSL maintains. The result is that, although you may be able to see only one network cable, that cable may be supporting two or more *virtual networks*. Let's see how virtual networks work.

Virtual Networks To deliver frames to the correct virtual LAN adapter, each adapter/protocol combination must be identified. As far as NetWare is concerned, each virtual LAN adapter is connected to a separate network cabling system. Each of these networks is identified by a *network number,* which is specified when the adapter is loaded. Although the IRQ, port, and frame parameters are utilized within the MLID, outside the MLID, the virtual network is identified by a network number that is unique within the entire internetwork. All NetWare servers that connect to this virtual network must identify the virtual network with the same network ID.

Figure 7.4 illustrates a network that consists of a single LAN cable segment. As far as NetWare is concerned, this physical network consists of three networks, associated with the Ethernet II, Ethernet 802.3, and Ethernet 802.2 frame types. Here is how the network functions from the perspective of each of the servers:

> ► NetWare server A (a NetWare 2 server) is connected to the Ethernet 802.3 virtual network.

▸ NetWare server B (a NetWare 3 server) is connected to the Ethernet 802.2 virtual network.

▸ NetWare server C (a NetWare 4 server) is connected to all three virtual networks.

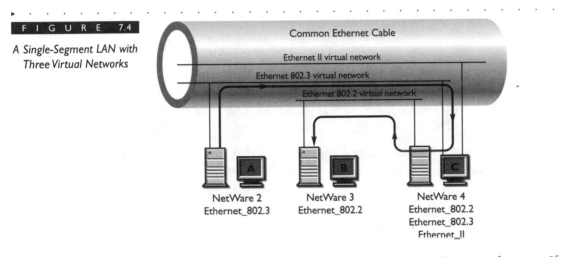

FIGURE 7.4

A Single-Segment LAN with Three Virtual Networks

Server C is the hub of the virtual network, serving as an IPX protocol router. If server A needs to communicate with server B, frames must be routed through server C. Even though A and B are attached to the same network cable, they cannot talk directly because they are using different frame types and therefore exist on different virtual networks.

Binding Protocols to Networks   Before a protocol may be bound to a network, two conditions must be met:

▸ An MLID must be loaded that defines a virtual network adapter for the physical adapter and frame type that will be used.

▸ The upper-layer protocol stack must be loaded.

By default, the IPX protocol stack is always loaded on a NetWare server, and no manual intervention is required on the part of the LAN administrator. However, NetWare supports two other upper-layer protocol stacks: TCP/IP and AppleTalk. The NLMs that support TCP/IP and AppleTalk must be explicitly loaded before the protocols can be bound to a network adapter. This is accomplished with a LOAD statement such as:

```
LOAD TCPIP
```

Now that the network adapters and protocols are defined, a binding can take place. Here is a complete sequence:

```
LOAD TCPIP
LOAD NE2000 NET=NE2000_1_EII FRAME=ETHERNET_II INT=A PORT=340
BIND IP NE2000_1_EII ARP=YES MASK=FF.FF.0.0 ADDRESS=128.1.0.1
```

Figure 7.5 illustrates the logical path that this command sequence establishes. Notice that the protocol being bound is IP, the lowest-level protocol in the TCP/IP protocol stack. The meaning of each parameter may already be clear to you if you have followed the discussion in the preceding chapters. Chapter 8 will examine the parameters in greater detail.

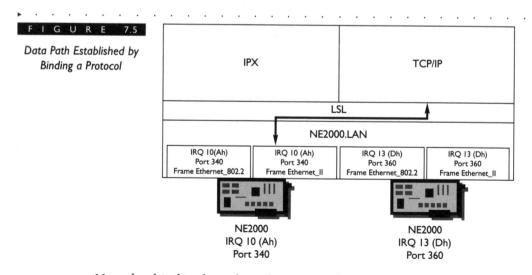

Data Path Established by Binding a Protocol

Now that binding has taken place, upper-layer processes can communicate with the network through the various network protocol layers.

UPPER-LAYER PROCESSES

NetWare supports three protocol stacks: IPX, TCP/IP, and AppleTalk. Specific upper-layer processes are associated with each protocol stack. As a result, users who access NetWare servers function in distinct process environments depending on the protocol stack that is employed. Figure 7.6 illustrates how upper-layer processes are supported for each protocol stack.

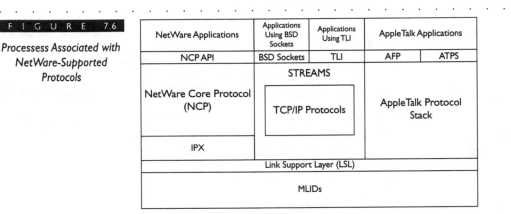

F I G U R E   7.6

Processess Associated with NetWare-Supported Protocols

For the IPX protocol stack, upper-layer processing is supported by the NetWare Core Protocol (NCP). The NCP provides all of the services traditionally made available to users by NetWare servers, including creating and releasing connections, directory and file services, NetWare Directory Services, and printing. NCP is the default NetWare service protocol and is loaded automatically on the server.

As included with NetWare server products, the TCP/IP protocols enable communications but provide little in the way of network services. Novell offers a variety of add-in software products that can be installed on a server to provide services over TCP/IP. Those products are described in the next section. TCP/IP protocol support has been included on all NetWare server platforms since NetWare 3.11, and it ships with NetWare 3.12 and NetWare 4.1.

NetWare TCP/IP supports two application program interfaces (APIs). 4.3 BSD Sockets is the widely used API popularized by BSD UNIX. Transport Layer Interface (TLI) is an API developed by AT&T. This choice of APIs provides developers with many options when porting programs to the NetWare environment. Figure 7.6 illustrates the NetWare API architecture. Both TCP/IP APIs are supported by the Streams interface, which provides a uniform interface to the transport layer protocols.

AppleTalk has its own upper-layer services. On a NetWare server, AppleTalk services are supported by two protocols: the AppleTalk Filing Protocol (AFP) and the AppleTalk Print Services (ATPS). These protocols enable users of AppleTalk-based computers to access files and printers on NetWare servers and are included with NetWare 3.12 and 4.1.

NetWare TCP/IP Products

NetWare 3.12 and 4.1 servers include modules that support the TCP/IP protocol stack. These protocols do not provide any network services, however, and meaningful connectivity requires add-in products. The remainder of this chapter examines the various products offered by Novell and discusses the place of each in the overall connectivity picture.

NETWARE NFS

The Network File System (NFS), developed by Sun Microsystems, is the de facto technology that enables TCP/IP hosts to share their resources on the network. NFS was described in Chapter 6 (The Process/Application Layer). Novell offers a variety of products that provide NFS connectivity:

- **NetWare NFS** enables NetWare servers to share files with UNIX and other NFS hosts. Novell's NFS technology works by providing an NFS *name space* on the NetWare server. Name spaces enable NetWare server file systems to masquerade as the file systems that are native to different end-user operating systems. By default, NetWare provides a name space that is compatible with MS-DOS. By loading additional name spaces, the same files can be provided under Macintosh, OS/2, and NFS name spaces.

- **NetWare NFS Services — NetWare 4 Edition** provides NFS name space support within the NetWare Directory Services environment of NetWare 4 along with a variety of other TCP/IP services. Among the services provided are:

- NFS version 2, enabling the server to share files with NFS clients.

- File Transfer Protocol, enabling a NetWare server to be an FTP server.

- Line Printer Daemon (LPD) protocol, enabling UNIX hosts to print through NetWare-managed printers.

- X Windows System support, enabling the server to function as an X Windows client. X Windows is a graphic user environment commonly employed in UNIX environments.

- VT100/200 terminal access to XCONSOLE.

- Domain Name Service, enabling a NetWare server to be a DNS name server.

- **NetWare NFS Gateway** enables NetWare IPX clients to access files that are stored on NFS servers.

NETWARE FLEX/IP

NetWare FleX/IP provides a more limited UNIX-to-NetWare connectivity solution than the various NetWare NFS products. FleX/IP enables NetWare servers to support the following:

- File Transfer Protocol, enabling the NetWare server to be an FTP server.

- Line Printer Daemon (LPD) protocol, enabling UNIX hosts to print to NetWare printers.

- X Windows System support, enabling administrators to manage NetWare servers through the X Windows interface of a UNIX host.

- VT100/200 terminal access to XCONSOLE.

LAN WORKPLACE AND LAN WORKGROUP

Some releases of NetWare client software (the protocol software running on the user workstation) include support for TCP/IP. However, this protocol support, like basic NetWare server TCP/IP protocol support, does not provide access to TCP/IP services. When NetWare DOS-based clients need access to TCP/IP services, turn to the LAN WorkPlace and LAN WorkGroup products. These products enable NetWare users to access NetWare and TCP/IP services simultaneously.

Both packages enable users of NetWare DOS and Windows clients to access a variety of TCP/IP services, including FTP, e-mail, NFS, and X Windows. The products also include a variety of Internet utilities such as the Netscape's Web browser and a Telnet client.

LAN Workplace is administered individually on each network workstation. Organizations that are heavily dependent on TCP/IP will probably choose the LAN WorkGroup product, which enables administrators to manage NetWare TCP/IP clients centrally. LAN WorkGroup software is installed on a NetWare server, and it is not necessary to install the software on each server.

In addition, LAN WorkGroup supports central administration of workstation TCP/IP configurations. Workstations can be assigned IP addresses dynamically rather than from static configuration files, greatly simplifying the task network administrators face when workstations move around the corporate internetwork.

LAN WorkPlace and LAN WorkGroup are discussed in detail in Chapter 9 (Installing TCP/IP on NetWare Clients).

NETWARE/IP

The network options we have looked at so far require that a NetWare network support two protocols: IPX/SPX for clients accessing NetWare services and TCP/IP for clients accessing TCP/IP services. Although Novell has made it possible to run both protocol stacks on NetWare servers and clients, some organizations want to boil down their protocol support to a single protocol, TCP/IP.

NetWare/IP eliminates IPX/SPX, enabling clients to access NetWare services using only the TCP/IP protocol stack. This makes it possible to construct a network that provides TCP/IP and NetWare services in a single-protocol environment. NetWare/IP also can be used as a gateway between TCP/IP and IPX networks.

NetWare/IP is examined in greater detail in Chapter 12 (NetWare/IP).

Let's Get Going

I promised this chapter would be short and (protocol) suite. Now, at last, you are ready to put theory into practice. The next two chapters focus on installing TCP/IP protocol support on NetWare servers and clients.

## CHAPTER 8

Implementing TCP/IP on NetWare Servers

Before any TCP/IP services can be installed on a NetWare server, the TCP/IP protocol stack must be configured and activated. When activating TCP/IP, you will find that 50 percent of your work will be in the planning phase, 40 percent will be configuration, and only about 10 percent will involve actually entering commands on the server. So, be prepared to be prepared. You can't just turn on TCP/IP like a light switch.

The first part of this chapter covers planning. You will discover that there are many issues that must be addressed such as planning addresses and host names. We will examine those issues, make some decisions, and fill in some planning forms that will guide the rest of the process.

The second part covers configuration. You will learn about the various files that are used to store TCP/IP configuration information. This chapter will examine a fairly basic configuration that ultimately will include two LAN segments and a single router. Chapter 10 (Internetworking NetWare TCP/IP) will extend the discussion to include more complex routed internetworks.

The final part covers activation. This section discusses how to load the TCP/IP protocols and bind them to network adapters. After completing this step, your NetWare server will be ready to talk TCP/IP.

Planning

I have addressed many of the implementation planning issues in earlier chapters, but now it is time to get real and plan an actual LAN. Here are the planning tasks that will be examined:

- ▸ Planning IP addressing

- ▸ Planning host names

- ▸ Planning the server hardware configuration

- ▸ Planning frame types and bindings

None of these tasks is terribly difficult on a single-segment LAN, but it is useful to see how the entire process works before getting into more complex cases. To illustrate the planning process, we will build a network for a hypothetical company, May's Berry Farm, a purveyor of fine fruit preserves. Management of this small company has set the following goals:

1 • The network's primary file services will be provided by a NetWare file server.

2 • The network will eventually obtain an Internet connection so that it can offer a Web server.

3 • The Web server will be run locally for now, functioning as a company bulletin board.

4 • Users will access the network using DOS/Windows clients.

At present, the following employees need to use the network:

▸ Drew, the president

▸ Blythe, manufacturing manager

▸ Woody, security

▸ Cyd, corporate communications

▸ Lauren, product testing

Figure 8.1 illustrates the network configuration, which consists of five workstations, a NetWare 4.1 server, and a UNIX host running the Web server software. Our task is to plan and implement the protocols on the network. Workstation installation will be covered in Chapter 9. In this chapter, we will configure and activate TCP/IP on the NetWare server.

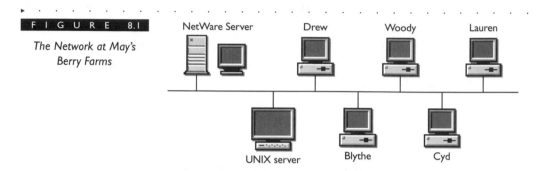

F I G U R E   8.1

The Network at May's
Berry Farms

PLANNING IP ADDRESSING

The first decision you need to make is whether you want to attach your network to the Internet any time within the next few years. Even class C addresses are getting scarce. If you are attaching now, or even think you might want to, obtain enough registered addresses to support your network. Because our network will soon be connected to the Internet, a registered address will be obtained.

> **WARNING**
>
> **The addresses used in the examples in this book are selected at random and may already be registered. You should not attempt to use them on your own LAN unless it is isolated from the Internet.**

If you will be connecting through a commercial Internet access provider, as is more often the case these days, the InterNIC expects you to obtain addresses from your service provider, which has been assigned blocks of IP addresses for use by their customers. If you will be connecting through another organization's network, you will need to register an IP address directly with the InterNIC Registration Services. Here is the contact information:

> Network Solutions
> InterNIC Registration Services
> 505 Huntmar Park Drive
> Herndon, VA 22070
> hostmaster@internic.net

Registration forms are available through the various resources described in Chapter 1. If you will never connect to the Internet, you have the luxury of selecting your own IP addresses. Go ahead, be a big shot and configure your office with a class A address. Why not?!

Now that you have an IP address, you need to decide whether your network will require subnetting. If the network will be segmented by routers, and you will have more segments than IP addresses, subnetting is a necessity. But you may want to plan for subnetting in the future even if you won't be subnetting now. To make your network subnetting easy to reconfigure, assign hostids starting with the low-order (rightmost) bits of the hostid field. For a class B address, you should begin assigning hostids in the following order:

```
00000000 00000001      0.1
00000000 00000010      0.2
00000000 00000011      0.3
00000000 00000100      0.4
```

...and so on. If you will be employing subnets, number your subnets from left to right. Again looking at a class B address, you would create subnets in the following order:

```
10000000 00000000      128.0
01000000 00000000      64.0
11000000 00000000      192.0
00100000 00000000      32.0
01100000 00000000      96.0
11100000 00000000      224.0
```

This approach creates a buffer of unassigned bits in the center of the hostid field. You have considerable freedom to add or remove bits from the subnetid field without running into bits that are already assigned as parts of existing subnetids or hostids. Yes, you have to change the subnet masks on your hosts, but the IP addresses you have assigned remain valid.

Figure 8.2 shows the example network, including the IP addresses that will be assigned to each host. You might find it convenient to reserve a few low hostids you can easily remember to identify servers and other hosts you need to access frequently.

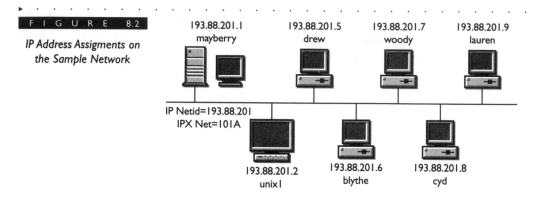

FIGURE   8.2

IP Address Assigments on the Sample Network

193.88.201.1 mayberry

193.88.201.5 drew

193.88.201.7 woody

193.88.201.9 lauren

IP Netid=193.88.201
IPX Net=101A

193.88.201.2 unix1

193.88.201.6 blythe

193.88.201.8 cyd

PLANNING HOST NAMES

Host names make the network easier to use and are required in some instances. Each host can be assigned a name along with up to ten aliases. Aliases are handy if the primary names are lengthy — if, for example, they are fully qualified domain names. Here are the IP addresses, host names, and aliases that will be configured in our example:

193.88.201.1	fs1.mayberry.com mayberry fs1
193.88.201.2	www.mayberry.com www unix1
193.88.201.5	drew.mayberry.com drew ws1 pres
193.88.201.6	blythe.mayberry.com blythe ws2 manuf
193.88.201.7	woody.mayberry.com woody ws3 security
193.88.201.8	cyd.mayberry.com cyd ws4 corpcom
193.88.201.9	lauren.mayberry.com lauren ws5 testing

Use of aliases clearly provides considerable flexibility, enabling you to identify hosts by function, location, primary user, and by other characteristics as well. Some, such as the ws names will be useful for network administrators. Others provide alternative names for users.

Next, you must decide how naming information will be made available. For a small network such as this, you might choose to use static HOSTS files. However, because the goal is to eventually connect to the Internet, this is a good time to contemplate establishing a name server.

The UNIX host is an ideal platform for the name server. BIND, by far the most popular DNS implementation, is widely and freely available for most UNIX platforms. If a pre-compiled version is not available for your UNIX server, you may need to acquire a copy of the BIND source code and compile it for your system. If you are unfamiliar with compiling C programs, you should be able to find a consultant who can provide the service for a fee.

Another choice is to install NetWare/IP on the NetWare server and use the DNS server that is included with that product. Chapter 12 will explore NetWare/IP and show you how to set up a name server.

If you will be configuring your hosts to obtain names from a name server, you will need to configure each host with the IP address of the name server. For our example, we will assume that the name server will be the UNIX host with the IP address 193.88.201.2.

Your network will be using a DNS name service. Should you go to the trouble of creating static HOSTS files as well? It might not be a bad idea. If you are running a single name server and the name server is down for any reason, your users can use HOSTS files to resolve names. If you are on the Internet, your local HOSTS files won't enable outside users to continue to resolve your domain names, but HOSTS files enable your local users to continue to function locally. Therefore, static HOSTS files that list at least the most critical hosts may be a good safety precaution.

PLANNING THE SERVER HARDWARE CONFIGURATION

The only hardware characteristic that concerns us in this chapter is the type of network adapter along with its hardware settings. You need to record the hardware settings of all your adapters, including IRQs, port addresses, and so forth. The adapter in the server has the following characteristics:

- Driver: NE2000.LAN

- IRQ:Bh (11 decimal)

- Port: 340h

PLANNING FRAME TYPES AND BINDINGS

Because the NetWare server will support both IPX and TCP/IP protocols, two protocol stacks must be bound to the NE2000 adapter. For IPX, the Ethernet_802.2 frame type will be used. NetWare TCP/IP is most commonly configured with the

Ethernet_II frame type, although Ethernet_SNAP may also be used. Ethernet II frames are required for the Internet, however, so that is the correct choice for this network. Each of these frame types will be assigned a name when it is loaded. The names chosen follow Novell's conventions:

- NE2000_1_E82 will be associated with the Ethernet_802.2 frame type

- NE2000_1_EII will be associated with the Ethernet_II frame type

The first part of the name (NE2000) is taken from the name of the LAN driver. The number (1 in this case) indicates that this is the first LAN adapter to be loaded. Finally, E82 and EII indicate the frame type.

Configuration

Some features of TCP/IP are configured by entering data into database files that are stored in the directory SYS:ETC. The files are:

- SYS:ETC\HOSTS

- SYS:ETC\NETWORKS

- SYS:ETC\GATEWAYS

- SYS:ETC\PROTOCOL

- SYS:ETC\SERVICES

When NetWare is installed, samples of these files are placed in the SYS:ETC\SAMPLES directory. Although you could create your own files from scratch, it is easier to use the sample files as templates. Some of the sample files may be used with little or no alteration. Before you begin to create the configuration database files for your network, copy the sample files from SYS:ETC\SAMPLES to SYS:ETC. All of the database files are simply text files that may be edited with any text editor.

The following sections will examine each of the configuration files along with any modifications required for the example network.

SYS:ETC\HOSTS

The HOSTS file associates IP addresses with host names and aliases. The sample HOSTS file illustrates the file format:

```
#
# SYS:ETC\HOSTS
#
#   Mappings of host names and host aliases to IP address.
#
127.0.0.1  loopback lb localhost # normal loopback address

#
# examples from Novell network
#
130.57.4.2     ta tahiti ta.novell.com loghost
130.57.6.40    osd-frog frog
130.57.6.144   sj-in5 in5
192.67.172.71 sj-in1 in1

#
# interesting addresses on the Internet
#
192.67.67.20   sri-nic.arpa nic.ddn.mil nic
26.2.0.74      wsmr-simtel20.army.mil simtel20
```

An entry in a HOSTS file has the following format:

```
ipaddress hostname [alias1] [alias2] [alias10] #comment
```

Each field must be separated from the next by at least one space or tab character. The *ipaddress* is the IP address of the host, which is ordinarily expressed in dotted decimal form. It can also be stated in dotted-hexadecimal. Using dotted-hex, the IP address 193.88.201.2 would be 0xC3.0x58.0xC9.0x2.

The *hostname* is a name for the system that owns the IP address. Host names cannot contain space, tab, or # characters. The *alias* is simply a nickname that may be used in place of the host name. Aliases follow the same character rules as host names and up to ten aliases may be specified. Host names and aliases must be unique within the HOSTS file. In other words, a given host name or alias must not be associated with more than one IP address.

A # character indicates the beginning of a comment. Any text between the # and the carriage return/line feed characters at the end of the line will be ignored.

Here is the HOSTS file for the MAYBERRY server:

```
#
# SYS:ETC\HOSTS
#
#IP Address        HOSTNAME              Aliases
127.0.0.1          loopback              lb localhost

193.88.201.1       fs1.mayberry.com      mayberry fs1
193.88.201.2       www.mayberry.com      www unix1
193.88.201.5       drew.mayberry.com     drew ws1 pres
193.88.201.6       blythe.mayberry.com   blythe ws2 manuf
193.88.201.7       woody.mayberry.com    woody ws3 security
193.88.201.8       cyd.mayberry.com      cyd ws4 corpcom
193.88.201.9       lauren.mayberry.com   lauren ws5 testing
```

NOTE

The HOSTS file conventionally includes an entry for the address 127.0.0.1, which is used for testing host TCP/IP configurations. Any datagrams sent to address 127.0.0.1 are reflected back and do not reach the network. This looping back demonstrates that lower-level protocol layers are properly configured and functioning.

The same HOSTS file may be used on all of the TCP/IP hosts on your network. You may wish to configure users' login scripts so that their local HOSTS file is updated periodically by copying it from a master file on the server.

SYS:ETC\NETWORKS

The NETWORKS file supplies logical names for networks much as HOSTS provides logical names for hosts. Following is the sample NETWORKS file. (If I remind you that the Bears are the football team at the University of California, Berkeley, can you guess the environment that originated this file?)

```
#
# SYS:ETC\NETWORKS
#
#              Network numbers
#
loopback    127      # fictitious internal loopback network
novellnet   130.57 # Novell's network number

#
# Internet networks
#
arpanet     10   arpa # historical network
milnet      26        # not so historical military net
ucb-ether   46        # Go bears!
```

The format of an entry in the NETWORKS file is as follows:

netname netid[/netmask] alias #comment

The *netname* is simply a logical name for the network. Network names must adhere to the the same rules as host names. The *alias* field enables each network name to be assigned an alias if desired.

The *netid* is the netid portion of the IP address associated with the network, expressed in dotted-decimal or hexadecimal form. If desired, a subnet mask can be specified using the optional *mask* parameter. If a subnet mask is not specified, the default subnet mask is used.

Networks don't really need names, but they can make the network administrator's life a lot easier. Among other things, network names can be used to identify routes in the GATEWAYS database, which is described in the next section. A NETWORKS file is not required for the mayberry network, but the following NETWORKS file will serve as an example:

```
#
# SYS:ETC\NETWORKS
#
#
loopback     127
mb1          193.88.201
```

SYS:ETC\GATEWAYS

The GATEWAYS database file includes static routing information. If a dynamic routing protocol (RIP or OSPF) is not loaded, static routes can be read into the server's routing tables using the IPCONFIG utility. Here is the sample GATEWAYS file:

```
#
# SYS:ETC\GATEWAYS
#
#  List of unusual routes which must be added to the routing
#  database statically.
#
# Normally you will not need this file, as most routing information
# should be available through the routing protocols.
#

# Examples.  These entries will not be useful to you.
#net milnet gateway sj-in5 metric 3 active  # to milnet through in5.
#net arpa gateway sj-in1 passive   # to arpanet.  in1 is passive.
#host 130.57.6.40 gateway 192.67.172.55   # route with numbers.
```

This file can define routes to remote hosts and networks. The syntax for a host route is as follows:

```
HOST {ipaddress | hostname} GATEWAY routeraddress
[METRIC cost] [ACTIVE | PASSIVE]
```

The syntax for a network route is as follows:

```
NET {netid | netname} GATEWAY routeraddress
[METRIC cost] [ACTIVE | PASSIVE]
```

Each entry states "to reach this remote destination, here is the next gateway to use." The HOST and NET keywords describe the type of address that the destination defines:

▸ For a HOST entry, the destination can be a host IP address, or it can be a host name that is defined in the HOSTS file.

▸ For a NET entry, the destination can be a netid (the network address portion only of the IP address), or it can be a network name that is defined in the NETWORKS file.

The *routeraddress* is the IP address of a router that is attached to a network that is connected directly to this host. Any datagrams that are directed to the destination network or host will be forwarded to this IP address. The optional *cost* represents the cost of this route. If a METRIC parameter is not specified, the default cost is 1.

By default, routes that the host receives from the GATEWAYS database are PASSIVE, meaning that they do not expire. Routes that are flagged as ACTIVE must be refreshed through ICMP protocol messages received from other routers. Active routes that are not refreshed will expire eventually and be purged from the database.

NOTE
Typically, each TCP/IP host will be defined with a default route, which states "any time I don't have a defined route to a destination, I will send the datagram to this default IP address." A default route is specified in a NET database entry with a netid of 0. The following entry defines a default route:

```
Net 0 Gateway 128.2.00.2 Metric 1 Passive
```

For an IP host that is attached to a single network (a host referred to as an end node), typically the GATEWAYS file will contain only a default route entry.

The GATEWAYS file has been described here so that all the configuration database files are defined together, but it is not required for the sample network. Static routing will be revisited in detail in Chapter 10. Unlike the other database files, which may be usable by all hosts without modification, the GATEWAYS file must be explicitly tailored to each host, depending on the host's location in the network topology.

SYS:ETC\PROTOCOL

The PROTOCOL database file identifies the names and numbers of TCP/IP protocols. Protocol numbers are used to complete the protocol ID field in the IP header, which identifies the upper-layer protocol associated with the datagram. For many protocols, the Internet Assigned Numbers Authority (IANA) has assigned official protocol numbers, which are recorded in the RFC titled "Assigned Numbers" (currently RFC 1700).

An entry in the PROTOCOL file has the following syntax:

```
protocol_name number [alias] [#comment]
```

The *protocol_name* states the name of the protocol. A protocol name cannot contain tab, space, or # characters. An alternate name for the protocol can be specified with the *alias* parameter. Service names and aliases must be unique within the PROTOCOL database. The *number* is the protocol number. Most are taken from the "Assigned Numbers" RFC. However, the PROTOCOL database file can be used to configure the host for new protocols that have not been assigned numbers by IANA. All characters between a # character and the end of a line are regarded as comment text and are not processed.

The sample PROTOCOL file follows. The sample file can typically be used without alteration but will require modification if additional TCP/IP protocols are installed.

```
#
#  SYS:ETC\PROTOCOL
#
#   Internet (IP) protocols
#
ip 0      IP        # internet protocol, pseudo protocol number
icmp      1    ICMP # internet control message protocol
igmp      2    IGMP # internet group multicast protocol
ggp       3    GGP  # gateway-gateway protocol
tcp       6    TCP  # transmission control protocol
pup       12   PUP  # PARC universal packet protocol
udp       17   UDP  # user datagram protocol
```

You should be able to use the sample PROTOCOL file without alteration.

SYS:ETC\SERVICES

Entries in the SERVICES file define services along with the transport protocols and ports the services utilize. For example, an entry in the SERVICES file for FTP will indicate that FTP will use port 21 with the TCP protocol. The syntax of an entry in the SERVICES file is as follows:

```
service port/transport [alias] [#comment]
```

The *service* parameter is the name of the service defined by the entry. Service names may not contain tab, space, or # characters, and each service must be uniquely named. The *port* parameter states the port number that will be used when the service uses the transport protocol defined by *transport*. All characters between a # character and the end of a line are regarded as comment text and are not processed.

The sample SERVICES file included with NetWare is lengthy, but you will get the gist of the file contents from the following sample:

```
#
# SYS:ETC\SERVICES
#
#       Network service mappings.  Maps service names to
#       transport protocol and transport protocol ports.
#
echo        7/udp
echo        7/tcp
discard     9/udp       sink null
discard     9/tcp       sink null
systat      11/tcp
daytime     13/udp
daytime     13/tcp
netstat     15/tcp
ftp-data    20/tcp
ftp         21/tcp
telnet      23/tcp
smtp        25/tcp      mail
time        37/tcp      timserver
time        37/udp      timserver
name        42/udp      nameserver
```

```
whois        43/tcp     nicname      # usually to sri-nic
domain       53/udp
domain       53/tcp
hostnames    101/tcp    hostname     # usually to sri-nic
sunrpc       111/udp
sunrpc       111/tcp
#
#
# Host specific functions
#
tftp         69/udp
rje          77/tcp
finger       79/tcp
link         87/tcp     ttylink
supdup       95/tcp
iso-tsap     102/tcp
x400         103/tcp                 # ISO Mail
x400-snd     104/tcp
csnet-ns     105/tcp
pop-2        109/tcp                 # Post Office
uucp-path    117/tcp
nntp         119/tcp    usenet       # Network News Transfer
ntp          123/tcp                 # Network Time Protocol
NeWS         144/tcp    news         # Window System
#
# UNIX specific services
#
# these are NOT officially assigned
#
exec         512/tcp
login        513/tcp
shell        514/tcp    cmd          # no passwords used
printer      515/tcp    spooler      # experimental
courier      530/tcp    rpc          # experimental
biff         512/udp    comsat
```

```
who        513/udp  whod
syslog     514/udp
talk       517/udp
route      520/udp  router routed
new-rwho   550/udp  new-who    # experimental
rmonitor   560/udp  rmonitord  # experimental
monitor    561/udp             # experimental
ingreslock 1524/tcp
snmp       161/udp             # Simple Network Mgmt Protocol
snmp-trap  162/udp  snmptrap   # SNMP trap (event) messages
```

Notice in the sample file that some services are listed twice, in association with both TCP and UDP. These services may run over either transport protocol, depending on the implementation. You should be able to use the sample SERVICES file without alteration.

Activation

Now that you have made your plans and configured the server database files, TCP/IP can be activated on the server. Activation is a three-step process:

1 • Loading the required protocols

2 • Loading MLIDs

3 • Binding protocols to MLIDs

With NetWare 3, the commands to perform these actions are stored in the AUTOEXEC.NCF file, which contains commands that execute whenever the server is restarted. The AUTOEXEC.NCF file must be manually edited by an administrator.

The approach of manually adding commands to AUTOEXEC.NCF works fine, but leaves something to be desired. The syntaxes of the commands are a bit involved, and administrators must understand the details of the command structure to make things work. Manual entry does not ensure that all necessary parameters will be present or that commands will execute in the correct order. And, because features like MLID logical names are entered as plain text, administrators often use different names and command sequences, making it difficult to maintain configuration consistency in a multi-server environment. Wouldn't it be nice if configuring networks was as easy as, say, managing users with SYSCON or NWADMIN?

INETCFG (Internetworking Configuration) is a menu-driven utility included with NetWare 4.1 that can be used to configure the networking characteristics of the server. The utility is quite comprehensive and eliminates the need to directly edit the commands in a NetWare command file.

Are NetWare 3 administrators doomed to manually configuring network configurations? No, because the NetWare MultiProtocol Router products, in addition to their advanced routing capabilities, include INETCFG. If your network is complex enough to make internetwork configuration a hassle, you probably need the capabilities of the MultiProtocol Router in any case, so either move to NetWare 4.1 or make the router upgrade.

Because a lot of NetWare 3 servers are in operation, you need to know how the manual commands work, so let's start by configuring the server manually. However, the discussion will be limited to examining features that are native to NetWare 3. When we look at configuration of NetWare 4 internetworking components, the INETCFG utility will be the focus of discussion.

Before looking at the procedures for configuring NetWare 3 and NetWare 4, a brief side trip is in order. As you configure LAN drivers, you may need to tune some of the server's parameters. This may involve changes to the STARTUP.NCF and AUTOEXEC.NCF startup files.

TUNING COMMUNICATION PARAMETERS

You should be aware of at least two server tuning parameters that can affect network performance. These parameters determine the maximum number of packet receive buffers and the maximum packet size that the server can receive.

Maximum Packet Receive Buffers

Receive buffers are used to temporarily store incoming data that must await server processing. If insufficient buffers are available to handle incoming data, frames may be lost, requiring upper-layer protocols to request retransmission. Clearly, retransmission of frames is inefficient and should be avoided.

You should have at least one packet receive buffer for each user and one for each application that is accessing the server. Each application that is accessing the server opens up a communication channel that requires an available packet receive buffer. For users of multitasking operating systems such as Windows and OS/2, who may have several applications running, you may need to allocate several packet receive buffers per user.

You can observe free packet receive buffers in the NetWare console MONITOR utility. On a NetWare 4.1 server, examine the Packet receive buffers field in the General Information window. If the value you observe consistently approaches the configured maximum, the value of Maximum Packet Receive Buffers should be increased.

The command to set the maximum number of packet receive buffers is

```
SET MAXIMUM PACKET RECEIVE BUFFERS=n
```

where n is a number in the range of 50-4000 (NetWare 4.1) or 50-2000 (NetWare 3.12). The default value is 100 for both NetWare versions. Configure higher values as required based on the number of users and running applications on your network.

Maximum Physical Receive Packet Size

Different physical networks have different maximum packet sizes. The Maximum Physical Receive Packet Receive Size should be configured to accommodate the largest frames possible for the network types that are employed. If the value is too small, large frames will be lost. If the value is too large, system memory will be used inefficiently.

As you learned in Chapter 3, the maximum size of an Ethernet packet is 1518 bytes, which is also Novell's recommendation for the Maximum Physical Receive Packet Size parameter with Ethernet Networks. The recommended value for token ring networks is 4202. If a server is connected to two network types, this parameter must be configured for the network with the largest maximum packet size.

Because the example network for May's Berry Farm currently is exclusively Ethernet, this parameter should be changed from its default value to a value of 1518.

The command to increase the maximum number of packet receive buffers is

```
SET MAXIMUM PHYSICAL RECEIVE PACKET SIZE=n
```

where n is a number between 618 and 24682 (for NetWare 4.1 or 3.12). The default value is 4202 for both NetWare versions. This parameter is entered in the

STARTUP.NCF file. To change the parameter, do one of the following:

▸ Use the server INSTALL utility to edit the STARTUP.NCF file. To activate the change, you must restart the server.

▸ On NetWare 4.1, you can modify the parameter using the SERVMAN utility. To activate the change, you must restart the server.

Setting Communication Parameters Using SERVMAN

The NetWare 4 SERVMAN utility is a more convenient way to update SET parameters. You cannot make an error in the command syntax or in the value assigned, and SERVMAN ensures that the changes are stored in the correct NCF file. To edit a communication parameter:

1 • Start SERVMAN with the console command **LOAD SERVMAN**.

2 • Select *Server parameters* in the Available Options window.

3 • Select *Communications* in the *Select a parameter category* window. This will open the Communications Parameters window shown in Figure 8.3.

4 • To edit a field, highlight the field and press Enter. A box at the bottom of the screen briefly describes the parameter, along with the range of values that can be assigned.

5 • After changing the field, press Enter.

6 • When changes have been completed, press Esc twice.

7 • If changes have been made, you will see an Update Options box. Select *Update AUTOEXEC.NCF and STARTUP.NCF now* to have SERVMAN write the changes to the startup files.

8 • When prompted, confirm the paths to your AUTOEXEC.NCF and STARTUP.NCF files.

9 • Press Esc to exit SERVMAN.

If changes have been made to the STARTUP.NCF file, you must restart the server to activate the changes.

FIGURE 8.3

Managing Communications
Parameters in SERVMAN

```
NetWare 4.10 Server Manager  4.14              NetWare Loadable Module

                          Communications Parameters

IPX NetBIOS Replication Option                 1
Maximum Packet Receive Buffers                 200
Minimum Packet Receive Buffers                 100
Maximum Physical Receive Packet Size           1508
Maximum Interrupt Events                       10
Reply To Get Nearest Server                    On
Number Of Watchdog Packets                     10
Delay Between Watchdog Packets                 59.3 Sec
Delay Before First Watchdog Packet             4 Min 56.6 Sec

        How the IPX router deals with NetBIOS replicated broadcasts:
        0 = don't replicate them; 1 = replicate them using the 'old'
        way; 2 = replicate them using the 'new' algorithm; 3 = same
        as the method 2, but don't replicate to the WAN links.
                            Setting: 1
                            Limits: 0 to 3

Enter=Edit field   Esc=Previous list   Alt+F10=Exit            F1=Help
```

NETWARE 3 NETWORK CONFIGURATION

IPX support will be configured when NetWare 3.12 or NetWare 4.1 are installed, so that when you add TCP/IP to a server it is unlikely that you will need to build the server communication configuration from scratch. But to illustrate all the pieces, that's what I'm going to do here. Assume that the hardware is installed, but that no MLIDs or protocols have been loaded.

After examining the basics of loading protocols and MLIDs, we will look at the procedures for configuring the network at May's Berry Farm.

Loading Communication Protocols

Figure 8.4 depicts the configuration of a server prior to configuring communications. The network adapter is installed, NetWare services are ready and waiting, and the Link Support Layer (LSL) sits in the middle. The only loaded protocol is IPX, which is always loaded on a NetWare server. The next steps will fill in the gaps in the communication layers.

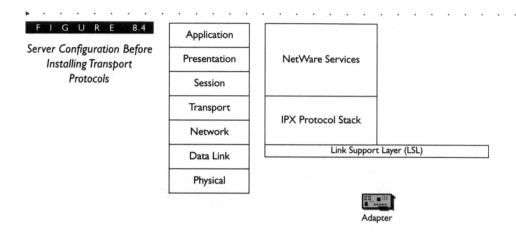

*Server Configuration Before
Installing Transport
Protocols*

The first step is to load the required communications protocols. The IPX protocol stack is loaded by default. Besides supporting user workstations, NetWare uses IPX to support lots of network houskeeping processes. The only configuration step required for IPX is to declare an internal network number, which is done with a statement in the AUTOEXEC.NCF file similar to this one:

```
ipx internal net 6a7fb123
```

Therefore, we don't have to worry about IPX. TCP/IP protocols, however, must be explicitly loaded.

The TCP/IP protocols are packaged in the file TCPIP.NLM. To load the TCP/IP protocol stack, type the command **LOAD TCPIP** at the server console. Loading TCPIP, or any NLM for that matter, dynamically links the NLM with the operating system.

Ordinarily, this command is stored in the AUTOEXEC.NCF file so that TCP/IP is loaded when the server restarts. The syntax of the LOAD TCPIP command is as follows:

```
LOAD TCPIP [FORWARD = {YES | NO}]
    [RIP = {YES | NO}]
    [TRAP = ip_address]
```

Table 8.1 describes the LOAD TCPIP parameters.

T A B L E 8.1	PARAMETER	VALUES	PURPOSE
Parameters for TCPIP.NLM	FORWARD	YES or NO	If this host has interfaces on two TCP/IP network segments, it will forward datagrams between network segments if FORWARD=YES. The default value is NO.
	RIP	YES or NO	If RIP=YES, this host will function as a RIP router. The default value is YES.
	TRAP	IP address	The IP address of a host to which SNMP trap messages should be sent.

NetWare servers that have a single network interface are referred to as *end nodes*. An end node cannot forward datagrams to other networks, which explains why the default value of FORWARD is NO. A host that is connected to two or more TCP/IP networks is referred to as a *multihomed* host. Multihomed NetWare servers can function as routers, and the value of FORWARD should be YES.

Because even an end node NetWare server may be a communication hub for the internetwork, it makes tremendous sense for the majority of NetWare servers to keep their routing tables up-to-date by running a routing protocol. This explains why the default value of the RIP parameter is YES. In Chapter 10, you will learn more about configuring RIP and about configuring OSPF as well.

The TRAP parameter enables the server to direct SNMP trap messages to an SNMP console. Chapter 11 will discuss SNMP management using the TCPCON utility, and you will see the TRAP parameter in action at that time.

To load TCP/IP with forwarding and RIP on, you would add the following command to the AUTOEXEC.NCF file:

```
LOAD TCPIP FORWARD=YES RIP=YES
```

Loading MLIDs

Figure 8.5 shows the server configuration after network protocols have been installed. The next step is to fill the gap between the LSL and the network adapter. This is done by installing driver software that communicates between the LSL and the network adapter hardware.

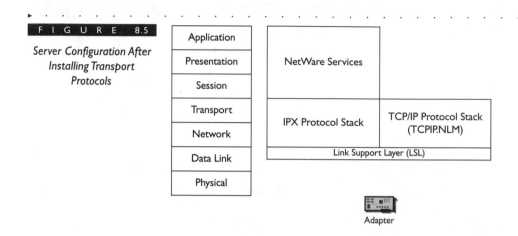

Server Configuration After Installing Transport Protocols

Each network interface adapter must be serviced by an MLID. NetWare includes a large number of MLIDs, packaged in NetWare Loadable Modules with the filename extension LAN. Like all NLMs, the LAN modules are activated on the server with the LOAD command. The syntax for loading an MLID is as follows:

```
LOAD [path]LAN_driver [parameter=value…]
```

The *LAN_driver* parameter is the filename of the NLM file containing the driver. The LAN extension is assumed. If the LAN file is not stored in the SYS:SYSTEM directory, the path to the driver file can be included as a *path* parameter.

Nearly all LAN driver modules are configured with default parameters, and you may be able to load the driver without parameters if the adapter is configured for the default settings. In practice, however, it is much better to explicitly include each parameter when the command is stored in the AUTOEXEC.NCF file, documenting the driver configuration.

Table 8.2 lists the MLID parameters. Consult the documentation for your hardware to determine which hardware parameters apply to your configuration. (Note: All hardware parameters for the TOKEN driver are optional.)

T A B L E   8.2

Parameters for LAN Driver NLMs

PARAMETER	VALUES	PURPOSE
DMA	Hardware defined	Reserves a DMA channel for use by the network board.
FRAME	Ethernet_802.2 Ethernet_802.3 Ethernet_II Ethernet_SNAP Token-Ring Token-Ring_SNAP	Specifies the frame encapsulation that is to be used with this logical network. For Ethernet drivers shipped with NetWare 3.12 and 4.1, the default frame type is Ethernet_802.2. For the TOKEN driver, the default frame type is Token-Ring. ARCnet has a single frame type for all transports.
INT	Hardware defined	Reserves an interrupt for use by the network board.
LS	Hardware defined	Specifies the number of 802.5 link stations to be configured for the TOKEN driver.
MEM	Hardware defined	Reserves a memory address for use by the driver.
NAME	Up to 17 characters	A name that identifies this logical network interface.
NODE	Node address	Can be used to override the physical addresses of some network adapter hardware.
PORT	Hardware defined	A memory address that is reserved for input/output use by this adapter.
RETRIES	0–255	Determines the number of times a LAN driver will attempt to retransmit a packet.
SAPS	Hardware defined	Specifies the 802.2 service access point for the TOKEN driver.
SLOT	1–8	On an EISA computer specifies the slot in which the target network board is installed. Hardware configuration parameters are taken from the EISA configuration.
TBC	0–2	Specifies the transmit buffer count for the TOKEN driver. The default value is 2.
TBZ	0 (use default) 96–65535	Specifies the transmit buffer size for the TOKEN driver. The default for this parameter is the value of the Maximum Physical Receive Packet Size parameter.

An example of a command that loads a LAN driver is:

```
LOAD NE2000 NAME=NE2000_1_E82 FRAME=Ethernet_802.2 INT=B PORT=340
```

Many drivers will prompt for required parameters that have not been specified. This is fine when the driver is entered from the command line, but the goal is to configure AUTOEXEC.NCF to start the server's communications automatically. Therefore, all parameters must be specified in the command line.

NOTE

I recommend that you always fully specify the parameters for LAN drivers, including a name and a frame type. This documents the server configuration and has the added benefit of shielding you from changes in default values as drivers evolve. The default frame type for Ethernet drivers was Ethernet_802.3 prior to NetWare 4.x and NetWare 3.12. Although such a change is unlikely in the future, specifying the frame type is cheap insurance.

Binding a Protocol to an MLID

At this point, the server is configured as shown in Figure 8.6. All of the communication layers are in place, but a crucial piece is missing. The LSL must be configured to serve as a communications link between specific network adapters and transport protocols.

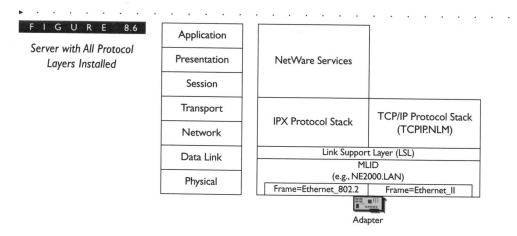

F I G U R E   8.6

Server with All Protocol Layers Installed

That link is established by binding a protocol stack to a virtual LAN adapter, a function performed by the BIND command. Because I am assuming that you will define a name each time you load a LAN driver, I will consider only the following syntax for binding IPX to a network adapter:

```
BIND IPX TO driver_name NET=network
```

The *driver_name* is the name you specified with the NAME parameter when the MLID was loaded. The *network* is a one-to-eight-digit hexadecimal number that identifies a given virtual network. An example of a BIND IPX command is the following:

```
BIND IPX TO NE2000_1_E82 NET=12FAA5
```

NOTE

All NetWare servers that connect to the same cable segment must be configured with the same network numbers for a given frame type. In other words, if one server assigns network number 12FAA5 to an Ethernet segment using the Ethernet_802.2 frame type, all servers using that frame type on the network segment must bind IPX with the network number 12FAA5.

When binding the IP protocol, considerably more parameters must be considered. The parameters for the BIND IP command are listed in Table 8.3. The syntax of the BIND IP command is as follows:

```
BIND IP TO board_name
        [ADDR=ip_address]
        [MASK=subnet_mask]
        [GATE=gateway_address]
        [BCAST=broadcast_address]
        [DEFROUTE={YES | NO}]
        [ARP={YES | NO}]
        [POISON={YES | NO}]
        [COST=hop_count]
```

	PARAMETER	VALUES	PURPOSE
TABLE 8.3 *Parameters for BIND IP*	ADDR	IP address	The value of *ip_address* specifies the IP address assigned to this interface.
	MASK	Subnet mask	The *subnet_mask* specifies the subnet mask used for addressing on the attached network.
	GATE	IP address	The *gateway_address* specifies a default gateway to be used on this network. If a default gateway is not specified, RIP is the source of routing information. This parameter may be entered in dotted decimal or dotted hexadecimal notation.
	DEFROUTE	YES or NO	If TCPIP was loaded with the FORWARD=YES parameter, DEFROUTE=YES configures this server to advertise itself as a default gateway through RIP. The default value is NO.
	ARP	YES or NO	Specifies whether ARP is to be used to resolve IP addresses to hardware addresses. The default value is YES.
	POISON	YES or NO	Specifies whether this node will use poison reverse for routing updates sent to this interface. If POISON=NO split horizon will be used. The default value is NO.
	COST	1–16	Specifies the cost metric for this interface. The default cost is 1.

An example of a BIND IP command is the following:

```
BIND IP TO NE2000_1_EII ADDR=155.28.2.100 MASK=255.255.255.0 RIP=NO
```

After protocols have been bound to network adapters, associations are established in the LSL layer that enable network adapters and protocols to communicate. NetWare communication configuration is complete, as shown in Figure 8.7.

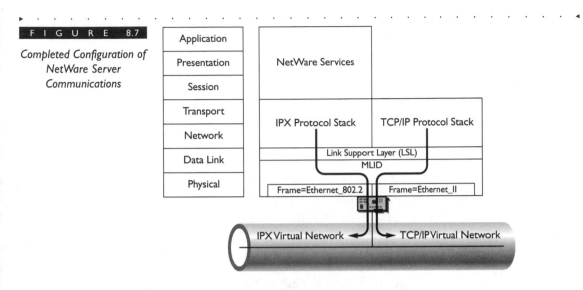

FIGURE 8.7

Completed Configuration of NetWare Server Communications

Examples of Network Configurations

Now it is time to look at some complete examples of server configurations. We will start with the basic configuration for May's Berry Farm, and then enhance the configuration as the network grows.

A Single-Segment Network The server configuration for the network in Figure 8.8 represents a simple case. Because the network has a single cable segment, TCPIP will be configured without RIP or forwarding. Forwarding is off by default, but RIP must be disabled with the RIP=NO parameter.

The TCP/IP database files that apply to this network were shown in the "Configuration" section earlier in this chapter. For this network, the server requires the files HOSTS, PROTOCOL, and SERVICES. Only the HOSTS file requires customization.

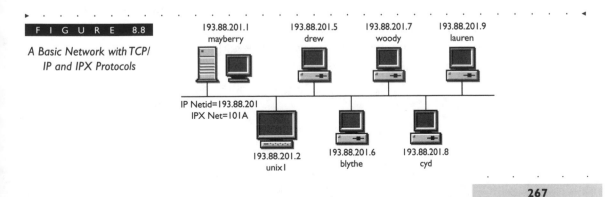

FIGURE 8.8

A Basic Network with TCP/IP and IPX Protocols

Because this server is connected to an Ethernet, the following command can be added to STARTUP.NCF:

```
SET MAXIMUM PHYSICAL RECEIVE PACKET SIZE=1508
```

The following commands will be placed in AUTOEXEC.NCF to configure the network:

```
LOAD TCPIP RIP=NO
LOAD NE2000 INT=B PORT=340 FRAME=ETHERNET_802.2 NAME=NE2000_1_E82
LOAD NE2000 INT=B PORT=340 FRAME=ETHERNET_II    NAME=NE2000_1_EII
BIND IPX TO NE2000_1_E82 NET=101A
BIND IP  TO NE2000_1_EII ADDR=193.88.201.1
```

Because subnet masking is not employed, a MASK parameter is not required, and the default class C subnet mask will be used (255.255.255.0). All other parameters can be left at their default values as well.

Configuring a Routed Network Few networks are as simple as the one shown in Figure 8.8, and we need to examine some more involved examples. Let's see what happens when May's Berry Farm expands.

Blythe's latest recipe, May's Kumquat Compote, is a rousing success, so successful that the manufacturing facilities need to be expanded. For the new manufacturing building, Blythe has decided to use a token ring. She doesn't want a batch of her patented preserves ruined because the Ethernet is saturated.

May's is still constrained to the original class C address. Therefore, it becomes necessary to subnet the network. To allow room for future growth, the MIS department has decided to allocate three bits for the subnet mask, resulting in a subnet mask of 255.255.255.224. The Ethernet will be subnet 193.88.201.32, and the token ring will be subnet 193.88.201.64. For each host on the network, the IP address must be updated and a subnet mask must be added to the configuration. The new network configuration is shown in Figure 8.9. (Refer to Table 4.4 for a summary of the available IP addresses for a class C network that allocates three bits for the subnetid.)

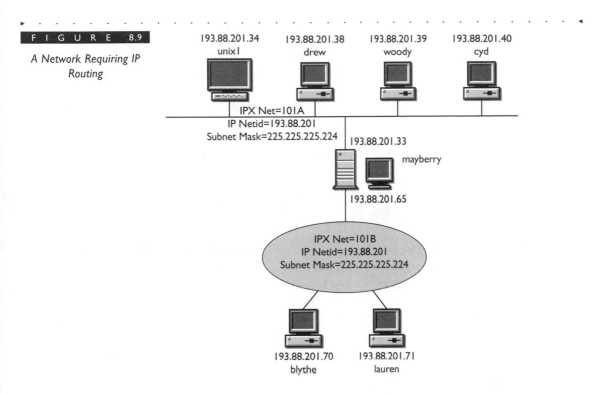

FIGURE 8.9

A Network Requiring IP Routing

The NetWare server will function as a router between the two networks. All of May's employees need to access the Web server, so the NetWare server must route IP (IPX is routed by default). Forwarding must be turned on (FORWARD=YES). It is not necessary to load RIP, however. RIP is responsible for exchanging route information between routers but does not perform the actual routing. Because the network has a single router, RIP is not needed. Loading RIP would just waste memory.

Because the token ring functions best with a larger frame, the following command will be entered in STARTUP.NCF to optimize the server for token ring:

```
SET MAXIMUM PHYSICAL RECEIVE PACKET SIZE=4202
```

Be aware that enlarging this parameter allocates somewhat more server memory to packet receive buffers. The administrator should pay close attention to server memory utilization to ensure that the server does not require additional memory in the new configuration. But the administrator should always pay close attention to server memory utilization, so this admonition should be unnecessary.

The configuration commands in the AUTOEXEC.NCF file are as follows:

```
LOAD TCPIP  FORWARD=YES    RIP=NO
LOAD NE2000 INT=B PORT=340 FRAME=ETHERNET_802.2   NAME=NE2000_1_E82
LOAD NE2000 INT=B PORT=340 FRAME=ETHERNET_II      NAME=NE2000_1_EII
LOAD TOKEN                 FRAME=TOKEN-RING        NAME=TOKEN_1_TOK
LOAD TOKEN                 FRAME=TOKEN-RING_SNAP   NAME=TOKEN_1_TSP
BIND IPX TO NE2000_1_E82   NET=101A
BIND IPX TO TOKEN_1_TOK    NET=101B
BIND IP  TO NE2000_1_EII   ADDR=193.88.201.33 MASK=255.255.255.224
BIND IP  TO TOKEN_1_TSP    ADDR=193.88.201.65 MASK=255.255.255.224
```

NOTE **If this network had been configured with two Ethernet segments, serviced by two NE2000 adapters, the configuration commands would resemble the following:**

```
LOAD TCPIP FORWARD=YES RIP=NO
LOAD NE2000 INT=B PORT=340 FRAME=ETHERNET_802.2 NAME=NE2000_1_E82
LOAD NE2000 INT=B PORT=340 FRAME=ETHERNET_II    NAME=NE2000_1_EII
LOAD NE2000 INT=C PORT=360 FRAME=ETHERNET_802.2 NAME=NE2000_2_E82
LOAD NE2000 INT=C PORT=360 FRAME=ETHERNET_II    NAME=NE2000_2_EII
BIND IPX TO NE2000_1_E82   NET=101A
BIND IPX TO NE2000_2_E82   NET=101B
BIND IP  TO NE2000_1_EII   ADDR=193.88.201.33 MASK=255.255.255.224
BIND IP  TO NE2000_2_EII   ADDR=193.88.201.65 MASK=255.255.255.224
```

Because the host IP addresses have changed to accommodate subnetting, the HOSTS and NETWORKS files must be updated. Here is the new HOSTS file:

```
#
# SYS:ETC\HOSTS
#
#IP Address      HOSTNAME             Aliases
127.0.0.1        loopback             lb localhost
```

```
193.88.201.33    fs1.mayberry.com      mayberry fs1e  #Ethernet
193.88.201.34    www.mayberry.com      www unix1
193.88.201.38    drew.mayberry.com     drew ws1 pres
193.88.201.39    woody.mayberry.com    woody ws3 security
193.88.201.40    cyd.mayberry.com      cyd ws4 corpcom
193.88.201.65    fs1t                                 #token ring
193.88.201.70    blythe.mayberry.com   blythe ws2 manuf
193.88.201.71    lauren.mayberry.com   lauren ws5 testing
```

Mayberry is a multihomed computer. A given host name can be resolved to only one IP address. For testing purposes, the network administrator chose to add an entry for the token ring interface on mayberry. When you learn about testing network communications in Chapter 11 you will appreciate the convenience this name offers.

To reflect the use of subnetting and the added network segment, the NETWORKS file would be updated to include the subnetid:

```
#
# SYS:ETC\NETWORKS
#
#
loopback    127
mb1         193.88.201.32
mb2         193.88.201.64
```

A Network Segment with Two NetWare File Servers   The MIS department at May's Berry Farm has decided to add a file server that will be used for testing new network hardware and software. Figure 8.10 shows how the MIS server will be attached. When installing a second server to a network segment, there are two major concerns. Servers on the same network segment must be configured with the same frame type and network addressing for each protocol stack. Also, routing must be properly configured.

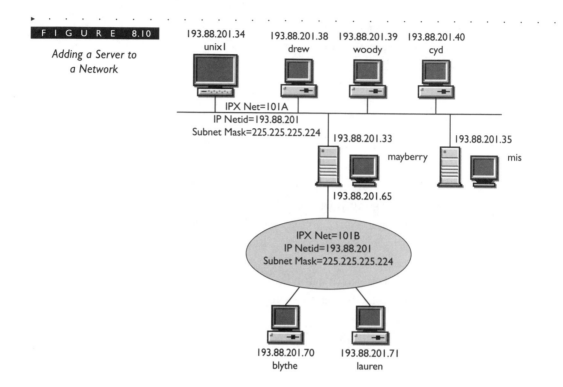

FIGURE 8.10

Adding a Server to a Network

The communications configuration for the new server would be established with the following commands in AUTOEXEC.NCF:

```
LOAD TCPIP RIP=YES
LOAD NE2000 INT=B PORT=340 FRAME=ETHERNET_802.2 NAME=NE2000_1_E82
LOAD NE2000 INT=B PORT=340 FRAME=ETHERNET_II    NAME=NE2000_1_EII
BIND IPX TO NE2000_1_E82 NET=101A
BIND IP  TO NE2000_1_EII ADDR=193.88.201.35 MASK=255.255.255.224
```

RIP has been turned on, even though this is an end node. This enables mis to learn routes from mayberry. Alternatively, static routes could be configured, a procedure that is described in Chapter 10.

Because RIP is being used it must be enabled on mayberry. The AUTOEXEC.NCF file on mayberry must be updated to load TCP/IP as follows:

```
LOAD TCPIP FORWARD=YES
```

The final required change is that the network HOSTS files must be updated with an entry for the new computer.

NOTE

NetWare 4 and the NetWare Multiprotocol Router support use of the ICMP Router Discovery Protocol, which would enable mis to discover mayberry as an available router. This would generate less overhead traffic than RIP, and would be the preferable configuration, but the router discovery feature is not available on NetWare 3, and this section focuses on configurations that can be achieved in NetWare 3 as well as NetWare 4.

NETWARE 4 NETWORK CONFIGURATION

If your server is running NetWare 4 (or NetWare 3 with the NetWare MultiProtocol Router) you should not even consider defining network communications from the command line. Manual configuration is tedious and error-prone, and many of the more advanced features offered by NetWare 4 cannot be configured from the command line.

Configuring network communication for NetWare 4 follows the same three steps that were used for NetWare 3, although a slightly different order will be followed here:

1 • Load and configure network boards.

2 • Load and configure network protocols.

3 • Bind protocols to network boards.

How NetWare 4 Configuration Works

To configure NetWare 4 you will use INETCFG, which puts a menu-driven interface on NetWare communications configuration. The first time you load INETCFG, it will ask you if you want to "Transfer LAN driver, protocol and remote access commands?" If you type *Yes*, INETCFG will examine the AUTOEXEC.NCF file to identify the statements that load and bind protocols and adapters. This configuration information is stored in the configuration database maintained by INETCFG. Then, the commands in AUTOEXEC.NCF are commented out.

Communications configuration data are stored in several files which are maintained by INETCFG. The following files are maintained by INETCFG and should not be modified with any other utility:

- ▸ AURP.CFG

- ▸ TCPIP.CFG

- ▸ IPXSPX.CFG

- ▸ NLSP.CFG

- ▸ NETINFO.CFG

In place of the original communications configuration commands, the following command is added to AUTOEXEC.NCF:

```
SYS:ETC\INITSYS.NCF
```

This NetWare command file contains the INITIALIZE SYSTEM command, which loads the communications configuration from the INETCFG database files.

Start INETCFG with the LOAD INETCFG command. The startup window is shown in Figure 8.11. In this section, you will use four of the options in this menu:

- ▸ The Boards option will be used to used to add and configure network board drivers.

- ▸ The Protocols option will be used to add and configure network protocols.

- ▸ The Bindings option will be used to bind protocols to boards.

- ▸ The View Configuration option will be used to view the configuration settings you choose.

FIGURE   8.11

The INETCFG Startup
Window

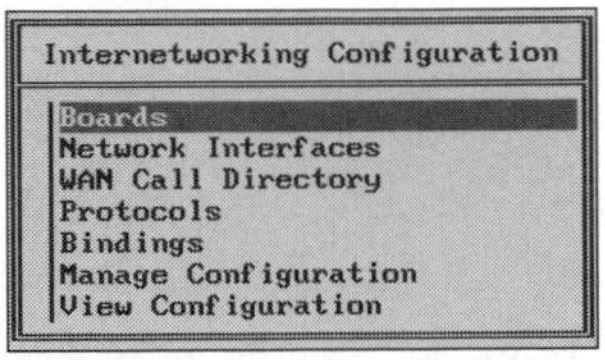

Managing Boards

To add a network board to the server configuration:

1 • Ensure that the network drivers for your network boards are in the
SYS:SYSTEM directory. These files are identified by the filename
extension LAN.

2 • Select *Boards* from the Internetworking Configuration menu. This will
open the Configured Boards window, which shows one configured
network board (see Figure 8.12).

FIGURE   8.12

Configured Boards in
INETCFG

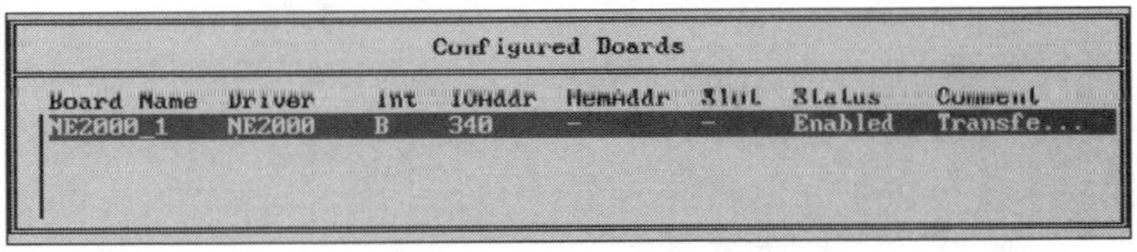

3 • Press Insert to open an Available Drivers window that lists all drivers
stored in SYS:SYSTEM. Select the driver you wish to configure, and
press Enter to open a configuration dialog box.

Figure 8.13 shows the configuration dialog box for the TOKEN driver,
and Figure 8.14 shows the configuration dialog box for the NE2000
driver. In each case, the administrator has specified a name for the
driver, consisting of the driver name and a number that identifies this
particular board. Don't try to specify the protocol part of the name in
this window. That will be added when the bindings are defined.

Many settings fields can be opened to produce lists of parameters. To
choose parameters for a field, select the field and press Enter. Select
the parameter from the list that is provided and press Enter.

FIGURE 8.13

The Configuration Dialog
for the TOKEN Driver

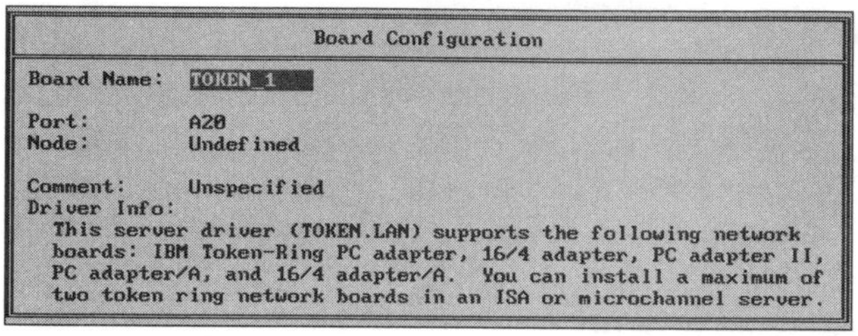

```
                          Board Configuration
Board Name:    TOKEN_1

Port:          A20
Node:          Undefined

Comment:       Unspecified
Driver Info:
   This server driver (TOKEN.LAN) supports the following network
   boards: IBM Token-Ring PC adapter, 16/4 adapter, PC adapter II,
   PC adapter/A, and 16/4 adapter/A. You can install a maximum of
   two token ring network boards in an ISA or microchannel server.
```

FIGURE 8.14

The Configuration Dialog
for the NE2000 Driver

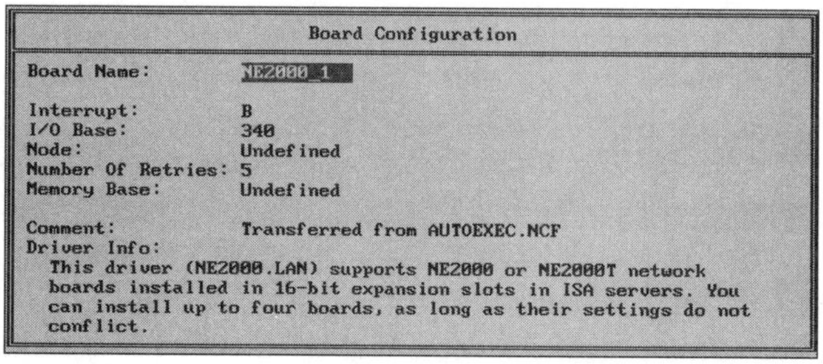

```
                          Board Configuration
Board Name:          NE2000_1

Interrupt:           B
I/O Base:            340
Node:                Undefined
Number Of Retries:   5
Memory Base:         Undefined

Comment:             Transferred from AUTOEXEC.NCF
Driver Info:
   This driver (NE2000.LAN) supports NE2000 or NE2000T network
   boards installed in 16-bit expansion slots in ISA servers. You
   can install up to four boards, as long as their settings do not
   conflict.
```

4 • After configuring the board, press Esc to exit the dialog window. To add the board to the server configuration, choose *Yes* when the Save Changes dialog box appears.

NOTE

Changes made in INETCFG are not activated as they are configured. To activate a communications configuration, you must exit INETCFG (press Esc several times) and do one of the following:

▸ **Type DOWN to stop the server. Type EXIT to return to DOS. Type SERVER to restart the server.**

▸ **Type the command REINITIALIZE SERVER at the server console.**

Either of these procedures will disrupt network communication. If users are connected to the server, have them log out before you shut down communication.

Managing Protocols

To load and configure TCP/IP:

1 • Select the *Protocols* option from the Internetworking Configuration menu to display the Protocol Configuration window, shown in Figure 8.15. This window lists the protocols along with a status: Enabled, Disabled, or Unconfigured.

```
            Protocol Configuration
  Protocol                 Status
  AppleTalk                Unconfigured
  IPX                      Enabled
  Source Route End Stn     Unconfigured
  TCP/IP                   Disabled
  User-specified Proto     Unconfigured
```

FIGURE 8.15

The Server Protocol Configuration

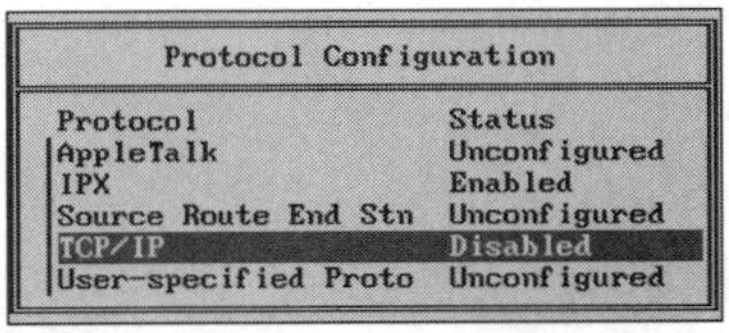

2 • Select *TCP/IP* in the Protocol Configuration window to open the dialog box shown in Figure 8.16. The options in this dialog box are described in Table 8.4. The following fields are required to configure the network for May's Berry Farm (shown in Figure 8.9):

> ▸ **TCP/IP Status (Enabled)**

> ▸ **IP Packet Forwarding (Enabled)**

> ▸ **RIP (Disabled)**

3 • After entering the TCP/IP configuration, press Esc.

4 • To save the new configuration, choose *Yes* when you see the prompt "Update TCP/IP Configuration?" Choose *No* to cancel changes.

```
             TCP/IP Protocol Configuration
  TCP/IP Status:                Enabled
  IP Packet Forwarding:         Enabled("Router")

  RIP:                          Disabled
  OSPF:                         Disabled
  OSPF Configuration:           (Select to View or Modify)

  Static Routing:               Disabled
  Static Routing Table:         (Select For List)

  SNMP Manager Table:           (Select For List)

  Filter Support:               Disabled
  Expert Configuration Options: (Select to View or Modify)
```

FIGURE 8.16

TCP/IP Protocol Configuration Options

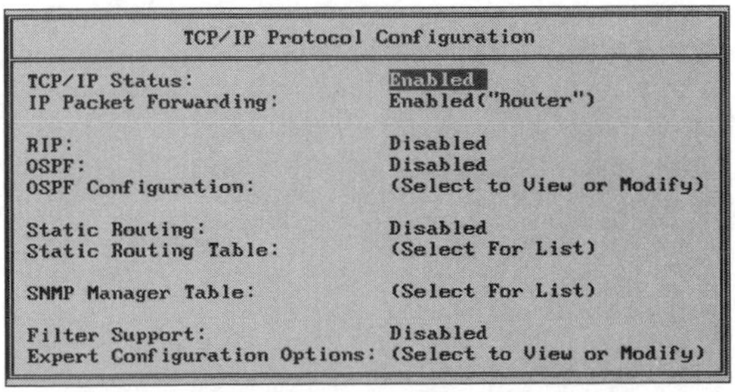

T A B L E 8.4

INETCFG TCP/IP Configuration
Options

PARAMETER	VALUES	PURPOSE
TCP/IP Status	Enabled/Disabled	Must be set to Enabled to activate TCP/IP protocols.
IP Packet Forwarding	Enabled/Disabled	If two or more network boards are installed on this server and IP Packet Forwarding is set to Enabled, the server functions as an IP router. On an end node (single adapter) host, this feature should be set to Disabled.
RIP	Enabled/Disabled	If RIP is set to Enabled, this server will exchange routing updates with other hosts running RIP.
OSPF	Enabled/Disabled	If OSPF is set to Enabled, this server will participate in OSPF routing. An OSPF configuration must be established. See Chapter 10 for information about configuring OSPF.
OSPF Configuration		Select this field to open the OSPF Configuration dialog window. (See Chapter 10.)
Static Routing	Enabled/Disabled	If set to Enabled, the server will read static routes from the static routing table when it is started or reinitialized.
Static Routing Table		Select this field to open the TCP/IP Static Routes list and manage the static routing table.
SNMP Manager Table		Select this field to open the SNMP Manager Table list and manage the list of hosts that will receive SNMP alerts from this host. (See Chapter 11.)
Filter Support	Enabled/Disabled	If set to Enabled, TCP/IP supports packet forwarding filters and routing information filters. (See Chapter 10.)
Expert Configuration Options		Select this field to open the TCP/IP Expert Configuration dialog window. (See Chapter 10.)

Binding Protocols to Network Boards

To bind TCP/IP to a network board:

I • Select *Bindings* from the Internetworking Configuration menu to open the Configured Protocol to Network Interface Bindings window shown in Figure 8.17.

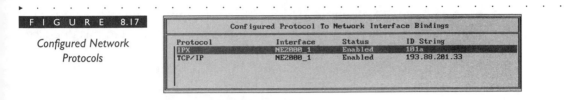

FIGURE 8.17

Configured Network Protocols

Configured Protocol To Network Interface Bindings

Protocol	Interface	Status	ID String
IPX	NE2000_1	Enabled	101a
TCP/IP	NE2000_1	Enabled	193.88.201.33

2 • To add a binding, press Insert to open a list of protocols that are enabled on the server (see Figure 8.18).

FIGURE 8.18

Enabled Protocols Available for Binding

Select from the list of configured protocols

Protocol	Status
IPX	Enabled
TCP/IP	Enabled

3 • Select *TCP/IP* from the list of enabled protocols to open a list of configured network interfaces (see Figure 8.19).

FIGURE 8.19

Configured Network Interfaces

Select from the list of configured network interfaces

Board Name	Port	Int. Name	Media	Status
NE2000_1	–	NE2000_1	Ethernet	Enabled
TOKEN_1	–	TOKEN_1	Token Ring	Enabled

4 • Select one of the configured network interfaces and press Enter to open a dialog box for binding the protocol (see Figure 8.20). Entries are required in the *Local IP Address* and *Subnetwork Mask of Connected Network* fields.

FIGURE 8.20

Options for Binding a Protocol

Binding TCP/IP to a LAN Interface

Network Interface: TOKEN_1

Local IP Address: 193.88.201.65
Subnetwork Mask of Connected Network: 255.255.255.224

RIP Bind Options: (Select to View or Modify)
OSPF Bind Options: (Select to View or Modify)
Expert TCP/IP Bind Options: (Select to View or Modify)

5 • Select the *Local IP Address* field and press Enter. Edit this field to reflect the IP address to be assigned to this host.

6 • Select the *Subnetwork Mask of Connected Network* field and press Enter. Edit this field to reflect the subnet mask to be applied to this interface.

7 • By default, TCP/IP will be bound using the Ethernet_II frame type for Ethernet and the Token-Ring_SNAP frame type for token ring, so you don't need to do anything else to configure TCP/IP on a basic network. To change the Ethernet frame type to Ethernet_SNAP, select *Expert TCP/IP Bind Options.* In the Expert TCP/IP LAN Options window, change the value of the Frame Type to the desired frame type. Remember: Ethernet_II is the overwhelming choice on TCP/IP networks!

8 • When binding parameters are entered, press Esc to exit the window. Respond *Yes* when you are asked, "Update TCP/IP Configuration?"

NOTE **Some of the other available options, such as RIP and OSPF bind options, will be examined in Chapter 10.**

To bind IPX to a network board:

1 • Select *Bindings* from the Internetworking Configuration menu to open the Configured Protocol to Network Interface Bindings window.

2 • Press Insert to open a list of protocols that are enabled on the server.

3 • Select *IPX* from the list of enabled protocols to open a list of configured network interfaces.

4 • Select the desired network adapter, and press Enter to open the Binding IPX to a LAN Interface window shown in Figure 8.21.

FIGURE 8.21

*Binding IPX to a
LAN interface*

```
          Binding IPX to a LAN Interface
Network Interface:   NE2000_1

IPX Network Number:  101a
Frame Type:          Ethernet_802.2
Expert Bind Options:
```

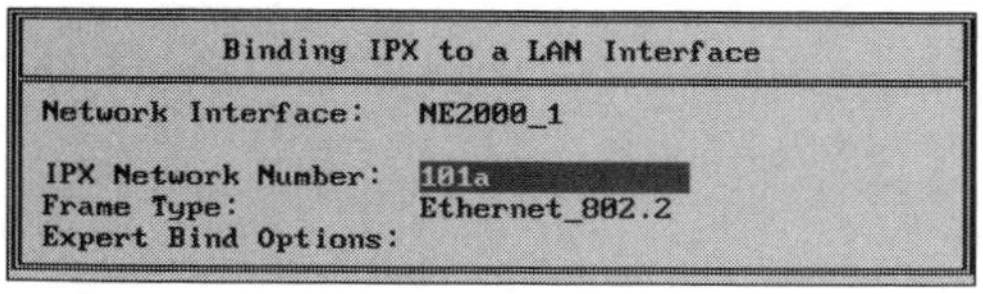

5 • Select the *IPX Network Number* field, and press Enter to edit the IPX network number.

6 • Select the *Frame Type* field, and press Enter to select a frame type.

7 • Press Esc. To save the binding, choose *Yes* when you are prompted, "Save IPX Bind Parameters?"

Figure 8.22 shows the status of the Configured Protocol to Network Interface Bindings window when all of the bindings have been entered for the network shown in Figure 8.9.

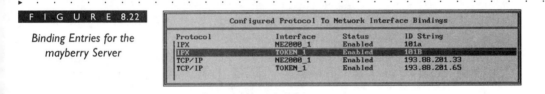

F I G U R E 8.22

Binding Entries for the mayberry Server

Configured Protocol To Network Interface Bindings			
Protocol	Interface	Status	ID String
IPX	NE2000_1	Enabled	101a
IPX	TOKEN_1	Enabled	101B
TCP/IP	NE2000_1	Enabled	193.88.201.33
TCP/IP	TOKEN_1	Enabled	193.88.201.65

Viewing the Network Configuration

After configuring communications in INETCFG, you can view the commands that INETCFG will generate. To view a menu of available options, choose *View Configuration* from the Internetworking Configuration menu. This choice will bring up the menu shown in Figure 8.23.

F I G U R E 8.23

Options for Viewing INETCFG Configurations

```
View Configuration
All INETCFG Commands
LAN Board Commands
WAN Board Commands
Protocol Commands
Protocol Bind Commands
Configuration Summary
Console Messages
```

The option *All INETCFG Commands* generates a display similar to the one in Figure 8.24. Most of the commands will be familiar to you if you think back to the discussion about entering configuration commands manually. However, some of the parameters that can be configured through INETCFG will not be reflected in this list.

F I G U R E   8.24

*Commands Generated
by INETCFG*

```
            View (Read-Only) All INETCFG-Generated Commands
LOAD SNMP
LOAD NE2000 NAME=NE2000_1_E82 FRAME=Ethernet_802.2 INT=B PORT=340 RETRIES=5

LOAD NE2000 NAME=NE2000_1_EII FRAME=Ethernet_II INT=B PORT=340 RETRIES=5
LOAD NE2000 NAME=NE2000_2_E82 FRAME=Ethernet_802.2 INT=C PORT=360 RETRIES=5

LOAD NE2000 NAME=NE2000_2_EII FRAME=Ethernet_II INT=C PORT=360 RETRIES=5
LOAD SPXCONFG Q=1 A=540 V=108 W=54 R=10 S=1000 I=1200
BIND IPX NE2000_1_E82 net=101A seq=1
BIND IPX NE2000_2_E82 net=101B seq=1
LOAD Tcpip RIP=No Forward=Yes
BIND IP NE2000_1_EII ARP=Yes Mask=255.255.255.224 Address=193.88.201.33
BIND IP NE2000_2_EII ARP=Yes Mask=255.255.255.224 Address=193.88.201.65
```

Activating the Network Configuration

Changes made in INETCFG are not activated as they are configured. After saving changes in INETCFG, you can put changes into effect in two ways.

The most effective way is to restart the server. Type **DOWN** to stop the server; type **EXIT** to return to DOS, and then type **SERVER** to restart the server. Of course, this will disrupt all communication with the server. Be sure to warn your users.

In many cases, changes can be activated typing **REINITIALIZE SYSTEM** at the server console. This command performs the following tasks:

- ► It compares the current NETINFO.CFG file to the NETINFO.CFG that was last used to start the system.

- ► If changes are identified, REINITIALIZE SYSTEM executes the new commands. REINITIALIZE SYSTEM is limited in two ways:

- ► If the new command is a LOAD command, REINITIALIZE SYSTEM must first unload the affected NLM. If the NLM cannot be unloaded because other loaded NLMs are dependent on it, the change cannot take effect. After unloading the NLM, it will be reloaded with the new configuration.

- ► Some communications changes are not reflected in the NETINFO.CFG file and will not be put into effect. Therefore, restarting the server remains the most effective way to put changes into effect.

Testing Connectivity

Before you go to a lot of trouble hooking up client software, it's a good idea to establish that basic TCP/IP connectivity exists between your hosts. Once you have configured two or more hosts you should make sure they can talk to one another. The most common tool for testing TCP/IP connectivity is PING.

PING uses ICMP messaging to establish that hosts can communicate. Because PING can resolve host names, it is a useful tool for testing out your name resolution mechanism as well. Ordinarily, PING is a command tool. To test connectivity with 193.88.201.38, you would enter the command PING 193.88.201.38 and wait for a reply. A command line PING utility is included with LAN WorkPlace, and you will see how it works in Chapter 9.

The PING utility for a NetWare 4 server has the capability of continuously pinging multiple hosts. PING sends an ICMP request packet at periodic intervals and waits for the target to return an ICMP response packet. If a response arrives, PING reports the statistics. If not, PING lets you know the host is unavailable.

Figure 8.25 shows PING in action. To start PING on a NetWare server, enter the command **LOAD PING**. Then, press the Insert key to add a target to be pinged. In the figure, the administrator is in the process of adding woody as a target. You can specify the interval at which pinging is to take place. Long intervals enable you to keep an eye on the network without generating outrageous traffic levels.

FIGURE 8.25
Pinging on a NetWare Server

```
Ping  1.02                                        NetWare Loadable Module

  Node        Sent   Received    High     Low    Last Average   Trend
  woody        114   114 100%   3.738s   0.0ms   1.1ms  1.206s  1.004s
  blythe        91    24  26%   3.380s   0.6ms   3.380s 487.0ms   Down
▶ cyd           96     0   0%                                   No data




 INS=Insert Target DEL=Delete Target ENTER=Modify Target ESC=Exit
```

In this figure, two hosts are not responding to pings. Blythe responded initially, but has stopped. You can see that received packets are far fewer than sent packets. Also, the Trend column indicates that this host is down. Cyd has never responded to a ping, and the Trend column shows no data.

For the responding hosts, PING reports high, low, last, and average response time. These values, with the trends, can tip you off on changes in network performance.

We're Only Part Way There

The network TCP/IP configuration is only partly completed. May's Berry Farm has a server that can talk TCP/IP. But the server doesn't have any clients it can talk to, and it doesn't have any TCP/IP services to offer.

Users need to get on the network and the next piece of the puzzle is to add TCP/IP protocols to the NetWare clients. For that we turn to the next chapter, which will examine Novell's TCP/IP clients for DOS and Windows, LAN WorkPlace and LAN Workgroup.

## CHAPTER 9

Installing TCP/IP on NetWare Clients

The servers on your network now can talk TCP/IP, but the network still lacks two crucial ingredients: applications to be used and workstations to use them on. Half of the client-server equation is missing. You have the servers; now you need to add the clients.

This chapter examines three of Novell's TCP/IP client solutions:

▸ The NetWare TCP/IP Transport add-on for the NetWare Client for DOS and MS Windows

▸ LAN WorkPlace

▸ LAN WorkGroup for DOS and Windows

The NetWare TCP/IP Transport add-on is a basic connectivity solution that enables NetWare clients to support a TCP/IP protocol stack. It doesn't include any applications, but the NetWare TCP/IP protocol stack supports many applications that are available for the DOS/Windows environment. Windows applications interface with TCP/IP using the Windows Sockets API, a variation of BSD Sockets that Microsoft has prepared for the Windows environment. The NetWare TCP/IP transport supports Windows Sockets and, therefore, is compatible with a huge number of Windows programs written for TCP/IP.

LAN WorkPlace is a complete TCP/IP connectivity package. It includes drivers for IPX and TCP/IP protocol stacks. LAN WorkPlace also includes a variety of TCP/IP applications, including an FTP client, an FTP server, a NFS client, Telnet, and the NetScape Navigator for the World Wide Web. LAN WorkPlace supports local LAN connectivity, but it also includes a remote client for connecting to dial-in Internet sites. These features make LAN WorkPlace a terrific tool for the road warrior who needs connectivity in the office and away. The procedures in this chapter describe LAN WorkPlace, version 5.

LAN WorkGroup is similar to LAN WorkPlace and includes nearly the same suite of applications. But LAN WorkGroup is designed for centralized LAN administration. All but a few client-specific files are stored on the LAN, greatly simplifying client software installation. LAN WorkGroup alleviates one of the most tedious tasks a TCP/IP administrator faces: assigning, configuring, and tracking IP addresses. Most LAN WorkGroup clients can obtain their addresses from a centrally administered pool, which eliminates the need to edit client configuration files when

IP addresses are assigned or changed. The procedures in this chapter describe LAN WorkGroup, version 5.

This chapter covers the installation and configuration of these three client packages so that you can determine which client best meets your organization's needs. We'll also take a look at how LAN WorkPlace can be configured as a dial-in TCP/IP client. Finally, we will examine some of the applications that are included with LAN WorkPlace and LAN WorkGroup.

Because these three clients are based on Novell's Open Datalink Interface (ODI) architecture, they have a great deal in common. Before getting down to the specifics of each package, let's take a basic tour of how NetWare client software is configured.

NOTE **As this book is nearing completion, Novell is beginning to ship its new NetWare 32-bit client software, which includes support for TCP/IP. A copy of the 32-bit client is included on the CD-ROM that accompanies this book. If you are using a 32-bit operating system such as Windows 95, you will want to use the new client software.**

Configuring the ODI Protocol Stack

Two factors determine the configuration of communication protocols on an ODI client:

- The order in which the drivers are loaded

- The configuration settings for the individual drivers.

The order in which the protocols are loaded is determined by the ODI architecture, which has the same basic layer structure on clients and servers. Figure 9.1 shows the software modules that implement the ODI protocol stack on DOS clients. For the IPX protocol stack, starting from the bottom of the protocol stack, the layers are:

- Network interface card drivers (MLIDs), implemented by hardware-specific software modules (e.g., NE2000.EXE).

▸ The Link Support Layer, implemented by the LSL.EXE program module.

▸ IPX protocols, implemented by the IPXODI.EXE program module.

▸ The DOS Requester, implemented by the VLM.EXE program module in conjunction with numerous virtual loadable modules (VLMs).

Each layer is established by executing a program module. The program modules that support the DOS client are stored in a directory on the client computer's hard drive, typically in C:\NWCLIENT.

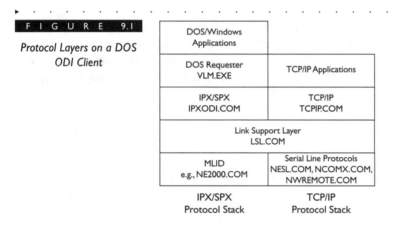

FIGURE 9.1

Protocol Layers on a DOS ODI Client

Figure 9.1 shows the NCOMX driver, which functions as an MLID when a modem is used to complete a TCP/IP network connection. Later in this chapter you will see how drivers are loaded to support network connections via modem.

Each protocol module can be configured by editing parameters in the NET.CFG file, which is usually stored in the same directory as the program files. Most of the work of configuring a NetWare client lies in editing the NET.CFG file. After looking at the basics of executing protocol modules on the client, we'll take a close look at the NET.CFG file.

LOADING PROTOCOL DRIVERS

The layers in the protocol stack are established by executing driver programs in a specific order. The following sequence of commands loads both IPX and TCP/IP protocol stacks using an NE2000 network interface board:

```
LSL
NE2000
IPXODI
VLM
TCPIP
```

As on the server, the Link Support Layer is loaded first, followed by drivers for the network interface cards. After network interfaces have been registered to the LSL, protocols can be bound to the interfaces.

The final step in configuring the IPX protocol stack is to load the DOS Requester, which sends network service requests to the network. The DOS Requester is loaded and configured by the VLM.EXE program. VLM stands for *virtual loadable modules*, and VLM.EXE performs much the same task on the client as the LOAD command does on the server: loading software modules and linking them to the network software. The TCP/IP protocols are loaded by executing the TCPIP.EXE program.

Loading protocol modules on the client typically is managed by placing the commands in a batch file. The commands can be added to the AUTOEXEC.BAT file; however, the INSTALL programs that accompany NetWare client products build separate batch files to load the client protocol stack. For example, the INSTALL program included with the NetWare Client for DOS and Windows creates a batch file named STARTNET.BAT, which is stored in the same directory as the driver files. The default client directory for the NetWare Client is C:\NWCLIENT.

To execute the batch file that loads the client software, INSTALL places a CALL statement in the AUTOEXEC.BAT file similar to the following:

```
CALL C:\NWCLIENT\STARTNET.BAT
```

A CALL statement enables batch files to execute other batch files. Each NetWare client package creates different batch files and different client directory structures, but the principle remains the same from package to package.

THE NET.CFG FILE

The NET.CFG file is a text file that is maintained with any standard text editor. If you install NetWare client software using any of the automated installation programs, a basic NET.CFG file will be created for you, but you should still know how to edit the file. Almost any change to client protocols requires you to modify NET.CFG.

My discussion of the NET.CFG file focuses on features that come into play when multiple protocol stacks or multiple drivers are employed, for example, when you configure TCP/IP alongside IPX on a workstation.

Take a look at the following sample NET.CFG file. For the sake of clarity, I've left out a lot of options that don't apply to the material covered in this book. Consult Novell's *NetWare Client for DOS and MS Windows* manual for information about the options for IPXODI and the DOS Requester.

```
Link Support
        Buffers          8 1500
        MemPool          4096
        Max Boards       4
        Max Stacks       4
Link Driver NE2000
        IRQ              5
        PORT             340
        MEM              D0000
        FRAME            ETHERNET_II
        FRAME            ETHERNET_802.2
        PROTOCOL IPX E0 ETHERNET_802.2
Protocol TCPIP
        PATH TCP_CFG     C:\NET\TCP
        ip_address       128.2.0.10      LOCAL_NET
        ip_netmask       255.255.0.0     LOCAL_NET
        ip_router        128.2.0.1       LOCAL_NET
        BIND NE2000 #1   Ethernet_II     LOCAL_NET
NetWare DOS Requester
        First Network Drive=F
```

The NET.CFG file format must follow these rules:

▸ Each section is identified by a header, which is entered flush with the left margin.

▸ The options within the sections must be indented using at least one space or tab character.

▸ Only one option should be entered per line.

▸ Parameters within the options must be separated by at least one space or tab character.

▸ Commands are not case sensitive, so you can use uppercase and lowercase letters to improve legibility.

Each section in NET.CFG, with the exception of the NetWare DOS Requester, gets involved in TCP/IP client configuration. Let's take a look at the sections.

The Link Support Section

Options in the Link Support section configure the ODI Link Support Layer (LSL), which is implemented by the file LSL.EXE. Table 9.1 describes the options that can appear in the Link Support section.

T A B L E 9.1

Link Support Section Options

OPTION	PARAMETER	PURPOSE
BUFFERS number [size]	number	Specifies the number and size of the receive buffers maintained by the LSL. The number parameter must specify enough buffers to hold all media headers together with the maximum amount of data specified by the size parameter. The buffer size is 618 bytes. The total buffer space (number × size) must be less than approximately 59 KB.
	size	Specifies the maximum amount of data accomodated by a receive buffer.
MAX BOARDS number	number	Specifies the number of logical boards the LSL will support. Each logical LAN driver uses one board resource. Any driver configured in a Link Driver section uses board resources. Range = 1 – 4. Default = 4.
MAX STACKS number	number	Specifies the maximum number of logical protocol stack IDs the LSL can support. Each protocol stack uses one or more stack ID resources. Increasing the number of stacks increases the memory requirements of the LSL. Range = 1 – 16. Default = 4.
MEMPOOL number [K]	number	Specifies the size of the memory pool buffer maintained by the LSL. The number parameter specifies memory in bytes unless the optional K parameter is included, indicating that the number parameter is multipled by 1024. This parameter is ignored by the IPXODI protocol stack.

Pay close attention to the MAX BOARDS and MAX STACKS options when configuring multiple protocol stacks. You can run out of resources fairly quickly. Suppose that you configure an NE2000 driver to support all four Ethernet frame types (Ethernet_II, Ethernet_802.3, Ethernet_802.2, and Ethernet_SNAP). That driver requires four board resources.

Some drivers that don't look like network board drivers also use board resources. When you see how LAN WorkPlace can be used to dial into an Internet access provider, you will run into the NCOM driver, which drives a serial port, not a network card. But NCOM still provides a network connection and uses a board resource.

The Link Driver Section

Each network interface is configured with a Link Driver section. Network interfaces most commonly are LAN interface cards, but with TCP/IP, serial connections can also be established that count as network interfaces.

Options in the Link Driver section fall into two categories: options that specify hardware characteristics of the network interface and options that specify software characteristics of the network driver. Table 9.2 summarizes the options you will encounter in this book. Examples of most options are provided in the sample NET.CFG file presented earlier in the chapter.

TABLE 9.2

Selected Link Driver Section Options

OPTION	PARAMETER VALUES	PURPOSE
DMA [#1|#2] *channel*	*channel*	Specifies the DMA channel the network interface is configured to use. Range: valid DMA for hardware.
FRAME *frame_type*	*frame_type*	For interfaces that can support more than one frame type, this option configures the driver to support a particular frame type. When multiple frame types are to be supported, a separate FRAME option is included for each frame type. (Early Ethernet drivers defaulted to Ethernet_802.3; current drivers default to Ethernet_802.2.) Range: valid frame type for hardware.
INT [#1|#2] *irq* or IRQ [#1|#2] *irq*	*irq*	Specifies the IRQ (in decimal) for which the network interface is configured. Newer clients use the IRQ keyword but continue to accept the older INT keyword. Range: valid IRQ for hardware.

OPTION	PARAMETER VALUES	PURPOSE
MEM [#1|#2] start_address	start_address	Specifies the starting memory address (in hex) of an area of memory that is reserved for use by this network interface.
[length]	length	Optionally specifies the length of the memory range.
PORT [#1|#2] start_address [ports]	start_address	Specifies the starting memory address (in hex) of a port, an area of memory that is used by this network interface for input/output.
	ports	A port size of up to 16 bytes can be specified by including a ports parameter, indicating the number of ports in hex.
PROTOCOL name protocol_id frametype	name	Specifies a protocol name for which a protocol number and frame type are to be declared. Example: IPX. (See the section "Specifying Protocol Frame Types" for more information.)
	protocol_id	Specifies a number in hex that identifies a protocol.
	frametype	Specifies a frame type that is valid for the protocol.
SLOT number	number	On slot-based systems, such as systems with EISA buses, specifies the slot in which the network interface hardware resides. The driver obtains network interface settings from the system configuration.

Configuring Multiple LAN Interfaces   The optional [#1|#2] parameter is seldom used, but because it appears in the option parameters and is placed in some NET.CFG files built by NetWare client INSTALL programs, it deserves an explanation. For network interfaces that support multiple channels, the channel hardware settings are identified by #1 and #2 parameters as in the following example:

```
Link Driver X
        IRQ     #1        5
        PORT    #1        340
        IRQ     #2        11
        PORT    #2        360
```

The first X driver that is loaded will be assigned the parameters identified by #1. The second X driver will be assigned the parameters identified by #2.

Workstations that require multiple LAN connections are more likely to be configured with two or more LAN cards, in which, each card must be configured with a Link Driver section, as shown in the following example:

```
Link Driver NE2000
       IRQ    5
       PORT   340

Link Driver NE2000
       IRQ    10
       PORT   360
```

Each driver is loaded separately in the protocol load sequence, for example:
```
LSL
NE2000
NE2000
IPXODI
VLM
```

Specifying Protocol Frame Types   You are unlikely to see a PROTOCOL option on an IPX-only network. This option serves an important function, however, when multiple protocol stacks and frame types are in use. In such cases, it enables the administrator to specify the frame type to which a protocol stack will be bound. The following example enables an NE2000 driver to support Ethernet_II and Ethernet_802.2 frames. To ensure that IPX will be configured with Ethernet_802.2 frames, a PROTOCOL IPX statement is added:

```
Link Driver NE2000
       IRQ               5
       PORT              340
       MEM               D0000
       FRAME             ETHERNET_II
       FRAME             ETHERNET_802.2
       PROTOCOL IPX E0 ETHERNET_802.2
```

Chapter 7 showed how ODI uses protocol IDs (PIDs) to associate data frames with upper-layer protocol stacks. Table 9.3 lists some of the protocol IDs that are established for protocols and frame types used with NetWare.

TABLE 9.3

Common Protocol IDs

PROTOCOL ID (HEX)	PROTOCOL	FRAME TYPE	DESCRIPTION
0	IPX/SPX	Ethernet_802.3	Raw Ethernet 802.3 encapsulation
E0	IPX/SPX	Ethernet_802.2	Ethernet 802.3, using IEEE 802.2 encapsulation
E0	IPX/SPX	Token-Ring	Token ring (IEEE 802.5), using IEEE 802.2 encapsulation
E0	IPX/SPX	FDDI_802.2	FDDI, using IEEE 802.2 encapsulation
800	IP	Ethernet_II	Ethernet, using an Ethernet II envelope
800	IP	Ethernet_SNAP	Ethernet 802.3, using an IEEE 802.2 envelope and SNAP encapsulation
800	IP	FDDI_SNAP	FDDI, using an IEEE 802.2 envelope and SNAP encapsulation
8137	IPX/SPX	Ethernet_II	Ethernet, using an Ethernet II envelope.
8137	IPX/SPX	Ethernet_SNAP	Ethernet 802.3, using an IEEE 802.2 envelope and SNAP encapsulation
8137	IPX/SPX	Token-Ring_SNAP	Token ring (IEEE 802.5), using an IEEE 802.2 envelope and SNAP encapsulation
8137	IPX/SPX	FDDI_SNAP	FDDI, using an IEEE 802.2 envelope and SNAP encapsulation

The Protocol Section

Each protocol can be configured by options in a Protocol section. The specific options depend on the protocol being configured. Table 9.4 summarizes the options used to configure the TCP/IP protocols. As you examine these parameters, you'll begin to realize why the operations of IP and TCP were covered so thoroughly in Chapters 4 and 5.

Protocol TCPIP Section Options

OPTION	PARAMETER	PURPOSE
BIND *driver* [*#board frame_type network_name*]		Specifies a binding between a network interface and a protocol stack. This option is required if more than one network interface driver will support a given protocol stack. If this parameter is not included, the TCPIP driver will bind using the Ethernet_II frame type.
	driver	Specifies the name of the ODI driver that is loaded for this board. If the MLID module is named NE2000.EXE, the driver parameter has the value NE2000.
	#board	This optional parameter specifies the number of the board to be bound. This parameter matches the physical load sequence of the driver, and is required only when more than one logical interface is defined. If this value is 0, TCPIP binds to the first board that supports TCP/IP and the frame type specified in the *frame_type* parameter.
	frame_type	Specifies the frame type to be used. This frame type is the same as the frame type specified in the Link Driver section for this driver.
	network_name	Specifies a logical name for this network connection. The *network_name* parameter is used to identify the network for the BIND, IP_ADDRESS, IP_ROUTER, and IP_NETMASK parameters.
IP_ADDRESS *address* [*network_name*]		This option specifies the IP address assigned to a network interface.
	address	Specifies an IP address, expressed in dotted-decimal notation. If this parameter is omitted, or has the value 0.0.0.0, the protocol uses BOOTP or Reverse ARP to determine an IP address.
	network_name	Specifies a logical name for this network connection. The *network_name* parameter is used to identify the network for the BIND, IP_ADDRESS, IP_ROUTER, and IP_NETMASK parameters.
IP_NETMASK *mask* [network_name]		Specifies the subnetwork mask to be used with this network interface.
	mask	Specifies a subnet mask, expressed in dotted-decimal notation.
	network_name	Specifies a logical name for this network connection. The *network_name* parameter is used to identify the network for the BIND, IP_ADDRESS, IP_ROUTER, and IP_NETMASK parameters.

OPTION	PARAMETER	PURPOSE
PATH LWP_CFG [[drive:] path [; ...]]	drive:path	Specifies the location of a directory that stores configuration files used by many LAN WorkPlace utilities.
PATH PROFILE [drive:] path	drive:path	Specifies the location of profile files used by LAN WorkPlace utilities such as the Host Presenter.
PATH SCRIPT [drive:] path	drive:path	Specifies the location of script files used by the Host Presenter.
PATH TCP_CFG [drive:] path	drive:path	Specifies one or more directories that contain the TCP/IP database configuration files HOSTS, NETWORKS, PROTOCOL, SERVICES, and RESOLVE.CFG. The default directory is \NET\TCP.
NO_BOOTP		Specifies that RARP should be used to identify a host's IP address, even if a BOOTP server is available.
TCP_WINDOW number	number	Specifies the maximum receive window size in bytes for the TCP protocol. The number parameter specifies a window size of up to 32,767 bytes.
TCP_MAXSEGSIZE number	number	Specifies the maximum size of segments constructed by TCP. The number parameter specifies a maximum segment size of 8192 bytes.
TCP_MINRXMIT number	number	Specifies the minimum number of timeouts allowed for TCP. The number parameter can specify a value of 1 to 540, with each timeout lasting 55 milliseconds.
TCP_MAXRXMIT number	number	Specifies the maximum number of timeouts allowed for TCP. The number parameter can specify a value from 1+TCP_MINRXMIT to 1080, with each timeout lasting 55 milliseconds.
TCP_SOCKETS number	number	Specifies the maximum number of concurrent TCP connections. If multiple TCPIP drivers are loaded, the number specified in this parameter is the total shared by all drivers. Range = 0 – 64. Default = 8.
UDP_SOCKETS number	number	Specifies the maximum number of concurrent UDP connections. If DNS is in use, at least one socket should be configured for each concurrently running UDP application. NetBIOS requires at least 2 UDP sockets. If multiple TCPIP drivers are loaded, the number parameter is the total shared by all drivers. Range = 0 – 32. Default = 8.
RAW_SOCKETS number	number	Specifies the maximum number of raw IP connections. At least one raw socket should be configured for applications using ICMP PING messages, including PING, Serving FTP, IP Resolver, and LWPCON. Default = 1.

By default, the TCP/IP protocol stack is configured with eight TCP sockets, eight UDP sockets, and one raw sockets. These numbers should be increased on clients that make heavy use of concurrent applications. Here are some guidelines:

- ▸ One TCP socket is required for each Telnet session

- ▸ Two TCP sockets are required for each FTP session

- ▸ One UDP socket is required for each application that uses DNS; however, UDP sockets are in use only when datagrams are actively sent and received, after which they are freed. The default number should be sufficient.

If a single network interface driver is loaded, IPX generally works fine with default values, and a Protocol IPXODI section is not required. You will see a need for a Protocol IPXODI section when IP tunneling is configured in Chapter 10, because multiple drivers will be loaded and it will be necessary to bind IPX to a specific driver.

Suppose that network interface drivers are loaded in the following order:

```
LSL
NE2000
NE2000
IPXODI
VLM
TCPIP
```

In the above example, two NE2000 drivers are loaded to correspond to two different network interface cards. The second card is attached to an IPX network, and you wish to ensure that IPX will be bound to the second device driver. To do that, include a BIND statement in a Protocol IPXODI section, like this:

```
Protocol IPXODI
        Bind #2
```

Installing NetWare TCP/IP Transport for DOS

The NetWare TCP/IP Transport for DOS is included with the NetWare Client for DOS and MS Windows. Several versions of the NetWare DOS client are available, and the versions included with NetWare 3.13 and 4.1 include TCP/IP support. The latest version of the DOS client is version 1.20, which is available from NetWire, Novell's forum on CompuServe.

You will need to supply your own TCP/IP applications, but that's not a difficult proposition. The TCP/IP Transport supports the Windows Sockets (WINSOCK) API and the Windows 3.x BSD socket API, which enables the TCP/IP Transport to work with the vast majority of DOS and Windows TCP/IP applications.

Other features of the TCP/IP Transport for DOS include:

- ▸ SLIP and PPP serial line drivers

- ▸ Reverse ARP (RARP) server

- ▸ PING

- ▸ IP tunnel driver

- ▸ SNMP agent

- ▸ LWPCON (an SNMP console)

This section covers installation and configuration of the TCP/IP transport. RARP is examined in the section "Central Assignment of IP Addresses"; SLIP and PPP drivers are covered later in this chapter in the section "Serial Connections for TCP/IP Clients"; and PING is covered in the section "Novell's TCP/IP Applications."

IP tunneling is covered in Chapter 10 (Internetworking NetWare TCP/IP), and you can learn about the SNMP agent and LWPCON in Chapter 11 (Managing NetWare TCP/IP).

INSTALLING THE NETWARE TCP/IP TRANSPORT

If you have installed any NetWare clients, this section holds no great surprises for you. The TCP/IP Transport is an add-on to the NetWare Client for DOS and MS Windows, so we'll examine installation of this NetWare client before getting down to TCP/IP.

Installing the NetWare Client for DOS and Windows

The NetWare Client for DOS and MS Windows, version 1.20, occupies five floppy disks. The software can be downloaded from CompuServe. At this writing, the files are in the NWOSFILES forum.

The client computer must meet the following minimum system requirements:

- ▸ 386-class or better CPU

- ▸ 4 MB of memory if Windows applications will be used

- ▸ MS-DOS 3.3 (or later), DR DOS 6.0 (or later), or Novell DOS 7.0 (or later)

- ▸ Windows 3.1 or later running in enhanced mode if Windows is used

In addition, a network interface card should be installed in the computer and configured with non-conflicting settings. If the network interface card is not supported by drivers included with the NetWare client, you will also require the drivers provided by the card's manufacturer.

To install the software, follow these steps:

1 • Insert Disk 1 in a diskette drive of the client computer.

2 • Enter the command **A:INSTALL** or **B:INSTALL** as appropriate. The installation program will open the NetWare Client Install form shown in Figure 9.2. This form organizes the installation procedure into six steps.

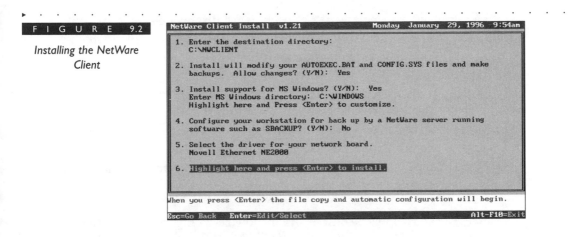

FIGURE   9.2

Installing the NetWare Client

3 • Step 1 specifies the directory in which client files will be placed. By default, the directory is C:\NWCLIENT. I recommend that you retain the default directory.

4 • Step 2 specifies whether CONFIG.SYS and AUTOEXEC.BAT should be updated automatically. I recommend that you retain the default response of *Yes*. If these files are modified by INSTALL, the original files are saved with the extension .BNW.

5 • Step 3 specifies whether Windows will be supported and identifies the Windows directory.

Windows installation allows you to customize two options. Select *Highlight here and Press <Enter> to customize* to change the following settings:

▶ **Additional country codes.** The country code configures the character set and keyboard layout. If this client will be using more than one country code, respond *Yes* to the prompt "Do you plan to use more country codes than the one currently running on your machine? (Y/N)."

▶ **Shared network path for Windows.** If this client will be using a shared windows directory, respond *Yes* to the prompt "Do you want to set the shared MS Windows Path? (Y/N)" Then specify the path to the shared directory in the field that is provided.

6 • Step 4 specifies whether backup agent software should be configured on this client. If you respond *Yes,* a form is displayed in which you enter SMS configuration information.

7 • Step 5 enables you to select and configure a network driver. Select *Highlight here and press <Enter> to see list* to select a network driver. Drivers may be loaded from the ODI LAN Drivers diskette that is included with the NetWare Client for DOS and MS Windows, or you can load drivers from a vendor's diskette for products that are not supported by the standard client disks.

8 • Step 6 initiates software installation. Select *Highlight here and press <Enter> to install* to install software. Change diskettes as prompted.

The client INSTALL program makes the following changes to the client file system:

▸ Creates the client directory if necessary. The default client directory is C:\NWCLIENT.

▸ Copies protocol and driver files to the client directory.

▸ Creates or modifies the NET.CFG file that establishes a basic protocol configuration, placing the file in C:\NWCLIENT.

▸ Creates or modifies the STARTNET.BAT file in the client directory.

▸ Adds the command CALL C:\NWCLIENT\STARTNET.BAT to the end of the AUTOEXEC.BAT file.

▸ Edits CONFIG.SYS as required.

Here is an example of the NET.CFG file that INSTALL will create:

```
Link Driver NE2000
        IRQ 5
        PORT 340
        FRAME Ethernet_802.2
```

```
NetWare DOS Requester
     FIRST NETWARE DRIVE = F
     NETWARE PROTOCOL = NDS BIND
```

The STARTNET.BAT file that INSTALL creates resembles the following:

```
SET NWLANGUATE=English
C:\NWCLIENT\LSL.COM
C:\NWCLIENT\NE2000.COM
C:\NWCLIENT\IPXODI.COM
C:\NWCLIENT\VLM.COM
```

The STARTNET.BAT file is executed when the client boots by a CALL C:\NWCLIENT\STARTNET.BAT statement that is added to the end of the AUTOEXEC.BAT file.

Installing TCP/IP Transport for DOS

After the DOS client has been installed and is verified to be operating properly in the IPX environment, you can install TCP/IP Transport for DOS. The procedure is as follows:

1 • Insert the TCP/IP Transport for DOS diskette in a diskette drive of the client computer.

2 • Enter the command **A:INSTALL** or **B:INSTALL** as appropriate.

3 • The first form that appears is named Destination Drive Selection. This form lists various known network and local drives on which the TCP/IP software can be installed. Select a drive and press Enter.

4 • Next, you are prompted to "Select the target directory." INSTALL proposes the \NET directory on the drive you chose in Step 3 (e.g., C:\NET). Select another directory if desired, but I recommend using the default. After you specify a directory, files will be copied.

5 • INSTALL then asks "Does your workstation boot from a file server?" Respond *Yes* or *No*.

6 • The next prompt asks "Do you want INSTALL to update your system files?" Respond *Yes* (the recommended response) if the AUTOEXEC.BAT, NET.CFG, and SYSTEM.INI (if Windows is installed) files should be updated. Your original AUTOEXEC.BAT and NET.CFG files will be saved with the extension .LWP.

INSTALL creates a file named LANWP.BAT in the root directory. If a LANWP.BAT file already exists, the old file is renamed OLANWP.BAT.

7 • Next you are asked "Are TCP/IP parameters provided automatically by a BOOTP server?" If a BOOTP server such as LAN WorkGroup is operating on your LAN, choose *Yes* if an IP address and other parameters should be obtained from BOOTP. Choose *No* if this host will be assigned a fixed IP configuration.

8 • If you responded *No* in step 7, you will be prompted for the following information:

▸ The IP address of the workstation.

▸ Whether the network has subnets.

▸ If subnets are used, the subnet mask for this workstation.

▸ Whether the network is equipped with an IP router.

▸ If an IP router is present, the IP address of the router.

▸ Whether the network has a Domain Name Server.

▸ If a Domain Name Server is available, the domain name and IP address of the primary DNS server.

9 • Next you will see the prompt, "Do you want to install the SLIP/PPP driver?" Choose Yes if this host will be connecting to a TCP/IP host or network through a serial connection.

10 • If you chose Yes in step 9, you will see a list of SLIP_PPP parameters. You do not need to configure these settings here. You will learn how to configure the SLIP-PPP driver with the Windows Dial-up utility in the section "Serial Connections for TCP/IP Clients."

Configuring NET.CFG for TCP/IP

Below is the NET.CFG file after TCP/IP Transport has been installed. In this case, SLIP_PPP protocol support was not configured. New lines appear in boldface Some comments have been added to explain the additions.

```
Link Driver NE2000
     IRQ 5
     PORT 340
PROTOCOL IPX E0 Ethernet_802.2 #Force IPX to use 802.2 frames
FRAME Ethernet_II                #Allows Ethernet_II frames
FRAME Ethernet_802.2             #Allows IEEE 802.2 frames

NetWare DOS Requester
     FIRST NETWARE DRIVE = F
     NETWARE PROTOCOL = NDS BIND

Link Support
     Buffers 8 1500
     MemPool 4096

Protocol TCPIP
     PATH SCRIPT     C:\NET\SCRIPT
     PATH PROFILE    C:\NET\PROFILE
     PATH LWP_CFG    C:\NET\HSTACC
     PATH TCP_CFG    C:\NET\TCP
     ip_router       128.1.0.1
     ip_netmask      255.255.0.0
     ip_address       128.1.0.10
```

The Link Support section is added to increase the resource allocation, as required by the additional protocol stack.

A new FRAME statement in the Link Driver section enables the NE2000 driver to support Ethernet_II frames, and a PROTOCOL IPX statement ensures that IPX is bound to the correct frame type.

The TCP/IP Transport software is a subset of software that is included with LAN WorkPlace for DOS and Windows. You can see vestiges of LAN Workplace in the PATH LWP_CFG statement, where LWP stands for LAN WorkPlace.

NOTE
The TCP/IP Transport INSTALL program creates the NET.CFG file in the root directory of the destination drive. You may wish to move this file to the \NWCLIENT directory. If you do, you need to ensure that program modules not stored in \NWCLIENT can find the NET.CFG file. TCPIP.EXE, which is installed in \NET\BIN will find NET.CFG if it is stored in the root or in the \NWCLIENT directory.

Loading TCP/IP Transport

When TCP/IP Transport is installed, a file named LANWP.BAT is created in the root directory of the destination drive. The contents of this file are as follows:

```
C:\NET\BIN\yesno "Do you want to load the TCP/IP transport? [Y/N] "
if errorlevel 1 goto noload
PATH C:\NET\BIN;%path%
tcpip.exe
break on
:noload
```

The first command line of the batch file calls a program named YESNO.EXE in C:\NET\BIN. This program accepts a keystroke and generates a DOS 1 error level code for N and a 0 error level code for Y. These error codes are used by the IF ERRORLEVEL statement to decide whether TCP/IP Transport will be loaded. A response of N generates an error code of 1 and bypasses loading of the transport by causing the execution of the GOTO NOLOAD statement. The YESNO utility also is used in configuration files generated for LAN WorkPlace and LAN WorkGroup.

The statement PATH C:\NET\BIN;%path% appends the C:\NET\BIN directory to the beginning of the existing PATH environment variable.

Installing LAN WorkPlace

LAN WorkPlace, version 5, includes everything you need to configure a DOS client for IPX/SPX and TCP/IP. Installation is quite simple. As an added benefit, LAN WorkPlace includes DOS and Windows tools for configuring the workstation protocols, in many cases eliminating the need to tinker with NET.CFG and startup batch files.

LAN WorkPlace is a client-centric package, designed to be installed entirely on the client computer. Installation can be made from floppy disks or CD-ROM. Be advised that LAN WorkPlace comes on a lot of floppies, and CD-ROM installation is by far the easiest route, particularly if you have a shared CD-ROM on your network. After taking you on a tour of the installation procedure, I'll show you how to use the client configuration utility.

INSTALLATION

The client computer must meet the following minimum system requirements:

- 386-class or better CPU

- 2 MB of memory if Windows applications will be used

- At least 400KB of hard drive space on an uncompressed volume, to be used during installation

- Sufficient free space on the hard drive to accept the modules that will be installed. See Figure 9.3 for the modules and their sizes.

- MS-DOS 3.3 (or later), DR DOS 6.0 (or later), or Novell DOS 7.0 (or later)

- Windows 3.1 or later running in enhanced mode

- VGA or better display

In the following installation procedures, it is assumed that no client software is installed on the computer. If a client is already installed, some of the configuration settings in the NET.CFG and startup batch files will be read into INSTALL, saving you some of the work shown here. To install LAN WorkPlace:

1 • Place the CD-ROM or Disk 1 in a drive.

2 • Type **<Drive>:INSTALL** as appropriate for the drive being used. This will open the installation form shown in Figure 9.3.

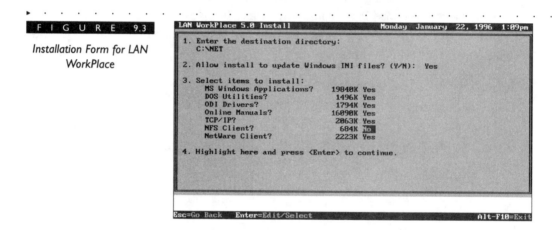

F I G U R E   9.3

Installation Form for LAN WorkPlace

3 • In Step 1, specify the directory in which LAN WorkPlace client files will be installed. I recommend accepting the default directory C:\NET.

4 • In Step 2, specify whether to allow install to update Windows INI files. I recommend selecting *Yes*.

5 • In Step 3, select the modules to install. Change the *Yes/No* field to *No* if a particular module should not be installed. The modules are as follows:

▸ **MS Windows Applications.** This module installs the suite of Windows applications included with LAN WorkPlace.

▸ **DOS Utilities.** This module installs the DOS Utilities.

▸ **ODI Drivers**. Install this module if the workstation does not have ODI drivers, or if you wish to overwrite existing drivers with the drivers provided with LAN WorkPlace. In general, you should install the LAN WorkPlace drivers to ensure compatibility.

▸ **Online Manuals**. Most of the documentation for LAN WorkPlace is provided in electronic manuals. Users may not need this information, but administrators certainly will.

▸ **TCP/IP**. This module installs TCP/IP protocols. This is the entire point of LAN WorkPlace, isn't it?

▸ **NFS Client**. Install this module if your network uses NFS.

▸ **NetWare Client**. Install this module if the workstation will log into NetWare servers in addition to connecting to TCP/IP.

6 • Select *Highlight here and press <Enter> to continue* when this form has been configured as desired. Files will be copied to the workstation. If you are installing from floppies, supply diskettes as requested.

7 • After files are copied, you will see a new screen headed with the message "The Install Utility is finished."

▸ Press Alt+F10 if you wish to build the client configuration files manually.

▸ Press Enter to start the LAN WorkPlace configuration program, which enables you to build the client configuration files using a graphical utility. (The remaining steps assume that Enter has been pressed.)

8 • If a NET.CFG file is in the C:\NWCLIENT directory, the settings will be read into the configuration program. Otherwise, you will see the message "Unable to open the configuration file C:\NWCLIENT\NET.CFG." Press Enter to open the configuration program.

The configuration program is shown in Figure 9.4. The program has nine configuration areas, which are opened by selecting an option in the Areas menu. Several areas should be examined while establishing a basic client configuration. You can move around in this screen by pressing the Tab key. Or, if a mouse driver is installed, you can use a mouse to select options directly.

In the fields that support choices from a list, highlight the field and press F4 to open the selection list. Most of the field names have one letter highlighted in yellow or inverse text. These fields can be selected by typing Alt along with the letter that is highlighted. For example, Alt+B selects the *Brand* field.

FIGURE 9.4

*The LAN WorkPlace
Configuration Utility*

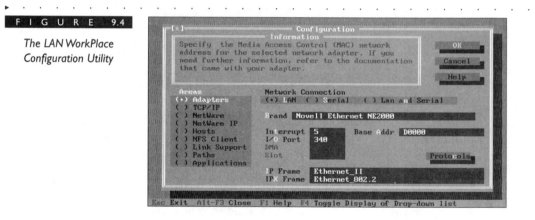

9 • The Adapters area configures options shown in Figure 9.4. The options in this area are:

▸ **Network Connection**. Network Connection. Choices here enable you to specify whether this will be a LAN, a serial client, or both. LAN clients can access network resources using IPX or TCP/IP protocols. Serial clients are configured to make direct or dial-in connections to TCP/IP hosts.

▸ **Brand**. Tab to this field and press F4 to select network card driver from a list. Press Enter to save the selection.

▸ **Link Driver settings.** Five Link Driver settings can be configured: Interrupt, I/O Port, DMA, Slot, and Base Address.

▸ **IP Frame.** Tab to this field and press F4 to select the frame type that will be used for TCP/IP. Of course, Ethernet_II is the heavy favorite, and Ethernet_SNAP is the only viable alternative.

▸ **IPX Frame.** Tab to this field and press F4 to select the frame type that will be used for IPX. The default is Ethernet_802.2.

▸ **Protocols.** Press Alt+C to open the adapter protocol configuration form shown in Figure 9.5. This frame configures PROTOCOL statements that appear in the Link Drivers section of the NET.CFG file.

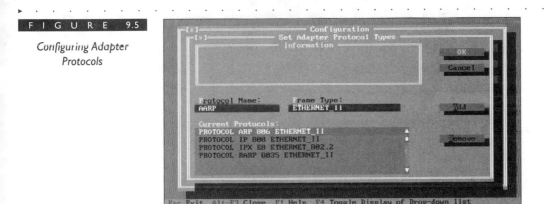

FIGURE 9.5

Configuring Adapter Protocols

10 • The Current Protocols list displays the PROTOCOL statements that are currently configured for the adapter. To add a protocol entry, tab to the Protocol Name field, press F4, and select a protocol. Then tab to Frame Type, press F4, and select a frame type. Finally, type Alt+A to add the entry. To delete a protocol entry, tab to the Current Protocols box, select the protocol to be deleted, and type Alt+D. After protocols have been configured, choose OK or press Esc to return to the main configuration screen.

11 • The TCP/IP area, shown in Figure 9.6, configures options that appear in the Protocol TCPIP section of the NET.CFG file. The parameters in this area are as follows:

▶ **Load TCP/IP**. Check this option if TCP/IP protocols are to be loaded. This option determines whether batch files will execute the TCPIP.EXE program when the system boots.

▶ **IP Address**. If the system will not use BOOTP to obtain an IP address, this field specifies the IP address that will be assumed by IP.

▶ **Subnet Mask.** If the system will not use BOOTP to obtain an IP address, this field specifies the subnet mask that will be used by IP.

▶ **Domain Name**. If this network uses DNS to resolve host names to IP addresses, this field specifies the domain in which this host resides.

▶ **Use BOOTP.** If this field is checked, this host will obtain its IP address and other address information from a BOOTP server.

▶ **DNS IP Addresses**. This field accepts IP addresses for primary, secondary, and tertiary DNS name servers.

▶ **Routing.** This field accepts IP addresses for primary, secondary, and tertiary routers.

FIGURE 9.6

Configuring the TCP/IP Protocols

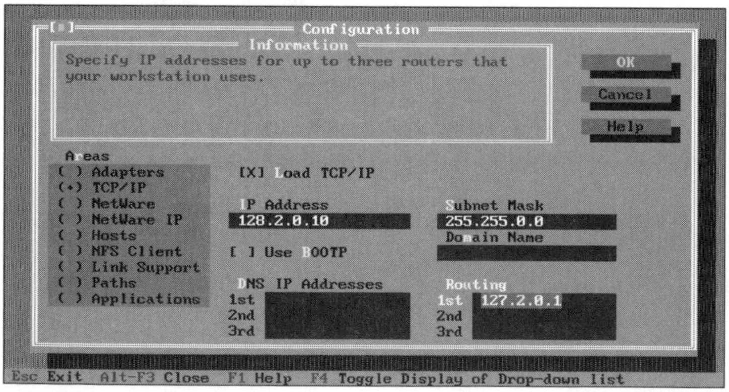

12 • The NetWare area is used to configure options in the NetWare Requester section of the NET.CFG file. The data entry form for this area is shown in Figure 9.7. The options that are part of a basic configuration are:

▸ **Load NetWare Client.** Check this option if the NetWare VLM client should be loaded after the protocol stack is loaded.

▸ **NetWare Protocol.** IPX usually should be selected. If NetWare/IP is in use, however, you can select IP to enable this client to access NetWare via the TCP/IP protocol stack.

▸ **First NetWare Drive.** This option determines the drive letter that will be mapped to the login directory when the NetWare requester connects with a server.

▸ **Preferred Server.** For NetWare 3 users, and users who access NetWare 4 in bindery mode, this option specifies the name of the server with which the DOS requester will first attempt to establish a connection.

▸ **Preferred Tree**. For users of NetWare 4 in NDS mode, this option specifies the name of the tree with which the DOS requester will first attempt to establish a connection.

Other options on this screen are used when the client will access NetWare via NetWare/IP. These options will be examined in Chapter 12.

Configuring the NetWare Requester

13 • The NetWare IP area configures the client to access NetWare using TCP/IP and NetWare/IP. See Chapter 12 for information on configuring NetWare/IP.

14 • The Hosts area can be used to build a hosts file. When you select this option, the configuration utility shows a list of entries in the hosts file. Type Alt+E to open to open the Editing the Host Table form shown in Figure 9.8. Complete the fields and choose OK to add an entry to the hosts file.

Adding an Entry to the hosts File

15 • The NFS Client area configures the NFS client software that is included with LAN WorkPlace. NFS configuration is beyond the scope of this book.

16 • The Link Support area (see Figure 9.9) configures five options that can appear in the Link Support section of the NET.CFG file. The parameters that can be configured from this form are:

▶ **Memory Pool**. Specifies the *number* parameter for the MEMPOOL option, which determines the size of the memory pool that will be available for buffering in the LSL.

▶ **Buffer Count**. Specifies the *number* parameter of the BUFFERS option, which determines the number of receive buffers that will be configured.

▶ **Buffer Size**. Specifies the *size* parameter of the BUFFERS option, which determines the size of each buffer.

▶ **Max Boards**. Specifies the *number* parameter for the MAX BOARDS option, which determines how many logical network interfaces the LSL will support.

▶ **Max Stacks**. Specifies the *number* parameter for the MAX STACKS option, which determines how many logical protocol stacks the LSL will support.

FIGURE 9.9

Configuring Link Support Options

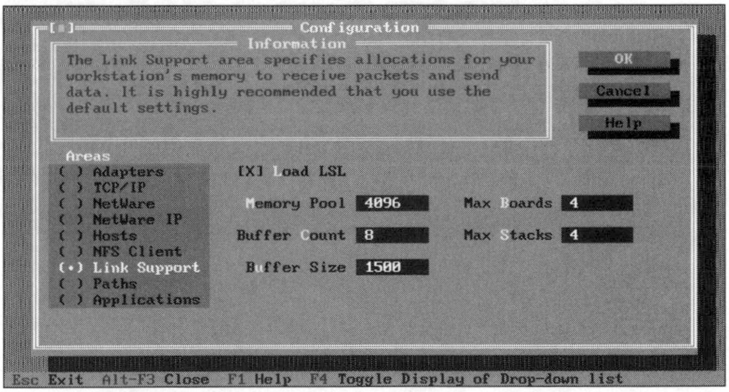

17 • The Paths area (see Figure 9.10) specifies paths to a number of LAN WorkPlace directories. The following directory paths can be configured:

▶ **Configuration**. This directory specifies the location of the LAN WorkPlace internal configuration and data files.

▶ **Profile.** This directory specifies the location of the profile files.

▶ **Script.** This directory specifies the location of scripts for the Script Directory, which is used to automate login procedures when making serial connections.

▶ **Spool.** This directory specifies the directory to be used when spooling print jobs that are handled by the LPR print client.

▶ **Xfonts.** This directory determines the location of fonts used by the X-Server application.

▶ **TCP/IP.** This directory contains the TCP/IP database files (e.g., hosts, networks, and gateways) and the RESOLVE.CFG file.

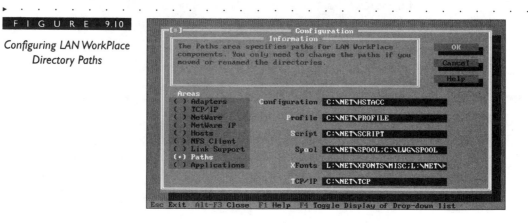

F I G U R E   9.10

*Configuring LAN WorkPlace
Directory Paths*

18 • The Applications area specifies settings used by several LAN WorkPlace applications. The fields shown in Figure 9.11 are used to configure the following settings:

▶ **Username.** Specifies the username that will be used with the Talk utility and several remote TCP/IP utilities. The username is case dependent. Be sure that all your hosts adhere to the same capitalization conventions.

▸ **Primary Terminal Emulation Protocol.** Specifies the protocol that is to be used for terminal emulators such as the Host Presenter.

▸ **XFonts**. If 100-dpi X-Server fonts are installed, this option specifies the font size that will be used.

▸ **Load LPR Print Client Network Driver.** Check this option if this host will support the LPR print services.

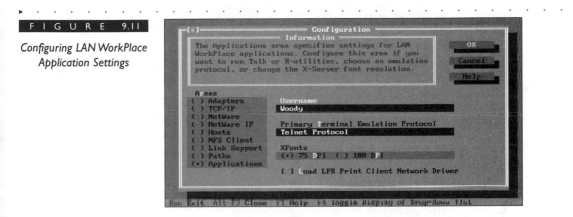

F I G U R E   9.11

*Configuring LAN WorkPlace
Application Settings*

19 • When all required areas have been configured, choose OK to save the configuration data and exit to DOS.

A Windows version of the configuration utility is included with LAN Workplace. Look for its icon in the LAN WorkPlace program group in Windows.

NOTE

CHANGES MADE WHEN INSTALLING LAN WORKPLACE

The LAN WorkPlace INSTALL program creates two directory structures:

▸ \NWCLIENT, containing the DOS client files, is created if it doesn't already exist

▸ \NET, containing the LAN WorkPlace files and all TCP/IP-related directories and files

In the \NET\BIN directory, INSTALL creates a batch file named STARTNET.BAT. This batch file contains the commands to load the protocol stacks and the DOS requester. In addition, if a serial connection was configured, STARTNET.BAT contains commands to load the NCOMX driver. We'll examine STARTNET.BAT in the next section. STARTNET.BAT is executed by the following line, which is added to the end of the AUTOEXEC.BAT file:

```
CALL C:\NET\BIN\STARTNET.BAT
```

A NET.CFG file is created in the \NWCLIENT directory. Here is a sample of the file INSTALL will create. I have moved things around a bit and lined up some columns to make the file easier to read:

```
Link Support
    Buffers             8 1500
    MemPool             4096
    Max Boards          4
    Max Stacks          4
Link Driver NE2000
    IRQ                 5
    PORT                340
    MEM                 D0000
    Frame               Ethernet_802.2
    Frame               Ethernet_II
Link Driver NCOMX
    IRQ         4
    PORT        3F8
Protocol TCPIP
    PATH TCP_CFG        C:\NET\TCP
    ip_address          128.1.0.10      LAN_NET
    ip_netmask          255.255.0.0     LAN_NET
    ip_router           128.1.0.1       LAN_NET
    Bind NE2000         #1 Ethernet_II  LAN_NET
    ip_address          0.0.0.0         PPP_NET
    Bind                NCOMX #1        PPP PPP_NET
```

```
NWIP
    AUTORETRIES       1
    AUTORETRY SECS    10
    NSQ_BROADCAST     ON
    NWIP1_1 COMPATIBILITY    OFF
NetWare DOS Requester
    First Network Drive = f
    Preferred Tree    iw
```

Much of this file should be familiar to you by now, so we'll only examine the new components. First is a new Link Driver NCOMX section. NCOMX is a serial driver that works in conjunction with the Dialer Windows utility, supporting dial-in access to TCP/IP hosts. NCOMX and the Dialer will be described in the section "Serial Connections for TCP/IP Clients."

The Protocol TCP/IP section makes extensive use of the *network_name* parameter. The LAN_NET identifies parameters associated with the connection to the local NE2000 network interface. The PPP_NET label identifies parameters associated with the NCOMX serial driver.

The parameters for LAN_NET are similar to parameters we have seen already, with a hard-configured IP address and other parameters. For PPP_NET, however, the ip_address statement declares an address of 0.0.0.0, which means that an address will be assigned when the connection is established.

The NWIP section defines options for the NetWare/IP client, described in Chapter 12.

STARTING THE LAN WORKPLACE CLIENT

After LAN Workplace is installed, the STARTNET.BAT file will be executed by AUTOEXEC.BAT when the client is booted. STARTNET.BAT offers several prompts to the user when it executes. Here are the prompts and the events that take place:

Load the LAN Support software [y/n]?   If the user responds **Y** to this prompt, the following commands are executed (assuming the system is configured with an NE2000 network adapter):

```
C:\NWCLIENT\LSL /C=C:\NWCLIENT\NET.CFG
C:\NWCLIENT\NE2000
```

The /C parameter for the LSL command specifies the location of the NET.CFG file that is to be used.

Do you want to load the SLIP/PPP Interface [y/n]?   This prompt appears if you have configured LAN Workgroup for both LAN and serial network connections (see Step 9 in the installation procedure). If you respond **Y** to this prompt, the following commands are executed:

```
C:\NWCLIENT\LSL /C=C:\NWCLIENT\NET.CFG
C:\NWCLIENT\NESL
C:\NWCLIENT\NCOMX
C:\NWCLIENT\NWREMOTE
```

The LSL.COM command is executed again in case the user responded **N** to loading LAN support software. The remaining commands load modules that support serial dial-up connections. These commands are described in the section "Serial Connections for TCP/IP Clients."

At this point, at least one network driver has been loaded (NE2000 or NCOMX) and possibly both have been loaded. The loaded driver(s) enable the workstation to support a protocol stack. If TCP/IP support has been enabled on this workstation, the following command is executed, regardless of the response to the previous prompt:

```
C:\NET\BIN\TCPIP
```

Do you want to load the NetWare Client Software [y/n]?   If you respond **Y** to this final prompt, the following commands are executed:

```
C:\NWCLIENT\IPXODI
C:\NWCLIENT\VLM
```

These commands load the IPX protocol stack and the NetWare Requester. Finally, a series of commands is executed that sets up the user's network environment:

```
PATH C:\NET\BIN;%PATH\
SET NAME=Woody
SET TELAPI_XPORT=Telnet
SET NWLANGUAGE=ENGLISH
```

These commands accomplish the following tasks:

▶ Append C:\NET\BIN to the beginning of the user's DOS PATH environment variable.

▶ Set the name variable that establishes the username for TCP/IP applications such as Talk and various R-utilities (so named because their program names start with the letter R).

▶ Specify the protocol to be used for terminal emulators.

▶ Set the NetWare NWLANGUAGE environment variable.

After STARTNET.BAT has completed, TCP/IP will be running over the LAN driver and/or the serial driver. Also, a NetWare Requester may be running over the IPX protocol stack. At this point, users can begin to work with the applications included with LAN WorkPlace (see "Novell's TCP/IP Applications" section).

Installing LAN WorkGroup

LAN WorkGroup, version 5, provides users with most of the features of LAN WorkPlace. The chief difference between these two products is that LAN WorkGroup is designed for central administration: Most files accessed by users are stored on the server. More important, however, is that LAN WorkGroup supports the BOOTP protocol, which enables TCP/IP clients to obtain their addresses and other configuration information from a central address server.

BOOTP is easy to configure and relieves network administrators of the tedious responsibility of managing IP address assignments manually. With manual IP address assignment, you can't just move a host to a new network and plug it in. You also have to give it a new and unique IP address. Errors are common, and the record keeping can be a pain. LAN WorkGroup may be the best present you can give yourself as a NetWare TCP/IP administrator. Automatic address assignment are discussed in detail in the section Central Assignment of IP Addresses.

LAN WorkGroup enables you to manage centrally several aspects of your TCP/IP clients. This is done by creating workstation types that determine the workstation configurations. Workstation type management isn't difficult. LAN WorkGroup also must be configured with information about the network. This area requires a bit of planning, but the process is relatively straightforward.

PLANNING LAN WORKGROUP CONFIGURATION

Planning for LAN Workgroup involves decisions in five areas:

- ▸ Defining workstation types

- ▸ Configuring subnetworks

- ▸ Setting LAN WorkGroup parameters

- ▸ Defining IP address assignment

- ▸ Entering excluded nodes

None of these areas is particularly complex. Let's examine them in turn.

Planning Workstation Types

When LAN WorkGroup is installed on a client, the installation is configured as a workstation type. A default workstation type, which is always present, is used when another workstation type is not specified, but administrators can create as many workstation types as necessary to match the characteristics of the clients on the LAN.

Most of the parameters defined when establishing a workstation type define settings in the NET.CFG file. The parameters in a workstation type are as follows:

- ▸ **Workstation Type Name.** A name specified by the network administrator. The default workstation type is named "!default".

- ▸ **Boot Drive.** The drive letter from which the client boots. The default is C:.

- ▸ **Link Driver Setup/Name.** The name of the MLID that will be loaded on the client.

- ▸ **Frame Type for IP.** Either Ethernet_II (the default) or Ethernet_SNAP.

- ▸ **Buffer Size.** Specifies the *size* parameter of the BUFFERS option in the Link Support section. Default = 1500.

▸ **Number of Buffers.** Specifies the *number* parameter of the BUFFERS option in the Link Support section. Default = 8.

▸ **Memory Pool Size.** Specifies the *number* parameter of the MEMPOOL option in the Link Support section. Default = 4096.

▸ **Maximum Number of Boards.** Specifies the *number* parameter of the MAX BOARDS option in the Link Support section. Default = 4.

▸ **Maximum Number of Stacks.** Specifies the *number* parameter of the MAX STACKS option in the Link Support section. Default = 4.

▸ **Primary Terminal Emulation.** Specifies the protocol that will be used in TCP/IP terminal emulators.

▸ **XFonts.** Sets the font size in dpi for fonts displayed by the X Windows Server application.

▸ **Load LPR Print Client Driver.** Determines whether the client will support TCP/IP printing by running the LPR client.

▸ **NFS Client Configuration.** Determines whether the client will load the NFS client.

You must define a workstation type for each group of workstations that has a unique combination of these parameters.

NOTE

Notice that none of the parameters relate to the Link Drivers, Protocol IPXODI, or NetWare DOS Requester sections of NET.CFG. To install LAN WorkGroup on a workstation, the workstation must be logged into NetWare, and it is assumed that network software is installed and configured. LAN WorkGroup INSTALL will add its own software and configuration files, but it won't affect files that are already in place.

Planning Subnetwork Configuration

LAN WorkGroup refers to each TCP/IP segment as a *subnet*, whether or not subnet addressing is involved. Throughout this book, I have used the term subnet to describe a network segment on which subnetting is configured. However, the use of the term subnet to describe any TCP/IP segment, subnetted or not, is extremely common in TCP/IP literature. Within the context of LAN WorkGroup, I'll fall in line and use the term subnet to describe a TCP/IP network segment.

Each subnet on your network must be entered into the LAN WorkGroup configuration. For each subnet, you must specify the following information:

- **Subnetwork Address**. The netid for the network segment.

- **Subnetwork Mask**. The subnet mask for the network segment. The default mask is entered if subnet addressing is not used.

- **Frame Type**. The frame type that will support IP on this network segment. The default is Ethernet_II.

- **Default Router**. You can specify up to three default routers for each network segment.

- **Domain Name System Used**. You can specify whether hosts on this segment may use DNS to resolve host names.

- **Domain Name**. If DNS is used, this field is displayed to specify the DNS domain name.

- **Primary, Secondary, and Tertiary Name Servers**. If DNS is used, the IP addresses of up to three name servers can be specified.

- **Automatic IP Address Assignment**. You can specify whether clients on this segment can obtain IP addresses from LAN WorkGroup.

- **Assign All Subnet IP Addresses**. You can specify whether all of the addresses on the segment are available for automatic assignment.

▶ **Start Address/End Address**. If not all addresses are available for automatic assignment, these fields can be used to specify a range of addresses that are available for automatic assignment. Otherwise, these fields indicate the full range of addresses on the subnet.

▶ **NetWare/IP Configuration**. You can specify whether NetWare/IP is supported on the subnet.

▶ **View Configured Workstations**. Allows you to view a list of the workstations that have already been registered on the subnet. No data entry is required for this field.

When multiple subnets are involved, setting up automatic IP address assignment requires a bit more work. See the section "Central Assignment of IP Addresses" for the details.

Planning LAN WorkGroup Parameters

LAN WorkGroup has three configuration parameters. You should determine the values of these parameters before you begin the installation program:

▶ **Private Path**. This parameter specifies the directory in which each user's private files will be stored. By default, this path is C:\LWG.

▶ **Shared Drive**. This parameter specifies a drive letter that is mapped to the directory containing the LAN WorkGroup files on the network. All users share this directory.

▶ **SYS Drive**. This parameter specifies a drive letter that is mapped to the SYS drive. If the LAN WorkGroup shared files are stored on the SYS drive, this parameter can have the same drive letter as the shared drive.

Planning IP Address Assignment

LAN WorkGroup allows you to assign fixed addresses to some or all of your hosts. Hosts need fixed IP addresses primarily when they are providing a service. Both of the naming systems covered in this book, HOSTS files and DNS, rely on static configuration files, which must be edited manually if a name-to-address relationship changes. Any host that is named in static HOSTS files or DNS requires a fixed address. If a host connects with a different IP address each time it enters the network, its name cannot be resolved by a static naming service. A LAN WorkGroup host that is functioning as an LPD print server or an FTP server, for example, would need a fixed address.

To create a fixed IP address, you need two pieces of information:

- ▸ The physical address of the hosts network adapter

- ▸ The IP address to be assigned.

In NetWare 3, you can discover the physical address of a logged-on workstation by using the USERLIST /A command. In NetWare 4, you can display a list of users with their physical addresses by using the NLIST USER /A command. In either case, the physical address will appear in the Node column.

As part of your preparation for LAN WorkGroup, you should make a list of the hosts that require fixed IP address assignments along with their physical addresses.

Planning Excluded Nodes

In the previous section, you learned that automatic address assignment can be configured to assign fixed addresses to selected hosts. Even though these hosts are assigned fixed addresses, they still obtain their addresses from BOOTP.

In some circumstances, it may be necessary to block hosts from accessing BOOTP altogether. If, for example, a router is sending invalid BOOTP requests, you can exclude it from BOOTP to prevent it from using up available IP addresses. If any hosts are to be excluded from BOOTP, you should make a list of the physical addresses of those nodes.

INSTALLING LAN WORKGROUP ON THE SERVER

Before workstations can connect to LAN WorkGroup, the LAN WorkGroup server must be installed and configured on a NetWare 3 or 4 server. The procedure to install LAN WorkGroup version 5 is as follows:

I • If you are installing from a CD-ROM, insert the CD-ROM in a drive that can be read from the server. This can be a drive that is supported by DOS drivers or it can be a drive that is running with the server-based CD-ROM driver.

If you are installing from floppy disks, place Disk 1 in a floppy disk drive.

NOTE

If you are already running an earlier version of LAN WorkGroup, you must uninstall it with the server INSTALL utility prior to installing LAN WorkGroup 5.

2 • At the server console, start the INSTALL utility by typing the command **LOAD INSTALL**.

3 • Select Product Options in the Installation Options menu.

4 • If you are installing LAN WorkGroup on a NetWare 4.1 server, select the "Install a product not listed" option in the Other Installation Actions menu.

5 • The default installation path is A:\. If you are installing from floppies, press Enter.

If you are installing from CD-ROM, press F3 to specify a different path. Then enter the path at the prompt "Specify a directory path." If your CD-ROM is drive D:, enter the path as **D:\DISK1**. Change the drive letter to match your drive.

6 • Follow the prompts until INSTALL displays a box labeled Destination Volume to Install. Select a volume from the list. LAN WorkGroup administration will be somewhat simpler if you install it on the SYS volume.

7 • Next, you will see the prompt "Install Online Documentation?" Most of the documentation for LAN WorkGroup is online. You should select *Yes* especially if this is your first LAN WorkGroup server.

8 • You will be asked for a login ID. For NetWare 3, enter a login name and password with Supervisor equivalence. For NetWare 4, enter a name and password for an account that has Admin rights to the root directory of the SYS volume.

9 • For NetWare 4, you will see the prompt 'Container for Object "LANWORKGROUP,"' which is the group to which all LAN WorkGroup users will belong. Press Enter to see a list of available containers. Specify an object path and press Enter.

10 • The installation is complete. Down, exit, and restart the server.

CONFIGURING LAN WORKGROUP ON THE SERVER

You must do three things to configure LAN WorkGroup:

1 • Add workstation types and other configuration data to LAN WorkGroup.

2 • Add users to the LANWORKGROUP group.

3 • Configure login scripts.

Let's take this one step at a time.

Adding Configuration Data to LAN WorkGroup

After you have planned your LAN WorkGroup configuration (see previous sections), entering the data is a piece of cake. The following sections describe how you configure LAN WorkGroup after the software has been installed and the server has been restarted.

Entering Workstation Types

1 • Type **LOAD LWGCON** at the server console. The LWGCON Configuration menu is shown in Figure 9.12.

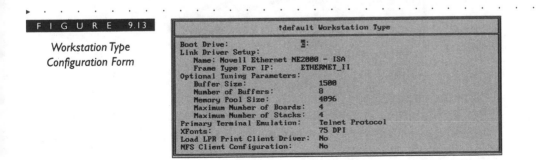

FIGURE 9.12

The LAN WorkGroup Configuration Menu

```
┌─────────────────────────────────────┐
│        Configuration Menu           │
├─────────────────────────────────────┤
│ Workstation Type                    │
│ Subnetwork Profile                  │
│ IP Address Assignment               │
│ LAN WorkGroup Parameters            │
│ Excluded Nodes                      │
│ Exit                                │
└─────────────────────────────────────┘
```

2 • Select the Workstation Type menu item to see a list of configured workstation types. At first, only one type, named !default, will appear in the list.

3 • Configure the !default workstation type to match the requirements of the largest possible number of your potential TCP/IP computers. To configure the !default workstation type, select the !default entry and press Enter to open the Workstation Type form, shown Figure 9.13. Configure this form as required and press Esc to return to the Workstation Types list.

4 • To create additional workstation types, press Insert in the Workstation Types box. At the Enter Workstation Type prompt specify a workstation type name. Then press Enter to open the Workstation Type form and configure the workstation type.

5 • Return to the LWGCON Configuration Menu after you have defined all required workstation types.

FIGURE 9.13

Workstation Type Configuration Form

```
┌──────────────────────────────────────────────────────┐
│                !default Workstation Type              │
├──────────────────────────────────────────────────────┤
│ Boot Drive:              C:                           │
│ Link Driver Setup:                                    │
│    Name: Novell Ethernet NE2000 - ISA                 │
│    Frame Type For IP:      ETHERNET_II                │
│ Optional Tuning Parameters:                           │
│    Buffer Size:            1500                        │
│    Number of Buffers:      8                          │
│    Memory Pool Size:       4096                        │
│    Maximum Number of Boards:   4                      │
│    Maximum Number of Stacks:   4                      │
│ Primary Terminal Emulation:    Telnet Protocol        │
│ XFonts:                    75 DPI                      │
│ Load LPR Print Client Driver:  No                     │
│ NFS Client Configuration:      No                     │
└──────────────────────────────────────────────────────┘
```

Entering Subnet Profiles

1 • To open the subnetwork profile list, select the Subnetwork Profile option from the LWGCON Configuration Menu (see Figure 9.14). The figure shows two defined subnets.

FIGURE 9.14

Configured Subnet Profiles

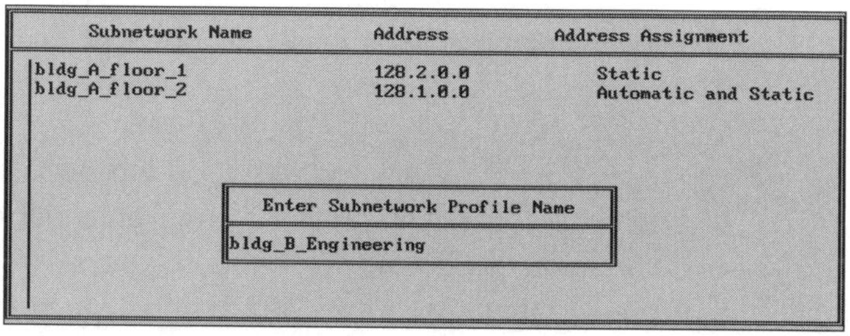

2 • To define a new subnet profile, press Insert and type the profile name at the "Enter Subnetwork Profile Name" prompt. You might name profiles after the subnet location (e.g., building and floor) or the department served. Press Enter after typing the name to open the Subnetwork Profile form shown in Figure 9.15.

FIGURE 9.15

Subnet Configuration Form

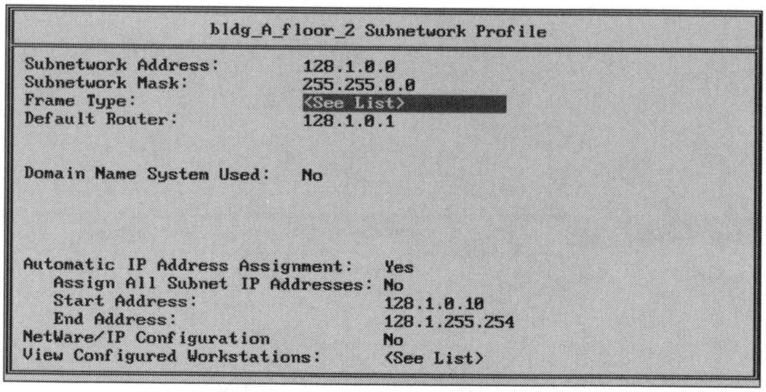

3 • In the *Subnetwork Address* field, type the network address of the subnet that is being profiled.

4 • In the *Subnetwork Mask* field, type a subnet mask or press Enter to select one from a menu.

5 • In the *Frame Type* field, press Enter to see a list of selected frame types. This list will be empty at first. Press Insert to add a frame type from a list of TCP/IP-compatible frame types. Press Esc to return to the Subnetwork Profile form.

6 • The *Default Router* entry has three fields, although only one is labeled clearly. Enter the IP addresses for up to three routers for this subnet.

7 • If hosts will use DNS, change the value of the *Domain Name System Used* field to *Yes*. A *Domain Name* field will be revealed in which you should enter the domain name. Three fields will then be displayed for the Primary, Secondary, and Tertiary Name Servers. Enter the IP addresses for up to three DNS servers.

8 • If automatic address assignment will be used, change the value of the Automatic IP Address Assignment field to *Yes*. An Assign All Subnet IP Addresses field is revealed, which should be set to *Yes* or *No*. If you select *Yes,* then *Start Address* and *End Address* fields are revealed. Complete these fields with the first and last IP addresses in the range that is available for assignment.

9 • The *NetWare/IP Configuration* field should be set to *No* unless the workstation will access the server using NetWare/IP. If this field is changed to *Yes*, a NetWare/IP Configuration form will open. See Chapter 12 for details about NetWare/IP.

10 • View Configured Workstations is a display-only field. No data entry is required.

11 • After this subnet is configured, press Esc to return to the Subnetwork list. Add any other requires subnets, and then return to the Configuration Menu.

Entering IP Address Assignments   If any LAN WorkGroup clients will be assigned fixed IP addresses, do the following:

1 • Choose *IP Address Assignment* from the Configuration Menu. This action will open the list shown in Figure 9.16, which will at first be empty.

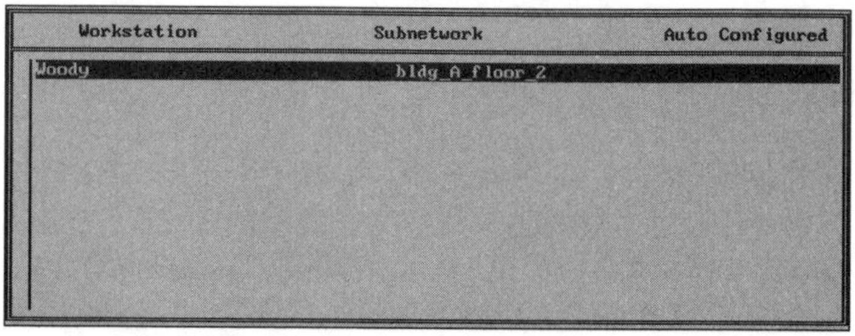

FIGURE 9.16

Configured Fixed IP Address Assignments

Workstation	Subnetwork	Auto Configured
Woody	bldg_A_floor_2	

2 • Press Insert to add an address assignment.

3 • You will be prompted to enter a workstation name. A Workstation IP Address Assignment form will then appear (see Figure 9.17).

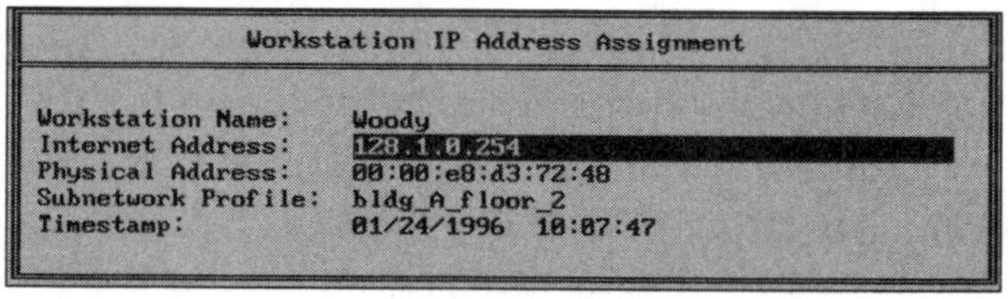

FIGURE 9.17

Defining an IP Address Assignment

```
                  Workstation IP Address Assignment

Workstation Name:    Woody
Internet Address:    128.1.0.254
Physical Address:    00:00:e8:d3:72:48
Subnetwork Profile:  bldg_A_floor_2
Timestamp:           01/24/1996  10:07:47
```

4 • In the *Internet Address* field, enter the IP address to be assigned to this workstation. The Subnetwork Profile field will be updated automatically to show the name of the subnet type that was defined for the network on which this workstation resides.

5 • In the *Physical Address* field, enter the hardware address of this workstation. This address must be a six-byte address, entered in hexadecimal format. Each pair of hex digits should be separated with a colon (:), and leading zeros should be added if the address is shorter than six bytes. (Example: 00:00:E8:D3:72:48.)

6 • When the required information has been entered, press Esc and save the entry.

7 • Repeat Steps 2 through 6 for each IP address assignment to be entered. When all required entries have been made, press Esc to return to the Configuration Menu.

Entering LAN WorkGroup Parameters   Three LAN WorkGroup parameters must be defined using the following procedures:

1 • Choose *LAN WorkGroup Parameters* from the Configuration Menu to open the LAN WorkGroup Parameters form shown in Figure 9.18.

F I G U R E   9.18

*LAN WorkGroup
Parameters Form*

2 • In the *Private Path* field, enter the drive and directory in which users' private files will be stored. The default is C:\LWG.

3 • In the *Shared Drive* field, enter the letter of a drive that will be mapped to the volume on which LAN WorkGroup will be installed.

4 • In the *SYS Drive* field, enter the letter of a drive that will be mapped to the SYS volume. If LAN WorkGroup was installed on the SYS volume, the *SYS Drive* field can have the same drive letter as the *Shared Drive* field.

5 • Press Esc and save the LAN WorkGroup Parameters. You will be returned to the Configuration Menu.

Entering Excluded Nodes   If any nodes are to be excluded from BOOTP address assignment, do the following:

1 • Choose *Excluded Nodes* from the Configuration Menu to open a list of excluded physical addresses.

2 • To add an address to the list, press Ins. At the "Enter Physical Address" prompt, enter the physical address of the excluded node.

This address must be a six-byte address, entered in hexadecimal format. Each pair of hex digits should be separated with a colon (:), and leading zeros should be added if the address is shorter than six bytes. (Example: 00:00:E8:D3:72:48.)

3 • Repeat Step 2 for all excluded nodes.

4 • Press Esc to return to the Configuration Menu.

This completes configuration of LAN WorkGroup. Quit LWGCON by pressing Esc. Restart the server to activate the features you have configured.

NOTE

If you have configured LAN WorkGroup to provide automatic IP address assignment, the LOAD BOOTPD -V command is added to the AUTOEXEC.NCF file. This command activates BOOTP and provides verbose messaging to the BOOTP monitor. After you are sure that BOOTP is operating properly, you may wish to remove the -V option to disable verbose messaging, which reports every BOOTP request and reply.

The LAN WorkPlace BOOTP Server protocol monitor is operational whenever BOOTPD is loaded. You can select this screen on the console (press Alt+Esc) to monitor BOOTP operation.

Preparing for Users

The LAN WorkGroup installation and configuration procedures accomplish the following:

▸ Install shared LAN WorkGroup files on the server.

▸ Create a group named LANWORKGROUP that has rights to the LAN WorkGroup directories.

▸ Creates login scripts appropriate for NetWare 3 and NetWare 4 users, placing them in the SYS:PUBLIC directory.

After LAN WorkGroup has been configured, two administrative tasks remain:

- ► All users who will access LAN WorkGroup must be added to the LANWORKGROUP group. Use SYSCON for NetWare 3 or NETADMIN for NetWare 4.

- ► The appropriate login file must be included in the login scripts that are executed when users log in to the server. The procedure differs depending on whether the server is running NetWare 3 or NetWare 4.

On NetWare 3 servers, add the following commands to the system login script, modifying the *servername* to specify the correct server:

```
INCLUDE servername/SYS:PUBLIC\SYSLOGIN.LWG
```

With NetWare 4, you must be sure to modify the system login script to accommodate bindery-mode users as well as the container login scripts of all users who will use LAN WorkGroup. Add the following command to the system login script, modifying the *servername* to specify the correct server:

```
INCLUDE servername/SYS:PUBLIC\SYSLOGIN.LWG
```

Add the following commands to the container login scripts that support LAN WorkGroup users:

```
IF MEMBER OF ".CN=LANWORKGROUP.OU=org_unit.O=org" THEN BEGIN
INCLUDE servername/SYS:PUBLIC\DSLOGIN.LWG
END
```

In the IF MEMBER OF statement, the quotation marks should enclose the distinguished name of the LANWORKGROUP object. Modify the *org_unit* and *org* as required. Modify the *servername* to specify the correct server.

If your network has a single router, you are ready to have your users connect to LAN WorkGroup. If your network has more than one router, you have one more job, configuring BOOTP forwarding. See the section "Central Assignment of IP Addresses" before you proceed setting up workstations.

SETTING UP LAN WORKGROUP WORKSTATIONS

Now that the server is set up, it is a simple matter to get your workstations connected to LAN WorkGroup.

The first step is to get the workstation logged in to the LAN WorkGroup server. This means that the workstation must be equipped with a fully configured IPX protocol stack. You can use the NetWare client software included with NetWare to make this basic connection. LAN WorkGroup won't look at your NET.CFG file at all, and your existing client software won't be affected by LAN WorkGroup setup.

After the workstation is logged in to the LAN WorkGroup server, use the command WGSETUP to configure the workstation with the !default workstation type. To configure the workstation with another workstation type, enter the command WGSETUP followed by the name of the workstation type to be used. WGSETUP does the following:

▶ Copies files to the designated private directory on the user's workstation.

▶ Creates the batch file C:\LWG\BIN\LANWG.BAT, which will load the TCP/IP protocol stack.

▶ Adds the command CALL C:\LWG\BIN\LANWG.BAT to the end of the AUTOEXEC.BAT file.

You should examine the LANWG.BAT file to ensure that it resembles the following:

```
@echo off
C:\LWG\BIN\yesno "Load the LAN WorkGroup Software [y/n]?"
if errorlevel == 1 goto notcpip
set name=Lauren
tcpip /C=L:\net\net.cfg
break on
:noload
```

The parameter /C=L:\net\net.cfg enables TCPIP.EXE to locate the NET.CFG file that is used by all LAN WorkGroup users. After LAN WorkGroup has been installed, reboot the workstation. After the IPX protocol stack and NetWare requester are installed, you will see the prompt:

```
Load the LAN WorkGroup Software [y/n]?
```

Type **Y** to load TCP/IP on the workstation. When TCPIP.EXE is loaded, you will see a display similar to the following:

```
Requesting my IP address from a BOOTP server ...
Novell TCP/IP Transport v5.0 (950430)
(C) Copyright 1992-1995 Novell, Inc.  All Rights Reserved.

Network Name: IP-NET          Bind: NE2000
IP Address: 128.1.0.254       Board Number: 2
Subnet Mask: 255.255.0.0      Board Instance: 1
Default Router: 128.1.0.1     Frame: ETHERNET_II
```

This workstation is configured for automatic address assignment and requests an IP address from a BOOTP server. BOOTP supplies the address and other configuration information as well, as shown in the rest of the information that is displayed.

Congratulations, LAN WorkGroup installation is complete!

Central Assignment of IP Addresses

Bootstrap protocol (BOOTP; RFC 951/1497) is a sophisticated address assignment method that also enables workstations to obtain an IP address, a subnet mask, and a router address. It provides other functions that are of most interest if you are using diskless workstations.

NetWare provides BOOTP services through the LAN WorkGroup product. The configuration of LAN WorkGroup to support BOOTP was covered in the section "Installing LAN WorkGroup." Two topics remain to be examined: configuration of NetWare clients to use BOOTP and configuration of routers to forward BOOTP messages.

CONFIGURING NETWARE TCP/IP CLIENTS FOR BOOTP

Once LAN WorkGroup has been installed and configured, it is incredibly easy to configure any NetWare TCP/IP client to use BOOTP. Simply edit the NET.CFG file to configure TCPIP with an IP address of 0.0.0.0. For example:

```
Protocol TCPIP
        ip_address 0.0.0.0
```

Alternatively, you can omit the ip_address option completely. That's it. Hardly deserved a whole section, didn't it?

CONFIGURING BOOTP FORWARDING

When a BOOTP server is not on the same network segment as a BOOTP client, BOOTP messages must be routed. This requires installation of a BOOTP forwarding process on the NetWare router. Figure 9.19 shows how BOOTP forwarding works.

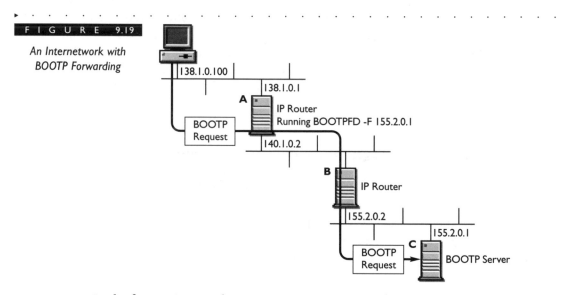

F I G U R E 9.19

An Internetwork with BOOTP Forwarding

In the figure, A, B, and C are NetWare servers configured as IP routers. Router C is the LAN WorkGroup BOOTP server, which has been configured with all of the subnets in the internetwork.

To enable its BOOTP requests to get to C, router A must have BOOTP forwarding enabled. BOOTP forwarding is enabled by loading the BOOTPFD NLM. When it is loaded, the IP address of the BOOTP server is declared like this:

```
LOAD BOOTPFD 155.2.0.1
```

The LOAD BOOTPFD command accepts two options, which should follow the IP address:

▸ -V generates verbose messages on the BOOTP monitor screen

▸ -Q turns off error logging to the SYS:ETC\BOOTP.LOG file

If the server is running NetWare 4 or the MultiProtocol Router, configure BOOTP using INETCFG with this procedure:

1 • Load INETCFG

2 • Select *Protocols* in the Internetworking Configuration menu

3 • Select *TCP/IP* in the Protocol Configuration menu

4 • Select *Expert Configuration Options* in the TCP/IP Protocol Configuration form

5 • Select *BOOTP Forwarding Configuration* in the TCP/IP Expert Configuration form. This will open the BootP Configuration Options form shown in Figure 9.20.

FIGURE 9.20

Configuring BOOTP in INETCFG

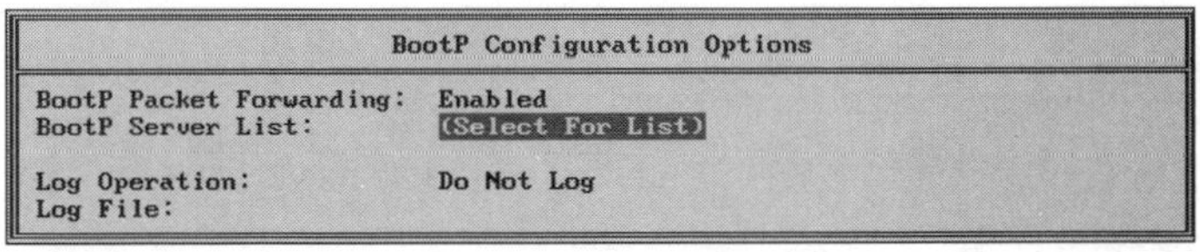

```
                      BootP Configuration Options

BootP Packet Forwarding:   Enabled
BootP Server List:         (Select For List)

Log Operation:             Do Not Log
Log File:
```

6 • Select the *BootP Servers List* to display a list of BOOTP server IP addresses. Press Insert to add an IP address to the list. At least one BOOTP server must be configured before BOOTP packet forwarding can been enabled.

7 • Change the *BootP Packet Forwarding* field to Enabled to have BOOTP loaded on the server.

8 • The *Log Operation* file accepts three values:

▸ **Do Not Log** disables logging. Logging should not be necessary unless troubleshooting is required.

> ► **Log to BootP Screen** logs messages to the BOOTP protocol monitor screen.

> ► **Log to File** logs messages to a file.

9 • If messages will be logged to a file, the *Log File* field specifies the path name of the log file. The default is SYS:\ETC\BOOTP.LOG.

Save changes to TCP/IP and restart the server to activate BOOTP forwarding.

Serial Connections for TCP/IP Clients

LAN WorkPlace includes an excellent utility called Dialer for dialing into remote TCP/IP hosts. This section shows you how to configure Dialer, but first you need to learn a bit about TCP/IP serial communication protocols.

UNDERSTANDING SLIP AND PPP

Two common serial line protocols are used with TCP/IP: SLIP and PPP. Both are supported for NetWare TCP/IP clients. You should be aware of the capabilities of these protocols.

SLIP

The Serial Line Internet Protocol (SLIP; RFC 1055) is the older of the two protocols, first implemented in 1984. SLIP is extremely basic and efficient and has been the most widely used serial line standard for TCP/IP.

A SLIP packet has a very simple format that contains three fields (see Figure 9.21):

> ► A leading delimiter with the value C0h

> ► A data section

> ► A trailing delimiter with the value C0h

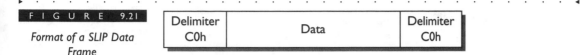

F I G U R E   9.21

Format of a SLIP Data Frame

| Delimiter C0h | Data | Delimiter C0h |

SLIP is an extremely rudimentary protocol that is easy to implement and that provides good performance; however, SLIP has several disadvantages. The lack of an error-check field prevents SLIP nodes from detecting or recovering from errors. Also, SLIP nodes must be statically configured to agree on all SLIP communications parameters. As a result, SLIP connections require fixed IP address assignments, so SLIP performs best when communicating between known peers.

Because if its limitations, SLIP has never entered the Internet standards track. Nevertheless, SLIP is implemented widely and has been eclipsed only recently by the newer PPP protocol.

PPP

The Point-to-Point protocol (PPP; RFC 1331/1332) is a more robust protocol that offers several administrative advantages over SLIP. Although PPP does more than SLIP and provides error recovery, it tends to be a bit slower than SLIP. Because it is more robust and versatile than SLIP, PPP is a standards-track Internet protocol.

A PPP packet contains the following fields (see Figure 9.22):

- **Flag.** One octet with the value 7Eh that functions as a frame separator.

- **Address.** One octet with the value FFh, the all-stations address. PPP does not assign individual station addresses.

- **Control.** One octet with the value 3h, designating unnumbered information.

- **Protocol.** Two octets, with the value identifying the protocol encapsulated in the information field.

- **Information.** The protocol data payload of the frame.

- **Frame Check Sequence (FCS).** A value used for error detection.

- **Flag.** A one-octet ending delimiter with the value 7Eh.

Delimiter 7Eh	Address FFh	Control 3h	Data	FCS	Delimiter 7Eh

F I G U R E   9.22

Format of a PPP Data Packet

Error recovery is made possible by the FCS field, and the protocol field enables PPP frames to carry data for multiple network protocols. PPP provides another advantage over SLIP: With PPP, you don't need to manually configure connection parameters between hosts. PPP includes protocols that enable the connection end-points to negotiate a variety of connection parameters, including IP addresses, router addresses, and data compression.

SETTING UP SERIAL CONNECTIONS

Three modules implement the network driver that supports serial connections:

- **NESL**. Provides a support layer called the NetWare Event Service Layer.

- **NCOMX**. Provides the serial connection.

- **NWREMOTE**. Provides the dial-connection function.

The NCOMX and NWREMOTE modules are configured via settings in the NET.CFG file; however, when using the Windows Dialer, very few NET.CFG commands are required.

Here is a sample NET.CFG file configured for use with Dialer. Most of the protocol information will be supplied by Dialer when you configure a dial-out entry.

```
LINK DRIVER NCOMX
     INT 4
     PORT 3F8


PROTOCOL TCPIP
     BIND NCOMX #1 PPP PPP_NET
```

That's really all that is required. If this station is also supporting a LAN connection, however, the Protocol TCPIP section will include two network definitions like this:

```
PROTOCOL TCPIP
        PATH TCP_CFG        C:\NET\TCP
        ip_address          0.0.0.0      LAN_NET
        ip_router           128.1.0.1    LAN_NET
        ip_mask             255.255.0.0  LAN_NET
        BIND NE2000 #1      Ethernet_II  LAN_NET
        BIND NCOMX #1       PPP          PPP_NET
```

When you specified serial network connections, INSTALL added the commands to your STARTNET.BAT file that are necessary to set up SLIP/PPP support. If you are using the STARTNET.BAT to set up your network software, do the following:

▸ Respond **N** when you see the prompt "Load the LAN Support software [y/n]?"

▸ Respond **Y** when you see the prompt "Do you want to load the SLIP/PPP Interface [y/n]?"

As a result, the following modules will be loaded:

LSL
NESL
NCOMX
NWREMOTE
TCPIP

That is all that is necessary to get ready to use Dialer.

Setting Up Dialer

Dialer is installed in the LAN WorkPlace 5 program group. The first time you start Dialer, you will be taken through a series of configuration screens. Here's what to expect:

1 • Start Dialer by double-clicking its icon in the LAN WorkPlace 5 program group.

2 • The first configuration option asks you to select Tone or Pulse depending on the dialing technology you use. The default is Tone. Select *Next Page* after making your decision.

3 • Next, in the screen shown in Figure 9.23, select a serial port (COM1 or COM2) in the *Port* box. Also, select a modem type in the *Modem Make and Model* box. Both boxes can be pulled down by clicking the arrow to reveal a list of choices. The modem selection list has been opened in the figure as an example. Choose *Next Page* after completing these entries.

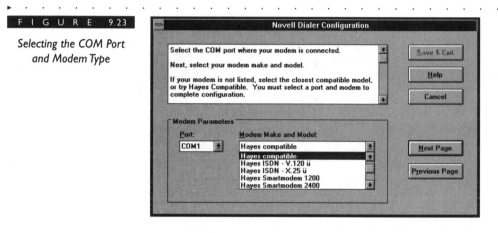

4 • Next, you will use the form shown in Figure 9.24 to define a first entry for the Dialer's connection directory:

▸ In the *Name for Dialing Entry* field, enter the name that will identify the entry in the directory.

▸ In the *Dial Before* field, add any characters or modem control codes that should be entered before dialing the phone number. This field can include long-distance access codes and modem control codes such as sequences from the AT modem command set.

▸ In the *Phone Number* field, enter the number to be dialed. Include an area code and any access codes not included in the Dial Before field.

▸ In the *Dial After* field, add any characters or modem control codes that should be entered after dialing the phone number.

Choose *Next Page* when the above entries are complete.

F I G U R E   9.24

*Configuring an Entry for
the Connection Directory*

5 • Select *PPP* or *SLIP* depending on the serial line protocol to be used. The default is PPP. Choose *Next Page* after making your selection.

6 • The next screen, shown in Figure 9.25, is used to enter your dial-up client TCP/IP parameters:

 ▸ For the majority of connections using PPP, addresses are assigned using IPCP, a protocol that is part of PPP. In this case, leave the IP Address field blank. Do, however, complete the Domain Name and DNS Server IP fields, because IPCP will not supply this information.

 ▸ If you are dialing an Internet access service that uses PPP with BOOTP for address assignment, check the Use BOOTP box.

 ▸ If you are using PPP and your provider does not use dynamic address assignment, enter the parameters supplied by your Internet provider.

 ▸ If you are using SLIP, you must enter all parameters. Obtain the correct values from your Internet provider.

 ▸ If you are dialing into a NetWare network that uses NetWare/IP, check the *Enable NetWare/IP* box.

 Choose Next Page to continue.

FIGURE 9.25

Configuring TCP/IP Session Parameters

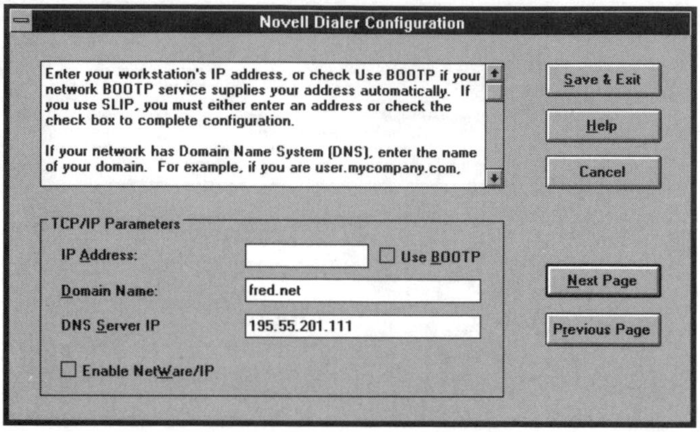

7 • The next screen you see is shown in Figure 9.26. You will see this screen if you selected PPP as the serial line protocol. Many PPP dial-in services are able to automate a user-authentication dialog using the Password Authentication Protocol (PAP).

▸ If PAP is supported at the site you are calling, check the Enable PAP Authentication box. Also enter your user account name in the UserName field.

▸ If you want your password entered for you, enter the password in the Password field. If you want to enter your password each time you connect, check the Prompt for Password box.

FIGURE 9.26

Configuring the Password Authentication Protocol

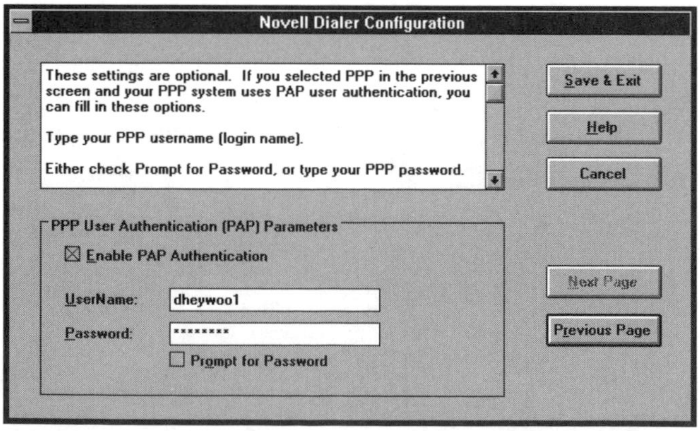

8 • When all entries are complete, choose *Save & Exit*. Restart Windows to activate your changes.

Getting Started with Dialer

When you start Dialer, you will see the window shown in Figure 9.27. Dialer has two windows. The Connection Directory contains your dial-out directory, starting with the entry you defined when Dialer was first started. The Login Window is active whenever you are put in terminal mode to complete a manual login dialog.

Most of Dialer is pretty easy to figure out, but you need to understand the configuration settings so that things work right. The online documentation includes a manual on Dialer if you want help with the basics or want to learn the more advanced features such as answering calls and scripting.

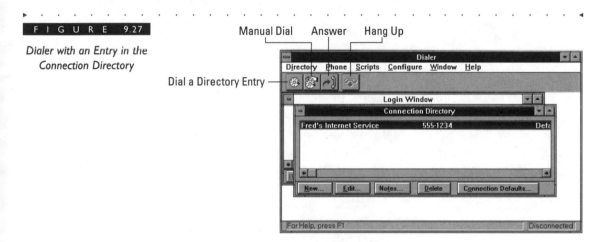

FIGURE 9.27

Dialer with an Entry in the Connection Directory

Assuming that the entry for Fred's Internet Service is properly configured, just double-click the entry to get a connection started. You will see a succession of dialog boxes as Dialer first dials the network and then completes the connection.

Once you are in session, you can use any of the TCP/IP tools that are included with LAN WorkPlace. When the session is completed, choose Hangup in the Phone menu, or click the correct icon to hang up the connection.

NOTE Dialer can be configured to start automatically anytime a LAN WorkGroup application needs access to network resources. To automate Dialer:

1 • Configure LAN WorkPlace for serial connections only. If necessary, you must disable LAN support in the Adapters area of the Configuration utility.

2 • Configure a default connection entry by choosing Connection Defaults in the Connection Directory window. You can configure a default entry for dialing out and for answering incoming calls.

3 • Place Dialer in the Windows Startup program group so that it will be running whenever a program needs to use it.

Adding and Modifying Connection Directory Entries

You may need to add new connection directory entries or to modify the entry you made when Dialer was configured. The entry you made when you first started Dialer was established with default settings. If any of the defaults don't work with the service you are connecting to, you will need to modify the entries.

To add or modify an entry to the connection directory:

1 • Choose *New* in the Connection Directory window to open the Connection Directory Entry form shown in Figure 9.28. Select an entry and choose *Edit* to modify the entry.

FIGURE 9.28

Creating a Connection Directory Entry

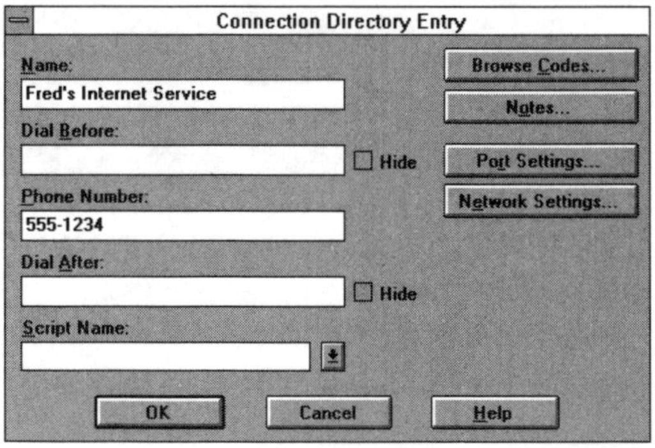

2 • Complete the entries in the Connection Directory Entry form as follows:

  ► **Name**. Enter a name to identify this entry.

▸ **Dial Before**. Enter any characters or modem control codes that should be entered before dialing the phone number. Check the Hide box if you don't want to see these codes as they execute.

▸ **Phone Number**. Enter the phone number. Include any area codes and long-distance access numbers that are required.

▸ **Dial After**. Enter any characters or modem control codes that should be entered after dialing the phone number. Check the Hide box if you don't want to see these codes as they execute.

▸ **Script Name**. If you have created a script for this destination, enter the name. Scripts should not be needed for most Internet providers.

3 • Choose *Port Settings* to review the port configuration, shown in Figure 9.29. Complete this form as follows:

▸ **Port.** Dialer is configured with a default serial port that is configured using the Port/Modem Setup command in the Configure menu. If you don't want to use the default serial port for this connection, change the value in this field.

▸ **Baud.** By default, Auto Select is checked, and modems will negotiate their baud rates when a connection is established. If you wish to configure a fixed baud rate, uncheck the Auto Select box and enter a baud rate.

NOTE

The key hardware component of a serial port is called a UART. Older serial ports for PC-compatibles used type 8250 UARTS, which run out of steam at about 19,200 bps. If you are operating at 19,200 bps or higher, be sure your serial port is equipped with a newer model 16550 UART.

FIGURE 9.29

Basic Port Settings

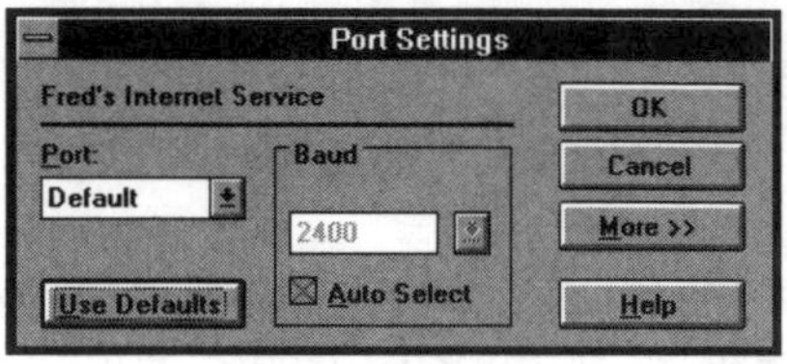

4 • Choose *More* in the Port Settings window to extend the port settings as shown in Figure 9.30. The additional port settings are:

▸ **Parity.** Determines the kind of parity checking that is used. The default is None, which is the most widely used setting.

▸ **Data.** Serial communication uses either 7- or 8-bit data sections. The default is 8, which is the most widely used setting.

▸ **Stop.** Determines whether a character has one or two stop bits. The default is 1, which is the more common setting.

▸ **Flow Control.** If the serial port can directly control the modem, select Hardware flow control; otherwise, select None.

▸ **Leased Line**. If you are using a direct lease line, rather than a dial-up connection, check this box, which is active only if the modem supports leased-line connections.

The most common serial setting (no parity, 8-bit data, and 1 stop bit) is commonly called 8-n-1. Consult with your dial-in service if the default settings don't work.

Choose OK when entries are completed to return to the Connection Directory Entry window.

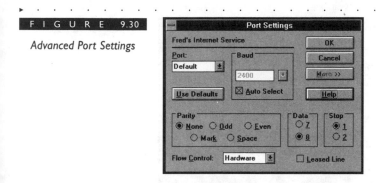

FIGURE 9.30

Advanced Port Settings

5 • In the Connection Directory Entry window, choose *Network Settings* to open the form shown in Figure 9.31. Complete the entries as follows:

▸ **Serial Line Protocol Options.** Select SLIP or PPP.

▸ **Enable NetWare/IP.** Check this box if you will be dialing into a NetWare network as a NetWare/IP client.

▸ **IP Address.** If this workstation will have a fixed IP address, enter it. If an address will be obtained from PPP, leave the field blank.

▸ **Use BOOTP for Address**. Check this box if the workstation will obtain its address from BOOTP.

▸ **Domain Name.** If this workstation will be in a DNS domain, enter the domain name.

▸ **Server IP Address.** If this workstation has access to a DNS name server, enter its IP address.

Network Options

Fred's Internet Service

[Advanced...]

┌─ Serial Line Protocol Options ──────────┐
│ Protocol to Use: ○ SLIP ⊙ PPP   │   [Authentication...]
└───┘   [Ne_t_Ware/IP...]

☐ Enable Net_W_are/IP

┌─ TCP/IP Options ──┐
│ _I_P Address: [   ]   ☐ Use _B_OOTP for Address │
└───┘

┌─ Domain Name System Options ────────────────────────────────┐
│ _D_omain Name: [fred.net   ] │
│ S_e_rver IP Addresses: [198.55.201.111   ] │
└───┘

[OK   ]   [Cancel]   [_U_se Defaults]   [_H_elp]

6 • Choose *Advanced* to open an advanced options window. The Advanced Options - PPP window is shown in Figure 9.32. The window for SLIP has only the top three options shown. The majority of PPP connections will work with default options, but changes may be needed in some cases. The options in this window are as follows:

▶ **Maximum Send/Receive Size (MRU).** For SLIP and PPP, this field determines the size in bytes of the largest packet that will be sent or accepted. The range of this parameter is 76 to 1500 bytes. The default value for PPP is 1500 bytes, and the default for SLIP is 1006 bytes.

▶ **Enable Header Compression.** For SLIP and PPP, check this option to enable Van Jacobson (VJ) header compression. VJ header compression is employed widely as a way to reduce transmitted packet size and is particularly useful when large numbers of small packets are sent (e.g., as with terminal emulators such as Telnet). This box is checked by default.

▶ **Compress Connection Identifiers.** For SLIP and PPP, check this option to enable VJ header compression for TCP/IP slot IDs that appear in packets. This box is checked by default.

▶ **Compress Header Address and Control Fields.** For PPP, check this option to enable compression for the address and control fields. This box is checked by default.

- **LCP and IPCP Open Mode.** For PPP, select Passive to force opening of the Login window during login authentication. Select Active if you have entered login information (username and password) and want PPP to authenticate using those settings. The default is Active.

- **Remote IP Address.** For PPP, enter an IP address in this field if you wish to force the remote peer to accept an address specified by this workstation. This field is blank by default.

- **Magic Number.** This number is used by PPP for error detection and internal datalink control. Enter a random hex number in the range of 00000000 to FFFFFFFF. The default is 00000000.

- **Asynchronous Control Character Map.** The ACCM is used to embed control characters in the data in mapped form. It is a bitmap of 8 bytes (64-bits) that allows control characters to be embedded in the data stream. See the online Help documentation for more information. The default is 00000000 (no mapping).

- **Retransmit Request Packets after...seconds.** This value determines how long PPP will wait before resending a request packet if no reply is received from the dial-in network. Enter a value in the range of 0 to 999. The default is 3.

- **Resend a Configuration Request...times.** This value specifies how many times PPP will request retransmission of messages if no response is received from the dial-in service. Enter a value in the range of 0 to 999. The default is 10.

- **Resend a Terminate Request...times.** This value specifies the how many times PPP will send a terminate request message if no response is received from the dial-in network. Enter a value in the range of 0 to 999. The default is 2.

▶ **Resend a Configuration NAK ... times.** This value specifies the number of negative acknowledgment (NAK) messages that PPP will send if no response is received from the dial-in service. Enter a value in the range of 0 to 999. The default is 10.

Choose OK when the parameters are configured.

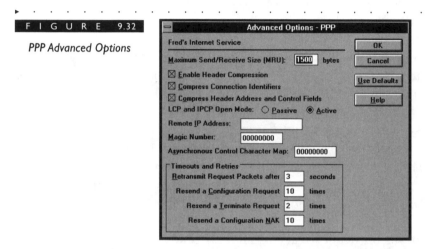

FIGURE 9.32

PPP Advanced Options

NOTE

Unless I miss my guess, you probably found several of these advanced parameters to be obscure at best. Well, I have good news — you probably won't need to change them. In fact, you can probably just click the Use Defaults button to set the default values in all fields. Take compression, for example. The benefits of compression on slow, modem-speed data lines are so pronounced that nearly all dial-in sites use all the compression they can muster. It turns out that CPU processing is no longer the bottleneck in data communication; the real tight spot is the serial line. So start with the defaults and check with your vendor before you make any changes.

7 • In the Network Options window, choose *Authentication* to open the PPP Authentication window shown in Figure 9.33. Complete the fields in this window as follows:

▶ **Enable PAP Authentication.** If PPP will use the Password Authentication Protocol (PAP) to authenticate your login, check this box.

▸ **User Name.** If PAP will be used, enter a user name.

▸ **Password.** If you wish PAP to authenticate your password automatically, enter the password here.

▸ **Prompt for Password.** Check this box if the password should be entered manually for each login attempt.

Choose OK when this form has been completed.

8 • This entry has been completed. Click OK repeatedly until you return to the Dialer main window.

FIGURE 9.33

*Configuring PPP
Authentication*

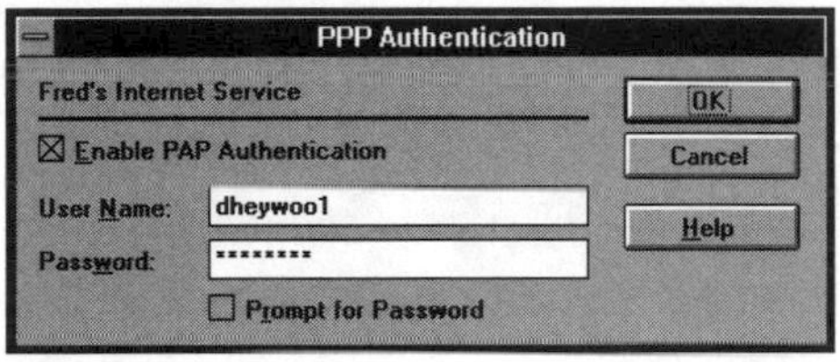

USING DIALER

After entries have been configured in the Connection Directory, using Dialer is a piece cake. Just double-click the entry in the Connection Directory window. Dialer will dial the remote number and step through the login procedures. For a PPP connection with PAP automatic authentication, the procedure requires no intervention on your part.

After Dialer is running, you can minimize the icon and use any of the TCP/IP applications that come with LAN WorkPlace. You can also use third-party applications that use the WINSOCK API. I've shown you the most basic essentials of Dialer. If you become a heavy user, be sure to read the online manual for more detailed information.

Novell's TCP/IP Applications

Figures 9.34 and 9.35 show the applications that LAN WorkPlace installs. All but the Windows Dialer application are included in LAN WorkGroup. As you can see, there are far too many to discuss in detail, so I'll take you for a drive-by tour with stopovers at some special places.

LAN WorkPlace Windows Applications

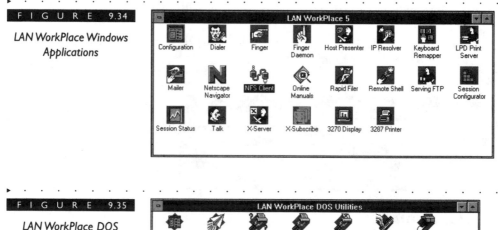

LAN WorkPlace DOS Applications

NOTE

In this section, you'll be running into an odd word that is bound tightly into UNIX folklore. A daemon is a process that runs in the background on a UNIX workstation. Some daemons perform system housekeeping, but others enable the workstation to provide services to outsiders. A line printer daemon, for example, enables a workstation to share its printer with other users on a network.

THE WINDOWS UTILITIES

The Windows utilities make LAN WorkPlace and LAN WorkGroup among the best packages for accessing the Internet. The basics such as file transfer, e-mail, and the Web are all covered. And, because Novell's Windows clients support WINSOCK, it's easy to add the applications you choose.

Configuration

This is a windows-based version of the LAN WorkPlace configuration utility. You can easily make configuration changes in Windows and restart the system, without needing to shell out to DOS to run the DOS configuration tool.

Dialer

This is the versatile dial-out access utility that was examined earlier in this chapter. Unless you have a direct connection to your destination network, the Dialer will be a vital tool in your remote computing activities.

Finger and Finger Daemon

Finger enables users to obtain information about other hosts. Figure 9.36 shows the results of pointing Finger at novell.com.

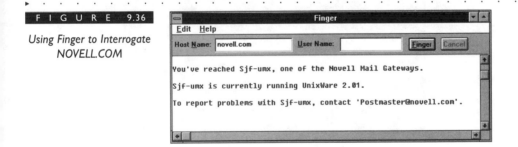

FIGURE 9.36

Using Finger to Interrogate NOVELL.COM

Run the Finger Daemon application to enable your computer to respond to Finger requests. Simply place the information you wish to provide in a file named PLAN.TXT and start the Finger Daemon. It's a piece of cake, really.

Host Presenter

This is a versatile terminal emulation program that enables you to run multiple terminal emulation sessions. A script facility enables you to automate tasks. See the online documentation or the *LAN WorkPlace for DOS User's Guide* for more information.

IP Resolver

IP Resolver does two things:

▶ It can be used to ping hosts by name or address.

▶ It can be used to resolve host names to IP addresses and vice versa.

Simply enter a host name or an IP address and click Ping or Resolve to get the process started. Figure 9.37 shows an example of using IP Resolver to resolve novell.com.

FIGURE 9.37

Using IP Resolver

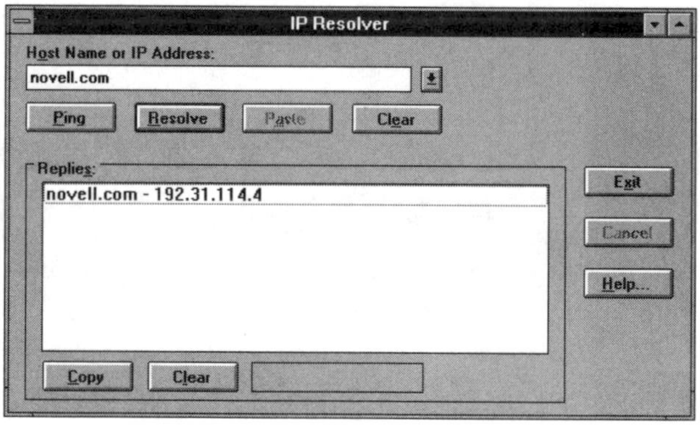

LPD Print Server

The Line Printer Daemon (LPD) Server application enables you to provide print services to remote users. You configure LPD print queues as destinations for remote print jobs. Consult the online documentation for more information.

Mailer

Mailer is a TCP/IP electronic mail application (I know, no big surprise there). Mailer supports SMTP for sending mail and the POP3 protocol for receiving mail. The online documentation includes a complete manual on Mailer.

Netscape Navigator

Netscape is perhaps the most popular software for browsing the World Wide Web. Figure 9.38 shows Novell's Web site viewed through Netscape. Netscape also can be used to read newsgroups and handle e-mail.

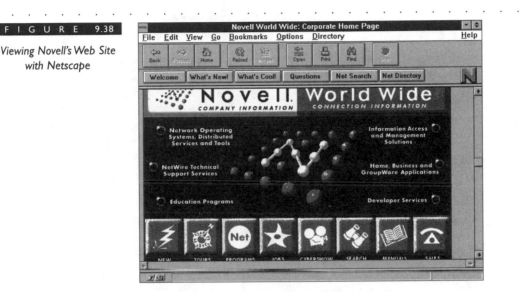

FIGURE 9.38

Viewing Novell's Web Site with Netscape

NFS Client

If you are integrated into a mixed NetWare and UNIX environment, you will appreciate having an NFS client. NFS is the de facto standard for sharing file resources on UNIX networks, and having an NFS client lets you interact with UNIX and NetWare NFS servers. See the online documentation for a manual on the NFS client. Chapter 6 includes a more extensive description of NFS.

Online Manuals

This icon leads you to Novell's DynaText documentation viewer. So that you can get an idea of the extent of the information, the opening screen of the LAN WorkPlace DynaText viewer is shown in Figure 9.39, listing all of the available manuals. In the figure, I've conducted a search to show you how they work. In this case, I was looking for instructions on using the Talk program (see below).

To conduct a basic search, just enter a key word in the Find field and press Enter. DynaText offers many advanced search options such as wildcards, boolean operations, and proximity searches. Consult the DynaText help for more information.

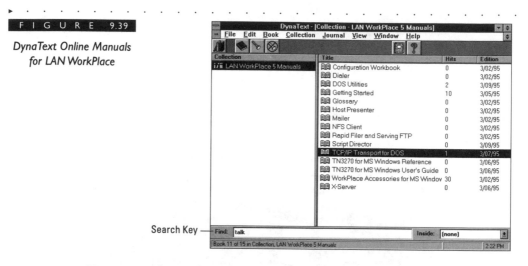

F I G U R E   9.39

DynaText Online Manuals
for LAN WorkPlace

Search Key

Figure 9.40 shows the DynaText reader after I opened up the *WorkPlace Accessories for MS Windows* manual, which generated the most hits on my search. The first hit for the search word *Talk* is highlighted. I could skip to other occurrences by clicking the Next or Previous buttons, or I could click through sections in the left-hand pane of the window to move through the document section by section. DynaText is too rich to cover briefly. Read the help files for more information.

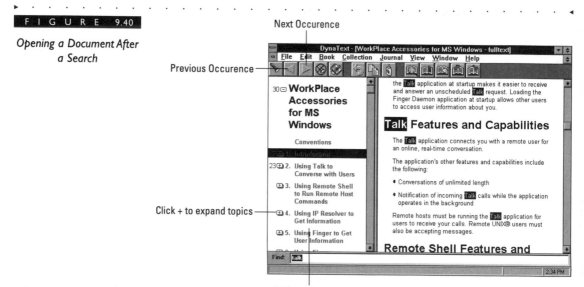

F I G U R E   9.40

Opening a Document After
a Search

Next Occurence

Previous Occurence

Click + to expand topics

Table of Contents

Remote Shell

This utility enables you to execute a command on a remote server that is running a remote shell (rsh) daemon. Remote shells can execute non-interactive commands, but they should not be used to run interactive programs such as text editors.

Serving FTP

This utility is a great way to prove to yourself that TCP/IP services aren't all that mysterious. Simply by running this Windows program and entering a little configuration data, you can configure your DOS/Windows workstation as an FTP server.

Configuration of the Serving FTP is quite simple. Start the program and do the following:

1 • Choose *Access Restrictions* in the Options menu to open the Restriction Setup form shown in Figure 9.41. Check Restrict Access if you wish to limit the users who can connect to your server. Click on the Change button if you want to change the name or location of the access control file that stores usernames and passwords.

F I G U R E   9.41

Configuring FTP Access Restrictions

2 • If access is restricted, choose *Usernames* to open the User Restriction Setup form shown in Figure 9.42. You can use this form to add usernames to the access control list and assign them guest access or to restrict access with a password. To permit anonymous FTP access, create the username anonymous and select Guest.

For user accounts that are assigned passwords, you can enter a password and restrict the user's directory rights. Click on *Directories* to open the User - Directory Rights Setup form, which allows you to establish directory access rights for each user.

F I G U R E   9.42

Setting up FTP User Restrictions

3 • Serving FTP has a home directory that is the first directory users access when they establish a connection. To define the home directory, return to the Serving FTP main window and choose *Change Home Directory* from the Options menu. Select a home directory by browsing the hard drive.

4 • Because FTP opens your system to access by others, it is a good idea to log activity. Choose *Logging* in the Options menu of the Serving FTP main window. You can then arrange to have log messages sent to the Serving FTP screen or to a log file.

5 • To determine the allowed number of concurrent FTP sessions, choose *Multiple Sessions* in the Options window and set the number of sessions. Of course, the higher the number of FTP connections the greater the demand on your system's processing power. If you will be working on the computer at the same time that Serving FTP is running, be careful not to let the number of sessions bog down your system.

Talk

Talk is a chat program that enables users to engage in typed dialogs, perfect for techie types who don't want to interface with real people. Figure 9.43 shows an example of a Talk dialog.

FIGURE 9.43

Example of a Talk Dialog

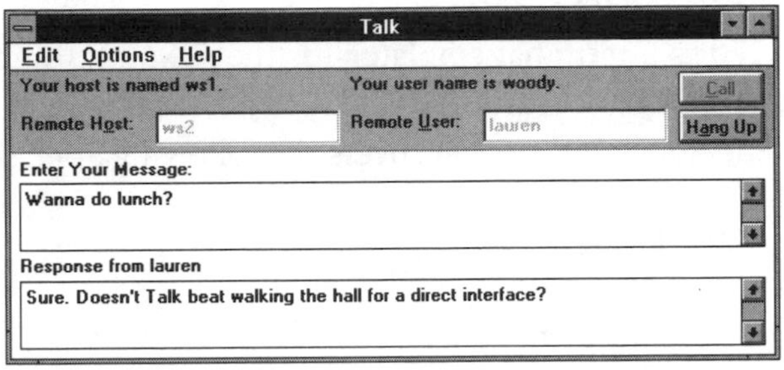

To call a host with Talk, enter the name of the remote host in the Remote Host field. (Host names are resolved using host files or DNS.) Then enter a username in the Remote User field, and finally, click Call.

To receive your call, the remote user must be running Talk or a Talk daemon. Also the name of the user that is logged in on the remote host must match the name specified in the Remote User field. When you receive a call, a dialog box pops up and you can accept or reject the call.

Talk is the first use you have seen for the username that was defined when LAN WorkPlace was configured. Please note that these usernames are case sensitive. It is very important for your organization to establish standards for usernames. Decide whether they will be initial-capped, all uppercase, or all lowercase? It doesn't matter, as long as you are consistent.

X-Server

The X Window System (usually referred to as X) is a popular graphical user environment that is similar to Windows. To start an X application, use an X server application to connect to an X client running on the remote computer. (Yes, this means that you are operating the server as far as X is concerned.) The X client interacts with the graphical display on the X server to generate program output, and the X server accepts user input, which is sent to the X client for processing.

To use the X server application to run X applications on remote hosts, you must have an account on the remote host, and you must be able to connect to the remote host using Telnet, RLOGIN, RSH, REXEC, X Console, XPC or XDM. The details of using the X Server application are beyond the scope of this book. Please consult the manual included in the online documentation. The X-Subscribe application works in conjunction with X-Server.

3270-Related Applications

TN3270 is a terminal emulator for the IBM 3270 terminal environment. For more information, consult the *TN3270 for MS Windows User's Guide* in the online documentation. This manual covers the following applications:

- ▸ 3287 Printer

- ▸ Keyboard Remapper

- ▸ Session Configurator

- ▸ Session Status

THE DOS UTILITIES

You will find several other utilities in the LAN WorkPlace DOS Utilities window.

Configuration

Configuration is the DOS setup utility that we examined in the section "Installing LAN WorkPlace." You may want to run this program from DOS so that you can reconfigure LAN WorkPlace without starting Windows. The program file is C:\NET\BIN\LWPCFGD.EXE (assuming a default installation).

File Transfer Utilities

FTP (see Chapter 6) and another file transfer utility called RCP (remote copy) are available included with LAN WorkPlace and LAN WorkGroup. RCP can be used to copy files and directories between local and remote hosts. The remote host must be running an rsh server and an rcp server.

LWPCON

LWPCON is the LAN WorkPlace console. Because LWPCON depends on SNMP, I've deferred coverage of it to Chapter 11, when I go over SNMP setup.

Ping

This is a Windows front-end to the DOS ping utility. Table 9.4 lists options for the PING command. The syntax is as follows:

```
PING hostname [ /R[N ] /Tn /Nn /Pn [ /Ln | /Sn [ /In ] ]
```

TABLE 9.4	OPTION	PARAMETER
Options for the PING Command	*hostname*	The IP address or hostname of the host to be pinged.
	/R[N]	Enables route tracing. The route of the ping request and reply will be reported. Use /RN to disable name resolution.
	/T*n*	Specifies a destination response timeout of *n* seconds.
	/N*n*	Specifies the number *n* of packets to send. 0 = continuous.
	/P*n*	Specifies the time between requests as *n* seconds. Usually, repeat request packets are sent as soon as a reply is received.
	/L*n*	Specifies the length of the packet in *n* bytes, with a range of 12 to 8192.
	/S*n*	Specifies a starting packet size of *n* bytes, with a range of 12 to 8192.
	/I*n*	Specifies the size increase of repeated packets to be an increment of *n* bytes.

Remote Printing Utilities

Several of the DOS utilities enable remote printing. TCP/IP remote printing involves sending jobs to *line printer daemons* such as the LPD Print Server, included with LAN WorkPlace and LAN WorkGroup, or a UNIX host running lpd server software. The LPD Print Server was described briefly in the "Windows Utilities" section and is covered by a manual in the online documentation. The following utilities work in conjunction with an lpd server:

- ▸ **LPR.** Prints a file to a remote LPD server.

- ▸ **LPRM.** Deletes a job from a queue on the LPD server.

- ▸ **LPQ.** Displays the status of a job on the LPD server.

- ▸ **RPD.** Deletes a job from the LPD server.

- ▸ **RPR.** Prints a job on a remote printer, working with an rsh server on the remote host.

Remote Command Utilities

UNIX offers several utilities for executing commands on remote systems. Novell has included several of these utilities for use with LAN WorkPlace and LAN WorkGroup. You were introduced to rsh in the "Windows Utilities" section. Here are the two DOS utilities:

- REXEC. Executes one command line on a remote host running rexec server software.

- RSH. Executes one command line on a remote host running an rsh server.

Telnet-Related Utilities

TNVT220 is a Telnet application designed to emulate a DEC VT220, VT100, or VT52 terminal. It requires a Telnet server on the remote host. TNVT220 is covered in the online *DOS Utiliites* manual.

XPC enables a remote X client or a Telnet client to access a workstation as a remote terminal. The remote terminal takes over the local host, and their screens mirror each other.

The TCP/IP Highway Is Complete

You now have a complete TCP/IP network environment, including servers, clients, and applications. That's not to say that you couldn't add quite a bit more. You could add an NFS server, for example, or use the printing utilities to set up TCP/IP print servers. But the infrastructure is in place. Network traffic is about the only thing left to add.

There is something you might want to do to your network first, though. Right now the NetWare network is running both IPX/SPX and TCP/IP protocols, which results in a lot of duplicated effort, such as the need to load two protocol stacks on your clients. If you'd like to simplify things a bit by moving everything over to TCP/IP, then the next chapter is for you. It describes NetWare/IP, Novell's product that enables you to run NetWare services over TCP/IP.

## CHAPTER 10

Internetworking NetWare TCP/IP

In the preceding chapters we have examined NetWare in the context of relatively simple networks. The most elaborate network seen so far consisted of two network segments, with a single NetWare server performing all routing functions. Few TCP/IP networks conform to such a simple model, however. This chapter examines two subjects that you will probably confront when your NetWare network grows beyond a single segment: routing and IP tunneling.

Most of this chapter is devoted to putting into practice the routing theory that you examined in Chapter 4 (The Internet Layer). You will learn how to configure NetWare servers with the following routing technologies:

- Static routing

- RIP

- OSPF

- ICMP Router Discovery Protocol

After RIP and OSPF have been examined separately, you will examine techniques that enable RIP and OSPF to coexist on the same internetwork.

The final topic in this chapter is IP tunneling, a neat trick that enables NetWare to route IPX packets through TCP/IP networks. This technique is especially useful when your network includes wide-area connections that are configured only for TCP/IP. You could, for example, connect two remote sites via the Internet and use IP tunneling to transport IPX traffic between the sites. Because IP tunneling only comes into action on a routed network, let's first see how NetWare can be used to construct complex internetworks.

NetWare Internetwork Support

NetWare's internetwork support is available at three levels:

- NetWare 3 provides basic internetwork support, with an emphasis on LANs.

► NetWare 4 provides more advanced internetwork support than NetWare 3, but NetWare 4 internetwork support remains focused on LANs.

► NetWare MultiProtocol Router is a family of add-in products for NetWare 3 and NetWare 4 that extends NetWare connectivity to a variety of WAN technologies.

The following sections describe the IP routing features of each product in greater detail.

NETWARE 3 ROUTING FEATURES

NetWare supports two techniques for maintaining routing tables: static routing using GATEWAYS files and dynamic routing using RIP.

NetWare 3 supports the first version of RIP (RIP I; RFC 1058), which does not directly support subnets. RIP I routers do not include subnet masks in their route broadcasts and must derive subnet mask information from their interfaces. Once a RIP I router determines the subnet mask for a local subnet, it assumes that the same subnet mask applies to all remote subnets that share the same netid.

NOTE

RIP I assumes that the same subnet mask applies to all remote subnets that are associated with the same network ID. Ordinarily this is a safe assumption. All examples of subnet masking that appear in this book assume that fixed-length subnet masks will be used. In Chapter 4, the discussion of subnet masks assumed that all subnets of a given netid would share the same subnet mask. However, some TCP/IP implementations, including NetWare 4, permit the use of variable-length subnet masks. Because the technique is tricky, I haven't examined it in this book. You should be aware of this factor when configuring RIP I routers, however, because they will be confused by variable-length subnet masks.

NETWARE 4 ROUTING ENHANCEMENTS

As you saw in Chapter 8, NetWare 3 connectivity is configured using commands that typically are embedded in the AUTOEXEC.NCF file. NetWare 4, in contrast, is configured with the INETCFG utility. The differences between NetWare 3 and NetWare 4 runs much deeper than their configuration methods. NetWare 4 provides a richer set of connectivity options, which become particularly obvious when routing is considered.

Here are some of the enhancements that NetWare 4 offers:

- ▸ **ICMP Router Discovery Protocol support.** This support enables servers to obtain updated routing information without using RIP or OSPF.

- ▸ **RIP I and RIP II.** RIP I, the version used by NetWare 3, has limited support for subnet masking and does not provide a mechanism that enables routers to authenticate routing packets received from other routers. RIP II supports subnet masking by including subnet masks in route advertisements, and also includes an authentication mechanism.

- ▸ **OSPF protocol support.**

- ▸ **BOOTP forwarding.** This feature enables routers to forward BOOTP address requests. BOOTP enables workstations to obtain their IP addresses from BOOTP servers, and is discussed along with NetWare LAN WorkGroup in Chapter 9.

- ▸ **IP filtering.** This feature enables network administrators to restrict the categories of datagrams that are permitted to cross the router.

- ▸ **Menu-based configuration of static routes.**

If your network is running NetWare 3, you can obtain these enhancements by upgrading to NetWare 4, a process made fairly painless with the introduction of NetWare 4.1. Alternatively, these same enhancements, along with WAN support, can be added to NetWare 3 by installing one of the NetWare MultiProtocol Router products described in the next section.

NETWARE MULTIPROTOCOL ROUTER

The NetWare MultiProtocol Router family can be used to configure sophisticated routers that are based on affordable 386, 486, and Pentium PCs. When WAN traffic is moderate, these products are an excellent alternative to expensive hardware-based routers. Also, because the MultiProtocol Router operates over NetWare, administrators can manage their WANS in a familiar environment. The Multiprotocol Router family includes these products:

- NetWare BranchLink Router, which offers two WAN ports.

- NetWare Enterprise Router, which offers 16 WAN ports.

- The WAN-Extensions package, which enables either router to connect to X.25 or frame relay networks.

- The SNA-Extensions package, which enables either router to communicate with SNA networks.

The WAN capabilities of the MultiProtocol Router products will be examined after we look at the configuration procedures for RIP and OSPF.

Configuring Static Routes

Static routes are defined by entries in the SYS:\ETC\GATEWAYS database file. This file is processed when the command LOAD IPCONFIG is issued, either in the AUTOEXEC.NCF file or from the command line. IPCONFIG reads the route entries in the GATEWAYS file and stores them in the server's IP routing table.

The GATEWAYS file can include entries that define routes to remote hosts and networks. It can also contain one entry that defines a default route that will be used when the routing table does not contain an entry for a destination. The default route is a special use of a network route entry that should appear only once in the GATEWAYS file. The formats used for entries in the GATEWAYS file were discussed in Chapter 8.

Contents of the GATEWAYS file can be modified in two ways:

- A text editor such as the EDIT NLM can be used to directly edit the file.

- INETCFG can be used to modify the file using menus and forms.

To see how static routing works, we will construct a routing table for a server on a sample network.

NOTE **Static routing is required only when a network is not running a dynamic routing protocol such as RIP or OSPF. A GATEWAYS file is not required when dynamic routing is employed.**

BUILDING A GATEWAYS FILE

Typically, static routes must be configured individually for each server. Figure 10.1 illustrates a somewhat artificial internetwork that illustrate several characteristics of database entries in the GATEWAYS file. The example makes use of subnetted and non-subnetted networks. Here is a GATEWAYS file that might be configured for server FS1:

```
#SYS:\ETC\GATEWAYS
#Server FS1-128.1.0.10
#Default route
NET 0 GATEWAY 128.1.0.2

NET 128.2 GATEWAY 128.1.0.1 METRIC 2
HOST FS3 GATEWAY 128.1.0.1
HOST FS5 GATEWAY 128.1.0.2
```

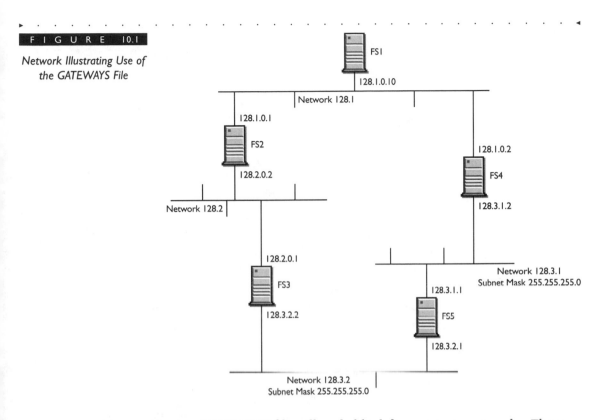

F I G U R E   10.1

*Network Illustrating Use of
the GATEWAYS File*

Most entries in a GATEWAYS file will probably define routes to networks. These entries have the following syntax:

```
NET {netid | netname} GATEWAY routeraddress [METRIC cost]
    [ACTIVE | PASSIVE]
```

Entries that define routes to hosts have this syntax:

```
HOST {ipaddress | hostname} GATEWAY routeraddress
    [METRIC cost] [ACTIVE | PASSIVE]
```

The NET and HOST keywords are used to specify whether the address defines a netid or the IP address of a host. The keywords also specify whether names should be resolved using the NETWORKS or the HOSTS database file.

Each entry states, "to reach this remote destination, here is the next gateway to use." The HOST and NET keywords describe the type of address that the destination defines:

- ▸ For a HOST entry, the destination can be a host IP address, or it can be a host name that is defined in the HOSTS file.

- ▸ For a NET entry, the destination can be a netid (the network address portion only of the IP address), or it can be a network name that is defined in the NETWORKS file.

A NET entry for netid 0 defines a default route to be used for datagrams that don't match destinations defined in the router table. Because a default route is established through 128.1.0.2, the only required entries are for routes that do not have 128.1.0.2 as the next hop.

The *routeraddress* is the IP address of a router that is attached to a network that is local (directly attached) to this host. Any datagrams that are directed to the destination network or host will be forwarded to this IP address.

The optional *cost* represents the cost of this route. If a METRIC parameter is not specified, the default cost is 1.

By default, routes that the host receives from the GATEWAYS database are flagged as PASSIVE, which means that they do not expire. Routes flagged as ACTIVE must be refreshed through ICMP protocol messages received from other routers. Active routes that are not refreshed by a routing protocol will expire eventually and be purged from the database. You should identify entries as PASSIVE when the route will not be advertised by a routing protocol.

If all routers are configured to advertise routes with ICMP, RIP, or OSPF, you should identify entries in the GATEWAYS file with the ACTIVE parameter. Passive entries are permanently loaded into the routing table and will not be adjusted as network conditions change.

Editing the GATEWAYS File

To edit the GATEWAYS file directly, enter the command **LOAD EDIT SYS:\ETC\GATEWAYS** at the server console. Make the required modifications and press Esc to save the changes. Separate the parameters with at least one space or tab character.

Managing the GATEWAYS File with INETCFG

If you have NetWare 4 or the MultiProtocol Router, you can use INETCFG to edit the GATEWAYS file. To manage static route do the following:

1 • Start INETCFG by typing **LOAD INETCFG** at the server console.

2 • Select the *Protocols* option in the Internetworking Configuration menu.

3 • Select *TCP/IP* in the Protocol Configuration menu.

4 • Highlight the *Static Routing Table* field in the TCP/IP Protocol Configuration form and press Enter to open the TCP/IP Static Routes list (see Figure 10.2).

F I G U R E   10.2

TCP/IP Static Routes Displayed in INETCFG

```
                     TCP/IP Static Routes
       Destination                        Next Hop
Default Route 0                            128.1.0.2
       Host 128.2.0.1                      128.1.0.1
       Network 193.88.201.96               193.88.201.34
```

5 • To add an entry, press Insert to open the Static Route Configuration form shown in Figure 10.3. To modify an existing entry, select the entry and press Enter to open the Static Route Configuration form. To delete an entry, select the entry and press Delete.

F I G U R E   10.3

Defining a Static Route in INETCFG

```
                    Static Route Configuration
Route to Network or Host:    Network
IP Address of Network/Host:  193.88.201.96
Subnetwork Mask:             255.255.255.224

Next Hop Type:               Gateway IP Address
Next Hop Router on Route:    193.88.201.34

Metric for this route:       2
Type of route:               Active
```

6 • In the *Route to Network or Host* field, press Enter and select a route type from the Route to Network or Host menu. The available choices are:

  ▸ **Default Route**. Specifies default route by creating a network route with a network ID of 0.

  ▸ **Host**. Creates a host route identified with the HOST keyword.

  ▸ **Network**. Creates a network route identified with the NET keyword.

7 • If you specified a host or network route, enter the address of the destination in the *IP Address of Network/Host* field. If subnetting is in use, enter the subnet mask in the *Subnetwork Mask* field. If a subnetwork mask is not specified, the route will use the default mask for the class of the address that was entered.

  If you selected *Default Route* in the *Route to Network or Host* field, the *IP Address of Network/Host and the Subnetwork Mask* fields will be inactive.

8 • The following values can be selected for the *Next Hop Type* field:

  ▸ **Gateway IP Address**. Specifies that the next hop is a router that is connected to the local network.

  ▸ **WAN Call Destination**. Specifies that the next hop is a call destination that has been defined in the INETCFG Internetworking Configuration menu.

9 • If you selected *Gateway IP Address* in the *Next Hop Type* field, in the *Next Hop Router on Route* field enter the IP address of the interface that will be used for the next router hop. The interface must be connected to a network segment that is connected directly to this host.

  If you selected *WAN Call Destination* in the *Next Hop Type* field, press Enter in the *Route to Network or Host* field to select a configured WAN interface.

10 • In the Metric for this route field, specify a number between 1 and 16 to specify the cost of this route. A cost of 16 disables the route.

11 • In the Type of route field specify whether the route entry is Passive or Active.

12 • Press Esc and save the new entry.

LOADING STATIC ROUTES

After the GATEWAYS file has been created, the static routes can be loaded into the server's router table, a function that is performed when the IPCONFIG utility is loaded on the server. IPCONFIG reads the SYS:\ETC\GATEWAYS file and stores static routes in the routing table. After populating the routing table, IPCONFIG exits. Changes that are made to the GATEWAYS file will not be reflected in the server's routing table until the next time IPCONFIG is loaded.

With NetWare 3, add the LOAD IPCONFIG command to the AUTOEXEC.NCF file following the TCP/IP LOAD and BIND statements.

With NetWare 4 or the NetWare MultiProtocol Router, activate static routing using INETCFG. The procedure is as follows:

1 • Start INETCFG by typing **LOAD INETCFG** at the server console.

2 • Select the *Protocols* option in the Internetworking Configuration menu.

3 • Select *TCP/IP* in the Protocol Configuration menu.

4 • In the TCP/IP Protocol Configuration form, set the value of the *Static Routing* field to Enabled.

5 • Exit INETCFG, saving changes, and updating the TCP/IP configuration when prompted. INETCFG will add the LOAD IPCONFIG command to the appropriate location in AUTOEXEC.NCF file.

6 • To load static routes from the GATEWAYS file, down and restart the server or type **LOAD IPCONFIG** at the server console.

USING DEFAULT ROUTES

If your network is fairly simple and seldom changes, static routing can be a useful technique that reduces the processing overhead and network traffic required to sustain dynamic routing. As you saw in the earlier example of a GATEWAYS file, in many cases a default route can eliminate the need to specify routes. The example file required a single NET routing specification to supplement the default route.

Unfortunately, default routes are inflexible and unthinking, and they can get you into trouble if you aren't careful. Let's examine some network configurations to see how default routes can cause a problem. We'll also take a look at possible solutions.

Figure 10.4 illustrates a network with three segments and two NetWare servers configured as routers. It is possible for all the TCP/IP hosts to communicate using only the default routers. Let's examine some situations:

- When A needs to send a datagram to C, A is aware that C's IP address, 2.0.0.3, is not on A's local network; therefore, A sends the datagram to its default router at 1.0.0.1. B receives the datagram and determines that it is to be delivered to a network to which it is directly attached. Therefore, B can deliver the datagram to C.

- When A needs to send a datagram to E, the process begins the same way, with A sending the datagram to B. B determines that the destination is not on a network to which it is attached; therefore, it sends the datagram to its default router at 2.0.0.2. D receives the datagram and can complete the delivery.

- When C needs to send a datagram to A, C begins by sending the datagram to its default router at 2.0.0.2. D receives the datagram and cannot deliver it to a local network; therefore, D sends the datagram to its default router at 2.0.0.1. B receives the datagram and determines that the destination is on a network to which B is directly attached; therefore, B can deliver the datagram to A.

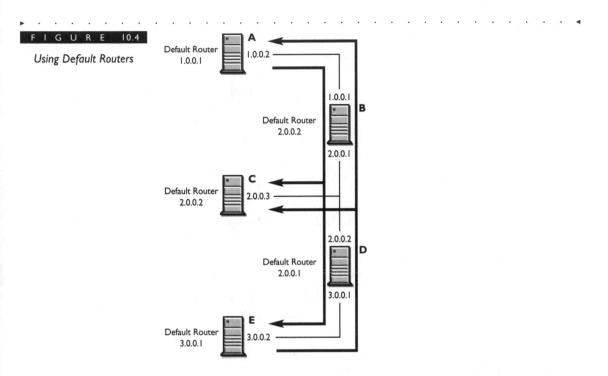

If you examine each possible pair of hosts, you will see that delivery can be achieved using the default routes. The routing tables of these hosts do not require any other entries.

A small change to the network blows this theory out of the water. Superficially, the network in Figure 10.5 looks like it should operate much like the network in Figure 10.4. That appears to be the case for datagrams that are moving down the figure. A, for example, can send datagrams successfully to any other host.

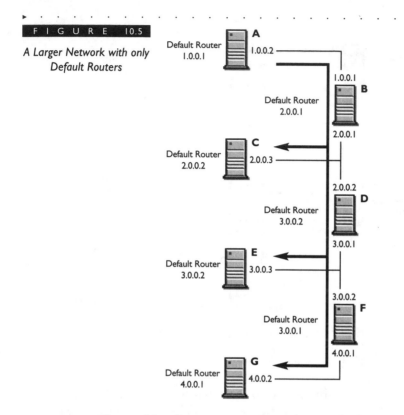

FIGURE 10.5

A Larger Network with only Default Routers

The problem becomes apparent when we look at what happens when G attempts to send a datagram to A (see Figure 10.6):

1 • A is not on a network that is local to G; therefore, G sends the datagram to its default router address 4.0.0.1.

2 • A is not on a network that is local to F; therefore, F sends the datagram to its default router address 3.0.0.1.

3 • A is not on a network that is local to D; therefore, D sends the datagram to its default router address 3.0.0.2.

As you can see, a loop has developed, and the datagram will circulate between D and F until its time-to-live expires.

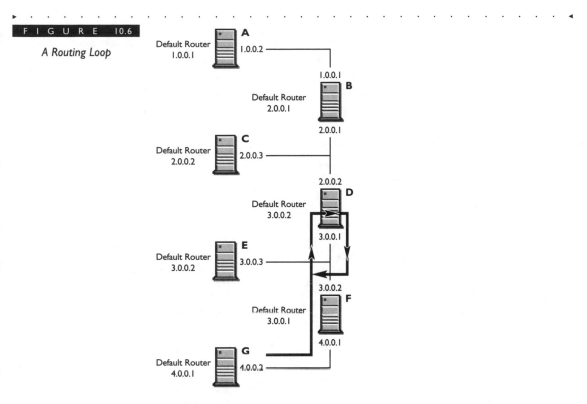

A Routing Loop

The loop develops because neither F nor D are aware of the location of Network 1.0.0.0. To correct the situation, the minimum fix is to add an entry to D's routing table by including the following line in its GATEWAYS file:

```
NET 1 GATEWAY=2.0.0.1
```

Static routing is not necessarily difficult to configure, but some caution obviously is needed. As you plan your network, try to "think like a router" to determine how datagrams will flow through the internetwork. Careful analysis will enable you to identify when additional static routes are required.

> **NOTE**
>
> **The networks in Figures 10.5 and 10.6 are perfect candidates for static routing. A single route exists between any given pair of networks. If a connection between the networks breaks, all traffic ceases. Therefore, no benefit would be gained by implementing dynamic routing, because a dynamic routing algorithm could not converge on a new route.**

NOTE

Internetworks that are configured around backbones often conform to this single-path limitation. In these cases, the deciding factor on whether to use dynamic routing is how frequently the network configuration changes. A stable, single-path network benefits little from dynamic routing, but performance may improve if routing traffic is eliminated.

That said, the decision to use static or dynamic routing is a fairly personal one that each network administrator will have to make on his or her own.

Configuring RIP

In Chapter 8 you saw that NetWare 3 communication configuration is a manual process, involving LOAD and BIND commands, which typically are embedded in the AUTOEXEC.NCF file. Configuring NetWare 3 RIP support involves adding some parameters to the LOAD TCPIP and BIND IP commands.

With NetWare 4, in contrast, RIP is configured entirely by using the INETCFG utility. That's a good thing, because NetWare 4 adds some features to RIP, including support for RIP II. These enhancements have added a number of configuration parameters, and the menu-driven nature of INETCFG makes it much easier to deal with all of the possibilities.

As in Chapter 8, before seeing how to configure RIP in INETCFG, this chapter examines the command-line approach used for NetWare 3. This discussion will highlight several scenarios for configuring RIP.

NETWARE 3 ROUTER CONFIGURATION

NetWare 3 routing is configured with the LOAD TCPIP and BIND IP commands. After reviewing the relevant options for the LOAD TCPIP command, we will examine the BIND IP options that are related to IP routing.

LOAD TCP/IP Routing Options

Two LOAD TCPIP options control routing functions:

- **RIP=YES|NO.** Determines whether RIP is active or inactive. The default value for the RIP parameter is YES.

- **FORWARD=YES|NO.** Determines whether the server will forward IP datagrams. The default value of the FORWARD parameter is NO.

Settings for these parameters are determined by the role of the server and by other routing protocols in use on the network. Let's look at some situations to determine the most appropriate configurations.

A NetWare Server on a Single-Segment Network   A single-homed server (see Figure 10.7) cannot forward traffic, so forwarding should be disabled. Because all servers are attached to the same network segment, there is no need for a routing protocol that enables servers on different segments to exchange routing information. Therefore, all servers that are attached to a single-segment network can be configured with RIP and forwarding can be disabled using this command:

```
LOAD TCPIP RIP=NO
```

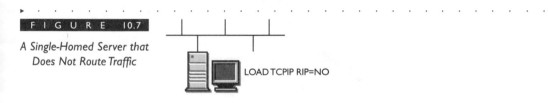

FIGURE 10.7

*A Single-Homed Server that
Does Not Route Traffic*

LOAD TCPIP RIP=NO

A Single NetWare Router on an Internetwork   Any NetWare TCP/IP server that is equipped with two network interface boards that are attached to different network segments (see Figure 10.8) can forward IP traffic between the network segments. If the server is the only router on the internetwork, it is unnecessary to run RIP, because there are no other routers with which routing data can be exchanged. Therefore, TCP/IP can be activated with this command:

```
LOAD TCPIP RIP=NO FORWARD=YES
```

▶ . . . . ◀

F I G U R E   10.8

A Multi-Homed Server that
Routes Traffic

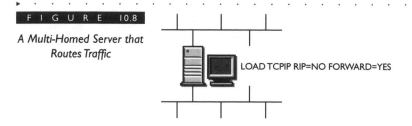

LOAD TCPIP RIP=NO FORWARD=YES

Multiple NetWare Routers on an Internetwork   If any other routers are present (see Figure 10.9), you must decide how the routers will be made aware of the routes that are available. You could configure static routes, or if you prefer to have the routers exchange dynamic routing information, you will need to enable RIP on all routers. RIP is the only mechanism NetWare 3 provides for exchanging routes. Under these circumstances, you would activate RIP by accepting the default value of the RIP parameter, and TCP/IP would be loaded with the following command:

```
LOAD TCPIP FORWARD=YES
```

▶ . . . . ◀

F I G U R E   10.9

A Multi-Homed Server that
Operates a Routing
Protocol

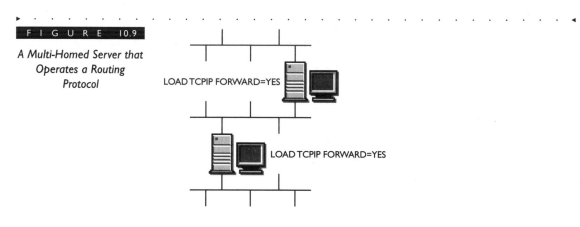

LOAD TCPIP FORWARD=YES

LOAD TCPIP FORWARD=YES

Single-Homed NetWare Servers on an Internetwork   Servers that do not forward datagrams may or may not benefit from participating in RIP broadcasts. Let's look at two situations.

In Figure 10.10, server S2 can reach remote networks only through a single path, via S1. If this path fails, S2 cannot learn another path. Therefore, it is not necessary for S2 to run a routing protocol. It is sufficient to configure S2 with a single static route that defines S1 as the default router for S2; therefore, TCP/IP would be loaded with the following command:

```
LOAD TCPIP RIP=NO
```

Because S1 will not be exchanging RIP advertisements with other routers, RIP can be deactivated on S1, as shown in the figure.

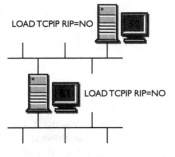

FIGURE 10.10

A Multi-Segment Network that Does Not Require RIP

In Figure 10.11, server S5 has two paths to network NET2, via S3 and S4. If S3 is configured as the default router for S5 and S3 fails, S5 can only learn a new route if it is receiving RIP broadcasts. Therefore, even though S5 is not routing datagrams, S5 would be configured with RIP enabled, with the following command:

```
LOAD TCPIP
```

Servers S3 should be configured with RIP and forwarding active using the command:

```
LOAD TCPIP FORWARD=YES
```

FIGURE 10.11

Configuring Routers on an Internetwork with Multiple Routes

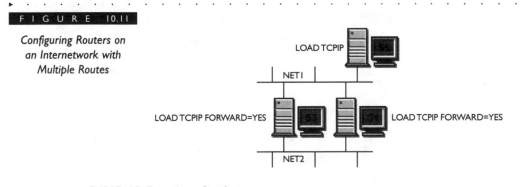

BIND IP Routing Options

Table 10.1 summarizes the options that can be used with the BIND IP command. Not all of the options are related to routing, but all have been included here for completeness. Four parameters are related to routing: GATE, DEFROUTE, COST, and POISON.

PARAMETER	VALUE	PURPOSE
ADDR	IP address	Specifies the IP address to be associated with the interface being bound.
MASK	Subnet mask	Specifies the IP network mask that applies to the network attached to the interface being bound.
ARP	YES or NO	Specifies whether the Address Resolution Protocol will be used to resolve IP addresses to hardware addresses. When the value is NO, the host part of the IP address is mapped to the local hardware address. It is strongly recommended that the value of this parameter be set to the default value of YES.
BCAST	IP address	Specifies an IP address to be used for broadcasting messages on this network. By default, the broadcast is 255.255.255.255 (0xFF.0xFF.0xFF.0xFF).
COST	1–15 (decimal)	The cost of this interface in hops that will be advertised by RIP. The default value is 1.
DEFROUTE	YES or NO	If TCP/IP is loaded with the FORWARD=YES parameter, this parameter causes the server to announce this node through RIP as a default gateway. The default value is NO.
GATE	IP address	Specifies the IP address of a default gateway (router) for this interface. This parameter is not recommended when RIP is active on the server, in which case, the server can obtain all routing information from RIP.
POISON	YES or NO	If the value of this parameter is YES, poison reverse is active and split horizon is inactive. If this parameter is NO (the default), poison reverse is inactive and split horizon is active.

Using the COST Parameter   A router will have at least two interfaces, and each interface could be assigned its own COST parameter, which specifies the cost that RIP will advertise for this interface. To see how costs are advertised, examine Figure 10.12. In this figure, Router R1 is equipped with two interfaces:

▶ The interface on Network 1 is configured with a cost of 2.

▶ The interface on Network 2 is configured with a cost of 5.

The cost R1 advertises for a given network is the cost that is assigned to the interface attached to that network. Consequently, R1 has a route to Network 1, which is advertised to Network 2 with a cost of 2. Also, R1 has a route to Network 2, which is advertised to Network 1 with a cost of 5.

Host H1 receives a route advertisement from R1 indicating that R1's cost to reach Network 2 is 5. H1's cost to reach Network 1 is 1. H1 adds its cost to reach Network 1 to R1's cost to reach Network 2 and concludes that H1 can reach Network 2 with a cost of 6.

Host H2 receives a route advertisement from R1, indicating that R1's cost to reach Network 1 is 2. H2's cost to reach Network 2 is 1. H2 adds its cost to reach Network 1 to R1's cost to reach Network 1 and concludes that H2 can reach Network 1 with a cost of 3.

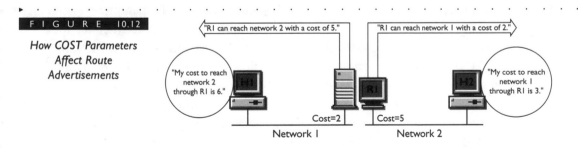

F I G U R E   10.12

How COST Parameters Affect Route Advertisements

The COST parameter can be used to encourage or discourage the use of certain routes. Consider the network in Figure 10.13. R1 is a dedicated router that has been put in place to handle the bulk of traffic between Network 1 and Network 2. S1 is a NetWare server that has been configured as a router (RIP=YES FORWARD=YES). The administrator wishes the majority of traffic to be routed through R1 to avoid loading down the server with routing duties. Therefore, when IP is bound on S1, the cost of the interface would be set to a value greater than 1, as in the following example:

```
BIND IP to NE2000_2_EII ADDR=2.0.0.1 COST=2
```

If the cost of R1 is 1, traffic normally will flow through R1. If R1 fails or is shut down for maintenance, hosts on Network 1 will begin to use S1 to reach Network 2.

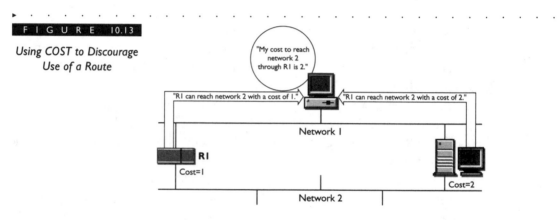

F I G U R E   10.13

Using COST to Discourage Use of a Route

Using the DEFROUTE Parameter   The DEFROUTE parameter takes effect only if the server is configured as a router by loading TCP/IP with the FORWARD=YES parameter. If the server is a router and the DEFROUTE=YES parameter is included with the BIND IP command, the server will advertise itself as a default router in RIP advertisements. That is to say, the server will advertise only the default route 0.0.0.0. Hosts that receive the default route announcement will add this server to their routing tables as a default router.

Careless use of the DEFROUTE parameter on multiple servers can result in network routing loops. As such, default route advertisements are very dangerous and should be used with extreme caution.

Using the GATE Parameter   If RIP is not active on a server, the GATE parameter can be used to specify a default gateway. Figure 10.14 illustrates a situation in which a default gateway might be configured. Server S1 must be configured with a default gateway address that enables it to send datagrams to S2 for routing. This is accomplished by using a BIND IP command similar to the following on S1:

```
BIND IP TO NE2000_1_EII ADDR=128.0.0.10 GATE=128.0.0.1
```

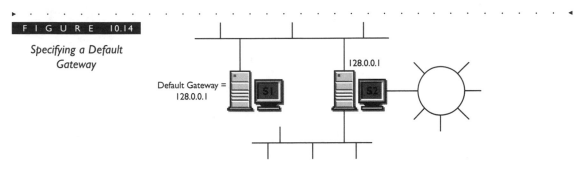

FIGURE 10.14

*Specifying a Default
Gateway*

As was shown during above discussion about static routing, a server that has only one possible routing path gains little by running a dynamic routing protocol. Use of the default gateway parameter can enhance performance in such situations.

Using the POISON Parameter   By default, NetWare routers are configured to use the split-horizon technique to limit the severity of the count-to-infinity problem. As you learned in Chapter 4, split-horizon breaks routing loops by preventing a router from advertising a route back to the interface from which the route was received.

Poison reverse is an alternative to split-horizon that enhances network stability but increases network traffic. Routers configured to use poison reverse advertise a route back to the interface from which the route was received, but they advertise the route with a metric of 16, indicating that the destination is unreachable. In this way, poison reverse immediately notifies routers of invalid routes.

Enable poison reverse with the POISON=YES parameter when you wish to promote network stability at the cost of increased network traffic. By default, poison reverse is disabled (POISON=NO) and split-horizon is enabled.

Example NetWare 3 Routing Configurations
Here are two examples that illustrate the use of TCP/IP configuration parameters.

Configuring a Server as an End Node   A NetWare server is to be configured with the following characteristics:

- ▸ The IP address is 153.12.8.20.

- ▸ The server is an end node (no forwarding).

- ▸ RIP will not be active.

▶ The server will use 153.12.8.1 as a default router.

▶ Subnet masking is not used on this network.

To configure TCP/IP on this server, the following commands would be included in the AUTOEXEC.NCF file:

```
LOAD NE2000 FRAME=ETHERNET_II NAME=NE2000_1_EII other parameters
LOAD TCPIP RIP=NO
BIND IP TO NE2000_1_EII ADDR=153.12.8.20 DEFROUTE=153.12.8.1
```

Configuring a Server as a Router   A server will be configured as a router with the following characteristics:

▶ The server is a router with two interfaces.

▶ The IP address of the first interface is 80.1.1.2 with a cost of 2.

▶ The IP address of the second interface is 80.2.2.5 with a cost of 1.

▶ Both interfaces will be configured with the subnet mask 255.255.0.0.

▶ RIP will be active.

▶ Forwarding will be active.

▶ Poison reverse will be active.

The commands to configure TCP/IP on this server are as follows:

```
LOAD NE2000 FRAME=ETHERNET_II NAME=NE2000_1_EII other parameters
LOAD NE2000 FRAME=ETHERNET_II NAME=NE2000_2_EII other parameters
LOAD TCPIP FORWARD=YES
BIND IP TO NE2000_1_EII ADDR=80.1.1.2 MASK=255.255.0.0
  POISON=YES COST=2
BIND IP TO NE2000_2_EII ADDR=80.2.2.5 MASK=255.255.0.0
  POISON=YES
```

NETWARE 4 ROUTER CONFIGURATION

NetWare 4 and the NetWare MultiProtocol Router include the INETCFG utility, which greatly simplifies configuration of routing parameters. The parameters for configuring RIP fall into two categories: TCP/IP load parameters and TCP/IP bind parameters. These groups of parameters are accessed through different menus in INETCFG.

Configuring TCP/IP Load Parameters for RIP

TCP/IP load parameter affect the settings of the RIP and FORWARD parameters in the LOAD TCPIP command.

To configure the TCP/IP load parameters for RIP, do the following:

1 • Start INETCFG by typing **LOAD INETCFG** at the server console.

2 • Select the *Protocols* option in the Internetworking Configuration menu.

3 • Select *TCP/IP* in the Protocol Configuration menu to open the TCP/IP Protocol Configuration form shown in Figure 10.15.

4 • If this server will be forwarding packets, set the value of the *IP Packet Forwarding* field to Enabled ("Router"). This setting adds the FORWARD=YES parameter to the LOAD TCPIP command.

If this server will not be forwarding packets, set the value of the *IP Packet Forwarding* field to Disabled ("End Node"). This setting adds the FORWARD=NO parameter to the LOAD TCPIP command.

5 • To enable RIP on this server, set the value of the *RIP* field to Enabled in the TCP/IP Protocol Configuration form. This setting adds the RIP=YES parameter to the LOAD TCPIP command.

To disable RIP on this server, set the value of the *RIP* field to Disabled in the TCP/IP Protocol Configuration form. This setting adds the RIP=NO parameter to the LOAD TCPIP command.

6 • After configuring these parameters, press Esc to exit the form. Choose *Yes* to update the TCP/IP protocol when prompted.

F I G U R E   10.15

TCP/IP Load Parameters

```
               TCP/IP Protocol Configuration
TCP/IP Status:                  Enabled
IP Packet Forwarding:           Disabled("End Node")

RIP:                            Disabled
OSPF:                           Enabled
OSPF Configuration:             (Select to View or Modify)

Static Routing:                 Disabled
Static Routing Table:           (Select For List)

SNMP Manager Table:             (Select For List)

Filter Support:                 Disabled
Expert Configuration Options:   (Select to View or Modify)
```

Configuring TCP/IP Bind Parameters for RIP

The TCP/IP bind parameters determine the parameters that configure individual interfaces when the BIND IP command is used. Some, but not all, parameters configured in INETCFG are reflected by parameters entered in the BIND IP command.

To configure TCP/IP bind parameters:

1 • Start INETCFG by typing LOAD INETCFG at the server console.

2 • Select the *Bindings* option in the Internetworking Configuration menu. This will open the Configured Protocol To Network Interface Bindings window, which lists bindings that have been configured.

3a • To add a new binding:

A. Press Insert in the Configured Protocol To Network Interface Bindings window.

B. Select *TCP/IP* from the list of configured protocols.

C. Select a network interface from the list of configured network interfaces. When you press Enter, INETCFG will open the Binding TCP/IP to a LAN Interface window.

3b • To reconfigure an existing binding, select the binding in the Configured Protocol To Network Interface Bindings window. When you press Enter, INETCFG will open the Binding TCP/IP to a LAN Interface window.

4 • Select the *RIP Bind Options* field in the Binding TCP/IP to a LAN Interface window. The RIP Bind Options window will be displayed (see Figure 10.16). The fields in this form are configured as follows:

▸ **Network Interface.** This is a read-only field that indicates which interface is being configured. The other fields are editable.

```
Internetworking Configuration  3.10a              NetWare Loadable Module

  ┌ Internetworking Configuration ┐
  ┌──────────────────────────────────────────────────────────────────┐
  │          Configured Protocol To Network Interface Bindings         │
 Pro┌────────────────────────────────────────────────────────────────┐
 IPX│               Binding TCP/IP to a LAN Interface                │
 IPX│ Netw ┌──────────────────────────────────────────────────────┐ │
 TCP│      │                  RIP Bind Options                     │ │
 TCP│ Loca │ Network Interface:        NE2000_1                    │ │
    │ Subn │                                                       │ │
    │      │ Status:               Enabled                         │ │
 RIP│      │ Cost of Interface:    2                               │ ┐│
 OSPF      │ Originate Default Route: Disable: Present Normal Routes│ )│
 Expe      │ Poison Reverse:       Disabled                        │ )│
           │ RIP Mode:             RIPI & RIPII                    │ │
           │ RIPII Options:        (Select to View or Modify)      │ │
           │ Neighbor List:        (Select For List)               │ │
           └──────────────────────────────────────────────────────┘ │
 Specify RIP metric to associate with this interface.
 ENTER=Select ESC=Previous Menu                                F1=Help
```

▸ **Status.** This field indicates whether RIP is enabled or disabled for this interface. This value is automatically set to Enabled when RIP is enabled for the server in the TCP/IP Protocol Configuration form.

You can enable or disable RIP for this interface by changing the value of the *Status* field. The effect of enabling or disabling RIP from this form depends on the TCP/IP load settings:

If the *IP Packet Forwarding* field is set to Enabled ("Router"), enabling RIP in the *Status* field configures this interface to participate in the exchange of RIP advertisements.

If the *IP Packet Forwarding* field is set to Disabled ("End Node"), enabling RIP in the *Status* field configures this interface to receive RIP advertisements from routers; however, this server will not generate RIP advertisements. This setting enables a non-routing host to update its routing table from RIP advertisements that it receives.

▸ **Cost of Interface.** This field specifies the cost that will be advertised for this interface. Enter a value between 1 and 16, where 16 indicates that routing is disabled for this interface. This parameter configures the COST parameter in the BIND IP command. See the section "Using the COST Parameter" for more information about how RIP advertises interface costs.

▸ **Originate Default Route.** This field determines whether this router will advertise itself as a default router.

Set the value to Disable: Present Normal Routes to have this router send normal RIP advertisements. This setting adds the DEFROUTE=NO parameter to the BIND IP command.

Set the value to Enable: Present Default Route to have this router advertise itself as a default router. This setting adds the DEFROUTE=YES parameter to the BIND IP command.

▸ **Poison Reverse.** This field determines whether this interface will use split-horizon or poison reverse to discourage routing loops.

Set the value to Disabled to configure the interface to use split horizon. This setting adds the POISON=NO parameter to the BIND IP command. RIP traffic is reduced at a cost of reduced stability.

Set the value to Enabled to configure the interface to use poison reverse. This setting adds the POISON=YES parameter to the BIND IP command. Stability is improved at a cost of increased RIP traffic.

▸ **RIP Mode.** This field has four possible values:

    ▸ **RIPI** configures the interface to use the RIP I only.

    ▸ **RIPII** configures the interface to use RIP II only. Choose this setting only if all routers on the network support RIP II.

▸ **RIPI & RIPII** configures the interface to operate with both levels of RIP.

▸ **Send Only** configures the interface to send RIP I packets announcing its routing table. Incoming RIP advertisements are discarded.

NOTE

The Send Only option commonly is used in environments that consist of OSPF and RIP routers. A router that is participating in OSPF routing can be configured to use Send Only mode so that it will announce its routing table to RIP routers on the network.

▸ **RIP II Options.** Selecting this field opens a RIP II Configuration form with two fields:

The *Authentication* field determines whether RIP II authentication is enabled or disabled. The default value is Disabled. Change the value to Enabled if you wish RIP II routers to use an authentication key to verify messages.

The *Authentication Key* field accepts a 16-byte string that functions as a password when authentication is enabled on the attached network.

▸ **Neighbor List.** Selecting this field opens a RIP Neighbors box listing the IP addresses of hosts that are configured as RIP neighbors. To add entries to this list, press Insert and enter an IP address. On broadcast networks such as Ethernet and token ring, it is unnecessary to configure RIP neighbors.

On networks that do not support broadcast messaging, such as X.25, frame relay, and PPP, it is necessary to configure RIP routers as neighbors. RIP neighbors exchange RIP advertisements as unicast messages rather than broadcast messages.

After RIP routing has been configured in INETCFG, the changes must be activated. Because not all changes are activated by the REINITIALIZE SERVER command, it is necessary to restart the server to activate the changes.

Configuring OSPF

Before you can make much sense out of OSPF, you need to be familiar with the alphabet soup that appears in OSPF verbage. Otherwise, you'll never make sense out of expressions such as "connecting an OSPF AS to a RIP AS requires an ASBR that has an interface in each AS." You see the acronyms ASBR, ABR, and AS quite frequently because the full terms are such tongue twisters. How many times do you want to say *autonomous system border router* in one day?

Let's take a moment to define some OSPF terms. This summary focuses on the components of an OSPF routing system and how they are related. See Chapter 4 for a more theoretical discussion of how OSPF builds routing tables.

A REVIEW OF OSPF TERMINOLOGY

Figure 10.17 shows a diagram of a network that uses OSPF routing. The diagram focuses on routers, and of course, many more TCP/IP hosts would appear on the networks that the routers join. Now, let's review the components of the network, with an emphasis on concepts that you must consider when configuring OSPF routers.

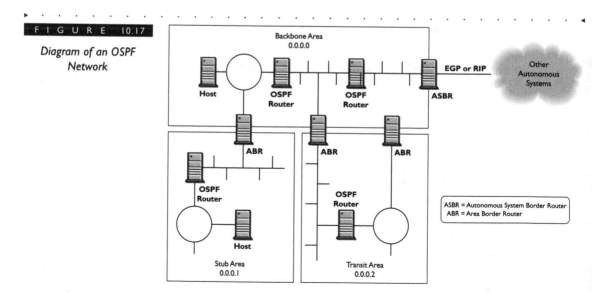

FIGURE 10.17

Diagram of an OSPF Network

An *autonomous system* (AS) is a collection of networks that share a common routing protocol. Figure 10.15 includes one OSPF AS.

Areas define groups of OSPF routers that share a common link-state database. OSPF advertises routes using *link-state advertisements (LSAs)*, which are flooded throughout an area. *Flooding* describes the process of distributing LSAs to all OSPF routers in an area. On small-to-medium size networks, the entire AS can be configured as a single area.

One router in an area is identified as the *designated router* through an election process that can be configured by setting priorities for individual routers. The designated router is responsible for preparing LSAs for the area.

Within an area, OSPF routers communicate with *neighbors*, which are peer OSPF routers. On broadcast networks, OSPF routers can discover their peers using Hello packets. Only routers that exchange Hello packets establish themselves as neighbors. On non-broadcast networks, such as X.25 and frame relay, the addresses of neighbors must be added manually to the routers' configurations.

As areas grow in size, OSPF performance diminishes in two areas: it takes longer to recompute the new routes that result from link-state changes, and increasing amounts of network traffic are devoted to distributing link-state advertisements. Consequently, the design of OSPF accommodates partitioning the AS into multiple areas. This has two advantages:

▸ Areas can be configured around organizational or geographical relationships, limiting the sharing of routing information and making the network more secure.

▸ The number of LSAs in the areas is reduced, and they are limited to the information users require most often.

NOTE

Novell recommends limiting the size of an AS to 200 routers.

Areas must be organized hiearchically, with one area designated as a *backbone area*. All other areas must connect to the backbone area. Each area is identified by an *area ID*, a four-byte number, which is usually expressed in dotted-decimal form. These area IDs are not IP addresses and don't need to follow IP address restrictions. The backbone area is always assigned the area ID 0.0.0.0.

Areas must be configured out of contiguous groups of routers and networks. In other words, parts of an area may not be separated by another area. Because most areas typically support a localized subset of hosts, it is seldom a problem to configure areas out of contiguous components. Because only one backbone is permitted, however, it may be difficult to configure a backbone contiguously on a geographically dispersed network.

It is possible to partition the backbone area into multiple physical areas, and to enable the backbone partitions to communicate using a *virtual link* through another area. The area that supports the virtual link is called a *virtual-link transit area*. Be aware that, in Novell's words, virtual links are "complicated and error-prone." Figure 10.18 illustrates a backbone that is partitioned to span a large area. In such cases a virtual link must be established to extend the backbone partition to the New York area. This approach enables Chicago and New York to share the same leased circuit between Chicago and Los Angeles.

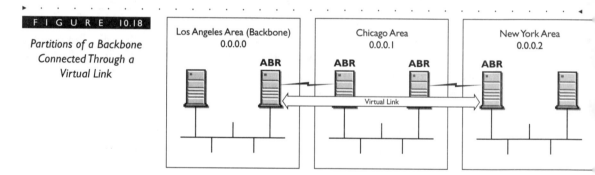

FIGURE 10.18

Partitions of a Backbone Connected Through a Virtual Link

Area border routers (ABRs) connect areas and advertise destinations across area boundaries in the form of *summary link advertisements*.

Two types of areas can connect to the backbone area:

> ► *Stub areas* connect to the backbone through a single ABR. The ABR of a stub area does not advertise external routes. Instead, because all external traffic must go through the ABR, a single default route is advertised. Configuration of stub areas reduces the memory, processing, and bandwidth requirements of the ABR but obviously makes the area subject to a single point of failure.

▶ *Transit areas* connect to the backbone with more than one ABR. Processing, memory, and bandwidth requirements are higher for ABRs that for support transit areas.

Routing within an area, called *intra-area routing* can take place without knowledge of external routes. Routing between areas, *inter-area routing*, requires ABRs to exchange routing information about their areas.

Autonomous system border routers (ASBRs) are responsible for routing traffic between the OSPF AS and AS's based on other routing protocols such as RIP or EGP. External routes are advertised through *external link advertisements*.

NOTE

OSPF gives different preferences to routes that are obtained from the local AS (internal routes) and from remote AS's (external routes). On a network that includes OSPF and RIP routers, for example, an OSPF router prefers a route that it learns internally from another OSPF router over a route that it learns externally from a RIP router.

If you are configuring your network using only NetWare routers, you don't need to be concerned with the preferences. If, however, your network includes third-party routers in addition to NetWare routers, you need to ensure that all routers employ the same preferences. Consult the TCP/IP Reference manual for more information about OSPF protocol preferences.

OSPF PROTOCOL CONFIGURATION

Setting up OSPF routing on a server involves the following steps:

1 • Enabling OSPF protocol support

2 • Configuring OSPF protocol settings

3 • Configuring areas

4 • Configuring virtual links (if applicable)

5 • Configuring OSPF interface bindings

6 • Activating the changes

These procedures are performed starting from the TCP/IP Protocol Configuration form in INETCFG. The following sections describe each procedure in detail.

Step 1. Enabling OSPF Protocol Support

Use the following steps to open the TCP/IP Protocol Configuration form:

1 • Start INETCFG by typing **LOAD INETCFG** at the server console.

2 • Select the *Protocols* option in the Internetworking Configuration menu.

3 • Select *TCP/IP* in the Protocol Configuration menu. This will open the TCP/IP Protocol Configuration form shown in Figure 10.14.

To enable OSPF protocol support, set the value of the *OSPF* field to Enabled.

Step 2. Configuring OSPF Protocol Settings

Select the OSPF Configuration field in the TCP/IP Protocol Configuration form to open the OSPF Configuration form shown in Figure 10.19. Two settings are configured on this form:

▸ The *Router ID* field uniquely identifies this router within the OSPF AS. The default value is First IP Interface, which identifies this router using the first IP address that is bound to an interface on the router.

Because the IP addresses on your internetwork should each be unique, they can be used to uniquely identify your routers as well. If you wish, however, press Enter in the *Router ID* field and enter a router ID, using four-byte, dotted-decimal notation.

▸ The *Autonomous System Boundary Router* field determines whether this router will serve as an ASBR. Any router on the backbone or in a transit area can function as an ASBR. Configuring a router as an ASBR increases the router's work and places greater demands on the router's memory and processing capabilities.

FIGURE 10.19

Configuring the OSPF
Protocol

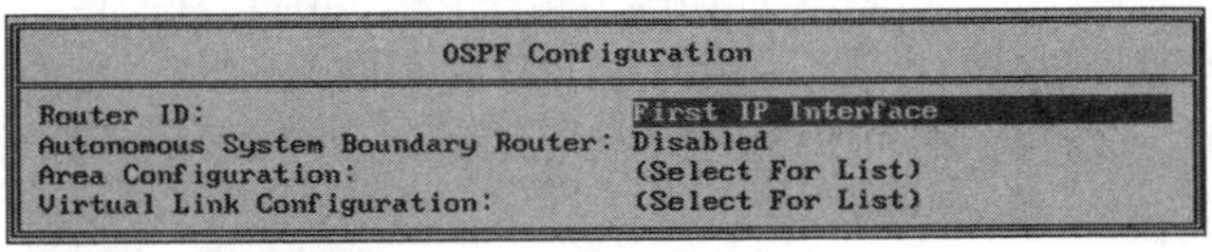

Step 3. Configuring Areas

To configure areas within the AS, select the *Area Configuration* field in the OSPF Configuration form. The OSPF Areas list shown in Figure 10.20 shows all areas that have been defined. If you are creating the first area, INETCFG assumes it is the backbone area and presents the area ID 0.0.0.0 as a default.

FIGURE 10.20

Configured OSPF Areas

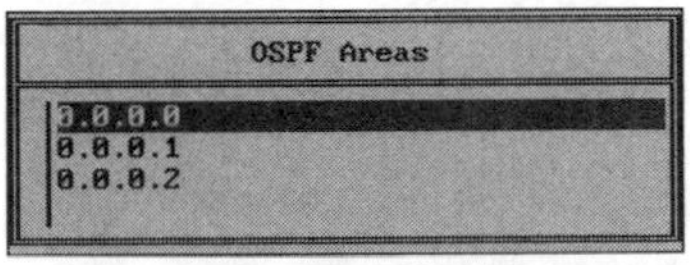

To modify an area, highlight the area in the list and press Enter to open the OSPF Area Configuration form shown in Figure 10.21. If you are configuring the first area in the AS, select the 0.0.0.0 entry and press Enter to configure the backbone area

To add an area, press Insert to open the OSPF Area Configuration form. To delete an area, highlight the area ID and press Delete.

FIGURE 10.21

Configuring an OSPF Area

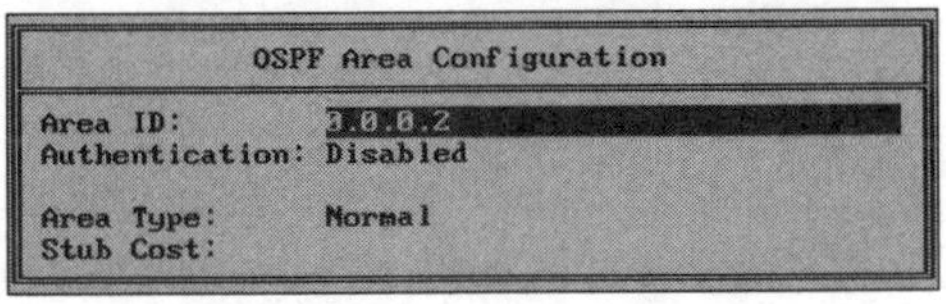

The OSPF Area Configuration form has four fields. Depending on the type of area that is being defined, some of the fields may be inactive. If, for example, you are configuring the backbone area by specifying 0.0.0.0 in the *Area ID* field, only the *Area ID* and *Authentication* fields will be active.

To activate authentication, change the value of the *Authentication* field to Enabled. When authentication is enabled, this router will accept only OSPF messages that are identified by an authentication key. The key is specified when OSPF is bound to a network interface. If authentication is activated, it must be activated for all routers in the area.

To configure a non-backbone area, edit the value of the *Area ID* field to specify a value other than 0.0.0.0, which can be assigned only to the backbone area. Assigning a non-zero value to the *Area ID* field will activate the *Area Type* field.

To configure a transit area, leave the value of the *Area Type* field with the default value of Normal.

To configure a stub area, change the value of the *Area Type* field to Stub. This will activate the *Stub Cost* field. Enter a value in the range of 1 through 16777215 in this field. The value you enter will be used to advertise the stub cost when the summary link advertisement is prepared for the stub area. The stub cost represents the cost of all datagrams routed to the area.

When OSPF areas have been configured, press Escape to return to the OSPF Configuration form.

Step 4. Configuring Virtual Links

If the backbone is not contiguous, a virtual link must be specified to connect the backbone partitions. To configure virtual links, select *Virtual Link Configuration* in the OSPF Configuration form and press Enter to present the OSPF Virtual Links list shown in Figure 10.22.

FIGURE 10.22

Configured OSPF Virtual Links

To add a virtual link, press Insert to open the OSPF Virtual Link Configuration form. To edit an existing link, select the link and press Enter to open the OSPF Virtual Link Configuration form. To delete an area, highlight the area ID and press Delete.

The OSPF Virtual Link Configuration form is shown in Figure 10.23. This form has five fields, which are configured as follows:

▸ **Router ID of Neighbor.** Specifies the IP address of the router at the other end of the virtual link. Press Insert in this field to present the list of host names that are defined in the HOSTS file, or enter an IP address.

▸ **Transit Area.** Specifies the area ID of the virtual link transit area that will support the virtual link.

▸ **Authentication Key.** This is an optional field. If authentication is enabled in the virtual link transit area, enter the eight-byte authentication key in this field.

▸ **Hello Interval.** Specifies the time in seconds between transmission of Hello packets to the network interface specified in the *Router ID of Neighbor* field. The default value is 10 seconds. This value must be the same for all routers on this network or virtual link.

▸ **Router Dead Interval.** Specifies the time in seconds between Hello packets that a router will wait before declaring dead the router at the other end of the virtual link. This value must be the same for all routers on this network or virtual link.

When virtual links have been configured, press Escape to return to the OSPF Configuration form.

FIGURE 10.23

Configuring an OSPF Virtual Link

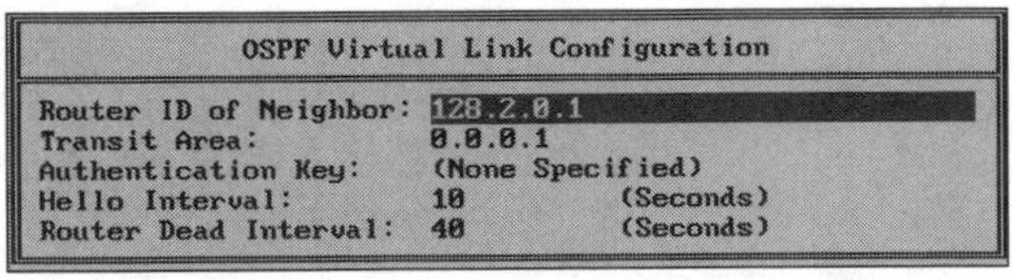

```
            OSPF Virtual Link Configuration
Router ID of Neighbor: 128.2.0.1
Transit Area:          0.0.0.1
Authentication Key:    (None Specified)
Hello Interval:        10          (Seconds)
Router Dead Interval:  40          (Seconds)
```

Step 5. Configuring OSPF Interface Bindings

When the OSPF protocol has been configured as discussed in Steps 1 through 4, OSPF can be bound to individual network interfaces as follows:

1 • Start INETCFG by typing **LOAD INETCFG** at the server console.

2 • Select the *Bindings* option in the Internetworking Configuration menu to open the Configured Protocols To Network Interface Bindings list.

3 • Select an existing TCP/IP binding or, if necessary, create a binding as described in Chapter 8.

4 • In the Binding TCP/IP to a LAN Interface form, select *OSPF Bind Options* and press Enter to open the OSPF Bind Options form shown in Figure 10.24. The fields in this form are completed as follows:

 ▶ **Network Interface.** Identifies the network interface for which OSPF is being configured (read-only).

 ▶ **Status.** When OSPF is enabled for the server, it is enabled for all interfaces on the server. To disable OSPF for a specific interface, change the value of this field to Disabled. When OSPF is disabled, this interface will not exchange route information with other OSPF routers.

 ▶ **Cost of Interface.** Specifies the cost OSPF associates with sending a datagram through this interface.

 ▶ **Area ID.** Specifies the OSPF area to which this router belongs. Areas must be defined in the OSPF Area Configuration form.

▶ **Priority.** Specifies the relative priorities that determine which router will be selected as the designated router for the area. Set the priority parameter to favor the selection of specific routers as the area designated router.

▶ **Authentication Key.** If authentication is enabled in this router's area, enter the eight-byte authentication string in this field.

▶ **Hello Interval.** Specifies the time in seconds between transmission of Hello packets to the network interface specified being configured. This value must be the same for all routers on this network or virtual link.

▶ **Router Dead Interval.** This field specifies the time in seconds between Hello packets that a router will wait before declaring a router dead. This value must be the same for all routers on this network or virtual link.

▶ **Neighbor List.** On broadcast networks such as Ethernet and token ring, routers can discover their neighbors dynamically using the Hello protocol. On non-broadcast networks such as X.25, frame relay, and PPP, neighbors must be added manually to the interface configuration. Select this field to open the OSPF Neighbors list and add the addresses of neighbors to the list.

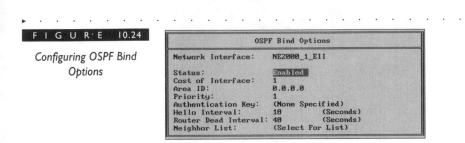

```
                    OSPF Bind Options

Network Interface:      NE2000_1_EII

Status:                 Enabled
Cost of Interface:      1
Area ID:                0.0.0.0
Priority:               1
Authentication Key:     (None Specified)
Hello Interval:         10          (Seconds)
Router Dead Interval:   40          (Seconds)
Neighbor List:          (Select For List)
```

Step 6. Activating the Changes

After configuring OSPF, restart the server to activate the changes.

MANAGING OSPF

Here are a few tips for tuning OSPF:

- ▸ OSPF generates less network traffic than RIP. To achieve that economy, OSPF needs more processor and memory than RIP. In high-traffic areas, consider setting up dedicated routers using the MultiProtocol Router.

- ▸ Use areas to reduce the levels of LSA traffic.

- ▸ Use interface costs to favor the most efficient routes. Consider characteristics such as bandwidth and reliability when establishing interface costs.

In Chapter 11 you learn how to use TCPCON to inspect the configurations of TCP/IP computers. TCPCON also has an option that enables you to observe the configuration of OSPF. Figure 10.25 shows the OSPF Protocol Information screen in TCPCON. Take some time to explore the information that can be reached from this screen.

FIGURE 10.25

OSPF Protocol Information in TCPCON

```
                    OSPF Protocol Information
   Router ID:                            193.88.201.65
   Administrative Status:                enable
   Version Number:                       2
   Area Border Router:                   false
   Autonomous System Border Router:.     false
   Type-of-Service Routing:              unsupported

   Areas:                                (Select to View)
   Interfaces:                           (Select to View)
   Neighbors:                            (Select to View)
   Virtual Interfaces:                   (Select to View)
   Virtual Neighbors:                    (Select to View)
   Hosts:                                (Select to View)
   Link State Advertisements:            (Select to View)

   OSPF Statistics:                      (Select to View)
```

I'll just highlight a few of the more interesting possibilities.

Select the *Neighbors* field to view routers with which this router has established a neighbor relationship. All neighbors should indicate a State of "full," showing they are synchronized with this router.

You can view the link-state database by selecting the *Link State Advertisements* field. Each entry can be opened up to show its parameters, as shown in Figure 10.26. The *Contents* field shows a dump of the LSA in hexadecimal, which isn't particularly useful to most of us. However, all routers should be receiving identical LSAs from this router. You can verify this by examining the *Checksum* field, which should be the same on each router.

```
     Link State Advertisement

Area ID:        0.0.0.0
Type:           Router
Link State ID:  193.88.201.65
Router ID:      193.88.201.65
Sequence:       80000007 (hex)
Age:            703      (seconds)
Checksum:       9177     (hex)

Contents:       (Select to View)
```

Running OSPF with RIP

A router that is running both RIP and OSPF does not necessarily forward routing information between the two environments. To enable OSPF to advertise routes derived from RIP, the OSPF router must be configured as an autonomous system border router (ASBR). The procedure is as follows:

1 • Start INETCFG by typing **LOAD INETCFG** at the server console.

2 • Select the *Protocols* option in the Internetworking Configuration menu to open the Protocol Configuration list.

3 • Select *TCP/IP* in the Protocol Configuration list to open the TCP/IP Protocol Configuration form.

4 • Select the *OSPF Configuration* field to open the OSPF Configuration form.

5 • Change the value of the *Autonomous System Border Router* field to Enabled.

6 • Press Escape to exit the form and save the changes.

Limit the number of routers that are configured as ASBRs. Functioning as an ASBR increases the processing overhead and memory requirement for the router. Also, each ASBR increases network traffic as the routers advertise the same routes. Novell recommends having at most two or three ASBRs between RIP and OSPF domains.

Configuring ICMP Router Discovery

If your TCP/IP network grows to significant size, you will probably have some NetWare servers and possible UNIX hosts that are not configured as IP routers. These hosts must be able to identify routers so that they can send datagrams to remote networks. What techniques are available for providing hosts with routing information?

One option is to configure the hosts with a default router address. But that approach is inefficient in many cases. For example, in the network shown in Figure 10.27, A has several routes available to it. Router R1 is not always the most efficient route, and if Router R1 fails, A is dead in the water if it has only a default router to work with.

F I G U R E   10.27

A Default Router Is Inefficient on this Network

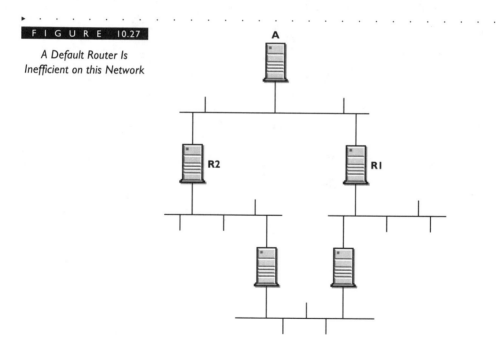

Another approach is to configure A with RIP. OSPF routers can be configured to broadcast their routing tables to RIP, enabling A to obtain routing data. But RIP broadcasts routing tables at 30-second intervals, which causes the traffic burden that we can avoid by using OSPF. Also, running RIP puts a load on A that might be undesirable.

A third approach is available if the host supports the ICMP Router Discover Protocol. The ICMP Router Discovery Protocol has two types of messages that enable hosts to obtain the addresses of routers on the local network without running a full-blown routing protocol:

- ► *ICMP Router Advertisement Messages* are used by routers to advertise their presence on the network. These messages are broadcast or multicast to all hosts, and carry the IP address of the router and its preference level. Hosts use these messages to determine next-hop addresses. The router with the highest preference is selected as a default router.

- ► *ICMP Router Solicitation Messages* enable hosts to solicit router advertisements from all routers on the local network.

The ICMP Router Discovery Protocol is supported by NetWare 4, the NetWare MultiProtocol Router, and many UNIX implementations.

To configure ICMP Router Discovery Protocol on a NetWare 4 server:

1 • Start INETCFG by typing **LOAD INETCFG** at the server console.

2 • Select the *Bindings* option in the Internetworking Configuration menu to open the Configured Protocols To Network Interface Bindings list.

3 • Select an existing TCP/IP binding or, if necessary, create a binding as described in Chapter 8.

4 • Select the *Expert TCP/IP Bind Options* field. Press Enter to open the Expert TCP/IP LAN Options window.

5 • Select the *Router Discovery Options* field in the Expert TCP/IP LAN Options window to open the Router Discovery form shown in Figure 10.28.

FIGURE 10.28

Configuring ICMP Router Discovery

6 • To enable router discovery, change the value of the *Status* field to Enabled.

7 • On networks that support multicasting, set the value of the *Destination Address* field to Router Discovery Multicast (the default value).

If the network does not support multicasting, change the value of the *Destination Address* field to Broadcast, which configures the router discovery protocol to use the address 255.255.255.255.

8 • Exit INETCFG, saving the configuration changes, and restart the server to activate the changes.

If IP packet forwarding and router discovery are both enabled, the server will send router discover advertisements and respond to router advertisement requests. If IP packet forwarding is disabled and router discovery is enabled, the server sends router discovery requests to identify routers.

Using IP Tunneling

Chapter 2 covered how protocol encapsulation functions within a protocol suite. For example, IP receives message segments from TCP and encapsulates those segments in IP datagrams. Encapsulation takes place at each layer as data are moved down the protocol stack.

But the Chapter 2 examples of encapsulation used protocols from the same protocol stack family. NetWare data are encapsulated in IPX packets, for example. And IPX packets are encapsulated in Ethernet frames. It was never suggested that protocols from one protocol stack could be encapsulated in another protocol stack, but that is exactly what *IP tunneling* does. IP tunneling encapsulates IPX packets in IP datagrams so that the IPX data can be delivered through a TCP/IP network. It's a pretty neat trick that enables you to connect your NetWare servers through any IP network, including the Internet.

A bit of theory is in order first. You need to understand how IP tunneling works before you can plan a configuration that puts it to work.

HOW IP TUNNELING WORKS

Figure 10.29 shows a simple network consisting of two IPX protocol segments that are connected by an IP segment. Computer A is running LAN WorkPlace, configured to use IP tunneling. Servers S1 and S2 are configured as routers, and they are configured to communicate through an IP tunnel. Server S3 is a conventional NetWare server, configured only for IPX communication.

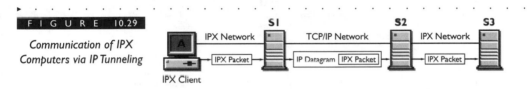

FIGURE 10.29

Communication of IPX Computers via IP Tunneling

Here is the sequence of events that enables A to send data to S3.

- Computer A places the data in an IPX packet and sends the packet to S1, which is advertised as a router on the local IPX network.

- S1 encapsulates the IPX packet in an IP datagram and sends the datagram to S2.

- S2 decapsulates the IP datagram to recover the IPX packet and routes the packet to S3.

S1 and S2 are configured as peers in an IP tunneling network. Between them, they establish a virtual tunnel through which IPX traffic can flow. An IP tunnel can include more than two peers, enabling you to configure a virtual IPX network within an IP network, as shown in Figure 10.30. In the figure, three servers are configured as peers. As far as the IPX clients of these servers are concerned, the complete setup operates as an IPX internetwork.

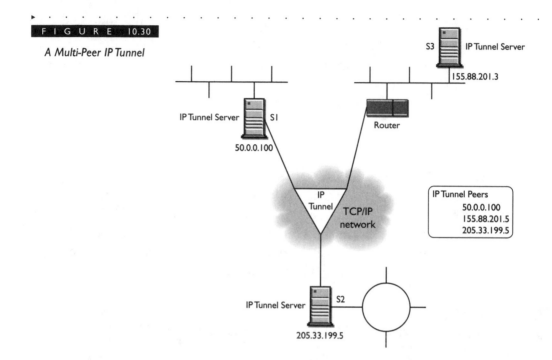

F I G U R E   10.30

A Multi-Peer IP Tunnel

The IP tunnel servers in Figure 10.30 are configured in two ways:

▸ S1 and S2 are configured as routers with two network interfaces. One interface on each server is bound to the IP tunnel, and one is bound to IPX. The LANs supported by S1 and S2 carry only IPX traffic. Workstations communicate with the IPX protocol only.

▸ S3 has only a single interface, which is bound to both IPX and the IP tunnel. The LAN supported by S3 carries both IP and IPX traffic, and communicates with the TCP/IP network via a standalone router. Workstations can communicate with IPX to communicate with NetWare servers through the IP tunnel, and they can communicate with IP to access TCP/IP services on the internetwork.

Although an IP tunnel can support many peers, Novell recommends a maximum of 10 peers for a given IP tunnel.

Figure 10.31 shows the protocol stack that permits IP tunneling to take place. The procedure for configuring IP tunneling on a server is as follows:

1 • Configuring and loading TCP/IP

2 • Configuring and loading the IP tunnel driver IPTUNNEL.LAN

3 • Binding IPX to IPTUNNEL

4 • Adding IP tunnel servers to the peer list

FIGURE 10.31

The Protocol Stack Supporting IP Tunneling

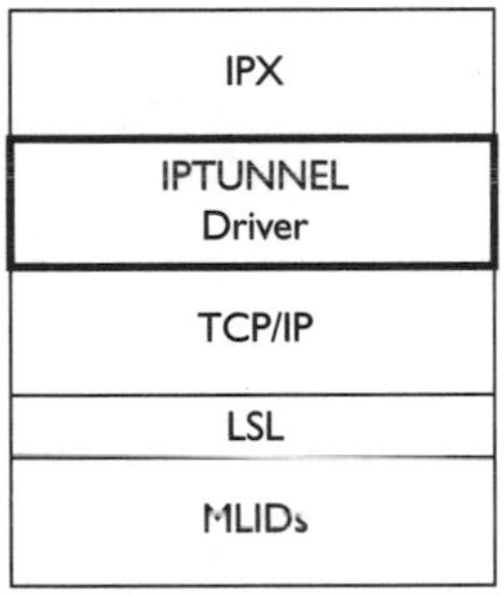

IPX
IPTUNNEL Driver
TCP/IP
LSL
MLIDs

Figure 10.32 shows the details of the IP datagram that encapsulates the IPX data. IPTUNNEL receives an IPX frame which it encapsulates in a UDP datagram. By default, IPTUNNEL is assigned the UDP port number 213. This port number is included in the source and destination port fields of the UDP datagram. The UDP datagram also includes a CRC field to ensure data integrity.

The UDP datagram is encapsulated in an IP datagram for delivery through the internetwork. At the receiving end, IP decapsulates the UDP datagram, and IPTUNNEL decapsulates the UDP datagram to recover the original IPX data. The IPX data is then routed to the IPX network.

FIGURE 10.32

Encapsulation via IP Tunneling of an IPX Packet in an IP Datagram

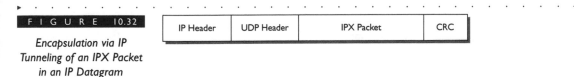

IP Header	UDP Header	IPX Packet	CRC

Workstations that support IP tunneling also can communicate with remote NetWare servers through IP networks. IP tunneling is supported by the following client products:

- ► Novell LAN WorkPlace

- ► Schneider & Koch SK-IPX/IP Gateway

- ► Schneider & Koch end-node product for DOS

CONFIGURING IP TUNNELING FOR NETWARE 3

The following commands will configure IP tunneling on a NetWare 3 server and should be added to the server's AUTOEXEC.NCF file:

```
LOAD TCPIP include any parameters required for the network
LOAD IPTUNNEL NAME=TUNNEL PEER=201.83.195.50
   LOCAL=193.88.201.34 CHKSUM=YES PORT=213
BIND IPX TO TUNNEL NET=200 SEQ=1
```

The IP tunnel must also be configured on the peer server. The commands are quite similar, although the IP addresses swap positions:

```
LOAD TCPIP include any parameters required for the network
LOAD IPTUNNEL NAME=TUNNEL PEER=193.88.201.34
   LOCAL=201.83.195.50 CHKSUM=YES PORT=213
BIND IPX TO TUNNEL NET=200 SEQ=1
```

The parameters for the LOAD IPTUNNEL command are listed in Table 10.2.

TABLE 10.2	PARAMETER	VALUES	PURPOSE
Parameters for LOAD IPTUNNEL	NAME	Up to 17 characters	A name that identifies this logical network interface.
	PEER	IP address	Specifies the IP address of a remote IP tunnel peer.
	LOCAL	IP address	Specifies the IP address of the local IP tunnel interface.
	CHKSUM	YES or NO	Specifies whether a checksum field is included (YES) or not included (NO).
	PORT	Valid port number	Specifies the UDP port that will identify this IP tunnel. The default port is 213. Specify a different port if port 213 is in use on your network. Consult product documentation for the appropriate values.
	SHOW	YES or NO	If YES, causes the LOAD IPTUNNEL command to display the current configuration. Default is NO.

The only parameter required for BIND IPX TO IPTUNNEL is NET, which specifies the IPX external network number that is associated with the IP tunnel. The address specified by NET is a one- to eight-digit hexadecimal number.

To include more than two peers for the IP tunnel, include a LOAD IPTUNNEL statement for each remote peer. The following commands configure a server to communicate through an IP tunnel with three other peers:

```
LOAD TCPIP include any parameters required for the network
LOAD IPTUNNEL NAME=TUNNEL PEER=201.83.195.50
  LOCAL=193.88.201.34 CHKSUM=YES PORT=213
LOAD IPTUNNEL PEER=53.0.105.8
LOAD IPTUNNEL PEER=130.8.99.205
BIND IPX TO TUNNEL NET=200 SEQ=1
```

As in the previous example, similar commands must be entered on all servers in the IP tunnel peer group.

CONFIGURING IP TUNNELING FOR NETWARE 4

INETCFG can configure IP tunneling on NetWare 4 servers and servers equipped with the MultiProtocol Router. TCP/IP configuration was examined in Chapter 8. This following discussion assumes that TCP/IP has been configured and loaded on the server.

Configuring and Loading the IPTUNNEL Driver

Configuring and loading IPTUNNEL is similar to configuring and loading a LAN interface driver. Here is the procedure:

1 • Start INETCFG by typing **LOAD INETCFG** at the server console.

2 • Select the *Boards* option in the Internetworking Configuration menu.

3 • Press Insert and select *IPTUNNEL* from the list drivers in the Available Drivers window.

4 • In the Board Configuration window, shown in Figure 10.33, configure the IP tunnel. The following fields can be configured:

▶ **Board Name.** Specify a name consisting of up to 10 characters for the IPTUNNEL driver.

▶ **Peer IP Address.** Specify the IP address of the first remote peer that will use the IP tunnel.

▶ **Local IP Address.** Specify the IP address that is associated with the local peer of the IP tunnel. This generally will be the IP address that is assigned to the interface board supporting the IP tunnel.

▶ **UDP Checksum.** If this field is set to Yes (the default), checksums will be included in UDP datagrams constructed by IPTUNNEL. If the field is set to No, checksums will not be calculated. Checksums are recommended for all WAN connections and for LANs unless the network is known to be reliable.

▶ **UDP Port**. If the default UDP port 213 is in use, change the port number to an unused port. All peers on the IP tunnel must be configured to use the same UDP port.

▶ **Comment**. An optional, freeform comment field.

5 • When the IPTUNNEL driver has been configured, press Escape, save the configuration changes, and return to the Internetworking Configuration menu.

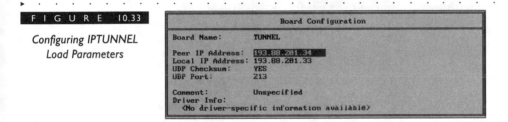

*Configuring IPTUNNEL
Load Parameters*

```
                      Board Configuration
Board Name:      TUNNEL

Peer IP Address: 193.88.201.34
Local IP Address: 193.88.201.33
UDP Checksum:    YES
UDP Port:        213

Comment:         Unspecified
Driver Info:
  <No driver-specific information available>
```

Binding IPX to the IP Tunnel

After the IPTUNNEL has been configured, specify the IPX binding as follows:

1 • Select the *Bindings* option in the INETCFG Internetworking Configuration menu.

2 • Press Insert in the Configured Protocol to Network Interface Bindings window.

3 • Select *IPX* in the protocol selection window.

4 • Select *IPTUNNEL* in the configured network interfaces window to open the Binding IPX to a LAN Interface window shown in Figure 10.34.

5 • Only the *IPX Network Number* must be configured. Enter the one- to six-digit hexadecimal number that is the IPX external network number for the IP tunnel.

6 • Exit INETCFG.

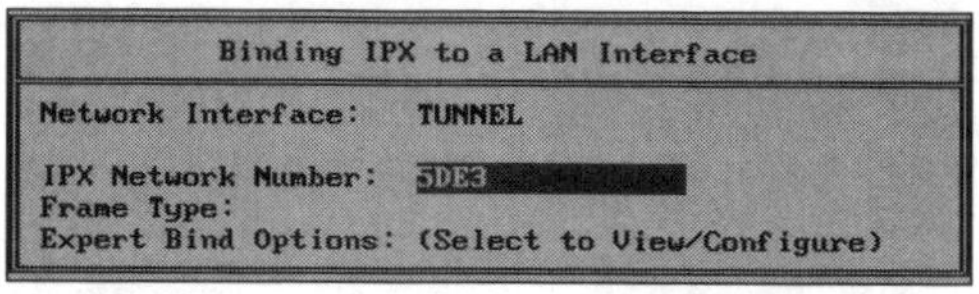

FIGURE 10.34

Configuring Bind Parameters for an IP Tunnel

```
              Binding IPX to a LAN Interface
Network Interface:    TUNNEL

IPX Network Number:  5DE3
Frame Type:
Expert Bind Options: (Select to View/Configure)
```

Only the first peer can be configured in INETCFG. If the IP tunnel supports more than one remote peer, you must add a LOAD IPTUNNEL command to the server's AUTOEXEC.NCF FILE after the line that executes INITSYS.NCF. For example:

```
sys:etc\initsys.ncf
LOAD IPTUNNEL PEER=53.0.105.8
LOAD IPTUNNEL PEER=130.8.99.205
```

Be sure to configure the IP tunnel on each peer.

VIEWING THE IP TUNNEL CONFIGURATION

After configuring an IP tunnel, you may wish to verify the configuration by typing **LOAD IPTUNNEL SHOW=YES** at the server console. Figure 10.35 shows an example of the output from this command.

FIGURE 10.35

Verifying the Configuration of an IP Tunnel

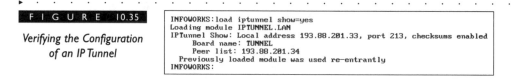

```
INFOWORKS:load iptunnel show=yes
Loading module IPTUNNEL.LAN
IPTunnel Show: Local address 193.88.201.33, port 213, checksums enabled
       Board name: TUNNEL
       Peer list: 193.88.201.34
  Previously loaded module was used re-entrantly
INFOWORKS:
```

To verify the IPX binding, type **CONFIG** at the server console. Figure 10.36 shows an example of the output from this command. Verify the following settings:

- ▸ **Hardware setting.** Displays the UDP port number in hex. The default port 213 will appear as D5h.

- ▸ **Node address.** Displays the IP address for the node, expressed in hex.

- ▸ **LAN protocol.** Displays the IPX external network number.

FIGURE 10.36

*Verifying the Binding
Configuration of an
IP Tunnel*

```
IP Tunnel for IPX
    Version 3.00    October 18, 1994
    Hardware setting: I/O Port D5h
    Node address: 0000C158C921
    Frame type: IP
    Board name: TUNNEL
    LAN protocol: IPX network 00005DE3
```

CONFIGURING LAN WORKPLACE CLIENTS FOR IP TUNNELING

LAN WorkPlace clients can be configured to access NetWare IPX services through an IP tunnel. Let's examine a LAN-only scenario and then one that involves a dial-up connection to the Internet.

Connecting a Workstation to an IP Tunnel on a LAN

In Figure 10.37, Network N2 supports only TCP/IP. Servers S1 and S2 are configured as peers, establishing an IP tunnel through N2. IPX computers C1 on N1 and C3 on N3 connect to both servers transparently via IPX. The client C2 on N2, however, must be configured to access NetWare services via an IP tunnel.

Client C2 is running LAN WorkPlace software, configured to enable TCP/IP. To enable IPX to run over the TCP/IP protocol stack, an IP tunnel driver must be configured. Here is a basic NET.CFG file for the client:

```
Link Driver NE2000
     IRQ    10
     PORT   340
     MEM    D0000
     FRAME    Ethernet_II
Protocol TCPIP
     IP_address 135.95.103.50
     IP_router  135.95.103.5
Protocol IPXODI
     Bind #2
Link driver IPTUNNEL
     gateway 135.95.103.5
     gateway 135.95.103.20
     checksum yes
     port 213
```

```
Link driver NCOMX
      IRQ 3
      PORT 3F8
      FRAME PPP

NetWare DOS Requester

   First NetWare Drive = F
```

The following command sequence would be used to load drivers on the workstation:

```
LSL
NE2000
TCPIP
IPTUNNEL
IPXODI
VLM
```

After loading LSL, NE2000 is loaded and becomes the first network interface. Then TCP/IP is bound to NE2000. Next, the IPTUNNEL driver is loaded above TCP/IP, providing network interface #2 to which IPX can be bound. When IPXODI is loaded, the IPX protocol is bound to interface #2 and is linked to the IP tunnel.

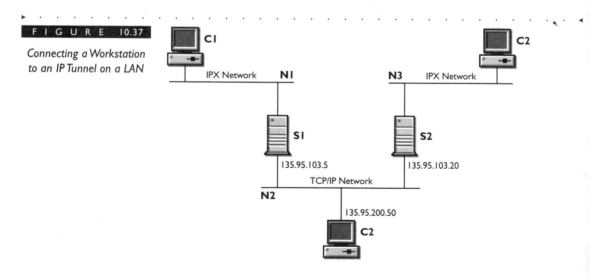

F I G U R E 10.37

Connecting a Workstation to an IP Tunnel on a LAN

Connecting a Workstation to an IP Tunnel on a WAN

Figure 10.38 shows how a LAN WorkPlace client could access a NetWare server through a TCP/IP network such as the Internet. Because the Internet is not configured with IPX, an IP tunnel is required.

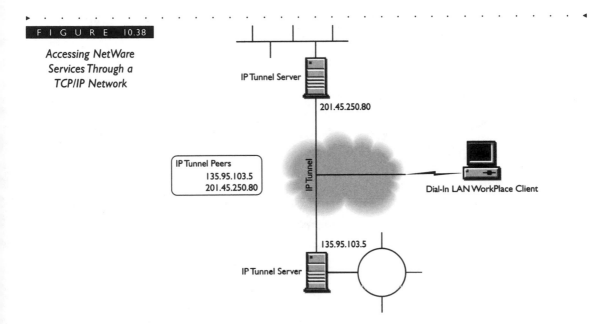

FIGURE 10.38

Accessing NetWare Services Through a TCP/IP Network

Servers S1 and S2 are connected to the Internet via WAN links using the NetWare MultiProtocol Router. The servers have been configured as peers in an IP tunnel.

Client computer C1 is equipped with LAN WorkPlace and accesses the Internet via PPP dial-up. LAN WorkPlace includes IP tunnel client protocols. The IPTUNNEL driver is configured in NET.CFG. Here are the critical sections of a NET.CFG file that enables the client to dial an Internet provider and connect to an IP tunnel:

```
Protocol TCPIP
    IP_address 0.0.0.0      PPP_NET
    BIND NCOM #1 PPP        PPP_NET

Protocol IPX
    Bind #2
```

```
Link driver IPTUNNEL
        gateway 135.95.103.5
        gateway 201.45.250.80
        checksum yes
        port 213

Link driver NCOMX
        IRQ 3
        PORT 3F8
        FRAME PPP

NetWare DOS Requester

        First NetWare Drive = F
```

The parameters for the Link driver IPTUNNEL section are quite similar to the parameters required to configure an IP tunnel on a server. The command sequence to configure protocols on the client is as follows:

```
LSL
NESL
NCOMX
NWREMOTE
TCPIP
IPTUNNEL
IPXODI
VLM
```

In this case, the first network interface is NCOM, to which TCP/IP is bound. Loading IPTUNNEL establishes a second network interface that supports IPX.

NOTE

Another way to enable users to access NetWare through the Internet would be to configure the servers with NetWare/IP, described in Chapter 12. NetWare/IP could be configured on a single server, without the need to establish an IP tunnel between two or more servers.

In a dial-up situation, NetWare/IP will perform about the same as an IP tunnel. Although NetWare/IP is more highly optimized than the IP tunnel client, end users will experience similar performance, because both technologies are limited by the throughput of the dial-up connection.

Big Network, Big Trouble

Now you know how to build a really big network. Well, bad news: Big networks are susceptible to problems that you'll never see on a simple LAN. Data can be misrouted, damaged, or lost. Network segments can become overloaded. One piece of flaky hardware can upset the entire network.

It's not enough to just build a big network. You also have to manage it. And that means getting SNMP up and running. The Simple Network Management Protocol is the standard protocol for monitoring and managing TCP/IP networks. Nearly all NetWare products can be configured as agents in an SNMP management system, and some basic SNMP management tools are included with NetWare. That's our next task: to learn how to put SNMP to work monitoring and managing the network.

## CHAPTER 11

Managing NetWare TCP/IP

The major pieces of your internetwork–servers, routers, and clients–are now in place. So, how's the network doing? Are there any performance bottlenecks? Are all devices functioning? Are any devices generating excessive errors? What? You don't know? But one of your responsibilities as a LAN administrator is to answer these and other important questions about your network's health. That's where the Simple Network Management Protocol (SNMP) comes in. SNMP agents are built into all NetWare platforms that support TCP/IP. SNMP is easy to configure and easy to monitor with tools that NetWare provides.

The TCP/IP Console (TCPCON) is a server-based utility for monitoring and managing TCP/IP nodes on your network. LAN WorkPlace and LAN Workgroup include a similar console called LWPCON.

NOTE

TCPCON and LWPCON provide very basic SNMP management capabilities. For networks that require a more powerful network management capability, Novell also offers the NetWare Management System (NMS), a separate product with much more powerful network management capabilities. Among its many capabilities, NMS is a full-function, extensible SNMP network management console that can manage all SNMP devices, regardless of the manufacturer.

The SNMP protocol is not exclusive to the TCP/IP protocol suite, and Novell has configured SNMP consoles to manage other NetWare-supported protocols. Similar utilities are available for managing IPX (IPXCON) and AppleTalk (ATCON).

The first task we'll look at in this chapter is how to configure SNMP agents so that we have something to monitor and manage. When that is done, we will examine TCPCON and LWPCON to learn the capabilities they offer.

Configuring SNMP Agents

SNMP managers communicate with SNMP agents, and an SNMP agent must be configured on each host that is to be managed. Configuration of an agent involves several activities:

▶ Loading the agent software

▶ Configuring SNMP communities

▶ Configuring SNMP node information

▶ Specifying trap destinations

This section examines the procedures required to activate and configure SNMP agents on NetWare 3 and NetWare 4 servers, as well as on NetWare DOS clients.

CONFIGURING SNMP AGENTS ON NETWARE SERVERS

On a NetWare 4 server, INETCFG is used to configure the SNMP agent. With a NetWare 3 server, the appropriate parameters must be added to the AUTOEXEC.NCF file. Both procedures are covered here.

NOTE

The NetWare server agent described in this section is the basic agent that is included with NetWare 3 and 4. The capabilities of this agent are a good fit if you will be managing the network with TCPCON and LWPCON. If you will be using a more powerful network management console such as Novell's NetWare Management System (NMS), you will want to obtain NetWare Management Agent, a set of NLMs that enhance the features of the SNMP agent, providing among other things configurable traps.

Loading the Agent Software

NetWare server–based protocols incorporate SNMP agents as standard features. Consequently, you don't need to do anything specific to load an SNMP agent on the server. The module SNMP.NLM provides SNMP agent functionality and is loaded for all server-based protocols.

Configuring SNMP Agent Communities

The SNMP agent can be configured with three SNMP community names. Community names determine which SNMP nodes will communicate to exchange management information and traps.

▶ The *monitor community* name grants Read access to an agent's MIB. Any SNMP manager that provides the correct monitor community name will be granted Read-only access to the MIB. By default, the monitor community name is set to "public."

▶ The *control community* name grants Read/Write access to an agent's MIB. An SNMP manager that supplies the correct control community name can modify some information in an agent's MIB. By default, the control community name is disabled.

▶ The *trap community* name is attached to all trap messages that an agent generates. An SNMP manager will receive only those trap messages that are identified by a specific trap community name. By default, the trap community name is set to "public."

Configuring Communities when Loading SNMP   Community names are specified when loading the SNMP NLM. Even though SNMP.NLM has been loaded previously, it can be reloaded to change the community names. The syntax to specify community names is as follows:

```
LOAD SNMP [MonitorCommunity=monitor_community]
          [ControlCommunity=control_community]
          [TrapCommunity=trap_community]
```

Any parameters that are not specified will be configured with default values. To configure SNMP with the monitor community "public," the trap communty "mayberry," and the control community disabled, load SNMP with the following command:

```
LOAD SNMP TrapCommunity=mayberry
```

Configuring Communities with INETCFG   With NetWare 4 or the NetWare MultiProtocol Router, you will want to configure SNMP communities using INETCFG. To configure SNMP communities:

1 • Load INETCFG.

2 • Select *Manage Configuration* from the Internetworking Configuration menu.

3 • Select *Configure SNMP Parameters* from the Manage Configuration menu to open the SNMP Parameters form shown in Figure 11.1.

Each of the State fields can be opened into a menu with three or four options. Press Enter to open the menu and select a configuration setting from the menu. The options for each of the State fields are described in the following steps.

```
                          SNMP Parameters
   Monitor State:       Specified Community May Read
   Monitor Community:   public

   Control State:       Specified Community May Write
   Control Community:   admin

   Trap State:          Send Traps with Specified Community
   Trap Community:      public

   Other SNMP Parameters: (None)
```

4 • Select one of the following settings in the Monitor State field:

▸ **Any Community May Read**. It will be unnecessary to specify a monitor community name.

▸ **Leave as Default Setting**. The monitor community name will be "public."

▸ **No Community May Read**. No community will have Read access to the MIB.

▸ **Specified Community May Read**. You must specify a community name in the Monitor Community field.

5 • If you selected *Specified Community May Read*, enter a monitor community name in the Monitor Community field.

6 • Select one of the following settings in the Control State field:

▸ **Any Community May Write**. It will be unnecessary to specify a control community name.

▸ **Leave as Default Setting**. Write access will be disabled.

▸ **No Community May Write**. Write access will be disabled

▸ **Specified Community May Write**. You must specify a community name in the Control Community field.

7 • If you selected *Specified Community May Write,* enter a monitor community name in the Control Community field.

8 • Select one of the following settings in the Control State field:

▸ **Do not send traps**. It will be unnecessary to specify a control community name.

▸ **Leave as Default Setting**. Traps will be sent to "public."

▸ **Send Traps with Specified Community**. You must specify a community name in the Trap Community field.

9 • If you selected *Send Traps with Specified Community,* enter a monitor community name in the Trap Community field.

10 • After configuring SNMP communities, press Esc. Complete any other required information before quitting INETCFG.

Configuring SNMP Node Information SNMP node information is descriptive information that enables managers to identify a node, its characteristics, and the person responsible for the node. This information is optional but can be handy when you are managing a large network with many nodes. Node information is specified using INETCFG as follows:

1 • Load INETCFG.

2 • Select *Manage Configuration* from the Internetworking
Configuration menu.

3 • Select *Configure SNMP Information* from the Manage Configuration
menu to open the SNMP Parameters form shown in Figure 11.2.

F I G U R E   11.2

*Configuring SNMP
Information for a
Server Node*

```
            General SNMP Information For This Node

Node Name for SNMP:      mayberry
Hardware Description:    (Select To View And Modify)
Physical Location:      (Select To View And Modify)
Human Contact:          (Select To View And Modify)
```

4 • If desired, enter a node name in the *Node Name for SNMP* field. By
default, the SNMP node name will be the same as the file server name
that is specified in the AUTOEXEC.NCF file.

5 • The *Hardware Description, Physical Location,* and *Human Contact* fields
can be selected to open forms that can be used to describe this node.
Figure 11.3 shows the form produced by selecting the Human
Contact field.

The information you enter in these forms is up to your discretion.
Ideally, when planning the LAN, you should define standard formats
for this information. If uniform formats are maintained on all
computers, it will be much easier for managers of large networks to
remain informed about the network configuration.

F I G U R E   11.3

*SNMP Information
Describing the
Human Contact*

```
            Human Contact Responsible For Node

Blythe Heywood
BHeywood@mayberry.com
x2356
```

6 • When the node information has been completed, press Esc. Complete
any other required information before quitting INETCFG.

Configuring Trap Addresses from the Command Line   When configuring an SNMP agent for NetWare 3, the LOAD TCPIP command must specify the address of the SNMP manager that will receive trap messages from this host. This involves adding to the command line a parameter such as the following:

```
LOAD TCPIP FORWARD=YES RIP=YES TRAP=193.88.201.33
```

Only one trap destination may be specified when configuring TCP/IP from the command line.

Configuring Trap Addresses with INETCFG   The final parameters to configure are the addresses to which this host will send trap messages. If the Trap Settings field in the SNMP Parameters has been configured with the setting "Do not send traps," it is unnecessary to specify trap addresses. In the majority of cases, however, trap messages will be generated and addresses should be configured. To specify TCP/IP trap addresses:

1 • Load INETCFG.

2 • Select *Protocols* from the Internetworking Configuration menu.

3 • Select *TCP/IP* from the Protocol Configuration menu.

4 • Select the *SNMP Manager Table* field to open the SNMP Manager Table window shown in Figure 11.4.

FIGURE   11.4

SNMP Manager Table Window

By default, a NetWare server will send trap messages to the loopback address 127.0.0.1, thereby sending trap messages to the server's local SNMP trap log. If a remote SNMP manager should receive trap messages, this address should be changed.

5 • To delete an address from the SNMP Manager Table window, highlight the address and press Delete. Choose *Yes* to confirm the deletion when you are prompted "Delete current entry from list?"

6 • To add an address to the SNMP Manager Table window, press Insert. In the IP Address of Manager window, enter the IP address of an SNMP manager. Press Enter to add the address to the SNMP Manager Table window.

7 • After the desired addresses have been deleted or added, press Esc. Complete any other required information before quitting INETCFG.

NOTE

Remember that configuration changes made in INETCFG do not take effect until the server has been restarted or the REINITIALIZE SERVER command has been executed from the server console.

CONFIGURING SNMP AGENTS ON NETWARE DOS CLIENTS

NetWare DOS clients can be configured as SNMP agents at two levels:

▶ The basic SNMP agent, included with LAN WorkPlace and LAN Workgroup, provides limited functionality, enabling SNMP managers to gain Read/Write access to the MIB. The basic SNMP agent matches the management capabilities of TCPCON and LWPCON.

▶ Desktop SNMP, included with the NetWare Client for DOS and MS Windows, provides richer functionality, including comprehensive MIB-II support and the ability to generate traps. Desktop SNMP supports the more advanced SNMP management capabilities of the NetWare Management System and other advanced network management consoles.

Because Desktop SNMP is required for products such as NMS, which are beyond the scope of this book, this section focuses on configuration of the basic SNMP agent. Details on configuring Desktop SNMP can be found in the *NetWare Client for DOS and MS Windows User Guide*.

The required agent software is included with the following products:

▸ LAN WorkPlace

▸ LAN WorkGroup

▸ NetWare Client for DOS and MS Windows, currently at version 1.2

The required files are installed whenever any of these products are installed on the client.

Configuration is a simple matter of adding a Protocol SNMP section to the NET.CFG file. Here is a sample of the Protocol SNMP section:

```
Protocol SNMP
    monitorCommunity      public
    controlCommunity      admin
    sysContact            Blythe Heywood
    sysName               BHeywood@mayberry.com
    sysLocation           Building A Room 105
```

The fields that appear in the Protocol SNMP section are summarized in Table 11.1.

After configuring the NET.CFG file, add the SNMP command to the STARTNET.BAT file following the TCPIP command. The structure of STARTNET.BAT will resemble the following:

```
lsl
ne2000
tcpip
snmp
```

When the SNMP agent loads, you will see a message similar to the following:

```
Novell SNMP Agent for TCP/IP Transport.
(C) Copyright 1992-1995 Novell, Inc. All Rights Reserved.
MonitorCommunity = public
ControlCommunity = admin
```

The SNMP agent may be unloaded with the SNMP U command.

T A B L E 11.1	PARAMETER	VALUES	PURPOSE
Parameters for TCPIP.NLM	monitorCommunity	32-character (not case sensitive)	The community name that permits text Read-only access to the MIB. The default value is "public." The community name "noAccess" disables the monitor community.
	controlCommunity	32-character (not case sensitive)	The community name that permits text Read/Write access to the MIB. This community is disabled by default. The community name "noAccess" disables the monitor community.
	sysContact	text	The name of the primary contact person for this host.
	sysName	text	Typically the primary contact's e-mail name, including the domain name.
	sysLocation	text	A description of the location of the host.

Using TCPCON

TCP/IP Console (TCPCON) can be used to monitor and manage the SNMP agents that were configured in the previous section. Many of the features of TCPCON are self-explanatory or are described in the context-sensitive help. Press F1 to obtain a description of the current field in any window. This discussion focuses on orienting you with TCPCON and highlighting specific features.

> **NOTE**
>
> **To enable a NetWare server to log SNMP trap messages, you must load the SNMPLOG NLM after loading the TCPIP NLM. SNMPLOG is a background process that collects trap messages and stores them in the file SYS:ETC\SNMP$LOG.BIN. This file can be read by TCPCON running on the local server. No size restrictions are placed on the SNMP$LOG.BIN file, and it will grow over time. If you are logging traps, you should monitor the size of this file and delete it periodically.**

To start TCPCON, enter the command **LOAD TCPCON** at the server console. The TCP/IP Console main window is shown in Figure 11.5.

```
TCP/IP Console  3.00                                    NetWare Loadable Module

  Host:    Local System
  Uptime: 1 Day   4 Hours 54 Minutes 17 Seconds
  System: Novell NetWare 4.10  November 8, 1994

  IP Received:  30,104          TCP Received:    0
  IP Sent:      16,629          TCP Sent:        0
  IP Forwarded: 13,401          TCP Connections: 0

                        Available Options
                      SNMP Access Configuration
                      Protocol Information
                      IP Routing Table
                      Statistics
                      Interfaces
                      Display Local Traps

  Display all network Interfaces supported by selected system.
  ENTER=Select ESC=Exit Menu                                    F1=Help
```

TCPCON can display data for a single host at one time. By default, TCPCON selects the local TCP/IP host, which is identified as the Local System in the *Host* field of the TCPCON main window. TCPCON displays some basic statistics for the selected host. The Available Options menu offers the following choices:

- **SNMP Access Configuration.** Selects the SNMP agent to be managed.

- **Protocol Information.** Used to display and configure protocols on the managed node.

- **IP Routing Table.** Used to display and configure the routing table on the managed node.

- **Statistics.** Enables you to observe protocol-related statistics on the managed node.

- **Interfaces.** Displays the network interface configuration of the managed node.

- **Display Local Traps.** Displays the traps that have been recorded in the local SNMP log file.

The following sections examine each of these functions briefly.

Selecting an SNMP Agent

The SNMP Access Configuration menu choice displays the window shown in Figure 11.6. This window is used to select the SNMP agent that will be managed and to set some management parameters.

*Setting the SNMP Access
Configuration*

```
                        SNMP Access Configuration
Transport Protocol: TCP/IP
Host:               andy
Community Name:     admin
Timeout:            5    (seconds)
Poll Interval:      5    (seconds)
```

The Transport Protocol field has three choices, revealed by selecting the field and pressing Enter:

- **Local System.** Configures TCPCON to manage the local server. If you pick this option, the Host field is inactive.

- **TCP/IP.** Configures TCPCON to manage the TCP/IP protocol stacks on computers running SNMP agents

- **IPX.** Configures TCPCON to access the selected node's TCP/IP information using SNMP over IPX. (Configuration of SNMP over IPX is not covered in this book.)

If you select either TCP/IP or IPX in the *Transport Protocol* field, the *Host* field will be active. In that field, you can specify the name or address of the host to be managed. For TCP/IP, press Insert to display a list of hosts taken from entries in the HOSTS file.

The *Community Name* field should be configured with the community name that matches the actions you wish to take. Enter the monitor community name to obtain Read-only access to the agent's MIB. Enter the control community name to obtain Read/Write access to the MIB. When managing a remote node, the community name will be used to authenticate your SNMP messages.

The *Timeout* field determines the number of seconds (with a range of 0 to 120 seconds) that TCPCON waits for a response after polling for information. If a response is not received, TCPCON will repeat the poll.

The *Poll Interval* field determines the interval in seconds (with a range of 0 to 900 seconds) between polls. Specifying a poll interval of 0 seconds configures TCPCON to poll the target as frequently as possible.

After configuring options in this window, press Esc. TCPCON displays the prompt "Save TCP/IP Console Options?" Type *Yes* to save the changes you have made.

Displaying Protocol Information

After selecting the *Protocol Information* option in the TCPCON Available Options menu, you will be presented with a list of protocols on which TCPCON can report. The following protocols are listed:

- ▸ EGP

- ▸ ICMP

- ▸ IP

- ▸ OSPF

- ▸ TCP

- ▸ UDP

The next window you see will depend on the protocol you select. Figure 11.7 shows the window that displays information for IP. This window illustrates the two types of fields that TCPCON presents:

- ▸ Editable fields are identified by an extra dot to the right of the colon following the field label. These fields can be edited, and the changes can be saved to the MIP of the node that is being managed. IP Packet Forwarding is an example of an editable field.

- ▸ Non-editable fields do not have the extra dot. These fields are for display purposes only and cannot be altered. IP Addresses is an example of a non-editable field.

FIGURE 11.7

IP Protocol Information

```
              IP Protocol Information
IP Packet Forwarding:.   Router
Default Time To Live:.   128
Reassembly Timeout:      15

IP Addresses:            (Select to View)
IP Address Translations: (Select to View or Modify)

IP Statistics:           (Select to View)
```

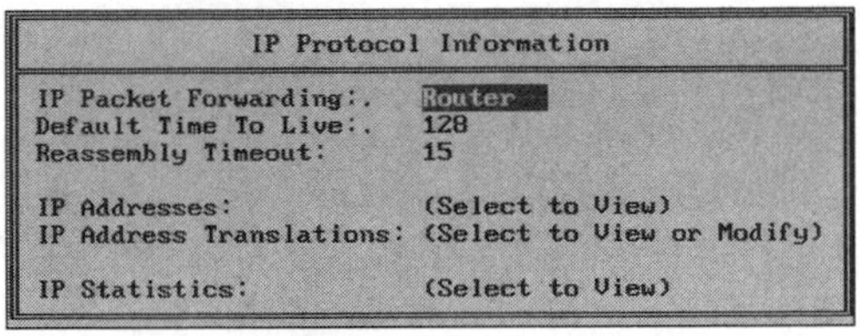

The *IP Packet Forwarding* field is significant because it enables you to remotely enable and disable forwarding on an IP router. This capability can be used to route traffic around a network segment that is generating errors or that must be shut down.

Select the *IP Statistics* field to generate a statistics display for the selected protocol. Figure 11.8 shows statistics for the IP protocol on a NetWare server.

FIGURE 11.8

Statistics for the IP Protocol

```
              IP Statistics
Datagrams
   Received:              30104
   Sent:                  16629
   Forwarded:             13401
   Delivered to IP users: 16698

Incoming Discarded Datagrams
   Local errors:          0
   IP errors:             3
   IP address errors:     0
   Unknown protocol errors: 0

Outgoing Discarded Datagrams
   Local errors:          0
   No route found:        2
```

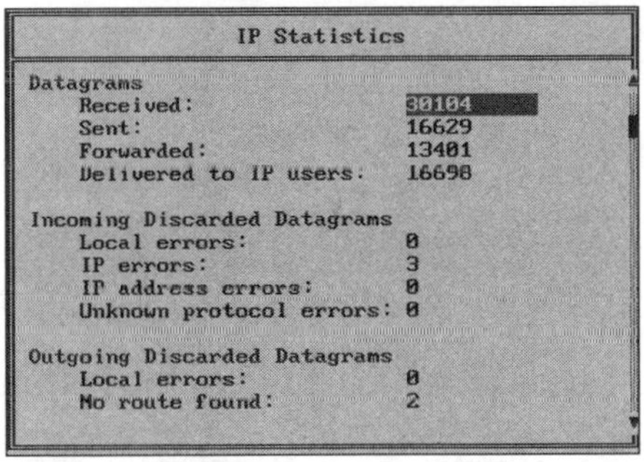

Be particularly attentive to errors that appear in the Local errors field. These errors reflect datagrams that were discarded because of limited buffer capacity. Errors in this field may indicate a need to increase the MAXIMUM PACKET RECEIVE BUFFERS parameter (see Chapter 8).

Managing Routing Tables

Select the *IP Routing Table* choice in the TCPCON Available Options menu to view the routing table of the host being managed. Figure 11.9 shows an example of a routing table for a multihomed server.

FIGURE 11.9

Routing Table for a Multihomed Server

Destination	Next Hop	Type	Cost	Interface
mb1	fs1	direct	1	2
mb2	193.88.201.65	direct	1	4
<End of Table>				

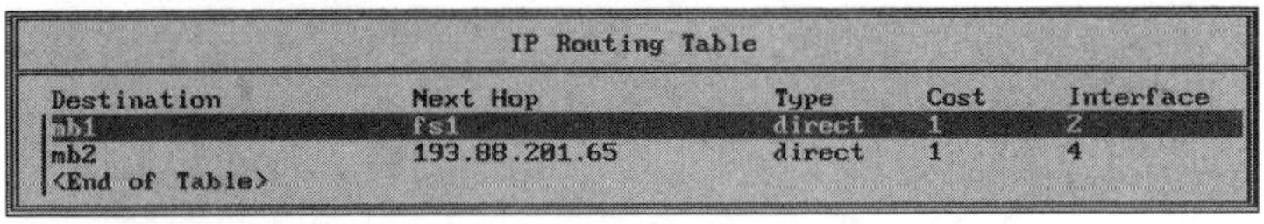

TIP

By default, the routing table will display host names, derived from the HOSTS file. You can toggle between listing table entries by IP address or host name by pressing the Tab key.

You can edit, delete, or add entries to routing table entries. To edit an entry, select the entry and press Enter. To add a new entry, press Insert. Figure 11.10 shows the IP Route Information form that is used to edit routing table entries.

F I G U R E   11.10

Detailed IP Route Information

```
            IP Route Information
   Destination:. nb1
   Mask:.        255.255.255.224
   Next Hop:.    fs1
   Type:.        direct
   Interface:.   2
   Protocol:     local
   Age:.         1:05:05:01
   Cost:.        1

   Metric 2:.    -1
   Metric 3:.    -1
   Metric 4:.    -1
   Metric 5:.    -1
```

The IP Route Information window contains the following fields:

- **Destination.** The address or name of the destination network or host. Names are taken from the NETWORKS and HOSTS database files. (Editable)

- **Mask.** The applicable subnet mask. (Editable)

- **Next Hop.** The host name or IP address that is the next hop to the destination. If the route was learned from an interface that is attached to a broadcast medium, this field has the value of the agent's IP address for the interface. (Editable)

- **Type.** This field has the value "direct" if the route is associated with a directly attached network. The value will be "remote" if the route is associated with an indirectly attached network. (Editable)

- **Interface.** The logical interface number on the host that is associated with the route. Use the Interfaces option in the TCPCON Available Options menu to determine the interfaces that are configured on this host. (Editable)

▸ **Protocol.** The protocol from which the route was learned (e.g., RIP or OSPF). For routes learned from local interfaces, the value will be "local." For routes entered manually, the value will be "netmgmt." (Not editable.)

▸ **Age.** The elapsed time since the route was established. (Editable)

▸ **Cost.** The primary cost metric associated with the route. (Editable)

▸ **Metric 2** through **Metric 5.** Additional cost metrics for protocols supporting them. (Editable)

After entering route configuration parameters, press Esc. To save the route entry, respond *Yes* when TCPCON displays the prompt "Save IP Route Entry?" New routes will be displayed in the IP Routing Table.

Examining Protocol Statistics

The *Statistics* option in the TCPCON Available Options menu produces statistics displays for the supported protocols (see Figure 11.8). These are the same displays we examined earlier in the section "Displaying Protocol Information."

Interfaces

Choose the *Interfaces* option in the TCPCON Available Options menu to display information about the interfaces that are configured on the managed host (see Figure 11.11).

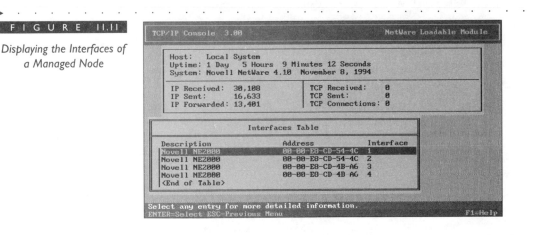

FIGURE 11.11

Displaying the Interfaces of a Managed Node

Select any interface and press Enter to obtain more information about the selected interface (see Figure 11.12). Note the Type field in this figure. The interface type is ISO88023, which is the international standard derived by the ISO from the IEEE 802.3 Ethernet.

F I G U R E   11.12

Details about a Host Interface

```
                          Interface Statistics
Last Change:            1 Day   5 Hours  8 Minutes 21 Seconds
Description:            Novell NE2000
Type:                  iso88023-csmacd
Physical Address:      00-00-E8-CD-54-4C
Interface:             1
MTU:                   1491
Speed:                 10000000
Administrative Status:. up
Operational Status:    up

                       Received           Sent
Octets:                10981              41135
Unicast Packets:       177                176
Non-Unicast Packets:   0                  7
Discarded Packets:     0                  0
Invalid Packets:       0                  0
```

NOTE

The Type field in Figure 11.12 does not match the NetWare Ethernet_802.3 frame type. The interface was, in fact, configured for Ethernet_802.2 frames. The value of the Type field will be iso88023-csmacd for all frame types based on IEEE 802.3 networks, including Ethernet_802.2, Ethernet_802.3, and Ethernet_SNAP. For an interface bound with the Ethernet_II frame type, the value of the Type field will be ethernet-csmacd.

The *Administrative Status* field can be used to enable and disable interfaces. Press Enter to select one of the following values for this field:

- **Up.** The interface functions normally.

- **Down.** The interface is disabled.

- **Testing.** The interface will not pass any operational packets.

The *Operational Status* field indicates the current status of the interface.

You can use the Administrative Status field to temporarily disable an interface. Suppose that the Invalid Packets field for a router interface indicates that the router is receiving a high number of bad packets. If an alternate route exists, you can disable this interface on the router without completely disabling forwarding for the entire router. Simply set the value of the Administrative Status field to "down" until the problem is corrected. Other interfaces on the router will continue to function, and the router will still forward packets among its other interfaces.

Displaying Traps

Choose the *Display Local Traps* option in the TCPCON Available Options menu to display trap messages that have been captured in the local SNMP trap database. Figure 11.13 shows a local trap table containing two entries that were generated when binding parameters were altered for a TCP/IP interface. The traps were generated when the REINITIALIZE SYSTEM command was used to activate the changes on the server.

FIGURE 11.13

Examples of Messages in the Traps Database

```
                                      Trap Log

Host Name                 Trap Type                      Timestamp
fs1                       Link Up [interface 4]          12-27-95 11:45:52pm
fs1                       Link Down [interface 4]        12-27-95 11:45:52pm
<End of Table>
```

Using LWPCON

LAN WorkPlace Console (LWPCON) is installed in the LAN WorkPlace DOS Utilities program group. Figure 11.14 shows the LWPCON Available Options menu. Your choices in this menu are:

- **Local Workstation**. Displays configuration and TCP/IP data for the local host. Provides the same information as Remote Host but offers a shortcut to the local host.

- **Remote Host**. Displays configuration and TCP/IP data for a remote host.

▸ **Services.** Accesses various tests and ascertains the status of a variety of network services.

Because the *Local Workstation* and *Remote Host* options provide essentially the same options, they are considered together in the section "TCP/IP Information and Statistics." Following that discussion, the options under Services are examined.

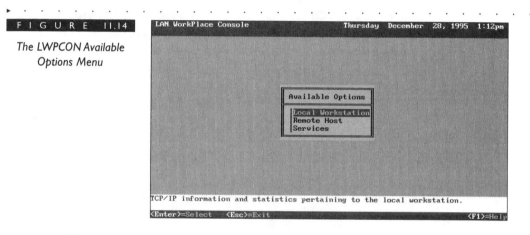

F I G U R E II.14

The LWPCON Available Options Menu

> LAN WorkPlace Console   Thursday December 28, 1995 1:12pm
>
>   ┌─ Available Options ─┐
>   │ Local Workstation   │
>   │ Remote Host   │
>   │ Services   │
>   └─────────────────────┘
>
> TCP/IP information and statistics pertaining to the local workstation.
> <Enter>=Select   <Esc>=Exit   <F1>=Help

NOTE

Before you begin using LWPCON, you should specify the community name that will be used to authenticate your SNMP messages. The procedure to specify a community name is as follows:

1 • **Select either** Local Workstation **or** Remote Host **in the Available Options menu.**

2 • **Select** SNMP **in the Local Workstation Options or Remote Host Options menu.**

3 • **Select** Options **in the SNMP Available Options Menu.**

4 • **Enter a community name in the** Community Name **field.**

5 • **Press Esc to return to the desired LWPCON menu.**

TCP/IP INFORMATION AND STATISTICS

The *Local Workstation* and *Remote Host* menu choices in the Available Options menu access essentially the same menu. The Remote Host Options menu is shown in Figure 11.15. If you chose *Remote Host,* before you see the Remote Host Options menu you will be prompted to specify the name or IP address of a host to be examined.

If you chose *Local Workstation,* the Local Workstation Options menu won't have a Change Host option. Otherwise, the menus have the same options: Overview, Interfaces, Protocols, Tables, and SNMP. Those five options are examined in the following sections.

FIGURE 11.15

The Remote Host Options Menu

Overview

The *Overview* menu choice provides a summary of the configuration characteristics of the target host. This display is shown in Figure 11.16.

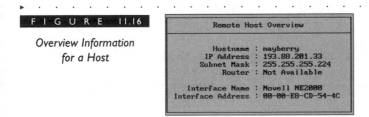

FIGURE 11.16

Overview Information for a Host

Interfaces

The *Interfaces* menu choice lists the interfaces that are configured on the target host. TCPCON produces essentially the same information, which you can examine in Figure 11.11. You can display details by selecting an interface and pressing Enter. The statistics in this display are less detailed than the detailed interface statistics produced by TCPCON.

Protocols

The *Protocols* menu choice generates the statistics shown in Figure 11.17. LWPCON reports on the IP, ICMP, TCP, and UDP protocols only.

FIGURE 11.17

LWPCON Protocol Statistics

```
              Remote Host Protocol Statistics

 IP Statistics                    ICMP Statistics
 Packets Received     30187       Packets Received     14663
 Packets Sent         16635       Packets Sent         14668
 Packets Discarded    0           Packets With Errors  0
 Packets With Errors  3

 TCP Statistics                   UDP Statistics
 Packets Received     0           Packets Received     2042
 Packets Sent         0           Packets Sent         1969
                                  Packets With Errors  0
```

Tables

The *Tables* menu choice opens a TCP/IP Tables submenu that can be used to examine five sets of tables. The options are:

- ▶ **Address Translation Table**

- ▶ **Interface Table**

- ▶ **Local IP Address Table**

- ▶ **Routing Table**

- ▶ **TCP Connection Table**

Some interesting features are lurking within these tables, and it is worth looking inside them.

Address Translation Table   As hosts use the Address Resolution Protocol (ARP) to resolve host names to IP addresses, they build an address translation table that caches recently resolved names. This table can be used to reduce the necessity of using ARP each time a datagram must be sent. Choose the *Address Translation Table* option to examine the table on the managed host (see Figure 11.18). Notice that this table does not include information that might be obtained from the HOSTS file. Only cached entries obtained from ARP will appear.

FIGURE 11.18

An Address Translation Table

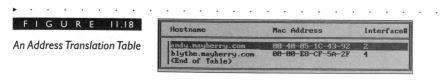

```
 Hostname               Mac Address          Interface#

 andy.mayberry.com      00-40-05-1C-43-92    2
 blythe.mayberry.com    00-00-E8-CF-5A-2F    4
 <End of Table>
```

Interface Tables   The *Interface Table* option produces a list of interfaces similar to lists you have seen elsewhere. When you select an interface and press Enter, a different set of statistics is reported (see Figure 11.19). Each of these fields corresponds to an object in the MIB and is described in the online help (press F1).

```
                        Interface Statistics
ifLastChange:      1 Day   5 Hours   8 Minutes 21 Seconds
ifDescr:           Novell NE2000
ifType:            ethernet-csmacd
ifPhysAddress:     00-00-E8-CD-54-4C  ifSpeed:           10000000
ifIndex:           2                  ifAdminStatus:     up
ifMtu:             1494               ifOperStatus:      up
ifInOctets:        275755             ifOutOctets:       2353572
ifInUcastPkts:     2817               ifOutUcastPkts:    4032
ifInNUcastPkts:    28                 ifOutNUcastPkts:   85
ifInDiscards:      0                  ifOutDiscards:     0
ifInErrors:        0                  ifOutErrors:       0
ifInUnknownProtos: 0                  ifOutQLen:         0
```

NOTE

As with TCPCON, Read-only fields are identified with a colon (:) following the field description. Read/Write fields are identified with a colon-dot (:.) following the field description.

You are permitted to change the value of the ifAdminStatus field to "up," "down," or "testing." These changes will have no effect on the managed nodes, however, because ifAdminStatus is not implemented as a Read/Write object in the SNMP client MIBs.

Local IP Address Table   The *Local IP Address Table* option lists IP addresses that are associated with local interfaces.

Routing Table   The *Routing Table* option lists entries in the routing table of the managed host. To see and details, select an entry and press Enter to open the Edit IP Routing Table Entry form shown in Figure 11.20.

```
        Edit IP Routing Table Entry
ipRouteDest:      193.80.201.32
ipRouteNextHop:   s1.mayberry.com
ipRouteIfIndex:   2
ipRouteType:      direct
ipRouteProto:     local
ipRouteAge:       0:00:40:51
ipRouteMetric1:   1
ipRouteMetric2:   -1
ipRouteMetric3:   -1
ipRouteMetric4:   -1
```

TCP Connection Table   The *TCP Connection Table* option lists active TCP connections on the managed host. Figure 11.21 shows a host with several active connections.

▶ · ◀

F I G U R E   11.21

Active TCP Connections

Local Host	Port	Remote Host	Port	State
unspecified	finger	unspecified	none	listen
unspecified	515	unspecified	none	listen
blythe.mayberry.com	ftp	woody.mayberry.com	1025	established
<End of Table>				

Two of the connections shown in Figure 11.21 resulted when services performed passive opens (see Chapter 5). For example, the finger service (the name is obtained from the SERVICES file, which maps services to ports (see Chapter 8) is prepared to accept an active open from a finger client. At this time, however, a remote host is not connected, and the value of the *Remote Host* field is unspecified. The *State* field has the value of "listen," indicating that the protocol is in a passive open state and will accept an active open from an outside host. The ftp service, on the other hand, is actively connected to a remote host. The remote host name is specified along with the remote port. The value of the *State* field is "established."

SNMP

The remaining option in the Local Workstation Options and Remote Host Options menus is *SNMP*. As Figure 11.22 shows, the SNMP menu choice produces its own Available Options menu.

▶ · ◀

F I G U R E   11.22

*Available Options
Under SNMP*

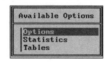

Each item in the SNMP menu is examined below:

SNMP Options   The *Options* choice in the SNMP Available Options menu opens the LWPCON Options form shown in Figure 11.23. This form is used to configure the following SNMP management parameters:

- ▶ **Community Name.** The community name that will be used by the managed host to authenticate SNMP messages.

▸ **Request Retry Count.** Specifies the number of times LWPCON will attempt to poll an interface before declaring that the interface is unreachable.

▸ **Request Poll Interval.** Specifies the interval in seconds (ranging from 0 to 900 seconds) between polling attempts. A value of 0 configures LWPCON to poll as frequently as possible.

▸ **Reply Timeout Interval.** Specifies the time LWPCON will wait for a response after polling an agent before classifying the poll as unanswered.

F I G U R E   11.23

LWPCON Options

```
                          LWPCON Options
Community Name:          public
Request Retry Count:     5
Request Poll Interval:   1    (seconds)
Reply Timeout Interval:  1    (seconds)
```

Statistics   The *Statistics* choice in the SNMP Available Options menu opens a submenu with the following choices:

▸ **ICMP Statistics**

▸ **IP Statistics**

▸ **TCP Statistics**

▸ **UDP Statistics**

Select one of these options to display statistics for that protocol. Figure 11.24 shows the statistics for IP.

F I G U R E   11.24

LWPCON Statistics for IP

```
                          IP Statistics
ipForwarding:      host        ipOutRequests:   2673
ipDefaultTTL:      60          ipOutDiscards:   0
ipInReceives:      2674        ipOutNoRoutes:   0
ipInHdrErrors:     0           ipReasmTimeout:  60
ipInAddrErrors:    0           ipReasmReqds:    0
ipForwDatagrams:   0           ipReasmOKs:      0
ipInUnknownProtos: 0           ipReasmFails:    0
ipInDiscards:      0           ipFragOks:       0
ipInDelivers:      2674        ipFragFails:     0
                               ipFragCreates:   0
```

Tables The *Tables* choice in the SNMP Available Options menu opens a submenu with the following choices:

- ▶ **Address Translation Table**

- ▶ **Interface Table**

- ▶ **Local IP Address Table**

- ▶ **Routing Table**

- ▶ **TCP Connection Table**

These are the same choices that were observed under the *Tables* option in the Local Workstation and Remote Host Options menus, and the available information is essentially the same.

Services The *Services* menu choice in the LWPCON Available Options menu opens the Services Options menu shown in Figure 11.25.

FIGURE 11.25

LWPCON Services Options

```
          Services Options
  Change Host
  Echo Test
  Display Name Server IP Addresses
  Check Active TCP Services
  Query Name Service
  Trace Route
```

The Services Options menu enables you to obtain information about services available on remote hosts. These options include:

- ▶ **Change Host.** Allows you to select the host you wish to observe.

- ▶ **Echo Test.** Pings the selected remote host.

- ▶ **Display Name Server IP Addresses.** Displays name server information in the RESOLV.CFG file.

▸ **Check Active TCP Services.** Opens a List of TCP Services menu. Select a service from this list to determine the status of the service on the selected remote host.

Figure 11.26 shows the status of the File Transfer Protocol service on a host. If the File Transfer Protocol service had been in use and did not have any available connections, LWPCON would have produced the message "File Transfer Protocol is not Active." In other words, LWPCON determines the status of the service by attempting to open a connection. The connection attempt may fail because the service is not operating or because the service has no free connections. In either case, LWPCON will report that the service is not active.

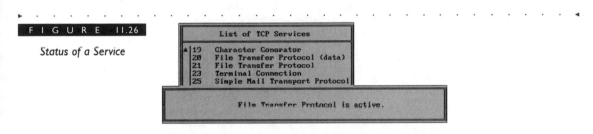

F I G U R E   11.26

Status of a Service

▸ **Query Name Service.** Used to resolve a name through a DNS name server.

▸ **Trace Route.** Displays the route between this host and the remote host. Figure 11.27 illustrates the route between this host and blythe.

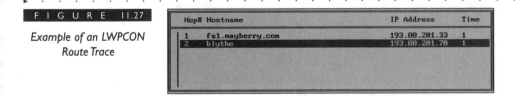

F I G U R E   11.27

*Example of an LWPCON
Route Trace*

Conclusion

This chapter rounds out our discussion of installing, configuring, and managing TCP/IP on NetWare servers and clients. At this point, the TCP/IP environment is quite distinct from the standard NetWare environment. TCP/IP is used to access TCP/IP services, and IPX is used to access NetWare services.

You may, however, want to design your network to use a single network protocol. Since TCP/IP must use IP, that means running NetWare over IP as well. NetWare/IP provides this capability and is our next stop in the exploration of NetWare TCP/IP.

## CHAPTER 12

NetWare/IP

This chapter rounds out our discussion of NetWare TCP/IP by introducing you to NetWare/IP, a product that enables NetWare services to run over a TCP/IP protocol stack. NetWare/IP also enables servers to function as gateways between IPX and IP networks. It takes a bit of work to set up NetWare/IP, but if you want a single-protocol NetWare LAN, the results can be worth it.

This chapter focuses on NetWare/IP version 2.1, which functions only with NetWare 4.01 and later. If you are working with NetWare 3, you will be using NetWare/IP version 1.1, which is similar to version 2.1 but is a much weaker implementation. If your organization is committed to NetWare/IP, I strongly recommend that you upgrade to NetWare 4 and use NetWare/IP version 2.

Introducing NetWare/IP

NetWare/IP has a simple purpose: to enable NetWare services to operate over the IP protocol. Figure 12.1 compares the NetWare client protocol stacks with and without NetWare/IP. Essentially, NetWare/IP emulates IPX using IP in conjunction with the UDP protocol. UDP is similar to IPX in that both are datagram-oriented protocols, but IPX and IP/UDP are unlike each other in key ways, and these differences complicated NetWare/IP's design. To see how, we need to examine the services that support NetWare/IP.

FIGURE 12.1

Client Protocols With and Without NetWare/IP

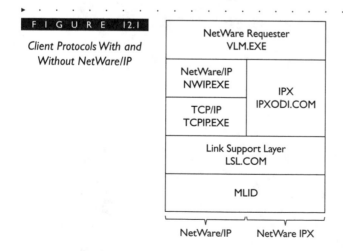

FIGURE 12.1

Client Protocols With and Without NetWare/IP

THE DOMAIN SAP/RIP SERVICE

The difference with the greatest effect on NetWare/IP's design is that IPX relies heavily on its ability to broadcast messages throughout the IPX internetwork, and IPX broadcast messages are forwarded by routers to other network segments. Broadcasts are used by two protocols:

▸ Service Advertising Protocol (SAP) uses broadcasts to announce the services available on NetWare servers.

▸ Routing Information Protocol (RIP) uses broadcasts to exchange routing information between IPX RIP routers.

IPX and IP handle broadcast messages differently. IP broadcasts are directed to a specific network and are not promulgated across routers. For this reason, IPX can't be emulated directly by IP. Instead, NetWare/IP uses a Domain SAP/RIP Service (DSS) to collect and share the information that SAP and RIP disseminate through broadcast messages.

A NetWare/IP network requires at least one computer that is configured as a DSS server. The DSS server can be a NetWare/IP server or it can be a system that is dedicated to providing the DSS service. A DSS server must be configured with a TCP/IP interface but need not be running IPX.

The DSS server collects SAP and RIP data from the network. NetWare/IP servers and clients that need service or route information query the DSS server for that information.

Primary and Secondary DSS Servers

A single DSS server can support an entire NetWare/IP internetwork, but relying on a single server for any critical service is a recipe for disaster. Therefore, NetWare/IP permits you to configure primary DSS servers, which serve as central data archives, and secondary DSS servers that automatically receive copies of the primary database. Similarly, changes made to the database of a secondary DSS server are registered automatically to the primary DSS. By default, primary and secondary DSS servers synchronize their databases at five-minute intervals.

The DSS server is the primary bottleneck in NetWare/IP's performance. In many cases, a computer should be dedicated to providing the primary DSS service; however, it is still desirable to include secondary DSS servers in the network configuration. Secondary DSS servers can offload processing from the primary DSS server by responding to DSS queries, and secondary DSS servers can take over if the primary DSS server fails or is shut down.

DOMAIN NAME SERVICE

Because NetWare/IP cannot use SAP to announce the existence of DSS servers, another mechanism is required. DSS servers are cataloged using the Domain Name Service (DNS).

Recall from Chapter 6 that a domain is a subtree of the overall DNS hierarchy. For example, a company with a presence on the Internet might be assigned the domain name widget.com.

When NetWare/IP is configured, a NetWare/IP domain must be designated, and all DSS servers in the NetWare/IP network must be registered as name servers in a NetWare/IP domain. Actually, a DSS server has a dual identity: It is registered as a name server in the NetWare/IP domain and as a host in organization's domain in the DNS hierarchy.

Figure 12.2 illustrates the characteristics of the NetWare/IP domain, using part of the directory for the company JazzIz, Inc., a publisher of jazz-related recordings, magazines, and books. The figure includes the various DNS and DSS servers, along with a sampling of the end-user hosts. Also shown is the NetWare/IP subdomain. This figure assumes that the company network is connected to the Internet. If the network is not connected to the Internet, the company has complete freedom to design the database tree from the root down.

NOTE

Forgive me if I hammer home a point that you may have understood perfectly in Chapter 6, but it is an important one. Names in the DNS hierarchy identify two types of entities. Domain names identify the nodes that define the hiearchy tree, but they do not identify hosts. Domain name nodes can contain subdomains and hosts. You will not find a host with the name jazziz.com, for example. In Figure 12.2, both jazziz.com and nwip.jazziz.com are names of domains.

Fully qualified host names append a host name to a domain name. A host name on the DNS tree is an end-point. Host names cannot contain subdomains or other hosts. In figure 12.2, an example of a host name is ella.jazziz.com.

The domain name is jazziz.com, which appears in the context of the Internet name space. The NetWare/IP domain is named nwip.jazziz.com in this directory tree. The NetWare/IP domain must reside at the bottom of the database tree. In other words, the NetWare/IP domain cannot contain any subdomains or hosts.

In the figure, all hosts including the DSS and DNS servers are registered as hosts in the jazziz.com domain. However, all DSS servers are identified as name servers in the NetWare/IP domain nwip.jazziz.com. Therefore, DSS servers will appear twice in the DNS database, as hosts and as name servers.

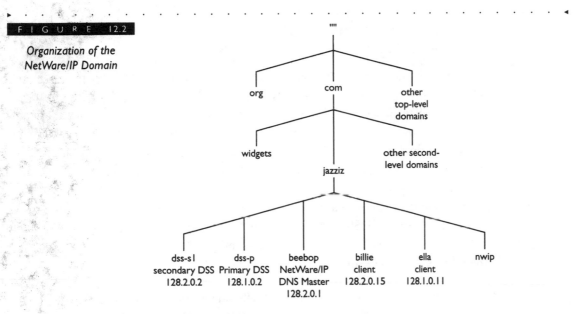

FIGURE 12.2

Organization of the NetWare/IP Domain

DNS Resource Records

An entry in a DNS database is called a *resource record*. A DNS database supports seven types of resource records, but only the following are critical to NetWare/IP:

> **Start of Authority (soa).** An soa record declares the domain for which this name server is authoritative.

> **Address (a).** An a record matches a host name with an IP address. These records are used by resolvers to derive IP addresses from host names.

> **Name Server (ns).** An ns record specifies a name server that is authoritative for a domain.

To see how these records are defined, examine the following entries, which would appear in the DNS database for the JazzIz network shown in Figure 12.2:

```
jazziz.com.          soa    beebop.jazziz.com.
nwip.jazziz.com.     ns     dss-p.jazziz.com.
nwip.jazziz.com.     ns     dss-s1.jazziz.com.
nwip.jazziz.com      ns     swing.jazziz.com.
dss-p.jazziz.com.    a      128.1.0.2.
dss-s1.jazziz.com.   a      128.2.0.2.
ella.jazziz.com.     a      128.1.0.11.
swing.jazziz.com.    a      128.2.0.1.
billie.jazziz.com.   a      128.2.0.15.
```

Domain names are not commonly shown with a trailing period, because a domain name usually is assumed to be fully qualified, describing all domains up to the root. In DNS resource records, however, the soa record establishes a context domain. Any domain name that is not terminated with a period is assumed to be a subdomain of the soa domain. In an NDS database, an entry for a domain nwip.jazziz.com (without the trailing period) would be assumed to be nwip.jazziz.com.jazziz.com. Therefore, all entries in the NetWare/IP DNS database are defined with fully qualified domain names ending in a period so that there is no ambiguity.

Notice that each DSS and DNS server is defined by a name server (ns) and an address (a) entry. The ns entry is used by NetWare/IP servers and clients to obtain the addresses of DSS servers.

NOTE

If you are using a NetWare DNS server, be sure to use the one included with NetWare/IP. Other products may not have the features required for NetWare/IP. However, you are free to use a non-NetWare DNS server as well, such as one running an implementation of Berkeley Internet Name Domain (BIND), the most popular DNS software on the Internet. Resource records in BIND have the same structure as resource records in NetWare/IP.

See the book *DNS and BIND* by Paul Albitz and Cricket Liu (O'Reilly & Associates, Inc.) for a thorough discussion of BIND resource records.

HOW DNS AND DSS WORK

Figure 12.3 illustrates how NetWare/IP servers and clients use DNS and DSS to support NetWare services. Here is how the process works:

1 • When a NetWare/IP server enters the network, it queries a DNS server to obtain a list of DSS servers, recorded in ns records.

2 • The NetWare/IP server registers with the DSS server, which maintains a database of all services provided by NetWare/IP servers on the network. If multiple DSS servers are active, they exchange databases periodically so that each DSS server has a complete record of available services.

3 • When a client enters the network, it queries a DNS server to obtain a list of DSS servers.

4 • When the client requires a service, it contacts a DSS server to obtain the address of a NetWare/IP server that can provide the service.

5 • When the client has the address of a server, it can initiate a direct dialog between itself and the server.

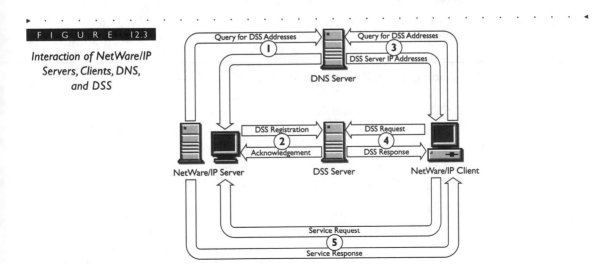

FIGURE 12.3

Interaction of NetWare/IP Servers, Clients, DNS, and DSS

Preferred DSS Servers

Strictly speaking, DNS is not required in this scenario. NetWare/IP 2.1 provides a mechanism that enables each NetWare/IP server and client to be configured with the IP addresses of up to five preferred DSS servers. If DNS is not available to provide a list of DSS servers, the server or client will try to contact the DSS servers in its preferred DSS servers list.

Static configurations are always somewhat difficult to administer, and preferred DSS server lists are no exception. Because preferred DSS server addresses must be reconfigured manually when a change takes place, it is preferable to configure a DNS server so that the network adapts dynamically to changes.

Registered and Unregistered DSS Servers

In most cases, DSS servers are registered in the DNS database, enabling servers and clients to identify available DSS servers by querying DSS. Under some circumstances, however, it may be desirable to have DSS servers that are not registered to DNS. A NetWare/IP computer can locate an unregistered DSS server only if its IP address appears in the list of preferred DSS servers for the NetWare/IP computer.

If a NetWare/IP domain spans a WAN link, it may be desirable to reduce the housekeeping traffic that traverses the WAN. If remote DSS servers are unregistered, local NetWare/IP computers cannot direct their DSS queries through the WAN link to the remote DSS server unless they are configured with the IP address of the DSS server. Clients and servers on the remote network can include the addresses of the unregistered DSS servers in their preferred DSS servers list, enabling them to query the unregistered DSS servers without the need for DNS.

The DSS Virtual-IPX Network

Even though NetWare/IP does not support IPX on the IP network segment, NetWare/IP does maintain a virtual IPX network that enables NetWare services to function. Therefore, just as each IPX network must be configured with a unique network number, DSS must be configured with an IPX network number that is unique among all IPX networks on the internetwork.

Architecture of a NetWare/IP Network

The design of a NetWare/IP network depends on the scope and requirements. Let's look at three different scenarios to see how NetWare/IP is adapted to varying network configurations.

A SINGLE SEGMENT NETWORK WITH IPX AND IP

When a NetWare network has been partially migrated to NetWare/IP, it must still be able to support IPX protocols. Figure 12.4 shows such a network, which includes two servers:

- COOLJAZZ is a standard NetWare server running IPX

- BEEBOP is a NetWare/IP server

One server could provide both IPX and IP protocol support, but in this example, let's keep things separate.

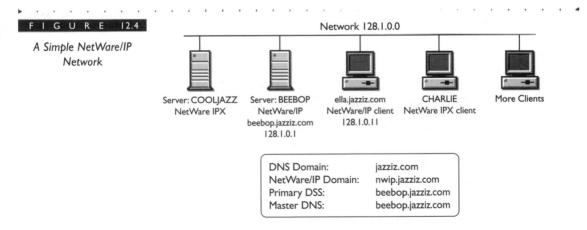

FIGURE 12.4

A Simple NetWare/IP Network

Network 128.1.0.0

Server: COOLJAZZ NetWare IPX	Server: BEEBOP NetWare/IP beebop.jazziz.com 128.1.0.1	ella.jazziz.com NetWare/IP client 128.1.0.11	CHARLIE NetWare IPX client	More Clients

DNS Domain: jazziz.com
NetWare/IP Domain: nwip.jazziz.com
Primary DSS: beebop.jazziz.com
Master DNS: beebop.jazziz.com

BEEBOP is the only server supporting TCP/IP, so it will provide all of the required NetWare/IP services, including DNS, DSS, and NetWare. When planning the network, you must specify the following information:

> ▸ **DNS Domain.** This is the topmost domain for this organization. The DNS domain is named jazziz.com.

> ▸ **NetWare/IP domain.** This domain supports all servers and clients that are using NetWare/IP. The NetWare/IP domain is nwip.jazziz.com.

> ▸ **Primary DSS.** The host that is the primary (and only) DSS server is beebop.jazziz.com.

> ▸ **Master DNS.** The host that provides the master DNS service is also beebop.jazziz.com.

As you can see, very little configuration data is required for this simple network.

The network shown in Figure 12.4 supports two distinct and separate virtual networks. CHARLIE, the IPX client can log into COOLJAZZ, the IPX server, but CHARLIE cannot log into BEEBOP, which has not loaded an IPX protocol stack. Similarly, the client ella cannot be configured to access the COOLJAZZ server. A NetWare/IP client can access only NetWare/IP servers.

Mixed IPX and IP networks of this type are not very desirable because they fragment the network. Some improvement can be had by configuring the NetWare/IP server as a gateway.

A SINGLE-SEGMENT NETWORK WITH A NON-FORWARDING GATEWAY

When designing a network that mixes IPX with IP, you need to determine whether IPX and IP computers need to interconnect. In Figure 12.4, IPX and IP computers are distinct and cannot communicate. It is difficult to imagine a real network where this would be a desirable characteristic, however. In most cases, all IPX workstations should be migrated to NetWare/IP. In cases when a complete migration is not possible, however, a NetWare/IP server can serve as a gateway between the IPX and IP environments. A *gateway* is a device that translates between two very different protocol stacks. Figure 12.5 shows how a NetWare/IP gateway functions.

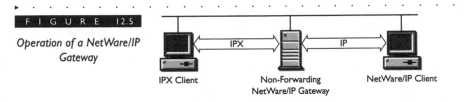

FIGURE 12.5

Operation of a NetWare/IP Gateway

To enable IP clients to access NetWare services on the IPX network, the gateway collects SAP and RIP advertisements from the IPX network and uploads the information to DSS. This information enables the IP clients to learn about services and routes on the IPX network.

To enable IPX clients to access services on the IP network, the gateway downloads SAP and RIP information from the DSS. This information is then advertised to the IPX network, enabling IPX clients to learn about services and routes on the IP network.

Figure 12.6 illustrates a network that incorporates a NetWare/IP gateway. To enable the NetWare/IP server in Figure 12.6 to function as a gateway, it is configured with both the IPX and TCP/IP protocol stacks. A NetWare/IP gateway that has a single network interface is classified as a *non-forwarding* gateway.

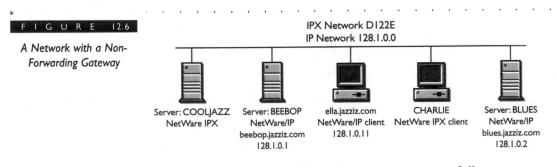

FIGURE 12.6

A Network with a Non-Forwarding Gateway

The capabilities provided by a non-forwarding gateway are as follows:

▸ IPX and IP clients can access services on the NetWare/IP gateway server.

▸ IPX and IP clients can access services on the NetWare IPX server. The user on ella.jazziz.com can be serviced by COOLJAZZ, an IPX server.

▸ IPX clients cannot be serviced by a non-gateway NetWare/IP server. CHARLIE cannot log into BLUES, which is not configured as a gateway.

As you can see, the connectivity supported by a non-forwarding gateway is not symmetrical in that NetWare IPX clients are barred from connecting to non-gateway NetWare/IP servers.

A MULTI-SEGMENT NETWORK WITH A FORWARDING GATEWAY

A NetWare/IP gateway can also be used to connect separate IPX and IP network segments, as in the network shown in Figure 12.7. A NetWare/IP gateway that has interfaces on two or more networks can forward traffic between the networks, converting protocols as required. This configuration is called a *forwarding gateway*.

A forwarding gateway is fully symmetrical. IPX clients can connect to NetWare/IP servers on the IP network, and IP clients can connect to NetWare IPX servers on the IPX network.

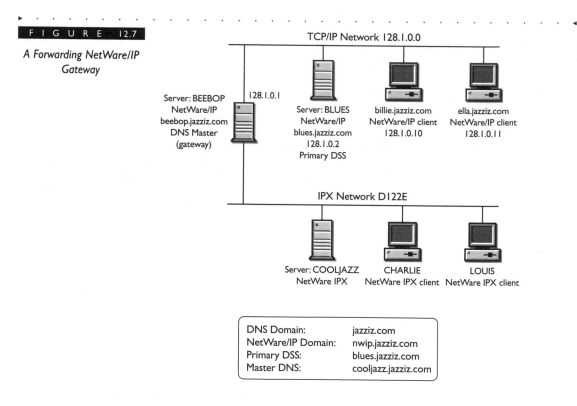

FIGURE 12.7

A Forwarding NetWare/IP Gateway

When a NetWare/IP server is functioning as a forwarding gateway, it is generally best to establish a separate DSS server, as in Figure 12.7. The gateway will be heavily burdened with the task of forwarding data between the networks, and performance will probably suffer if it is also responsible for DSS.

AN INTERNETWORK

Figure 12.8 illustrates a larger network, incorporating two IP segment and one IPX segment. A NetWare/IP forwarding gateway connects the IPX segment to the IP network.

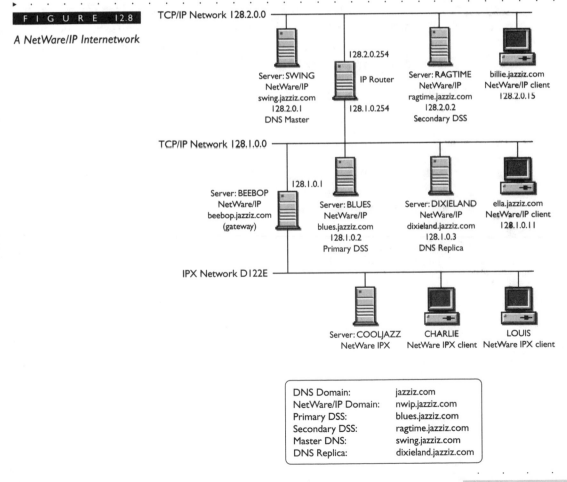

FIGURE 12.8

A NetWare/IP Internetwork

TCP/IP Network 128.2.0.0

128.2.0.254

Server: SWING
NetWare/IP
swing.jazziz.com
128.2.0.1
DNS Master

IP Router

128.1.0.254

Server: RAGTIME
NetWare/IP
ragtime.jazziz.com
128.2.0.2
Secondary DSS

billie.jazziz.com
NetWare/IP client
128.2.0.15

TCP/IP Network 128.1.0.0

128.1.0.1

Server: BEEBOP
NetWare/IP
beebop.jazziz.com
(gateway)

Server: BLUES
NetWare/IP
blues.jazziz.com
128.1.0.2
Primary DSS

Server: DIXIELAND
NetWare/IP
dixieland.jazziz.com
128.1.0.3
DNS Replica

ella.jazziz.com
NetWare/IP client
128.1.0.11

IPX Network D122E

Server: COOLJAZZ
NetWare IPX

CHARLIE
NetWare IPX client

LOUIS
NetWare IPX client

DNS Domain:	jazziz.com
NetWare/IP Domain:	nwip.jazziz.com
Primary DSS:	blues.jazziz.com
Secondary DSS:	ragtime.jazziz.com
Master DNS:	swing.jazziz.com
DNS Replica:	dixieland.jazziz.com

In this network, separate servers have been established for DNS and for DSS, and each service has been replicated. DNS is supported by a master and a replica server, and DSS is supported by a primary and a secondary server. The NetWare/IP gateway functions only as a gateway, and other servers provide NetWare services to clients.

AN INTERNETWORK WITH A WAN LINK

In Figure 12.9, one of the TCP/IP segments is separated by a WAN link. Because WAN links generally are slower and have less capacity than LANs, the design must be adapted in several ways:

- The remote TCP/IP network includes an unregistered DSS server, which is known only to its local NetWare/IP servers and clients. Servers and clients on the other side of the WAN link will not be able to access this DSS server because it will not be registered to DNS.

- Each NetWare/IP server and client on the remote TCP/IP network is configured with a preferred DSS server address of the unregistered DSS server.

- The frequency with which DSS servers synchronize their databases is increased from 5-minute to 30-minute intervals, again with the goal of reducing WAN traffic.

- Timing parameters (tick counts) are adjusted to accommodate the slower data rates of the WAN link.

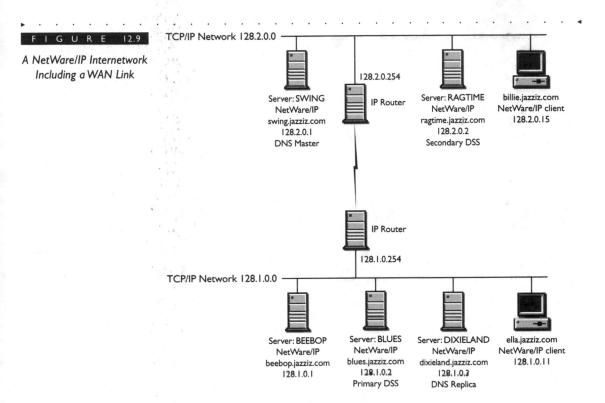

A NetWare/IP Internetwork Including a WAN Link

Configuring Tick Counts

Several NetWare/IP operations are time dependent. For example, NetWare/IP can be configured to determine how long it will wait before retransmitting an unacknowledged packet. If the retransmit time is too short, NetWare/IP may resend a packet before it is possible for the acknowledgment to be returned, generating excess network traffic. If the retransmit time is too long, NetWare/IP will await an acknowledgment for an excessive amount of time, and performance will suffer when packets are lost or damaged.

Time-dependent operations are measured in *ticks*, where a tick is 1/18 second (a long time to a computer). To determine the required tick count between two network end-points, use PING, which is described in Chapter 8. Ping a destination and note the average time that is reported. Divide this value by 110 to determine the number of ticks required for a packet to travel one way to the remote host. This value can be used to configure the tick count parameters.

You can configure the tick counts between nodes on the:

- ▶ Same IP subnetwork

- ▶ Same IP network

- ▶ Different IP networks

Planning NetWare/IP Installation

Depending on the size of the network, NetWare/IP planning can get fairly involved. Planning requires examination of three areas:

- ▶ DNS

- ▶ DSS

- ▶ NetWare/IP

The extremely simple network shown in Figure 12.10 is used to illustrate the process of planning and configuring NetWare/IP.

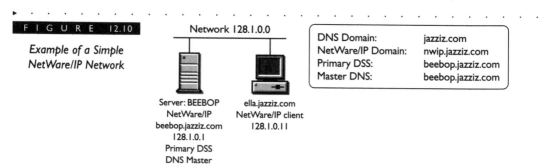

FIGURE 12.10

Example of a Simple NetWare/IP Network

Network 128.1.0.0

DNS Domain: jazziz.com
NetWare/IP Domain: nwip.jazziz.com
Primary DSS: beebop.jazziz.com
Master DNS: beebop.jazziz.com

Server: BEEBOP
NetWare/IP
beebop.jazziz.com
128.1.0.1
Primary DSS
DNS Master

ella.jazziz.com
NetWare/IP client
128.1.0.11

The first step in planning DNS is to determine the scheme of the domain. Will all hosts be entered at the same level, or will the domain be organized in subdomains? From the user's viewpoint, a single domain is easiest because it simplifies names. From an administrative standpoint, however, subdomains may be necessary. The advantage of creating subdomains is that they can be organized into zones (described in Chapter 6) that can be supported by different name servers. On large networks, zones reduce the demand on a given group of name servers. They can also be organized to reflect the network geography, so that more names can be resolved without crossing WAN links.

The JazzIz network is modest in scope and can be organized safely into a single zone. Therefore, all hosts can be placed in the jazziz.com domain. The design of the JazzIz name space is shown in Figure 12.11.

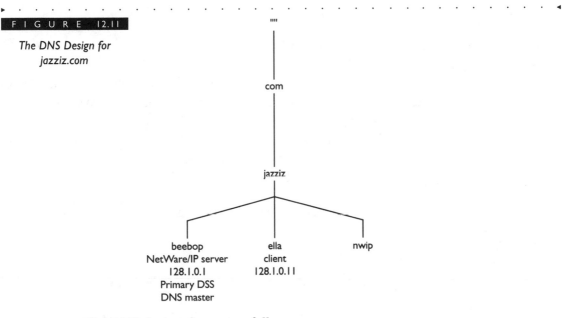

The DNS design data are as follows:

- ▶ DNS Domain: jazziz.com

- ▶ NetWare/IP Domain: nwip.jazziz.com

- ▶ Master DNS Server: beebop.jazziz.com

- ▶ Primary DSS Server: beebop.jazziz.com

- ▶ DSS IPX Network Number: d122e

Because the network is simple, all other NetWare/IP parameters can be left at their default values.

Obtaining NetWare/IP

As this book is being written, NetWare/IP is available in two versions:

- NetWare/IP 1.1 for NetWare 3

- NetWare/IP 2.1 for NetWare 4

Novell has announced its intention to incorporate NetWare/IP into future releases of NetWare. For that reason, NetWare/IP 2.1 is a free upgrade to NetWare 4, available from NetWire on CompuServe or from Novell's FTP server (ftp.novell.com) via anonymous FTP or the World Wide Web (http://www.novell.com). For NetWare 3, NetWare/IP version 1.1 remains available as a commercial product. For NetWare/IP 2.1, you need to retrieve two files:

- NIPS21.EXE, which contains the server files

- NIPW21.EXE, which contains the client files

The installation procedures described below will assume that you have these files.

NOTE

NetWare/IP 2.1 was upgraded to version 2.2, just before this book became available, and it remains a free upgrade. If your organization is committed to NetWare/IP, I strongly recommend that you migrate to NetWare 4 if necessary to take advantage of version 2.x, which is considerably more sophisticated than version 1.1. Only NetWare/IP 2.1 will be considered in this chapter, although the full working version of NetWare/IP 2.2 is available on the CD that comes with this book . Some of the new features to look for in version 2.2 include:

- **Dynamic Host Configuration Protocol (DHCP), a sophisticated method of centrally managing host configurations.**

▸ **NetWare-to-UNIX Printing, a capability currently available only in other NetWare TCP/IP products.**

▸ **Filtering, the capability of determining which messages will be sent to specific interfaces.**

▸ **Spoofing, a technique that reduces traffic on WAN links.**

Installing and Configuring the NetWare/IP Server

Before installing NetWare/IP, you should do the following:

▸ **Test the network using IPX.** Fewer configuration mistakes are possible, and IPX operation demonstrates that the server and client are operational. Later, if IPX operation is not required, the IPX protocol may be unbound from the network interfaces.

▸ **Install NDS on the server.** You will need to log in using the admin user object to configure NetWare/IP.

▸ **Install TCP/IP on the server and on at least one client.** Ensure that IP is functioning properly by pinging the server and client. TCP/IP must be functioning on the server before NetWare/IP can be installed.

▸ **Obtain the file NIPS21.EXE** from one of the sources mentioned in the previous section.

▸ **Ensure that the Maximum Physical Receive Packet Size parameter on the server is set to the default value of 4202.** This parameter is configured in the STARTUP.NCF file.

▸ **Edit the SYS:ETC\HOSTS file.** Delete any entries that you do not wish to have copied into the NDS database.

There are a few caveats regarding NetWare/IP 2.1:

NOTE

▸ **All computers that are sharing a NetWare/IP domain should be defined in the same NDS domain. Computers in the NetWare/IP domain must be able to communicate, and computers in different NDS trees cannot communicate via NetWare.**

▸ **NetWare/IP does not support SFT III and should not be installed on an SFT III server.**

▸ **Only English messages are supported, regardless of the setting of the NWLANGUAGE variable.**

The procedures for installing and configuring the NetWare/IP server are described in the following sections. Although the exact order of steps can vary in many instances, the sequence presented in this section will enable you to successfully configure a NetWare/IP server.

INSTALLING THE NETWARE/IP SERVER SOFTWARE
To install NetWare/IP on NetWare :

1 • Log into the server from a NetWare client.

2 • Create a directory at the root of a server volume to receive the installation files. I named my directory \NWIPS.

3 • Copy the NIPS21.EXE file to the directory you created.

4 • Execute NIPS21. The file will unpack itself and create the installation directories and files.

5 • Read the NIPS21.TXT file that is placed in the \NWIPS directory. This document describes procedures for installing the product remotely through a TCP/IP network.

6 • If an earlier version of NetWare/IP is running, or if it is running the NUC.NLM included with UnixWare, enter the command **UNISTOP** at the server to unload running software.

7 • At the console prompt, load INSTALL.

8 • Select *Product options* in the Installation Options menu.

9 • Select *Install a product not listed* in the Other Installation Options menu.

10 • Because you will be installing from a server volume, you must specify a custom installation path. When prompted for a path, press F3.

At the prompt "Specify a directory path" enter the path to the installation you created, for example, SYS:NWIPS\NWIP1. Edit the path as needed to identify the NWIP1 subdirectory.

11 • You are warned that a README.TXT file is found in the installation directory. You should have read this file in Step 5, so you can press Esc and then respond No to the prompt "Do you want to stop the installation to read the readme file?"

12 • INSTALL will display the prompt "Enter Local Host Name." As a default name, INSTALL will suggest the server name that is defined in the AUTOEXEC.NCF file. Change the host name if you wish, or press Enter to accept the name that is suggested.

13 • Next you will see the prompt "Enter drive and/or path for booting NetWare." Drive C: is supplied as a default. Press Enter to accept drive C:, or edit the path as required.

14 • Now INSTALL asks "Install Online Documentation?" Unless you already have installed the documentation on another server, respond Yes. Most of the documentation for NetWare/IP is supplied in the online documentation.

15 • If a viewer is already present on the server, you will see the prompt "Viewer Exists. Overwrite?" All viewers supplied with NetWare 4 products should be compatible with the online document files supplied with NetWare IP, so you can respond No at this prompt.

16 • An Information box will confirm that NetWare/IP has been installed. After you clear the box by pressing Esc, you will receive the prompt, "Do you want to configure NetWare/IP Server?" Despite the warnings, you can safely respond No. Configuration of the NetWare/IP server will be covered in the next section, along with configuration of the other components.

17 • When you see the prompt "Exit NetWare/IP Server Configuration Utility," respond Yes.

18 • When you see the Server Login box (see Figure 12.12) enter the server name and the password for the admin user object on that server. This will log you into the UNICON utility used to administer NetWare/IP.

FIGURE 12.12

Logging into UNICON

19 • When UNICON is first started after NetWare/IP installation, a product initialization procedure is initiated. Progress is reported in the Product Initialization Status box shown in Figure 12.13. If the sequence of events ends with the message "Product Initialization Complete," NetWare/IP is ready to go. Press Esc to continue.

20 • After a few more messages scroll through the Product Initialization Status box, you are prompted to restart the server. Execute the commands DOWN and EXIT from the server console. Then restart the server by entering the command SERVER at the DOS prompt.

NetWare/IP is now ready to be configured.

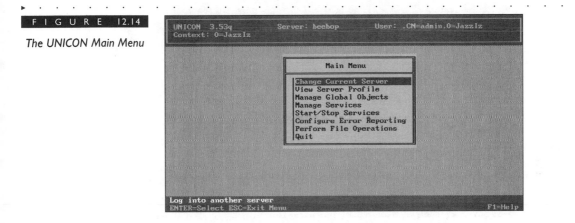

FIGURE 12.13

The NetWare/IP Product Installation Status Messages

Product Initialization Status

Creating Imported Groups group succeeded.
Creating UNICON Management groups...
Creating UNICON Groups succeeded.
Creating NDS user accounts...
Creating NDS user accounts succeeded.
Granting the UNIX Service Handler object rights in the NDS tree...
NDS UNIX Service Handler modified successfully.

Product Initialization complete.
<Press ESC to Continue>

CREATING UNICON ADMINISTRATORS

NetWare/IP is administered using the UNICON server utility. The main menu of UNICON is shown in Figure 12.14. Although any user can start UNICON, he/she must be given specific rights to perform certain UNICON functions.

FIGURE 12.14

The UNICON Main Menu

UNICON 3.53q   Server: beebop   User: .CN=admin.O=JazzIz
Context: O=JazzIz

Main Menu

Change Current Server
View Server Profile
Manage Global Objects
Manage Services
Start/Stop Services
Configure Error Reporting
Perform File Operations
Quit

Log into another server
ENTER=Select ESC=Exit Menu   F1=Help

When NetWare/IP is installed, four group objects are created that convey different sets of UNICON capabilities. These groups are:

▸ **UNICON MANAGER.** Membership in this group enables full use of the UNICON utility and access to all menu options. (However, users must be members of the UNICON HOST MANAGER group to manage hosts in the DNS database.)

▸ **UNICON SERVICES MANAGER.** Membership in this group gives the user access to the Start/Stop Services and Manage Services menu options, enabling the user to start, stop, and manage services.

▸ **UNICON HOST MANAGER.** Membership in this group gives the user access to the Manage Global Objects and Manage Hosts menu options, enabling the user to create, delete, and modify host entries.

▸ **UNICON USER/GROUP MANAGER.** Membership in this group enables the user to manage UNICON users and groups.

To assign specific UNICON capabilities to users, use the NetWare Administrator (NWADMIN in WINDOWS) or NETADMIN (DOS) to assign the appropriate group memberships to their user objects.

MANAGING THE MASTER DNS SERVER

The master DNS server is the primary administration point for DNS. Later, you will see how to administer replica DNS servers, but the primary task here is to get the master server configured and running.

Initializing the DNS Master Database

Before you begin to administer DNS, you must initialize the DNS master database. This operation can also be performed should the database become corrupt. The database can be backed up to text files when configuration is completed. A corrupt database can be reconstructed from the text files by this procedure.

Before you initialize the DNS master database, use a text editor to remove unwanted records from the SYS:ETC\HOSTS file. The file that is installed with NetWare/IP contains many records that you don't want in your database. To edit the file using the editor on the server:

1 • Enter the command **LOAD EDIT SYS:ETC\HOSTS.**

2 • Use standard NetWare editor procedures to remove undesired entries from the file.

3 • When NetWare/IP was installed, an entry for the current server was added to SYS:ETC/HOSTS, assuming that the NetWare server name would be the TCP/IP host name. Leave this entry if desired, or edit the name if necessary.

4 • Exit the editor by pressing Escape. Save the file when prompted.

To initialize the DNS master database:

1 • Load UNICON and log in with a user account that is a member of the UNICON MANAGER group.

2 • Select the *Manage Services* option in the Main Menu to open the Managing Services menu.

3 • Select *DNS* in the Managing Services menu to open the DNS menu shown in Figure 12.15.

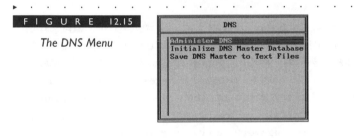

FIGURE 12.15

The DNS Menu

4 • Select *Initialize DNS Master Database* in the DNS menu.

5 • At the "Select Name Servers" prompt, specify the DNS domain for which this server is authoritative (see Figure 12.16). This domain will be specified in the start of authority (soa) record in the DNS database.

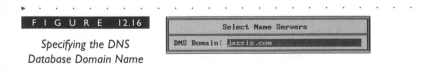

FIGURE 12.16

Specifying the DNS Database Domain Name

6 • Press Esc to continue. A series of messages will track the process of the database initialization. A successful initialization is shown in Figure 12.17.

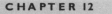

UNICON After Initialization of the DNS Master Database

```
Generated zone jazziz.com. database.
Generated zone 1.128.in-addr.arpa for address to hostname lookups.
Configured domain jazziz.com for DNS client access.
Successfully created DNS database.
Starting DNS Server.
<Press ESC to Continue>
```

7 • Press Esc to return to the UNICON Main Menu.

Adding Hosts

Each host that will function as a DNS or DSS server must be registered to the DNS database. Registration can be done in two ways. We'll examine one approach here. The other approach will be demonstrated in the section "Managing DNS Data."

NOTE

Why two procedures? Probably so that you can delegate management of hosts without granting full access to the DNS database. Any member of the UNICON HOST MANAGER group can add or delete hosts, so you could delegate the task to another if necessary, without also delegating full control of the database. Once NetWare/IP is running, adding and removing hosts will be the primary administrative tasks, so the ability to delegate this work can be very handy.

When NetWare/IP is installed on a server, the server is registered in the DNS database using its NetWare server name. In the case of the JazzIz sample network, NetWare/IP was installed on the server named BEEBOP. As a result, an entry for beebop.jazziz.com was added to the NDS database. To manage hosts in the NDS database:

1 • Load UNICON and log in. The user must be a member of the UNICON HOST MANAGER group to manage hosts using this technique.

2 • Choose the *Manage Global Objects* option in the Main Menu to open the Manage Global Objects menu.

3 • Choose *Manage Hosts* in the Manage Global Objects menu to open the Manage Hosts menu.

4 • Choose *Hosts* in the Manage Hosts menu to open the Hosts in the Local Domain box shown in Figure 12.18. At the bottom of the screen, confirm that the legend states "Update Rights: Granted." If update rights are denied, you cannot modify host entries from this box.

As mentioned above, beebop was registered in the local domain when NetWare/IP was installed on the BEEBOP server.

F I G U R E   12.18

Hosts Registered to the Local Domain

```
                    Hosts in the Local Domain
  beebop
  ella
```

5 • To add a host:

A. Press Insert.

B. Enter a host name at the "Hostname" prompt. (Do not enter a fully qualified domain name. Enter only the host name, for example, ella, not ella.jazziz.com. The host name will be added to the local domain.)

C. Enter an IP address at the "IP Address" prompt.

D. When you press Enter, the Host Information form, shown in Figure 12.19, will be displayed. All necessary information has been entered. Consult the online documentation for information about the remaining fields.

E. Press Esc to exit the Host Information field and add the host to the domain.

F·I G U R E   12.19

Entering Host Information

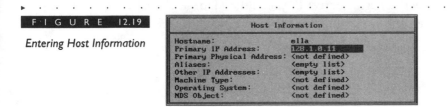

```
                      Host Information
  Hostname:                    ella
  Primary IP Address:          128.1.0.11
  Primary Physical Address:    <not defined>
  Aliases:                     <empty list>
  Other IP Addresses:          <empty list>
  Machine Type:                <not defined>
  Operating System:            <not defined>
  NDS Object:                  <not defined>
```

6 • To remove a host, select the host and press Delete. When you see the prompt "Delete?," enter *Yes* to confirm deletion of a host.

7 • To modify a host, select the host and press Enter to open the Host Information form. The *Hostname* field cannot be modified, but all other fields in the form can be edited. Press Esc when changes are complete and respond *Yes* to the "Save Changes?" prompt to save your edits.

8 • Add all hosts that will function as DNS servers or as DSS servers. If desired, you can also add non-servers such as NetWare/IP clients to the hosts list. Servers and clients can use the names in the DNS database to resolve host names to IP addresses.

9 • When changes are complete, press Esc to exit the Hosts in the Local Domain box.

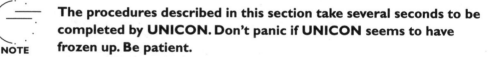 **The procedures described in this section take several seconds to be completed by UNICON. Don't panic if UNICON seems to have frozen up. Be patient.**

NOTE

Configuring the Server Profile

The server profile defines the DNS name server characteristics for this NetWare/IP server. Many of the parameters in the server profile were defined when NetWare/IP was installed, but you may need to add DNS name servers to the configuration or update the server profile. To configure the server profile:

1 • Load UNICON and log in. The user must be a member of the UNICON MANAGER or the UNICON HOST MANAGER group.

2 • Select *Manage Global Objects* in the Main Menu.

3 • Select *Configure Server Profile* in the Manage Global Objects Menu to open the Server Profile Configuration form shown in Figure 12.20.

FIGURE 12.20

*Configuring the Server
Profile*

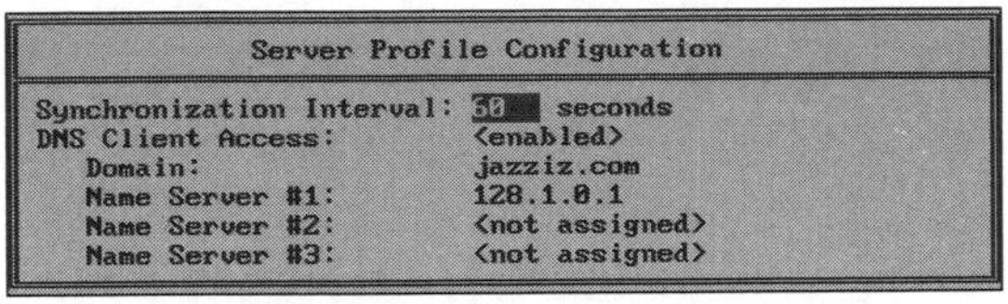

```
                    Server Profile Configuration
Synchronization Interval: 60   seconds
DNS Client Access:        <enabled>
   Domain:                jazziz.com
   Name Server #1:        128.1.0.1
   Name Server #2:        <not assigned>
   Name Server #3:        <not assigned>
```

4 • The fields in this form are as follows:

▸ **Synchronization Interval.** This parameter determines how often the DNS server checks its configuration files for changes. The default interval (60 seconds) is generally adequate.

▸ **DNS Client Access.** Set this parameter to <enabled> (the default) to permit this server to access the global DNS database. If this parameter is set to <not enabled> this server can obtain information only from its local files.

▸ **Domain.** This field specifies the domain this server will access to obtain DNS information. Change the domain to have the server obtain DNS information from another domain

▸ **Name Server #1, #2, and #3**. These fields permit you to specify three name servers that will be used to resolve names.

5 • After any required changes have been made, press Esc to exit the form and save the changes.

Clearly, entering the wrong values in this form can severely disrupt the NetWare/IP server. In most cases, you should edit only the *Name Server* fields as the addresses of DNS servers change.

Delegating Subzone authority
After the DNS master database has been initialized, the first step in configuring the DNS server is to specify the domains for which the server is authoritative:

1 • Load UNICON and log in. The user must be a member of the UNICON MANAGER group.

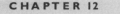
2 • Choose *Manage Services* in the Main Menu.

3 • Choose *DNS* in the Manage Services menu.

4 • Choose *Administer DNS* in the DNS menu to open the DNS Server Administration menu shown in Figure 12.21.

FIGURE 12.21

The DNS Server Administration Menu

5 • Choose *Manage Master Database* in the DNS Server Administration menu to open the Manage Master Database menu shown in Figure 12.22.

FIGURE 12.22

The Manage Master Database Menu

6 • Choose *Delegate Subzone Authority* in the Manage Master database menu to open the Master Zone and Subzones list shown in Figure 12.23.

At first, this list will include only the domain name that was specified when the database was initialized, in this case, jazziz.com. You must add any other domains this server will support, including the NetWare/IP domain.

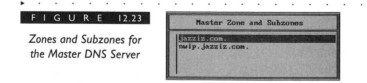

FIGURE 12.23

Zones and Subzones for the Master DNS Server

The product documentation can be a bit confusing in its terminology and misleadingly defines zones and domains as the same thing. In this step you are defining an administrative zone, which can encompass your entire corporate DNS subtree, or just a few of the domains in your subtree. Identify each domain and subdomain that this DNS server will support and add it to the list.

7 • To add the NetWare/IP domain:

  ▸ Press Insert to display the "Domain Name" prompt.

  ▸ At this prompt, enter the name of the NetWare/IP domain. In the example network, the NetWare/IP domain is nwip.jazziz.com.

  ▸ Press Enter to open the Available Hosts list, which lists hosts that have been defined in the DNS database. Select a host from this list to specify the DNS master name server for the domain you are adding. The domain will be added to the Master Zone and Subzones list.

8 • Repeat step 7 to add any other required zones. In many cases, however, the organization domain and the NetWare/IP domain will be the only required entries.

9 • Press Esc to return to the Main Menu when all domains and subdomains have been entered.

Managing the DNS Database

Until now, you have been configuring DNS, but you haven't done much about the data in DNS that describes the name space itself. In this step you will directly manage the resource records that are stored in the DNS database:

1 • Load UNICON and log in. The user must be a member of the UNICON MANAGER group.

2 • Choose *Manage Services* in the Main Menu.

3 • Choose *DNS* in the Manage Services menu.

4 • Choose *Administer DNS* in the DNS menu to open the DNS Server Administration menu.

5 • Choose *Manage Master Database* in the DNS Server Administration menu.

6 • Choose *Manage Data* in the Manage Master Database menu to open the Contents of Database box shown in Figure 12.24.

F I G U R E   12.24

Contents of the jazziz.com Database

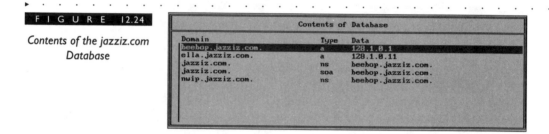

At this point, three types of records appear in the database:

▸ The start of authority (soa) record was created when the DNS database was initialized. Recall that a domain name was specified at that time. That domain name was used to define the soa record. The soa record may be created only by initializing the database and cannot be modified here.

▸ An address (a) entry exists for each host. The entry for this server (beebop.com) was created when the database was initialized. Other host entries (e.g., ella.jazziz.com.) were added to the hosts list, as described in the section "Adding Hosts." You can add hosts in this box by adding more a records to the database.

▸ A name server (ns) entry exists for this host, which is being configured as a master DNS server. This entry was also created when the database was initialized. An ns entry also exists for each DSS server, which is defined as a name server in the NetWare/IP domain (e.g., beebop.jazziz.com. is a name server in the nwip.jazziz.com. domain).

Each DSS must be defined by two entries in the database: an address record in its DNS domain and a name server record in the NetWare/IP domain.

7 • To create an address record:

A. Press Insert to open a the Record Type list. Only a and ns records are required. Other record types are described on the online help. Press F1 for descriptions.

B. Select a and press Enter to open the Resource Record Information form shown in Figure 12.25. (The fields that appear in the form depend on the type of the resource record being defined.) Complete the form as follows:

▸ **Record Name**. For an a record specify the fully qualified domain name of the host that is being defined, e.g., beebop.jazziz.com.

▸ **Record Type**. This field cannot be modified in the Resource Record Information form.

▸ **Caching Period**. Records are cached for a minimum amount of time, as defined by the Minimum Caching Interval parameter in the soa record, before they are refreshed. This parameter can be used to extend the minimum caching period for an individual resource record.

▸ **Address**. Enter the IP address that is associated with the host name specified in the Record Name field.

C. Press Esc to save the entry to the database.

FIGURE 12.25	Resource Record Information
Creating an Address Resource Record	Record Name: ella.jazziz.com. Record Type: a Caching Period: 0 seconds Address: 128.1.0.11

8 • To create a name server record:

    A. Press Insert to open a the Record Type list.

    B. Select a and press Enter to open the Resource Record Information form shown in Figure 12.26. (The fields that appear in the form depend on the type of the resource record being defined.) Complete the form as follows:

      ▶ **Record Name**. For an ns record, specify the domain in which the name server is being defined. A DSS server, for example, must be defined in the NetWare/IP domain.

      ▶ **Record Type**. This field cannot be modified in the Resource Record Information form.

      ▶ **Caching Period**. Specifies the time this record will be cached in addition to the minimum caching interval specified in the soa record.

      ▶ **Name Server**. Enter the fully qualified domain name of the name server's host.

    C. Press Esc to save the entry to the database.

FIGURE 12.26

Defining a Name Server Resource Record

```
          Resource Record Information
Record Name:   nwip.jazziz.com.
Record Type:   ns
Caching Period: 0                        seconds
Name Server:   beebop.jazziz.com.
```

9 • To edit a record, select the record in the Contents of Database list and press Enter to open the Resource Record Information form.

10 • To delete a record, select the record in the Contents of Database list and press Delete.

11 • When all resource records have been defined, press Esc to exit the Contents of Database box.

The Start of Authority Record

We have not examined the soa record, and we should take a look at the soa Resource Record Information form, shown in Figure 12.27:

- **Record Name**. Specifies the domain for which this name server is authoritative.

- **Record Type**. This field cannot be modified in the Resource Record Information form.

- **Caching Period**. Specifies the time this record will be cached in addition to the Minimum Caching Interval parameter in the soa record.

- **Domain**. Specifies the master name server.

- **Zone Supervisor**. The address of the person responsible for this zone. The default is root.<domain_name>, e.g., root.jazziz.com.

- **Serial Number.** A serial number for the database, which is incremented each time the database is changed This number enables secondary servers to determine when they need to retrieve a new copy of the database.

- **Refresh Interval.** The interval in seconds at which a secondary server checks the accuracy of its database.

- **Refresh Retry Interval.** The number of seconds a secondary server waits to retry after a failed attempt to refresh its data database.

- **Refresh Validity Period.** The number of seconds a secondary server waits after a failed attempt to reach a master before it stops responding to queries.

- **Minimum Caching Interval.** The minimum number of seconds that information is held in cache by a master server. This value can be extended for individual records by entering a value in the Caching Period field that is included with all records.

F I G U R E 12.27

The Start of Authority Record

Resource Record Information		
Record Name:	jazziz.com.	
Record Type:	soa	
Caching Period:	0	seconds
Domain:	beebop.jazziz.com.	
Zone Supervisor:	root.jazziz.com.	
Serial Number:	0	
Refresh Interval:	3600	seconds
Refresh Retry Interval:	300	seconds
Refresh Validity Period:	3600000	seconds
Minimum Caching Interval:	86400	seconds

Starting and Stopping the DNS Service

The DNS master has now been configured. Before the rest of NetWare/IP can be made operational, it is necessary to have DNS in operation. The procedures to stop and start DNS are as follows:

1 • Load UNICON and log in. The user must be a member of the UNICON MANAGER or the UNICON SERVICES MANAGER group.

2 • Choose the *Start/Stop Services* option in the Main Menu to open the Running Services box shown in Figure 12.28. In the figure, all services have been started so that you can see what the entries look like. At first, however, no services will be running, and the box will be empty.

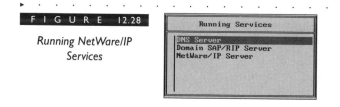

F I G U R E 12.28

Running NetWare/IP Services

3 • To start the DNS service on this host:

A. Press Insert to open the Available Services list.

B. Select DNS Server and press Enter. After a brief time, the service will be started and will be listed in the Running Services box.

4 • To stop the DNS service you need to jump through some hoops, because stopping DNS can stop DSS as well. The procedure is as follows:

A. Select DNS Server in the Running Services list and press Delete.

B. Select Yes when you see the prompt "Stop Service."

C. Press Enter when you see the magenta warning box, "Stopping the DNS Server will stop other NLMs (such as DSS) dependent on it."

D. Select Yes when you see the prompt "Stop Service."

Well, if you make a mistake, at least you can't say you weren't warned.

Linking to Outside DNS Servers

If the domain you are configuring is a subdomain of a larger DNS name space such as the Internet, you need to do a few more things to enable outside users to query your DNS servers. You may also want to install some shortcuts that make it faster for your users to query specific outside domains.

If your network will be connected to the Internet, you must register your domain with the authorities for your parent domain. Chapter 6 explains how to identify the administrative authority for your parent domain and register your DNS domain. When you register your DNS domain, the administrator of the parent domain will record your DNS server as the server that is authoritative for your domain, enabling all users on the Internet to query your domain. JazzIs, for example, must register jazziz.com with the authorities for the com domain.

No special action is required to enable your users to query outside domains. NetWare/IP includes the file SYS:ETC\DNS\ROOT.DB, which includes entries for the Internet root domain name servers. Because the contents of the ROOT.DB file are current when the NetWare/IP product was finalized, it is possible (although unlikely) that Internet root name servers may have changed. Take the time to verify the contents of ROOT.DB by conducting a WHOIS query on the Internet root domain using the procedure described in Chapter 6.

To manage the ROOT.DB file:

1 • Load UNICON and log in. The user must be a member of the UNICON MANAGER group.

2 • Choose *Manage Services* in the Main Menu.

3 • Choose *DNS* in the Manage Services menu.

4 • Choose *Administer DNS* in the DNS menu to open the DNS Server Administration menu.

5 • Choose *Link to Existing DNS Hierarchy* to open the Link to Existing DNS Hierarchy menu. It is possible to link to outside DNS hierarchies via DNS forwarders. Consult the online manuals for more information about linking through forwarders.

6 • Choose *Link Direct* in the Link to Existing Hierarchy menu to open a Root Domains list that includes outside domains for which links have been defined. The root domain is indicated by a period (.).

7 • To add a domain to the Root Domains list, press Insert and follow the prompts to enter the domain information.

8 • Select a domain in the Root Domains list to view the name servers that are associated with that domain. To view or edit the address for the name server, select the host name and press Enter.

Setting up DNS Replicas

Each zone should also be supported by a DNS replica server. A DNS replica is a read-only copy of a DNS master database. The replica database is updated only by copying information from the DNS master. DNS clients can query the replica as well as the master. To add a replica database to a DNS server:

1 • Load UNICON and log in. The user must be a member of the UNICON MANAGER group.

2 • Choose *Manage Services* in the Main Menu.

3 • Choose *DNS* in the Manage Services menu.

4 • Choose *Administer DNS* in the DNS menu to open the DNS Server Administration menu.

5 • Choose *Manage Replica Databases* in the DNS Server Administration menu to open the Replica Databases list shown in Figure 12.29. At first this list will be empty. The figure shows the list after a replica database has been created.

F I G U R E   12.29

List of Replica Domains

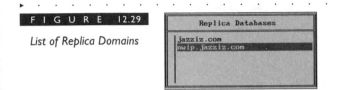

6 • Press Insert in the Replica Databases box to open the Replica Database Information form shown in Figure 12.30. Complete the fields in this form as follows:

▶ **Domain**. Enter the fully qualified domain name of the domain for which a replica will be maintained.

▶ **Name Server #1**. Enter the IP address of the DNS master name server for the domain.

▶ **Name Server #2 and #3**. Enter the IP addresses of up to two other DNS replica servers for this domain.

Press Esc to save the information you have entered.

F I G U R E   12.30

Configuring a DNS Replica

Backing Up the DNS Database to Text Files

When changes are made to the DNS database, it is a good idea to back up the database by copying the data to text files. These files can be used to reinitialize the database if files are lost or corrupted. To back up the DNS master database:

1 • Load UNICON and log in. The user must be a member of the UNICON MANAGER group.

2 • Choose *Manage Services* in the Main Menu.

3 • Choose *DNS* in the Manage Services menu.

4 • Choose *Save DNS Master to Text Files* in the DNS menu.

5 • After data are backed up, press Esc to return to the Main Menu.

MANAGING NETWARE/IP

After DNS is running, the next step is to configure and start the DSS servers and NetWare/IP itself. These procedures are closely related and will be covered together in this section.

Although your network will probably include secondary DSS servers, most of the configuration work is performed when setting up the primary DSS. Before you begin, DNS must be configured and running, as described in the previous section.

Configuring a Primary DSS

To configure a primary DSS:

1 • Load UNICON and log in. The user must be a member of the UNICON MANAGER group.

2 • Select *Manage Services* in the Main Menu.

3 • Select *NetWare/IP* in the Manage Services box to open the NetWare/IP Administration menu shown in Figure 12.31.

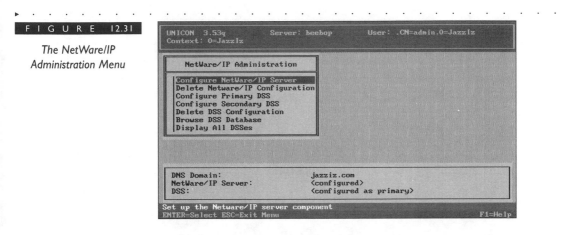

FIGURE 12.31

The NetWare/IP Administration Menu

4 • Select *Configure Primary DSS* in the NetWare/IP Administration menu to open the Primary DSS Configuration form shown in Figure 12.32.

FIGURE 12.32

The Primary DSS Configuration Form

5 • At first, the first three configurable fields will read <none assigned>. Configure the primary DSS as follows:

▸ **NetWare/IP Domain**. Enter the fully qualified name of the NetWare/IP domain.

▸ **Primary DSS Host Name**. Enter the fully qualified name of the host on which the primary DSS will be running.

▸ **IPX Network Number (in hex)**. Enter a network number that identifies the virtual IPX network that will be supported by NetWare/IP. This network number must be unique among all IPX network numbers in use on your internetwork.

6 • To configure the DSS tunable parameters, select the *Tunable Parameters* field in the Primary DSS Configuration form and press Enter to open the Tunable Parameters form shown in Figure 12.33. On most LANs and many WANs, the default settings will be adequate. The parameters are as follows:

▸ **UDP Port Number for NetWare/IP Services**. NetWare/IP requires the use of two consecutively-numbered UDP ports, which must not be used by other services on your network. Change the value of this parameter if port 43981 or 43982 is in use on your network. The default is 43981, and the range is from 1 to 65535.

▸ **DSS-NetWare/IP Server Synchronization Interval**. This parameter determines how often NetWare/IP servers will query DSS for updated information. The default is 5 minutes, and the range is 1 to 60 minutes.

▸ **Primary-Secondary DSS Synchronization Interval**. This parameter determines how often secondary DSS servers will synchronize their databases with the primary DSS. The default is 5 minutes, and the range is 1 to 240 minutes.

▸ **Maximum UDP Retransmissions**. This parameter determines the number of times an unacknowledged packet is sent before it is dropped. The default is 3 times, and the range is 1 to 48 times.

▸ **UDP Checksum?** If this field is set to Yes, a checksum field is added to the UDP datagram and error checking is performed, improving reliability but degrading performance. By default, this field is set to No, and error checking is not performed.

▸ **Ticks between Nodes on the Same IP Subnet**. This parameter determines the number of ticks (1/18 second) DSS will allow for a packet that is being delivered to the local subnet. (Default is 2 ticks.)

▸ **Ticks between Nodes on the Same IP Net**. This parameter determines the number of ticks (1/18 second) DSS will allow for a packet that is being delivered to the local network. (Default is 4 ticks.)

▸ **Ticks between Nodes on the Different IP Networks**. This parameter determines the number of ticks (1/18 second) DSS will allow for a packet that is being delivered to the local subnet. (Default is 6 ticks.)

```
                          Tunable Parameters
UDP Port Number for NetWare/IP Service:          43981
DSS-NetWare/IP Server Synchronization Interval:  5    minutes
Primary-Secondary DSS Synchronization Interval:  5    minutes
Maximum UDP Retransmissions:                     3
UDP Checksum?                                     No
Ticks between Nodes on the Same IP Subnet:       2
Ticks between Nodes on the Same IP Net:          4
Ticks between Nodes on Different IP Nets:         6
```

7 • Press Esc to return to the Main Menu when the primary DSS has been configured, saving the configuration changes when prompted. When you save the DSS configuration data, you will be shown a reminder that the DNS database should have records that specify this host as a name server in the NetWare/IP domain.

8 • Start the DSS server on this host, using the procedure described in the section "Starting and Stopping the DSS Server."

Configuring a Secondary DSS Server

Before you can configure a secondary DSS server, a primary DSS server must be in operation, and this server must be configured for DNS access. To configure a secondary DSS server:

1 • Load UNICON and log in. The user must be a member of the UNICON MANAGER group.

2 • Select *Manage Services* in the Main Menu.

3 • Select *NetWare/IP* in the Manage Services box to open the NetWare/IP Administration menu.

4 • Select *Configure Secondary DSS* in the NetWare/IP Administration menu to open the Secondary DSS Configuration form shown in Figure 12.34 Complete the fields in this form as follows:

▶ **NetWare/IP Domain**. Enter the NetWare/IP domain name.

▶ **Primary DSS Host**. Enter the fully qualified domain name of the primary DSS host.

```
                  Secondary DSS Configuration
  NetWare/IP Domain: nwip.jazziz.com
  Primary DSS Host: beebop.jazziz.com
```

5 • Press Esc when the server is configured and save the changes. Return to the Main Menu.

6 • Start the DSS server on this host, using the procedure described in the section "Starting and Stopping the DSS Server."

Starting and Stopping the DSS Server

Like all NetWare/IP services, the DSS must be started to become active. To start the DSS:

1 • Load UNICON and log in. The user must be a member of the UNICON MANAGER or the UNICON SERVICES MANAGER group.

2 • Choose the *Start/Stop Services* option in the Main Menu to open the Running Services box.

3 • To start the DSS service on this host:

A. Press Insert to open the Available Services list.

B. Select Domain SAP/RIP Server and press Enter. After a brief time, the service will be started and will be listed in the Running Services box.

4 • To stop the DSS service:

A. Select Domain SAP/RIP Server in the Running Services list and press Delete.

B. Select Yes when you see the prompt "Stop Service."

Configuring the NetWare/IP Server

To configure the NetWare/IP server:

1 • Load UNICON and log in. The user must be a member of the UNICON MANAGER group.

2 • Select *Manage Services* in the Main Menu.

3 • Select *NetWare/IP* in the Manage Services box to open the NetWare/IP Administration menu.

4 • Select *Configure NetWare/IP Server* in the NetWare/IP Administration menu to open the NetWare/IP Server Configuration form shown in Figure 12.35.

FIGURE 12.35

The NetWare/IP Server Configuration Form

```
                        NetWare/IP Server Configuration
    NetWare/IP Domain:               nwip.jazziz.com
    Preferred IP Address:            128.1.0.1
    Preferred DSSes:                 <see form>
    Initial DSS Contact Retries:     1
    Retry Interval:                  10  seconds
    Slow Link Customizations:        <none>
    Forward IPX Information to DSS?   No
```

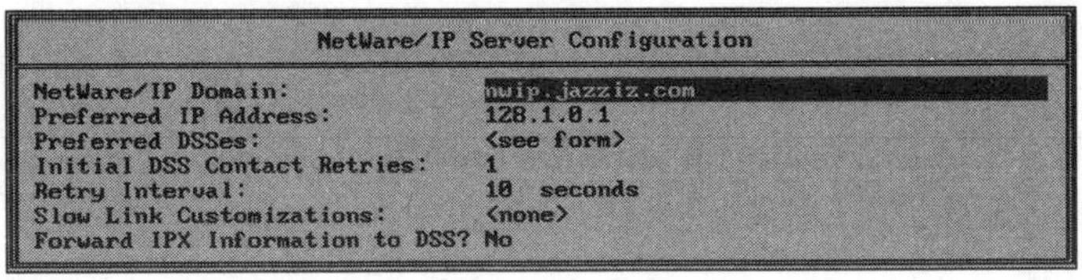

5 • Configure the primary DSS as follows:

▶ **NetWare/IP Domain**. Enter the fully qualified name of the NetWare/IP domain.

▶ **Preferred IP Address**. If NetWare/IP is running on a server that is equipped with multiple network interfaces, this field specifies the interface that will be associated with NetWare/IP. Press Enter and select an IP address from the list that is provided.

▸ **Preferred DSSes**. Select this form to specify the IP address of five preferred DSSes. This list will be used if this NetWare/IP server is unable to identify DSSes by querying DNS.

▸ **Initial DSS Contact Retries**. This parameter specifies the number of times the NetWare/IP server will retransmit an unacknowledged query to a given DSS server when it starts up. The default is 1 try, and the range is 1 to 50.

▸ **Retry Interval**. This parameter specifies the time in seconds that the NetWare/IP server will wait before retransmitting an unacknowledged query to a DSS server when it starts up. The default is 10 seconds, and the range is 5 to 100 seconds.

▸ **Slow Link Customizations**. Press Enter to open the Remote Access Via Slow Links form shown in Figure 12.36. Use this form to specify tick counts required to reach remote networks through slow links. The tick count specifies the time in ticks (1/18 second) required for a packet to travel one way between this NetWare/IP server and a remote server. Slow link customization is required only if NetWare/IP servers are timing out when trying to access services over specific links.

▸ **Forward IPX Information to DSS**. This field determines whether this NetWare server will function as a forwarding IP-IPX gateway. If this parameter is set to Yes this server will function as a forwarding gateway. The default is No.

Specifying slow link tick counts.

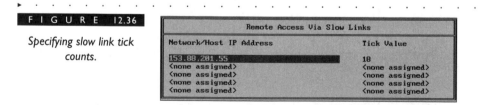

6 • When the NetWare/IP server configuration parameters have been entered, press Escape, save the changes, and return to the Main Menu.

Starting and Stopping the NetWare/IP Server

Like all NetWare/IP services, the NetWare/IP server must be started to become active. To start NetWare/IP:

1 • Load UNICON and log in. The user must be a member of the UNICON MANAGER or the UNICON SERVICES MANAGER group.

2 • Choose the *Start/Stop Services* option in the Main Menu to open the Running Services box.

3 • To start the NetWare/IP server on this host:

A. Press Insert to open the Available Services list.

B. Select **NetWare/IP Server** and press Enter. After a brief time, the service will be started and will be listed in the Running Services box.

4 • To stop the NetWare/IP server:

A. Select **NetWare/IP Server** in the Running Services list and press Delete.

B. Select Yes when you see the prompt "Stop Service."

NOTE

When NetWare/IP is installed, a file named UNISTART.NCF is created that is used to start the NetWare/IP server and related processes when the NetWare server is restarted. The command UNISTART.NCF is placed in the AUTOEXEC.NCF file by the INSTALL program.

The UNISTOP.NCF file contains the commands necessary to shut down NetWare/IP. Execute the command UNISTOP from the server console. You will need to execute UNISTOP.NCF if it is necessary to remove or reinstall NetWare/IP.

Installing and Configuring the NetWare/IP 2.1 Client

The NetWare/IP version 2.1 client is distributed in the file NIPW21.EXE, available from NetWire on CompuServe or from Novell's FTP server (`ftp.novell.com`). This section describes how to prepare the installation files and install the client software.

PREPARING THE INSTALLATION DISKS

You must prepare client installation disks from the files in NIPW21.EXE. The procedure is as follows:

1. • Obtain five freshly formatted high-density diskettes. Label the disks WSDOS_1 through WSDOS_5.

2. • Copy the NIPW21.EXE file to an empty directory and execute it to unpack the files.

3. • Subdirectories WSDOS_1 through WSDOS_5 will be created, and the appropriate files will be unpacked into each directory.

4. • Copy the contents of each directory to the appropriate floppy disk. Use the XCOPY command to retain the subdirectory structure (for example, type **XCOPY WSDOS_1 A: /S**).

INSTALLING THE CLIENT SOFTWARE

Before you install the client software, read the NIPW21.TXT file that was placed in the working directory when NIPW21.EXE was unpacked. This file describes procedures for using the client with NetWare versions other than 4.1 and describes procedures for merging the client software with LAN WorkPlace.

You may also wish to review the NetWare/IP Client Guide, which is included with the online manual set for the NetWare/IP server software. The NetWare/IP client has the following requirements:

▸ MS-DOS or PC-DOS version 3.3 or later, or Novell DOS 6.0 or later

▶ DOS must be configured to support at least 40 open files and 20 buffers by including the statements FILES=40 and BUFFERS=20 in the CONFIG.SYS file.

▶ If the APPEND command is in use, it must be disabled prior to installing the client software.

▶ If the SHARE command is in use, it must be disabled prior to installing the client software.

Installation of the client software is very similar to installation of the NetWare Client for DOS and Windows, which was described in Chapter 9. This chapter focuses on the special steps required to configure the client for NetWare/IP.
To install the NetWare/IP 2.1 client software:

1 • Insert the WSDOS_1 diskette into a drive, and execute the INSTALL program on the diskette (for example, type **A:INSTALL**). The initial installation screen is shown in Figure 12.37.

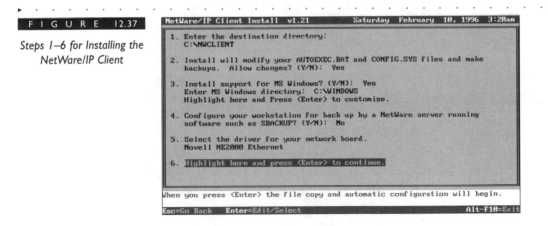

FIGURE 12.37

Steps 1–6 for Installing the NetWare/IP Client

2 • Complete Steps 1–4 as for the Client for DOS.

3 • In Step 5, after selecting a driver, select the driver name and press Enter. Then select the driver in the Network Board list and press Enter again. Inspect the parameters for the driver to ensure that the Ethernet_II frame type is supported.

4 • In Step 6, after you press Enter, INSTALL will open the form shown in Figure 12.38.

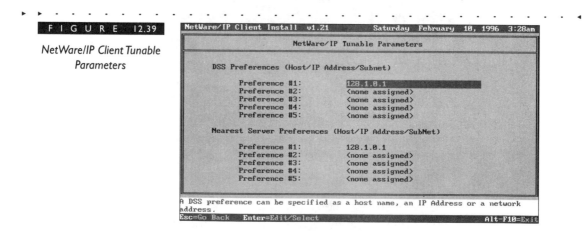

FIGURE 12.38

Steps 7–9 for Installing the NetWare/IP Client

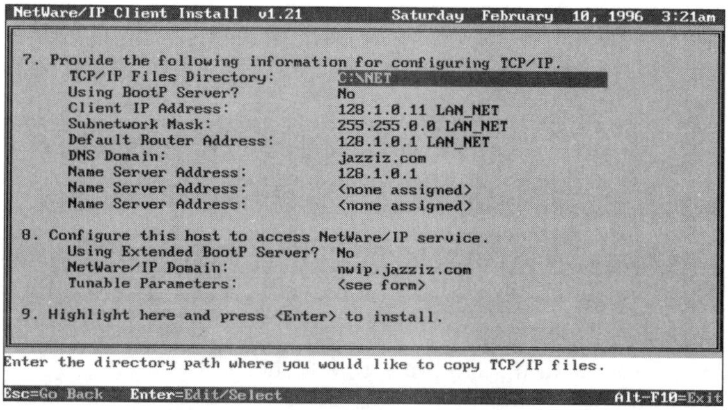

5 • In Step 7, configure the client parameters. Be sure to configure the DNS Domain field and to specify the address of at least one name server.

6 • In Step 8, specify the NetWare/IP domain.

7 • In Step 8, select the *Tunable Parameters* field, and press Enter to open the NetWare/IP Tunable Parameters form shown in Figure 12.39.

FIGURE 12.39

NetWare/IP Client Tunable Parameters

8 • In the DSS Preferences section, enter up to five IP addresses (or host names) that identify DSS servers. These servers will be used if the client is unable to obtain DSS server addresses from DNS.

9 • In the Nearest Server Preferences section enter up to five IP addresses (or host names) to specify the NetWare/IP servers closest to this client.

10 • Select Step 9, Highlight here and press <Enter> to install to begin copying files. Change diskettes as requested.

RESULTS OF INSTALLING THE NETWARE/IP CLIENT

The NetWare/IP client installation follows the pattern established by the NetWare Client for DOS and Windows. By default, NetWare client files are placed in the C:\NWCLIENT directory, and NetWare TCP/IP client files are placed in C:\NET.

A STARTNET.BAT file is created and is placed in the C:\NWCLIENT directory, and the command @CALL C:\STARTNET.BAT is placed in the AUTOEXEC.BAT file. The contents of the STARTNET.BAT file are as follows:

```
SET NWLANGUAGE=english
C:\NWCLIENT\LSL.COM
C:\NWCLIENT\NE2000.COM
REM C:\NWCLIENT\IPXODI.COM
C:\NET\BIN\TCPIP.EXE
C:\NWCLIENT\NWIP.EXE
if errorlevel -1 goto end_startnet
C:\NWCLIENT\VLM.EXE
:end_startnet
```

This batch file demonstrates the order in which modules are loaded to support the NetWare/IP client:

1 • Link Support Layer (LSL.COM)

2 • MLID (e.g., NE2000.COM)

3 • TCP/IP (TCPIP.EXE)

4 • NetWare/IP (NWIP.EXE)

5 • DOS Redirectory (VLM.EXE)

It is worth taking a look at the messages returned by the modules as they load:

```
C:> LSL
NetWare Link Support Layer v2.14 (941011)
(C) Copyright 1990-1994 Novell, Inc. All Rights Reserved.
BUFFERS 8 1500
MEMPOOL 4096
MAX BOARDS 4
MAX STACKS 4
The configuration file used was "C:\NWCLIENT\NET.CFG".
Max Boards 4, Max Stacks 4
Buffers 8, Buffer size 1500 bytes, Memory pool 4096 bytes.

C:> NE2000
Novell NE2000 Ethernet MLID v2.02 (941014)
(C) Copyright 1991 - 1994 Novell, Inc.  All Rights Reserved.
IRQ 5, Port 340, Mem D0000, Node Address E8D37248 L
Max Frame 1514 bytes, Line Speed 10 Mbps, Bus ID 0
Board 1, Frame ETHERNET_II, LSB Mode

C:> TCPIP
Novell TCP/IP Transport v5.0 (950430)
(C) Copyright 1992-1995 Novell, Inc.  All Rights Reserved.
Network Name: LAN_NET          Bind: NE2000
IP Address: 128.1.0.11         Board Number: 2
Subnet Mask: 255.255.0.0       Board Instance: 1
Default Router: 128.1.0.1      Frame: ETHERNET_II

C:> NWIP
NetWare/IP IPX Far Call Interface Emulator v2.10  (950322)
(C) Copyright 1990-1995 Novell, Inc.  All Rights Reserved.
NWIP Domain Name: NWIP.JAZZIZ.COM.
Configuration: Node address: 128.1.0.11
```

```
C:> VLM
VLM.EXE       - NetWare virtual loadable module manager
v1.20              (941108)
(C) Copyright 1994 Novell, Inc.  All Rights Reserved.
Patent pending.
The VLM.EXE file is pre-initializing the VLMs.............
The VLM.EXE file is using extended memory (XMS).
You are attached to server BEEBOP
```

Notice that the DOS requester (VLM.EXE) loads over NWIP exactly as it would load over IPXODI. NWIP presents a virtual IPX network to the requester.

If you experience difficulty getting the NetWare/IP client to connect, examine these messages to ensure that the configuration data are correct. Some client modules report the configuration file they are using; others report the parameters with which they are configured.

USING LAN WORKPLACE

LAN WorkPlace includes NetWare/IP client capability. Changing over to NetWare/IP requires only minor changes in the Configuration utility. Use the Windows or DOS version as you prefer. To configure NetWare/IP support for LAN WorkPlace, make the following changes with the Configuration utility:

1 • In the Adapter area, change the IPX Frame parameter to Ethernet_II.

2 • In the TCP/IP area:

   A. Enter your organization's domain name in the Domain Name field.

   B. Specify the IP addresses of at least one DNS server. Up to three addresses can be entered.

3 • In the NetWare area:

   A. Ensure that the NetWare Protocol is configured to use the IP frame type.

   B. Enter the name of the NetWare/IP domain in the NetWare/IP Domain field.

4 • In the NetWare/IP area:

A. Enter the name of the most easily accessed NetWare/IP server in the Nearest NWIP Server field.

B Enter the IP address of one preferred DSS server in the Preferred DSS field.

C. Check the box Support NetWare IP 1.1 Compatibility if NetWare/IP 1.1 servers are operating on your network.

The LAN WorkPlace STARTNET.BAT file will be reconfigured to load NWIP instead of IPXODI. The next time you restart the workstation, it will access NetWare using NetWare/IP.

The End?

If you have made it this far, you have learned a lot about TCP/IP in general and NetWare TCP/IP in particular. Some of it is pretty rough going, and I applaud you for sticking with it. Your skills and experience with TCP/IP will be valuable additions to your resume.

You may have reached the end of this book, but you haven't reached the end of the potential of NetWare TCP/IP. In Chapter 7 you learned about a plethora of products that can enable your NetWare TCP/IP network to do more for more users. Your network infrastructure is in place, and the features you add from this point on are up to you. If you need NFS support or TCP/IP printing support, select the product that meets your needs and get going. There's not much about TCP/IP that you can't do with NetWare products.

It's time to close this connection, and I want to end by thanking you for staying the course. I sincerely hope that you have found between these covers the information you need to understand and apply TCP/IP to your NetWare LAN.

Understanding Decimal, Binary, and Hexadecimal Numbers

How most human societies settled on a numbering system based on multiples of 10 is lost in history. The most probable explanation is that 10-based numbering came about as a natural extension of the way we kept track of livestock and pots: by counting them on our fingers. But whatever the explanation, most humans have become comfortable with decimal numbers, or the system called *base 10*.

Humans abandoned counting with fingers long ago because ten fingers just wasn't enough to deal with the real world. Ten grains of wheat isn't a lot of wheat, for example. The problem of representing large numbers was solved by Arab mathematicians who introduced the concept of zero, a hole that stood for an empty place. Combining the use of zero with multiples of ten produced the decimal numbering system we use today, which allows us to represent values of any magnitude.

But the digits in digital computers aren't the same as the digits we call fingers. The way that computers count is very different from the way that humans do. Computers, which use large arrays of switches that are either on or off, are called *binary computers* because of this two-state operation. Yes, these switches could have been used to count like fingers, with each switch in a bank of ten representing a finger that was counted in sequence, but that wouldn't have permitted computers to handle large numeric values. Instead, the developers of computers needed a numbering system that was as natural to computers as base 10 is to humans.

The branch of mathematics that became the foundation for computer operation was established in 1854 by George Boole. Boolean algebra, as it came to be called, is based on binary logic (for example, true/false, on/off, yes/no) and fits quite nicely with the on/off character of digital computers. For the pioneers of digital computers, mathematical geniuses all, boolean algebra was mother's milk. They had no trepidation's whatsoever in using binary boolean logic to solve complex problems.

Unfortunately, that gives us network administrators big headaches, because few of us were math majors. However, we have no choice but to accept the computer for what it is and learn a bit of its binary logic. If you take it in small steps, the process isn't difficult. But before looking at the binary and hexadecimal numbering systems that are closely allied with computers, let's take a refresher course on decimal numbers.

How Decimal Numbers Work

The decimal numbering system is based on powers of ten. For example:

```
10⁰ = 1 (any integer to the 0 power = 1)
10¹ = 10 × 1 = 10
10² = 10 × 10 = 100
10³ = 10 × 10 × 10 = 1,000
10⁴ = 10 × 10 × 10 × 10 = 10,000
```

The position of a digit in a decimal number determines its magnitude in powers of ten. For the number 6,812, the digits represent the following values:

```
6 represents 6 × 10³ = 6 × 10 × 10 × 10 = 6 × 1000 = 6,000
8 represents 6 × 10² = 6 × 10 × 10 = 6 × 100 = 800
1 represents 1 × 10¹ = 1 × 10 = 1 × 10 = 10
2 represents 2 × 10⁰ = 2 × 1 = 2
```

That's enough for grade-school arithmetic. Let's see how binary numbers follow the same principle.

How Binary Numbers Work

Base 10 (decimal) numbers use digits 0 through 9 to represent digits. Base 2 (binary) digits are restricted to the values 1 and 0. As with base 10 numbers, the values of base 2 numbers are associated with powers of the base. The first few powers of 2 are as follows:

```
2⁰ = 1
2¹ = 2 × 1            = 2  decimal
2² = 2 × 2            = 4  decimal
2³ = 2 × 2 × 2        = 8  decimal
2⁴ = 2 × 2 × 2 × 2    = 16 decimal
```

These powers of 2 can be used to evaluate binary numbers. This example evaluates the binary number 1101:

```
1 represents 1 × 2³ = 1 × 2 × 2 × 2 = 1 × 8 = 8
1 represents 1 × 2² = 1 × 2 × 2 = 1 × 4 = 4
0 represents 0 × 2¹ = 0 × 2 = 0 × 2 = 0
1 represents 1 × 2⁰ = 1 × 1 = 1
```

Therefore, 13 is the decimal equivalent of the binary number 1101.

Binary digits (bits) typically are organized in terms of groups of eight, comprising the familiar *byte*, also referred to as an *octet* in some network standards. A byte can range in value from 0 through 11111111 binary, equivalent to a range of 0 through 255 decimal. That's how dotted-decimal IP address representation (discussed in Chapter 4) works—each group of eight bits is represented by a decimal value from 0 through 255.

How Hexadecimal Works

Decimal representation is used as a way to make binary numbers more palatable to humans. Which of these numbers is easier for you to comprehend:

01001110110011101111101100010001 binary
or
78.206. 251.71 dotted-decimal

The act of converting binary to decimal and back isn't something we can all do in our heads. Unless you're very good at head math, you'll probably resort to a conversion table (such as the one in Appendix B) or to a scientific calculator. That's why the hexadecimal numbering system is more commonly used as an alternative to binary representation. Hexadecimal looks weird and foreboding, but it's really an easier way to go if you work a lot with computer numbers.

Hexadecimal, or hex, has a base of 16. Because a hex digit can have one of 16 values, letters are used to represent the hex digits equivalent to decimal 10 through 15. Table A.1 shows the digits used in hex, with their decimal equivalents.

UNDERSTANDING DECIMAL, BINARY, AND HEXADECIMAL NUMBERS

T A B L E   A.1

Hex Digits with Decimal Equivalents

HEX DIGIT	DECIMAL EQUIVALENT	HEX DIGIT	DECIMAL EQUIVALENT
0	0	8	8
1	1	9	9
2	2	A	10
3	3	B	11
4	4	C	12
5	5	D	13
6	6	E	14
7	7	F	15

The values represented by digits in a hex number are determined by powers of 16. Here are the first few powers of 16:

$$16^0 = 1 \ (2^0)$$
$$16^1 = 16 \times 1 \qquad = 16 \text{ decimal } (2^4)$$
$$16^2 = 16 \times 16 \qquad = 256 \text{ decimal } (2^8)$$
$$16^3 = 16 \times 16 \times 16 \qquad = 4{,}096 \text{ decimal } (2^{16})$$
$$16^4 = 16 \times 16 \times 16 \times 16 \quad = 65{,}536 \text{ decimal } (2^{32})$$

Here is how the hex number E40A evaluates:

```
E represents E × 16³ = E × 16 × 16 × 16 = E × 4,096 = 57,344 decimal
4 represents 4 × 16² = 4 × 16 × 16 = 4 × 256 = 1,024 decimal
0 represents 0 × 16¹ = 0 × 16 = 0 × 16 = 0 decimal
A represents A × 16⁰ = A × 1 = 10 decimal
```

As a result, 58,378 (57,344+1,024+10) is the decimal equivalent of the hex number E40A.

Converting Binary to Hex

As things develop, it is a piece of cake to convert binary numbers to hex, all in your head.

Take the binary number 1111, which is decimal 15. Referring to the list of hex digits presented in Table A.1, it becomes clear that binary 1111 represented in hex is F. Therefore, any four-bit binary number can be represented by a single hex digit as shown in Table A.2:

T A B L E A.2 *Binary Numbers with Hex Equivalents*	FOUR-BIT BINARY NUMBER	HEX DIGIT EQUIVALENT
	1	1
	10	2
	11	3
	100	4
	101	5
	110	6
	111	7
	1000	8
	1001	9
	1010	A
	1011	B
	1100	C
	1101	D
	1110	E
	1111	F

To convert longer binary numbers to hex, just break the binary number into groups of four bits, and represent each group with a hex digit. For example:

0100	1110	1100	1110	1111	1011	0001	0001
4	E	C	E	F	B	1	1

As you can see, if you can memorize just 16 bit patterns and their hex equivalents, you can convert binary to hex and back without a net.

Most commonly, hex numbers are organized in groups of two digits, with each group representing one byte. You might see the above number written something like this:

4E CE FB 11

However, hex numbers can easily look like decimal. For example, is the number 1025 decimal or hex? As a result, it is important to have a way of unambiguously identifying hex numbers.

Representing Hex Numbers

In Chapter 4's discussion of subnet masks, you learn that it is extremely important to consider the bit pattern that the subnet mask represents. Subnet masks often are shown in dotted-decimal form, for example, 255.255.240.0. To make it easier to convert subnet masks to their binary forms, however, you often will see subnet masks represented in hex. For example, the subnet mask 255.255.240.0 might be written in hex as:

0xFF.0xFF.0xE0.0x0

The 0x part is taken from the C programming language, which identifies a hex digit with the 0x prefix. Hex numbers also are frequently identified with a lower-case letter h, for example: 4Eh. Expect to see both forms as you read about TCP/IP.

Decimal, Binary, and Hexadecimal Equivalents

T A B L E

DECIMAL	BINARY	HEX
0	0	0
1	1	1
2	10	2
3	11	3
4	100	4
5	101	5
6	110	6
7	111	7
8	1000	8
9	1001	9
10	1010	A
11	1011	B
12	1100	C
13	1101	D
14	1110	E
15	1111	F
16	10000	10
17	10001	11
18	10010	12
19	10011	13
20	10100	14
21	10101	15
22	10110	16
23	10111	17
24	11000	18
25	11001	19

DECIMAL	BINARY	HEX
26	11010	1A
27	11011	1B
28	11100	1C
29	11101	1D
30	11110	1E
31	11111	1F
32	100000	20
33	100001	21
34	100010	22
35	100011	23
36	100100	24
37	100101	25
38	100110	26
39	100111	27
40	101000	28
41	101001	29
42	101010	2A
43	101011	2B
44	101100	2C
45	101101	2D
46	101110	2E
47	101111	2F
48	110000	30
49	110001	31
50	110010	32
51	110011	33

T A B L E

DECIMAL	BINARY	HEX	DECIMAL	BINARY	HEX
52	110100	34	78	1001110	4E
53	110101	35	79	1001111	4F
54	110110	36	80	1010000	50
55	110111	37	81	1010001	51
56	111000	38	82	1010010	52
57	111001	39	83	1010011	53
58	111010	3A	84	1010100	54
59	111011	3B	85	1010101	55
60	111100	3C	86	1010110	56
61	111101	3D	87	1010111	57
62	111110	3E	88	1011000	58
63	111111	3F	89	1011001	59
64	1000000	40	90	1011010	5A
65	100000	41	91	1011011	5B
66	1000010	42	92	1011100	5C
67	1000011	43	93	1011101	5D
68	1000100	44	94	1011110	5E
69	1000101	45	95	1011111	5F
70	1000110	46	96	1100000	60
71	1000111	47	97	1100001	61
72	1001000	48	98	1100010	62
73	1001001	49	99	1100011	63
74	1001010	4A	100	1100100	64
75	100101	4B	101	1100101	65
76	1001100	4C	102	1100110	66
77	100110	4D	103	1100111	67

T A B L E

(continued)

DECIMAL	BINARY	HEX		DECIMAL	BINARY	HEX
104	1101000	68		130	10000010	82
105	1101001	69		131	10000011	83
106	1101010	6A		132	10000100	84
107	1101011	6B		133	10000101	85
108	1101100	6C		134	10000110	86
109	1101101	6D		135	10000111	87
110	1101110	6E		136	10001000	88
111	1101111	6F		137	10001001	89
112	1110000	70		138	10001010	8A
113	1110001	71		139	10001011	8B
114	1110010	72		140	10001100	8C
115	1110011	73		141	10001101	8D
116	1110100	74		142	10001110	8E
117	1110101	75		143	10001111	8F
118	1110110	76		144	10010000	90
119	1110111	77		145	10010001	91
120	1111000	78		146	10010010	92
121	1111001	79		147	10010011	93
122	1111010	7A		148	10010100	94
123	1111011	7B		149	10010101	95
124	1111100	7C		150	10010110	96
125	1111101	7D		151	10010111	97
126	1111110	7E		152	10011000	98
127	1111111	7F		153	10011001	99
128	10000000	80		154	10011010	9A
129	10000001	81		155	10011011	9B

DECIMAL, BINARY, AND HEXADECIMAL EQUIVALENTS

T A B L E

(continued)

DECIMAL	BINARY	HEX	DECIMAL	BINARY	HEX
156	10011100	9C	182	10110110	B6
157	10011101	9D	183	10110111	B7
158	10011110	9E	184	10111000	B8
159	10011111	9F	185	10111001	B9
160	10100000	A0	186	10111010	BA
161	10100001	A1	187	10111011	BB
162	10100010	A2	188	10111100	BC
163	10100011	A3	189	10111101	BD
164	10100100	A4	190	10111110	BE
165	10100101	A5	191	10111111	BF
166	10100110	A6	192	11000000	C0
167	10100111	A7	193	11000001	C1
168	10101000	A8	194	11000010	C2
169	10101001	A9	195	11000011	C3
170	10101010	AA	196	11000100	C4
171	10101011	AB	197	11000101	C5
172	10101100	AC	198	11000110	C6
173	10101101	AD	199	11000111	C7
174	10101110	AE	200	11001000	C8
175	10101111	AF	201	11001001	C9
176	10110000	B0	202	11001010	CA
177	10110001	B1	203	11001011	CB
178	10110010	B2	204	11001100	CC
179	10110011	B3	205	11001101	CD
180	10110100	B4	206	11001110	CE
181	10110101	B5	207	11001111	CF

T A B L E

(continued)

DECIMAL	BINARY	HEX	DECIMAL	BINARY	HEX
208	11010000	D0	232	11101000	E8
209	11010001	DI	233	11101001	E9
210	11010010	D2	234	11101010	EA
211	11010011	D3	235	11101011	EB
212	11010100	D4	236	11101100	EC
213	11010101	D5	237	11101101	ED
214	11010110	D6	238	11101110	EE
215	11010111	D7	239	11101111	EF
216	11011000	D8	240	11110000	F0
217	11011001	D9	241	11110001	FI
218	11011010	DA	242	11110010	F2
219	11011011	DB	243	11110011	F3
220	11011100	DC	244	11110100	F4
221	11011101	DD	245	11110101	F5
222	11011110	DE	246	11110110	F6
223	11011111	DF	247	11110111	F7
224	11100000	E0	248	11111000	F8
225	11100001	EI	249	11111001	F9
226	11100010	E2	250	11111010	FA
227	11100011	E3	251	11111011	FB
228	11100100	E4	252	11111100	FC
229	11100101	E5	253	11111101	FD
230	11100110	E6	254	11111110	FE
231	11100111	E7	255	11111111	FF

Internet Top-Level Domains

The following table lists the country codes for country domains in the Internet domain name space. These codes were obtained from the WHOIS service at rs.internic.net in September 1995.

DOMAIN	COUNTRY
AE	United Arab Emirates
AG	Antigua and Barbuda
AI	Anguilla
AL	Albania (Republic of)
AM	Armenia (Republic of)
AN	Netherlands Antilles
AQ	Antarctica
AR	Argentina (Argentine Republic)
ARPA	Advanced Projects Research Agency Domain
AT	Austria (Republic of)
AU	Australia
AZ	Azerbaijan
BB	Barbados
BE	Belgium (Kingdom of)
BF	Burkina Faso
BG	Bulgaria top level domain
BH	Bahrain (State of)
BM	Bermuda
BO	Bolivia (Republic of)
BR	Brazil (Federative Republic of)
BS	Bahamas (Commonwealth of the)
BW	Botswana (Republic of)
BY	Belarus
BZ	Belize

T A B L E

DOMAIN	COUNTRY
CA	Canada
CH	Switzerland (Swiss Confederation)
CI	Cote d'Ivoire (Republic of)
CK	Cook Islands
CL	Chile (Republic of)
CM	Cameroon
CN	China (People's Republic of)
CO	Colombia (Republic of)
COM	Commercial
CR	Costa Rica (Republic of)
CU	Cuba (Republic of)
CY	Cyprus (Republic of)
CZ	Czech Republic
DE	Germany (Federal Republic of)
DK	Denmark (Kingdom of)
DM	Dominica (Commonwealth of)
DO	Dominican Republic
DZ	Algeria (People's Democratic Republic of)
EC	Ecuador (Republic of)
EDU	Education
EE	Estonia (Republic of)
EG	Egypt (Arab Republic of)
ES	Spain (Kingdom of)
FI	Finland (Republic of)
FJ	Fiji (Republic of)
FM	Micronesia (Federated States of)
FO	Faroe Islands
FR	France (French Republic)

DOMAIN	COUNTRY
GB	Great Britain (United Kingdom of)
GD	Grenada (Republic of)
GE	Georgia (Republic of)
GH	Ghana
GL	Greenland
GN	Guinea (Republic of)
GOV	Government
GR	Greece (Hellenic Republic)
GT	Guatemala (Republic of)
GU	Guam
GY	Guyana
HK	Hong Kong (Hisiangkang, Xianggang)
HN	Honduras (Republic of)
HR	Croatia / Hrvatska (Republic of)
HU	Hungary (Republic of)
ID	Indonesia
IE	Ireland
IL	Israel (State of)
IN	India (Republic of)
INT	International
IR	Iran (Islamic Republic of)
IS	Iceland (Republic of)
IT	Italy (Italian Republic)
JM	Jamaica
JO	Jordan (The Hashemite Kingdom of)
JP	Japan
KE	Kenya (Republic of)
KI	Kiribati

TABLE

DOMAIN	COUNTRY
KN	Saint Kitts & Nevis
KR	Korea (Republic of)
KW	Kuwait (State of)
KY	Cayman Islands
KZ	Kazakhstan
LB	Lebanon (Lebanese Republic)
LC	Saint Lucia
LI	Liechtenstein (Principality of)
LK	Sri Lanka (Democratic Socialist Republic of)
LS	Lesotho (Kingdom of)
LT	Lithuania (Republic of)
LU	Luxembourg (Grand Duchy of)
LV	Latvia (Republic of)
MA	Morocco (Kingdom of)
MC	Monaco (Principality of)
MD	Moldova (Republic of)
MG	Madagascar
MIL	Military
MK	Macedonia (The former Yugoslav Republic of)
ML	Mali (Republic of)
MN	Mongolia
MO	Macau (Ao-me'n)
MT	Malta (Republic of)
MX	Mexico (United Mexican States)
MY	Malaysia top level domain
MZ	Mozambique (People's Republic of)
NA	Namibia (Republic of)
NATO	NATO (North Atlantic Treaty Organization)

(continued)

DOMAIN	COUNTRY
NC	New Caledonia (Nourvelle Caledonie)
NET	Network
NG	Nigeria
NI	Nicaragua (Republic of)
NL	Netherlands
NO	Norway (Kingdom of)
NP	Nepal
NZ	New Zealand
ORG	Organization
PA	Panama (Republic of)
PE	Peru (Republic of)
PG	Papua New Guinea
PH	Philippines (Republic of the)
PK	Pakistan (Islamic Republic of)
PL	Poland (Republic of)
PR	Puerto Rico
PT	Portugal (Portuguese Republic)
PY	Paraguay (Republic of)
RO	Romainia
RU	Russia (Russian Federation)
SA	Saudi Arabia (Kingdom of)
SB	Solomon Islands
SE	Sweden (Kingdom of)
SG	Singapore (Republic of)
SI	Slovenia
SK	Slovakia
SM	San Marino (Republic of)
SN	Senegal (Republic of)

TABLE	DOMAIN	COUNTRY
	SR	Suriname (Republic of)
	SU	Soviet Union (Union of Soviet Socialist Republics)
	SV	El Salvador
	SZ	Swaziland (Kingdom of)
	TH	Thailand (Kingdom of)
	TN	Tunisia
	TR	Turkey (Republic of)
	TT	Trinidad & Tobago (Republic of)
	TW	Taiwan
	TZ	Tanzania (United Republic of)
	UA	Ukraine
	UG	Uganda (Republic of)
	UK	United Kingdom of Great Britain
	US	United States of America
	UY	Uruguay (Eastern Republic of)
	UZ	Uzbekistan
	VA	Vatican City State
	VC	Saint Vincent & the Grenadines
	VE	Venezuela (Republic of)
	VI	Virgin Islands (US)
	VN	Vietnam (Socialist Republic of)
	VU	Vanuatu
	WS	Samoa
	YU	Yugoslavia (Federal Republic of)
	ZA	South Africa (Republic of)
	ZM	Zambia (Republic of)
	ZW	Zimbabwe (Republic of)

CD-ROM Contents

NetWare Client 32 for Windows 95

The CD-ROM bound into the front of this book contains a full working version of Novell's NetWare Client 32 for Windows 95. This product offers users access to networking services through native Windows 95 interfaces and networking extensions to the Windows 95 desktop. The NetWare Client 32 architecture enables users to maximize the value of new 32-bit operating systems such as Windows 95 by tightly integrating the desktop with NetWare services.

NetWare Client 32 for Windows 95 includes all the features users are familiar with in the NetWare Clients they are using today and builds on these features to deliver:

- ▶ Easy installation and upgrades for NetWare clients

- ▶ Optimal access to NetWare Directory Services (NDS)

- ▶ Access to innovative new features built on NDS

- ▶ Easier node management to help reduce the costs of managing desktop operating systems on the network

- ▶ High-performance networking connectivity based on proven technology

- ▶ Seamless integration with native Windows 95 interfaces

SYSTEM REQUIREMENTS

- ▶ PC with an Intel (or compatible) 80386 or later processor

- ▶ A hard disk with 6 MB of free storage space

- ▶ 6 MB or more of RAM

- ▶ A network board installed in your workstation

- ▶ A cable connection to the network

- ▶ Windows 95 installed

INSTALLATION INSTRUCTIONS

1 • Review the above system requirements.

2 • Insert CD-ROM.

3 • Change to the ENGLISH folder in the NWCLIENT directory.

4 • Run SETUP.EXE.

5 • Follow the instructions on the screen. Choose Help for online assistance.

6 • Reboot the workstation.

TROUBLESHOOTING TIPS

Ensure the following:

▸ The server patches shipped with Client 32 are installed.

▸ Your preferred server is set (for NetWare 3). Your preferred tree and name context, or your preferred server is set (for NetWare 4).

▸ Your network adapter is set up correctly.

▸ Network cabling is within IEEE specifications and is properly installed and connected.

▸ All network software is the most recent version available.

NetWare/IP 2.2

The CD-ROM also contains a full working version of NetWare/IP 2.2. This product is a set of server and client software modules that provide access to NetWare networks using TCP/IP transport instead of or in addition to the IPX protocol used in traditional NetWare environments. NetWare/IP enables you to:

- Extend NetWare services and applications to nodes on an existing IP network in a manner that is transparent to users

- Migrate your network from IPX to TCP/IP

- Interconnect TCP/IP and IPX networks, enabling users on both networks to access NetWare resources on either network

With NetWare/IP NetWare applications and services look the same to the user regardless of whether IPX or IP is the transport protocol. In addition, the same datalink-level drivers service both protocols, so both can share the same cabling system.

INSTALLING NETWARE/IP 2.2

Before installing NetWare/IP 2.2 from the CD-ROM, be sure you are in the NETIP22 directory. The directory contains a README.1ST file that provides detailed information about installing NetWare/IP 2.2. The NetWare/IP software must be installed and configured in a specific manner, and prior to installing a NetWare/IP network, you should read Chapters 1 through 5 of the online *NetWare/IP Administrator's Guide*. This guide is contained as postscript files in the NETIP22\PSFILES directory on the CD.

Index

(continued)

(continued)

M

(continued)

(continued)

S

(continued)

X

Z

IDG BOOKS WORLDWIDE LICENSE AGREEMENT

Important — read carefully before opening the software packet. This is a legal agreement between you (either an individual or an entity) and IDG Books Worldwide, Inc. (IDG). By opening the accompanying sealed packet containing the software disc, you acknowledge that you have read and accept the following IDG License Agreement. If you do not agree and do not want to be bound by the terms of this Agreement, promptly return the book and the unopened software packet(s) to the place you obtained them for a full refund.

1. **License.** This License Agreement (Agreement) permits you to use one copy of the enclosed Software program(s) on a single computer. The Software is in "use" on a computer when it is loaded into temporary memory (i.e., RAM) or installed into permanent memory (e.g., hard disk, CD-ROM, or other storage device) of that computer.

2. **Copyright.** The entire contents of this disc and the compilation of the Software are copyrighted and protected by both United States copyright laws and international treaty provisions. You may only (a) make one copy of the Software for backup or archival purposes, or (b) transfer the Software to a single hard disk, provided that you keep the original for backup or archival purposes. The individual programs on the disc are copyrighted by the authors of each program respectively. Each program has its own use permissions and limitations. To use each program, you must follow the individual requirements and restrictions detailed in Appendix D of this Book. Do not use a program if you do not want to follow its Licensing Agreement. None of the material on this disc or listed in this Book may ever be distributed, in original or modified form, for commercial purposes.

3. **Other Restrictions.** You may not rent or lease the Software. You may transfer the Software and user documentation on a permanent basis provided you retain no copies and the recipient agrees to the terms of this Agreement. You may not reverse engineer, decompile, or disassemble the Software except to the extent that the foregoing restriction is expressly prohibited by applicable law. If the Software is an update or has been updated, any transfer must include the most recent update and all prior versions. Each shareware program has its own use permissions and limitations. These limitations are contained in the individual license agreements that are on the software discs. The restrictions include a requirement that after using the program for a period of time specified in its text, the user must pay a

registration fee or discontinue use. By opening the package which contains the software disc, you will be agreeing to abide by the licenses and restrictions for these programs. Do not open the software package unless you agree to be bound by the license agreements.

4. <u>Limited Warranty</u>. IDG warrants that the Software and disc are free from defects in materials and workmanship for a period of sixty (60) days from the date of purchase of this Book. If IDG receives notification within the warranty period of defects in material or workmanship, IDG will replace the defective disc. IDG's entire liability and your exclusive remedy shall be limited to replacement of the Software, which is returned to IDG with a copy of your receipt. This Limited Warranty is void if failure of the Software has resulted from accident, abuse, or misapplication. Any replacement Software will be warranted for the remainder of the original warranty period or thirty (30) days, whichever is longer.

5. <u>No Other Warranties</u>. To the maximum extent permitted by applicable law, IDG and the author disclaim all other warranties, express or implied, including but not limited to implied warranties of merchantability and fitness for a particular purpose, with respect to the Software, the programs, the source code contained therein and/or the techniques described in this Book. This limited warranty gives you specific legal rights. You may have others which vary from state/jurisdiction to state/jurisdiction.

6. <u>No Liability For Consequential Damages</u>. To the extent permitted by applicable law, in no event shall IDG or the author be liable for any damages whatsoever (including without limitation, damages for loss of business profits, business interruption, loss of business information, or any other pecuniary loss) arising out of the use of or inability to use the Book or the Software, even if IDG has been advised of the possibility of such damages. Because some states/jurisdictions do not allow the exclusion or limitation of liability for consequential or incidental damages, the above limitation may not apply to you.

7. <u>U.S.Government Restricted Rights</u>. Use, duplication, or disclosure of the Software by the U.S. Government is subject to restrictions stated in paragraph (c) (1) (ii) of the Rights in Technical Data and Computer Software clause of DFARS 252.227-7013, and in subparagraphs (a) through (d) of the Commercial Computer — Restricted Rights clause at FAR 52.227-19, and in similar clauses in the NASA FAR supplement, when applicable.

IDG BOOKS WORLDWIDE REGISTRATION CARD

Visit our Web site at http://www.idgbooks.com

ISBN Number: 1-56884-818-8

Title of this book: Novell's Guide to integrating Netware ®and TCP/IP

My overall rating of this book: ❑ Very good [1] ❑ Good [2] ❑ Satisfactory [3] ❑ Fair [4] ❑ Poor [5]

How I first heard about this book:

❑ Found in bookstore; name: [6] _____

❑ Advertisement: [8] _____

❑ Word of mouth; heard about book from friend, co-worker, etc.: [10] _____

❑ Book review: [7] _____

❑ Catalog: [9] _____

❑ Other: [11] _____

What I liked most about this book: _____

What I would change, add, delete, etc., in future editions of this book: _____

Other comments: _____

Number of computer books I purchase in a year: ❑ 1 [12] ❑ 2-5 [13] ❑ 6-10 [14] ❑ More than 10 [15]

I would characterize my computer skills as: ❑ Beginner [16] ❑ Intermediate [17] ❑ Advanced [18] ❑ Professional [19]

I use ❑ DOS [20] ❑ Windows [21] ❑ OS/2 [22] ❑ UNIX [23] ❑ Macintosh [24] ❑ Other: [25]_____

(please specify)

I would be interested in new books on the following subjects:

(please check all that apply, and use the spaces provided to identify specific software)

❑ Word processing: [26] _____

❑ Data bases: [28] _____

❑ File Utilities: [30] _____

❑ Networking: [32] _____

❑ Other: [34] _____

❑ Spreadsheets: [27] _____

❑ Desktop publishing: [29] _____

❑ Money management: [31] _____

❑ Programming languages: [33] _____

I use a PC at (please check all that apply): ❑ home [35] ❑ work [36] ❑ school [37] ❑ other: [38]_____

The disks I prefer to use are ❑ 5.25 [39] ❑ 3.5 [40] ❑ other: [41]_____

I have a CD ROM: ❑ yes [42] ❑ no [43]

I plan to buy or upgrade computer hardware this year: ❑ yes [44] ❑ no [45]

I plan to buy or upgrade computer software this year: ❑ yes [46] ❑ no [47]

Name: _____ **Business title:** [48] _____ **Type of Business:** [49] _____

Address (❑ home [50] ❑ work [51]**/Company name:** _____)

Street/Suite# _____

City [52]**/State** [53]**/Zip code** [54]: _____ **Country** [55] _____

❑ **I liked this book!** You may quote me by name in future IDG Books Worldwide promotional materials.

My daytime phone number is _____

IDG BOOKS WORLDWIDE
THE WORLD OF COMPUTER KNOWLEDGE®

❑ YES!

Please keep me informed about IDG Books Worldwide's World of Computer Knowledge. Send me your latest catalog.

…SECRETS®

…FOR DUMMIES™

BESTSELLING BOOK SERIES FROM IDG

INFO WORLD
TECHNICAL BOOKS

3-D Visual

Macworld® Books